THE JUNG–WHITE LETTERS

The Jung–White Letters charts 15 years of correspondence between C.G. Jung and Victor White, an English Dominican priest and theologian. The dialogue between the two provides valuable insights into the development of Jung's thought, and the relationship between psychology and religion.

Jung hoped that his correspondence with White would help him to reinterpret the classic Christian symbols and White sought Jung's support of his project to integrate analytical psychology into Catholic theology Although both Jung and White were committed to a productive collaboration, the letters trace a trajectory toward a crisis of misunderstanding and betrayal, culminating in a sharpening of disagreements after publication of Jung's *Answer to Job*.

The letters are presented with great attention to authenticity, and Jung's previously published letters have been restored to their original style. The text is helpfully annotated throughout with historical, literary and personal references. A wealth of editorial material is also included to set the letters in context, including an authoritative memoir of Victor White.

Jung's engagement with White was an essential dialogue that contributed importantly to his late writings, forcing him to refine his critique of classical theology. This volume will be of great interest to all Jungian analysts, psychoanalysts and psychotherapists and anyone interested in investigating the complex relationship between analytical psychology and religion.

THE JUNG–WHITE LETTERS

Edited by Ann Conrad Lammers and Adrian Cunningham

Consulting editor Murray Stein

Routledge
Taylor & Francis Group
LONDON AND NEW YORK

PHILEMON SERIES

First published 2007
by Routledge
27 Church Road, Hove, East Sussex BN3 2FA

Simultaneously published in the USA and Canada
by Routledge
711 Third Avenue, New York, NY 10017

Routledge is an imprint of the Taylor & Francis Group, an informa business

Typeset in Times by
RefineCatch Ltd, Bungay, Suffolk
Jacket design by Sandra Heath

British Library Cataloguing in Publication Data
A catalogue record for this book is available from the British Library

Library of Congress Cataloging in Publication Data
Jung, C. G. (Carl Gustav), 1875–1961.
[Correspondence. Selections]
The Jung–White letters / edited by Ann Conrad Lammers and Adrian Cunningham.—1st ed.
p. cm.
Includes bibliographical references and index.
ISBN–13: 978-1-58391-194-5 (hardback)
ISBN–10: 1-58391-194-4 (hardback)
1. Jung, C. G. (Carl Gustav), 1875–1961—Correspondence. 2. White, Victor, 1902–1960—Correspondence. 3. Psychoanalysis and religion. 4. Catholic Church and psychoanalysis. I. Lammers, Ann Conrad. II. Cunningham, Adrian. III. White, Victor, 1902–1960. Correspondence. Selections. IV. Title.
BF109.J8A4 2007
150.19′54092—dc22
[B] 2006100288

ISBN 978-1-58391-194-5

CONTENTS

CONTENTS

ILLUSTRATIONS

FOREWORD

By Murray Stein

This edition of the letters between Prof. C.G. Jung and Fr. Victor White is the third major collection of Jung's correspondences to be published. The first was the famous exchange between Jung and Freud (McGuire).[1] The second was that between Jung and Wolfgang Pauli, the physicist (Meier).[2] Now in this correspondence with White we see Jung in dialogue with a theologian.

All three collections of letters tell us a great deal about the human matrix underlying the formal theoretical and scientific writings that in some measure derive from and surely are deeply influenced by these important relationships. With respect to Jung's side of the equation, in each collection, too, we discover a different side of his complex personality and another facet of his brilliant mind. It is noteworthy that he was able to carry on such significant exchanges with three figures of the highest standing in their own fields of expertise, each having completely different backgrounds and specializations. Each set of letters shows a complex and personal human connection between the correspondents as well as an intellectual dialogue of the highest caliber.

From these letters between Jung and White, we can see that the main subject matter of their discussions was the relationship between psychology and religion. However, the correspondence also reflects the trajectory of their personal relationship, from the high excitement of mutual recognition at the beginning, through the realization of crucial differences in attitude and philosophical commitments in the middle, to a mutual feeling of betrayal and misunderstanding as it unwound. In the end there is a note of empathy and healing, but that came muted and late.

Psychology was, of course, Jung's chief concern, and all other interests

1 William McGuire, ed., *The Freud–Jung Letters: The Correspondence between Sigmund Freud and C.G. Jung*, trans. Ralph Mannheim & R.F.C. Hull, PUP/Bollingen, 1974. (Hereafter *FJL*.)

2 C.A. Meier, ed., *Atom and Archetype: The Pauli/Jung Letters 1932–1958*, PUP, 2001.

consistently were inspected and interpreted through the lens of his psychological understandings. In the dialogue with White, this eventually caused a major and, as it turned out, insoluble conflict. Theology and psychology are quite distinct disciplines that proceed from widely different assumptions and employ incompatible methodologies, and the consequences of this Jung and White did not know quite as profoundly at the outset as at the conclusion of their exchanges. On the question of evil, their thoughts diverged irrevocably. When Jung put forward his most distinctive and forthright psychological reflections on Biblical theology and Christian doctrine in *Answer to Job* – which was also his answer to White! – much of it flew directly in the face of the received doctrine that had anchored White's life and career.

Many of Jung's more substantial letters in this correspondence have been published previously in the collection edited by Gerhard Adler.[3] None of White's side of the correspondence, however, has previously been available. Until now, one had to read between the lines and do a lot of guesswork to discern the fullness of their personal relationship and the details of their intellectual exchange. With this publication of the complete correspondence, it becomes quite evident that the engagement with White was for Jung an essential dialogue that contributed importantly to his late writings. Their tortured argument over the place of evil in theological doctrines (White maintaining the church's teaching that evil is merely secondary, a "*privatio boni*," over against Jung's conviction that good and evil are equal opposites, two halves of a reality) pushed Jung toward refining and deepening his critique of classical theology, which then appeared in full force in *Aion* (1951)[4] and *Answer to Job* (1952).[5] White, one could say, sharpened Jung's sword by dueling with him for several years before Jung entered the public arena with his published writings.

For White, Jung was a teacher and the very figure of an archetypal "wise old man." They first met when Jung was 70 years old. For Jung, White was a "raven" (see Jung's second letter in the correspondence), like the ones sent by God to Elijah in the wilderness, come to feed him with spiritual nourishment

3 Gerhard Adler, ed., *C.G. Jung Letters, Vol.1: 1906–1950; Vol.2: 1951–1961*, in collaboration with Aniela Jaffé, PUP/Bollingen, 1973. (Hereafter, *Letters I, II.*)

4 C.G. Jung, *Aion: Untersuchungen zur Symbolgeschichte* [Researches into the History of a Symbol], Psychologische Abhandlungen, 8, Zürich: Rascher Verlag, 1951. Later German edition titled, *Aion: Beiträge zur Symbolik des Selbst* [Contributions to the Symbolism of the Self], Gesammelte Werke, 9,ii, 1976. In English, *Aion: Researches into the Phenomenology of the Self*, Collected Works, Vol. 9.ii, trans. R.F.C. Hull, PUP/Bollingen, 1959/1968. (Hereafter *Aion*, CW 9.ii.)

5 C.G. Jung, *Antwort auf Hiob*, Zürich: Rascher Verlag, 1952. First generally available English edition: *Answer to Job*, trans. R.F.C. Hull, London: Routledge & Kegan Paul, 1954. (Cf., *Psychology and Religion: West and East*, Collected Works, Vol. 11, PUP/Bollingen, 1958/1969; hereafter *Psych. & Rel.*, CW 11.)

from abroad. Jung had longed for this kind of connection with a theologian. Not that Jung would use White as a confessor or a professor, although he did pick his brain on various fine points of Thomistic thought and Catholic doctrine, about which White was an expert. Rather, Jung looked on White as an invaluable interlocutor on matters that had preoccupied and bothered him for nearly his whole lifetime. Growing up in the home of a pastor father who could not answer his difficult questions about the meaning of such abstruse theological doctrines as the Trinity (see *Memories, Dreams, Reflections*, pp. 52ff),[6] Jung found in White a Catholic father who could not only match his questions with keen answers from his learned intellect but who also could challenge him to change some of his (by this time) ingrained attitudes and views. Strangely, however, Jung also discovered in White a similar set of conflicts to those he had earlier perceived in his father, Paul Jung, who was torn apart by the battle raging in his day between science and religion. As with his father, so too with White, Jung was not able to solve the other man's dilemmas. For himself Jung had found a solution to the problem of the historical split in the Christian West between matter and spirit in a type of psychology that has the potential to heal it.

Jung's frail health during the years of corresponding with White is a constant theme in these letters. Yet, paradoxically, he outlived the younger man by a year.

Jung was correct in his intuition that White was a godsend, for it was through White's provocations that he produced some of his most impassioned and stimulating writings. This is not a particularly happy story, though, for in the end each man felt rather abused and misunderstood by the other.

White died with his Christian faith intact, perhaps even strengthened by his engagement with Analytical Psychology. Jung passed away in another state of grace. In the end, they were of different faiths.

6 C.G. Jung, *Memories, Dreams, Reflections*. New York: Vintage Books, 1961. (Hereafter, *MDR*.)

ACKNOWLEDGMENTS

Many people have generously assisted in the creation of this work, and the editors are profoundly grateful. We have done our best to include all the names, and can only beg forgiveness if an oversight nevertheless occurs.

The primary source for the main text of this volume is the ETH Library archive: Korrespondenz C.G. Jung–Victor White (HS 1056), C.G.Jung-Arbeitsarchiv, Hauptabteilung Handschriften und Nachlässe des Archivs der ETH Zürich (C.G. Jung Archive, Department of Manuscripts and Legacies, Archive of the Swiss Institute of Technology, Zurich). Other cited correspondences, located in the same archive, include Jung's letters to and from John Layard, Gerhard Adler, Barbara Robb, and the Mother Prioress. Permission to receive copies of the Jung–White letters, to study and photograph selected originals, and for access to the other cited correspondences, was given by Ulrich Hoerni and Peter Jung for the C.G. Jung Estate, and by Rudolf Mumenthaler and Yvonne Voegeli for the C.G.Jung-Arbeitsarchiv and the ETH-Bibliothek.

Access to Jung's library and family information was kindly given by Ulrich Hoerni, Peter Jung, and Andreas Jung. Other archives and special collections were made available by Fr. Bede Bailey, archivist of the English Dominican Province, Edinburgh; Fr. Richard Finn, librarian at Blackfriars, Oxford: St. Mark's Library, The General Theological Seminary, New York; the librarians of the Analytical Psychology Club, San Francisco.

Opportunities for sustained dialogue about the Jung–White letters, often leading to the happy resolution of textual mysteries, were provided in recent years by the C.G. Jung Institute of San Francisco (thanks to Thomas Kirsch); the C.G. Jung Institute of Chicago (thanks to Murray Stein); the Guild of Pastoral Psychology, Oxford (thanks to Lyn Phillips and Diana Grace-Jones, and special appreciation to Molly Tuby, Ean Begg, Paula Monahan, Nick Lewin); the Psychological Club of Zurich (thanks to Emmanuel Kennedy); the Jung Society of Seattle (thanks to Connie Eichenlaub); the North Pacific Institute of Analytical Psychology (thanks to Michael Horne and Joseph Rutte).

Hundreds of annotations in this volume were made possible by the indispensable technical assistance of Luis Gutierrez. Other scholars assisted in specific areas. William Countryman deciphered Jung's Greek writing, translated and proofread Greek portions of the text. Additional help with Greek (particularly the sermon of St. Basil) was kindly given by Darren Miner, Paula Monahan, and Fritz Böbel. Help with Latin was generously provided by Arthur Holder and Richard Corney. For consultation on the Kabbalah, gratitude to Steven Joseph. For advice on Dominican history and Catholic doctrine, thanks to Fr. Bede Bailey, Fr. Fergus Kerr, John Giannini, and Ean Begg.

Franz Jung, while he lived, and later Ulrich Hoerni and Peter Jung, generously provided primary materials for research and brought forward information for countless "mosaic stones." For help with Jung's literary deposit, thanks to Sonu Shamdasani, Brewster Beach, Charles H. Taylor, and the Kristine Mann Library of the C.G. Jung Foundation, New York. Profound thanks to Angela Cunningham for her close reading of the primary texts, and to Ulrich Hoerni for his critical review of text and notes. For the Whites' family history, thanks to Douglas Smith. Others who provided information include: the archivist, Bloxham School; the Rector of the English College, Valladolid, Revd. Mgr. Canon Peter Dooling; Alexandra Cohen of the information office of the Royal College of Psychiatrists; Fr. Jean Paillard, O.P.; Christina Megroz.

Copyright permissions to print the primary materials in this volume were kindly granted by the following. For the writings of Victor White, the English Dominican Province, with special thanks to Fr. Timothy Radcliffe, Fr. Malcolm McMahon and Fr. Allan White, successive Prior Provincials. Special appreciation to Fr. Paul Philibert, O.P., who helped at an early stage. For the writings of C.G. and Emma Jung, the C.G. Jung Estate, with special thanks to the late Franz Jung, and to Peter Jung and Ulrich Hoerni for the Executive Committee of the C.G. Jung Estate.

Other copyright permissions were sought and given by the following. The estate of Marie-Jeanne Schmid-Boller; the estate of Toni Wolff; Emmanuel Kennedy, Hansueli Etter, and the Stiftung für Jung'sche Psychologie for the estates of Marie-Louise von Franz and Barbara Hannah; Robert Hinshaw for the estate of Aniela Jaffé; Professor Lord Layard for the estate of John Layard; Harriet Francis for the estate of Barbara Robb; Lady Chitty for the estate of Antonia White; Michael Strathern for the estate of Catherine Ginsberg.

Reprint permission for previously published letters of C.G. Jung, in this edition, reverting to Jung's original English, was kindly granted by Princeton University Press:

Reprint permission for Victor White's 1955 *Blackfriars* review, "Jung on 'Job'," was kindly granted by Fr. Fergus Kerr for New Blackfriars.

Materials used in the illustrations were provided by Fr. Bede Bailey, English Dominican Province, ETH Library archive, Andreas Jung, Peter Jung. Copyright permissions for the illustrations were kindly granted by the C.G. Jung Estate; the English Dominican Province; Eureka Cartographers, Berkeley, California. Pre-publication preparation of the illustrations was by Wilsted & Taylor, Oakland, California; Eureka Cartographers, Berkeley, California; and Clone Art, Berkeley, California. For a detailed list of credits, cf. Illustrations, pp. vii f.

The editors wish to express our sincere gratitude to the publisher, Routledge, especially to Kate Hawes, Michael Forster, Joanne Forshaw, Claire Lipscombe, and Dawn Harris, for graciously seeing this complex project through the many stages of its always slower-than-expected development and delivery.

Funding for The Jung-White Letters was very generously provided by several sources, including the C.G. Jung Estate, Zurich; the Donald Cooper Fund, ETH-Bibliothek, Zurich; the Ann and Erlo van Waveren Foundation, New York; the Marie-Louise von Franz Stiftung, Zurich; the Stiftung für Jung'sche Psychologie, Zurich; and finally, during the project's last two years, the Philemon Foundation, Philadelphia.

We are honored by this volume's inclusion in the recently created Philemon Series. Our heartfelt thanks go to Dr. Stephen Martin, President, and Dr. Sonu Shamdasani, General Editor, for their steady encouragement, as well as for their unfailing confidence, patience, and diplomacy.

Every effort has been made to trace the copyright holders and obtain permission to reproduce extracts from other sources. Any omissions brought to our attention will be remedied in future editions or reprints.

ABBREVIATIONS

Aion	C.G. Jung, *Aion: Researches into the Phenomenology of the Self*. Trans. R.F.C. Hull. PUP/Bollingen, 1959. CW 9.ii. (*Aion: Untersuchungen zur Symbolgeschichte*, Zürich: Rascher-Verlag, 1951.)
APC	Analytical Psychology Club (of Zurich, London, New York, Los Angeles, San Francisco, etc.).
Briefe I, II, III	*C.G. Jung Briefe. I, 1906–1945; II, 1946–1955; III, 1956–1961* Herausgegeben von Aniela Jaffé, in Zusammenarbeit mit Gerhard Adler. Olten und Freiburg im Breisgau: Walter-Verlag, 1972/1980.
Contributions	C.G. Jung, *Contributions to Analytical Psychology*. Trans. (from *Energetik* 1928) H.G. & Cary F. Baynes. New York: Harcourt Brace, 1928; London: Kegan Paul, Trench, Trubner, 1928.
CW	*The Collected Works of C.G. Jung*, 21 volumes. (Cf. Selected Bibliography, p. 367.)
EJ	*Eranos-Jahrbuch, -Jahrbücher*, herausgegeben von Olga Fröbe-Kapteyn. Zürich: Rhein-Verlag, 1933–.
Energetik 1928	C.G. Jung, *Über die Energetik der Seele und andere psychologische Abhandlungen*. Zürich: Rascher Verlag, 1928.
Energetik 1948	C.G. Jung, *Die psychische Energetik und das Wesen der Träume*. Zürich: Rascher Verlag, 1948.
ETH	Eidgenössische Technische Hochschule (Swiss Federal Institute of Technology), Zurich.
ETH Library archive	C.G.Jung-Arbeitsarchiv, Hauptabteilung Handschriften und Nachlässe des Archivs der ETH, Zürich. (C.G. Jung Archive, Department of Manuscripts and Legacies, Archive of the Swiss Federal Institute of Technology, Zurich).
FJL	*The Freud/Jung Letters*. Ed. William McGuire, trans. R. Mannheim & R.F.C. Hull. PUP/London: Hogarth Press, Routledge & Kegan Paul, 1974.

God & Unc.	Victor White, *God and the Unconscious*. London: Harvill Press, 1952; revised ed., Dallas, Texas: Spring Publications, 1982.
GPP	The Guild of Pastoral Psychology, London/Oxford, founded 1937.
GW	*Die Gesammelten Werke von C.G. Jung*, 21 volumes. (Cf. Selected Bibliography, p. 367.)
Hiob	C.G. Jung, *Antwort auf Hiob*. Zürich: Rascher Verlag, 1952.
IGS	Ann Conrad Lammers, *In God's Shadow: The Collaboration of Victor White and C.G. Jung*. Mahwah, NJ: Paulist Press, 1994.
Integration	C.G. Jung, *The Integration of the Personality*. Trans. Stanley Dell. New York: Farrar & Rinehart, 1939.
Job	C.G. Jung, *Answer to Job*. Trans. R.F.C. Hull. London: Routledge & Kegan Paul, 1954.
Jungians	Thomas B. Kirsch, *The Jungians: A Comparative and Historical Perspective*. London & Philadelphia: Routledge, 2000.
Letters I, II	*C.G. Jung Letters. Vol. I: 1906–1950; Vol. II: 1951–1961*. Selected and edited by Gerhard Adler in collaboration with Aniela Jaffé, trans. R.F.C. Hull. PUP/London: Routledge, 1973, 1975.
MDR	C.G. Jung, *Memories, Dreams, Reflections*. Written with Aniela Jaffé, trans. Richard & Clara Winston, revised ed. New York: Vintage Books, 1961.
Mysterium	C.G. Jung, *Mysterium Coniunctionis: An Inquiry in the Separation and Synthesis of Psychic Opposites in Alchemy*, CW 14. (Corresponds to GW 14, Band I & II.)
ODCC	*Oxford Dictionary of the Christian Church*. Eds Cross & Livingstone, 2nd ed. Oxford: Oxford University Press, 1974.
Psych & Alch.	C.G. Jung, *Psychologie und Alchemie*. Zürich: Rascher-Verlag, 1944. CW 12, *Psychology and Alchemy*. Trans. R.F.C. Hull. PUP/Bollingen; London: Routledge & Kegan Paul, 1953/1968.
Psych & Rel.	C.G. Jung, *Psychology and Religion: West and East*, CW 11, 1958/1969.
PUP	Princeton University Press, Princeton, NJ.
ST	St. Thomas Aquinas, *Summa Theologiae*. Oxford: Blackfriars, in conjunction with New York: McGraw-Hill, and London: Eyre & Spottiswode, 1964–1975.
Structure & Dynamics	C.G. Jung, *The Structure and Dynamics of the Psyche*, CW 8, 1960/1969.

Symbolik	C.G. Jung, *Symbolik des Geistes: Studien über psychische Phänomenologie*, 1948.
Transference	C.G. Jung, *The Practice of Psychotherapy: Essays on the Psychology of the Transference and Other Subjects*, CW 16, 1954/1966.
Two Essays	C.G. Jung, *Two Essays on Analytical Psychology*, CW 7, 1953/1956.
Types	C.G. Jung, *Psychological Types*, CW 6, 1971.
Wandlungen	C.G. Jung, *Wandlungen und Symbole der Libido: Beiträge zur Entwicklungsgeschichte des Denkens*. Leipzig and Vienna: Franz Deuticke, 1912.

INTRODUCTION

It has been pointed out that Jung's literary deposit includes letters, most still unpublished, numbering in the tens of thousands.[1] According to Aniela Jaffé, who served as Jung's secretary at the end of his life and edited the German edition of his collected letters,[2] the preservation of his letters began in earnest in the 1930s (*Briefe I*, p. 8). In the mid-1950s, at the urging of friends, Jung began to envision publishing parts of what had already grown into a virtual library of correspondence. Jaffé recalls the day in 1956 when Gerhard Adler, later the editor of Jung's collected letters in English, came to visit Jung, then 81, and an agreement was finally struck: a selection of his letters should be prepared for publication (*Briefe I*, p. 7). In his account of this important visit (*Letters I*, p. ix),[3] Adler recalls that Jung handed him a file of letters labelled *Pfarrerbriefe*. These "clergy letters," he urged, should be considered first for publication.

The present volume fulfils, if not that exact wish of Jung's, a closely related one. One of Jung's collections of clergy letters was of such singular importance to him that he made special arrangements for its safekeeping before he died. This was his correspondence with Father Victor White, the English Dominican priest and theologian who became, for several years at the end of both their lives, Jung's most important theological conversation partner, and his friend.

When he himself was already an old man, Franz Jung told me the story[4] of

1 Sonu Shamdasani, *Jung and the Making of Modern Psychology: The Dream of a Science* (Cambridge, UK: Cambridge University Press, 2003), pp. 22f.

2 *C.G. Jung Briefe, Band I, 1906–1945; Band II, 1946–1955; Band III, 1956–1961*. Herausgegeben von Aniela Jaffé, in Zusammenarbeit mit Gerhard Adler. Zürich: Walter-Verlag, 1972/1981. (Hereafter, *Briefe I, II, III*.)

3 To a large extent Adler's "Introduction" and Jaffé's "Vorwort" run parallel; but passages also diverge, as here, reflecting the editors' separate sensibilities and experiences.

4 Private communication, Franz Jung, 17 August 1991. Cf. also Lammers, *In God's Shadow: The Collaboration of Victor White and C.G. Jung* (Mahwah, NJ: Paulist Press, 1994; hereafter, *IGS*), Appendix A, "The Letters of Victor White," pp. 257ff.

how his father, at the end of his life, had handed to him a zippered leather case, containing some 150 letters and related papers, the epistolary remains of a once inspiring, later conflictual, finally tragic relationship. Jung gave solemn instructions to keep these letters from the eyes of the world until a suitable editor could be found. So the letters of Jung and White, with their addenda and enclosures (journal offprints, dreams, drawings, typescripts, writings by third parties), were kept safe by Franz Jung for 30 years after his father's death. Access to them during these years was highly restricted.[5]

Jung's care with White's letters and his double injunction, to conceal and to publish them, recall his complicated instructions about whether and when to publish his correspondence with Freud. Having appointed the original Editorial Committee for his letters in 1956, he charged them to treat his correspondence with Freud separately, withholding it from publication "as long as the waves of hostility are still running so high."[6] Jung proposed a delay of 30 years after his death, Jaffé recalls, in order to establish Freud and himself as "historical personalities" (*Briefe I*, pp. 9f). William McGuire, editor of *The Freud–Jung Letters*, has reported that at various times Jung wanted his letters to and from Freud withheld from publication for periods of up to 100 years (*FJL*, p. xxxiii). In the event, however, for the reasons laid out in McGuire's Introduction to that volume, they were published only 13 years after Jung's death.

Jung was of two minds about publishing any of his correspondence.[7] In the course of corresponding with White, however, he became convinced that at least some of their letters belonged to the public discourse about psychology and religion. Starting in 1953 his handwritten notes appear on particular letters to and from White: *für die Pfarrerbriefe!* ("for the clergy letters!"). The holograph of one of his major letters to White includes instructions to make multiple copies, to be filed with other papers intended for publication.

Still one might ask, granted that Jung meant to publish some of these letters, what justifies publishing all of them? The decision is justified on several

5 The restriction was not absolute, however. Between Jung's death and the release of the Jung–White letters for publication, carefully chosen readers had access to them. About two-thirds of Jung's letters to White have been published previously (cf. List of Letters, p. 363.) In the late 1960s, while editing Jung's letters, Gerhard Adler had access to both sides of the correspondence and was able to quote or paraphrase White's letters to Jung in the annotations to Jung's letters to White. In 1986 Franz Jung also read through the correspondence in order to answer questions I had asked about White's letters. His answer was incorporated into my dissertation and later published (cf. *IGS*, pp. 259f).

6 *"so lange die Wogen der Gehässigkeit noch so hoch schlagen"* (*Briefe I*, p. 9, trans. ACL).

7 Jaffé writes, "Jung was ambivalent about publishing his letters. Neverthless in later years, when the publication plan was already established, he would sometimes remark that what he had just dictated was intended not only as a communication to the addressee, but was first and foremost 'for the Letters' " (Ibid., p. 7, trans. ACL).

grounds. One is Jung's own decision, at the end of his life, to hand over to his son not only the small portion of White's letters he had previously marked for publicaton but the entire correspondence, including addenda and enclosures. Next, the requirements of historical scholarship argue for full publication. These letters are irreplaceable primary documents, and their textual integrity is essential to the research on which all historical knowledge rests. On this basis, the editors must show strong reasons for omitting even a single word.[8] Finally, there is the argument of the heart. The letters of Jung and White, read in their entirety, tell a riveting human story and show us the writers as full human beings. We would lose that glimpse of them, and the soul of their story, if only their "professional/scientific" letters were published.[9]

If the concerns of Franz Jung[10] about the Jung–White correspondence reflected those of his father, it is fair to say that Jung hoped these letters would be given to editors who, in addition to observing clinical confidentiality and privacy, would maintain equal relationships with both sides in a painful, many-faceted conflict. The adversarial division which undermined the friendship of Jung and White, revolving around their divergent ideas of God and the Self, arose from a thicket of misunderstandings and led to mutual wounding and increasingly bitter reproach. Editing the Jung–White letters for publication has been an ongoing process of "holding the opposites together," with all the perils and imperfections this endeavor implies.

Victor White was a thinker. He was 27 years younger than Jung but was also, like Jung, a pioneer in his field, which was Catholic (Thomistic) theology. For personal reasons White entered Jungian analysis in Oxford during the Second World War. He plunged into reading Jung's published

8 The argument is made, by Ernst Falzeder, Sonu Shamdasani and others, that it is wrong to omit even a single word when publishing texts such as these, on grounds that it obstructs the advance of learning; and further, unless original documents are defaced, in the long run it is pointless (cf. Ernst Falzeder, "Some Reflections on Editing Freud's Correspondence," in *Behind the Scenes: Freud in Correspondence*, eds C. Bonomi, P. Mahoney, J. Stensson. Scandinavian Press, 1997). I am grateful to Dr. Shamdasani for raising my awareness on these issues while this book was in preparation. I often find, however, that I am guided by more than one set of concerns, coexisting and sometimes conflicting with the commitment to pure science, and therefore I have not always been able to make editorial decisions that were simply and clearly right. When forced to choose between two errors, I have tried to make the error I could best defend.

9 Aniela Jaffé likewise expressed her hope that Jung's letters to members of his family might be published someday, because they "surpass the factual/scientific" to reveal *"eine wenig bekannte Seite im Wesen Jungs"* ("a little-known side of Jung's nature") (*Briefe I*, p. 9, trans. ACL).

10 Private communication, Franz Jung, 19 September 1992. After this conversation Mr. Jung also wrote an account of the Jung Heirs' decision to release the Jung–White letters from the locked family archive (cf. Editorial Note, p. 357). Writing in English, he asked me to edit his statement for style and return it for approval (private correspondence, Franz Jung, 1 Nov. 1992). The edited account was later published (*IGS*, pp. 261ff).

works in both English and German and was excited to discover key points of contact between Jung's thought and the Thomistic theology that was his own creative field. His long-term, ambitious goal was to point the way toward a new Thomistic synthesis between orthodox Catholic doctrine and the best of modern science, which he had found, he believed, in Jung's psychology.

White first wrote to Jung in August 1945, when the international mail service was working after the war, and enclosed four journal articles he had written in the meantime about his proposed synthesis. In these essays White explored key writings by Jung and criticized the work of fellow theologians who had tried, with mixed success, to discuss the psychologies of Freud and Jung from a theological standpoint. Jung digested these offprints and then, with unwonted speed, welcomed White as the long-sought answer to a beleaguered scientist's prayer. The rest of their story occupies the pages that follow.

Since this is a story of interdisciplinary collaboration, readers on either side of the theology–psychology divide, not to mention those in different fields, may wonder what tempted representatives of such different professions into the risky process of theoretical bridge-building. The theology–psychology dialogue occupies no-man's-land, a territory mined with risks of misunderstanding and threatened by political crossfire. What historical factors propelled this psychologist and this theologian to gamble their personal resources and professional reputations in the debate between faith and science?

The relationship between theologians and psychologists has long been one of suspicion, if not outright hostility. In White's case, as a Catholic religious and priest, and a teacher of future priests, the professional stakes were especially high. After he first visited Jung in Bollingen, White dreamed they were sailing at great speed among rocks. Jung wrote back, "We are indeed on an adventurous and dangerous journey!"[11] One might suspect that a philosophically trained theologian and a medically trained psychologist, having been schooled in such different modes of reaching and defending conclusions, would quickly encounter theoretical problems, their basic assumptions being so mismatched. In fact, this turned out to be the case with Jung and White. They experienced difficulties at the levels of doctrine and interpretation. Underneath, controlling both these levels of discourse, their epistemologies (theories of knowledge) were in conflict.[12]

Jung is firmly committed to a theory of knowledge that springs from a neo-Kantian philosophy and views the soul (or psyche) as the primary organ

11 Cf. White, 13 Oct. 1946, p. 45; Jung, 6 Nov. 1946, p. 53.

12 The theoretical and historical observations offered in this paragraph and those following are thoroughly explored in my earlier work. For a deeper discussion of the roots and ramifications of the two men's divergent epistemologies, cf. *IGS*, especially ch. 1, "Builders of Bridges" (pp. 11ff); ch. 2, "Thomism and the Warrants of Experience" (pp. 40ff); and ch. 4, "Jung's Relationship to Christian Thought" (pp. 114ff).

of knowing. Jung always starts from and returns to his conviction that the psyche is the only available lens through which images of reality are experienced and interpreted. By this theory everything – even such unfathomable realities as the soul, nature, and God – is known subjectively, experientially or, as Jung likes to say, empirically. By contrast White's theological method begins with the church's three classic sources of authority: revelation, tradition, and reason, to which he adds an important fourth: experience. This fourth source of knowledge, experience, did not occupy the same place of importance for many of White's Dominican contemporaries. But it was, as I argue elsewhere,[13] a very important part of White's theology, and the part which made him genuinely open to Jung's thought.

Jung's epistemology made him suspicious of most theologians, for what he saw as their tendency to dodge reality and flee into metaphysical realms where they could assert doctrinal and credal claims as true, whether or not these claims made a pragmatic connection with experience, in a subjective or psychological sense. At times Jung was merely amused, but often he was angrily impatient with what he saw as the "medieval" frame of mind that could ignore facts, if necessary, to defend a truth that existed only in the abstract.

Yet as he grew older Jung also experienced a powerful sense that he was called to treat the spiritual and religious ills of patients who, as he wrote, were suffering psychologically for lack of an authentic spiritual life. He began to reach out to theologians, especially to Catholics, whose ancient symbols and creeds he found both alien and compelling. From his father, a Swiss Reformed pastor, Jung felt he had absorbed enough Protestantism to last a lifetime. For the sake of his patients, however, and for his collective "patient," Western Christianity,[14] he came to a point where he had to ask for help, to gain access to the symbolic language of Catholicism.

When White wrote to him, Jung had long been yearning to carry on a truly psychological dialogue with his Catholic consultants. So White's apparent grasp of and openness to empirical reasoning surprised and pleased him enormously. He could not have known, in advance of their debate, that White's commitment to experiential thought was not absolute but was balanced by his enduring respect for revelation, tradition, and reason, the three authorities invoked in classical Christian discourse. White's epistemology thus had four roots, whereas Jung's, arguably, had only one.

The two men quickly acknowledged their different educations and work

13 Cf. *IGS*, ch. 2, "Thomism and the Warrants of Experience," especially pp. 48ff.

14 For a thorough discussion of how Jung developed his sense of mission to the broken soul of Western civilization, cf. Murray Stein, *Jung's Treatment of Christianity: The Psychotherapy of a Religious Tradition* (Wilmette, IL: Chiron Publications, 1985). The theme is discussed also in my book, *IGS*, ch. 4, pp. 144ff, "Saving the Christian West."

environments, but they did not take time to test the depth of those differences. They felt the pressure of Jung's advancing age, and they were also laboring under the impact of all the revelations of evil and suffering in the war just ended. For these and other reasons they rushed into collaboration, believing they could build a solid bridge between their divergent modes of thought. White was particularly optimistic on this count. He observed that they used language and concepts differently but thought that with diligence their differences could be resolved. Later, when the relationship was undergoing acute strains, he still pointed to their typological differences, as if hoping that they faced no irreconcilable contradiction, but were simply viewing the same reality from two angles.

Jung and White agreed at the outset about what constituted the inner experience and objective welfare of the human soul but disagreed about many other things which would have been essential to their shared task, such as the source and extent of human knowledge about God, the definition and foundation of faith, and the grounds for ultimate hopefulness about the destiny of creation. These disagreements proved so vast that, even if all the other variables affecting their relationship had been positive, the conceptual divide would perhaps have been unbridgeable. Their falling out, which erupted in earnest after Jung's publication of *Answer to Job*, only laid bare the fundamental barriers to their collaboration. For all White's distress about it, *Job* did not create these obstacles; they were present from the start.

In his earliest letters White "writes up" to Jung, as if addressing a great master whose goodwill he dreads to lose. He emphasizes their points of convergence and avoids mentioning passages in Jung's writings with which he disagrees. One of these was Jung's broadside attack, in the published text of his 1940 lecture on the Trinity, against the Catholic doctrine treating evil as the "privation of good." When White finally takes Jung to task for inferior theology, in his fierce review of Jung's 1948 lecture about the Self, he writes as if to a first-year Dominican, referring Jung to texts that will correct his fundamental error. It is a crucial turning point in the relationship. As the two men discover more about each other, their disagreements become tougher and more frustrating, until it becomes evident that their opposing views of God, evil, and the human soul are based not only on conflicting theories of knowledge but on their deepest personal commitments, the nondebatable ground in which their respective epistemologies are rooted.

Jung and White were brought together by shared, passionate convictions concerning the spiritual healing of individuals and collectives. Each one, using his own language, related spiritual health to psychological wholeness, interpreting the latter as the integration of opposites within the personality. White was enthusiastically willing to embrace Jungian psychology, as far as he understood it, and saw himself as a proto-analyst. In this respect their relationship was asymmetrical: Jung did not reciprocate. His rejection of metaphysical arguments, despite his own commitment to Kantian idealism,[15] and his resistance to collective authority – especially when this authority spoke in a voice of religious orthodoxy – made it highly unlikely that he would ever enter White's world, as White longed to enter his.

Jung had grown up with the sinewy individualism of the Swiss Reformed tradition, which holds the soul's relationship to God to be solitary and direct, unmediated by any outer authority; although the local pastor's interpretation of the Bible (in Zwingli's translation) would be taken into account. Jung never repudiated this tradition, of which his pastor father had been his most influential, if ambivalent, teacher. White, meanwhile, son of an Anglican priest, had converted to Catholicism in his teens and treasured the credal and metaphysical thought-world which was his heritage.[16] He held a complex, sacramental view of the church's communal body, his inner world having been shaped by his Dominican education and by decades of service to his community of faith. He could neither overcome Jung's resistance to credal and doctrinal statements nor share it. His appropriation of Jung's psychology was based on his prior conviction that truth, like God, is unitary.[17] He could only wring his hands at Jung's insistence that unconsciousness and evil are intrinsic to the very nature of God.

Historical contingencies also impinged heavily on the relationship. The collaboration of White and Jung unfolded during a period in the twentieth century when many Catholic theologians, not just White, felt the ground of ecclesial politics shift beneath them. White depended on his Order, in which he had lived since young adulthood; yet he also suffered repeatedly from wrenching vocational conflicts. With these internal struggles as a backdrop, he recognized the bitter irony of the blow dealt to him in the summer of 1954 when suddenly and without explanation he was deprived of his appointment as Regent of Studies at Oxford Blackfriars.

White had confided his renewed vocational doubts to Jung late in 1953 and early in 1954, when he came close to leaving the Order. With Jung's support and counsel he had concluded it was right to stay where he was, even though this would mean again signing an anti-modernist oath, with which he

15 Cf. Marilyn Nagy, *Philosophical Issues in the Psychology of C.G. Jung* (Albany, NY: State University of New York Press, 1991), especially ch. 1, ch. 3, and ch. 7, "Two Epistemological Discussions by Jung."

16 Cf. Adrian Cunningham, "Victor White, a Memoir," Appendix 2, pp. 307ff, below. Cf. also Adrian Cunningham, "Victor White and C.G. Jung, the fateful encounter of the White Raven and the Gnostic" (*New Blackfriars*, July/August 1981, pp. 320–334).

17 White treats this theme in a foundational essay, written before he met Jung's thought, which concludes that the medieval synthesis of St. Anselm, St. Albert, and St. Thomas Aquinas must be re-created in a new form for modern people. Faith and science do not conflict, he argues, but point to the same truth ("Scholasticism," London: Catholic Truth Society, 1934, esp. pp. 18–26; 30f).

emphatically disagreed, as the price of his new position. White had just made his peace with this decision when he experienced his public humiliation. This series of events should be kept in mind, I believe, when considering the rupture of the Jung–White friendship in mid-1955. This was the time, as it happens, when C.G. and Emma Jung were facing the terminal cancer diagnosis which had just been delivered to her. Jung's capacity to deal kindly with a troubled and troubling friend was doubtless less than it might have been. For whatever reason, his need to separate himself from White at this point was apparently so absolute that, had it not been for the mediation that came later from an extraordinary direction, during White's final illness, their story would have ended, like the Freud–Jung story, in silence.

In the annotations to Jung's collected letters, Adler and Jaffé clarify themes and references, making the letters accessible to an educated but not necessarily "Jungian" readership. These editors had the advantage of personal acquaintance with Jung, combined with practical knowledge of and dedication to his psychology. By today's standards their work may lack something in historical or scholarly rigor; but they provided a footnote apparatus of psychological depth and integrity, which for 40 years many serious readers – myself included – have found immensely valuable.

Being an English-speaker, and working on letters written originally in English, I have always leaned on Adler's annotations more than Jaffé's. When I began to edit the Jung–White correspondence, it was the height of my intention at first simply to "do as Adler did," or try. But sincere imitation soon led to differentiation, for I found it impossible to follow Adler's example in detail. My departure from Adler's model was inevitable, it has dawned on me, because *C.G. Jung Letters* and *The Jung–White Letters* are of different genres. Jung's collected letters provide a rich overview of his thought and feeling on myriad topics, through a thousand letters, addressed to hundreds of correspondents, over five and a half decades. Yet for all its riches, *C.G. Jung Letters* is necessarily a one-sided work. Apart from the summaries, paraphrases and quotations in its footnotes, the voices of Jung's correspondents are silent. This establishes a certain terrain for the reader to travel on, and a certain frame around the editor's work. *The Jung–White Letters*, on the other hand, is a close-knit dialogue; so its terrain is different, and the editor's framework changes accordingly.

Likewise, although I expected to borrow heavily from Adler's notes for Jung's letters to White, the tightly woven fabric of *The Jung–White Letters* creates its own intellectual and cultural context, to which Adler's notes are not always attuned. To take a contrast which seems obvious once pointed out, Adler's notes on Jung's letters to White are predicated on the absence of White's letters to Jung. As soon as White's letters become part of the primary text, the flow of information in the book undergoes a radical transformation. In the simplest case, a person, book or idea may be named first by White. Annotation is generally provided where a thing is first mentioned; so by the time Jung addresses it, much of the necessary information has already been provided, in a context which takes both White's cultural world and Jung's into account. For this reason alone, I often found it impossible to adopt Adler's notes verbatim.

With certain exceptions, the annotations in this volume are mine. For the sake of stylistic consistency, strands from Adler's notes are sometimes woven into my own. In these instances, as when other scholarly sources are quoted or paraphrased, credit is given in the normal fashion, citing author and source. Notes written by Adrian Cunningham or Murray Stein, in whole or in part, are also marked as such.

For the last three decades *C.G. Jung Letters* has been a valued work partly because it provides such a lively portrait of a brilliant personality, through the medium of his correspondence. As a portrait, though, it is the work of a court painter, because Jung's words in English are not left as he wrote them. With a great deal of help from R.F.C. Hull, whom Adler thanks for his assistance with these "improvements" (*Letters I*, p. xviii), Jung's English is smoothed over. Through a thousand small emendations, his rough edges, grammatical errors and eccentricities are trimmed away, his diction corrected. Ironically, given Jung's desire to embrace his shadow at all costs, with such improvements the individuality of the writer is subtly diminished.

An example may illustrate. Jung wrote to White from his sickbed in December 1946, with a shaky hand, that his "haleness" had been tested but he was now "hale" again. In the Adler/PUP edition these words are silently corrected to "wholeness" and "whole" (*Letters I*, p. 450). The likely reason for such a change was to standardize Jung's English, by removing the unexpected word, as a practiced portraitist might remove a blemish from an honored subject's face. One change in wording was not so harmless, however. It is hard to understand why, in a passage referring to human hubris, an editor (more likely Hull than Adler) corrected Jung's intended meaning, substituting the word "Evil" for Jung's plainly written "Good" (*Letters I*, p. 540 and note).[18] The overall result of most such changes was to heighten the impression of Jung's mastery of English (already astonishingly good), in order to present his letters as a polished literary work.

Perhaps there is such a thing as leaning too far the other way. If so, the editors of this book will be judged accordingly. Adler defended his policy, pointing out that "Jung submitted all of his English lectures and writings to the criticism of English-speaking people for revision" (*Letters I*, p. xvi). I would simply refer once again to the distinction between one work of "letters" and another. Adler may have been fully justified in treating Jung's collected letters as belonging to the same literary genre as his published lectures and essays. In the correspondence of Jung and White, however, we

18 Compare below, Jung, 31 Dec. 1949, p. 142 and note.

find a different type of literature, not magisterial but personal, relational, intimate. The authority of these letters rests on their trustworthiness as accurate reproductions of the letters two people actually sent each other.[19]

For this reason the editors of this volume have followed the model of scribes, copying out precious originals that might otherwise be lost. Conscious that the printed page is already a reduction, a loss of information, I transcribed the letters as if I were the writers' servant. If they drew attention to their errors and found meaning in them, who was I to find a particular error too insignificant to preserve? At an early point in the editing, Adrian and Angela Cunningham checked my transcriptions of the primary texts with enormous care, and thus not only established the text but also confirmed the policy of making these printed letters reflect the originals as fully as possible.

That discrete task aside, it would be hard to overstate the overall contribution of my co-editor. Adrian Cunningham has worked in countless ways over the months to bring this volume to a level of clear and responsible scholarship. Our consulting editor has worked strategically, putting his wide knowledge, wisdom and tact into the project. Without his help I doubt this work would have reached publication. After all our efforts, however, if errors still remain in text or notes, they are on my account.

It is true, but inadequate, to say that White and Jung corresponded in English. The use of English on both sides of the correspondence is vigorous, literate and fluent, although Jung's often has (like his spoken English) a strong Swiss accent. But their letters are enriched by words and phrases, sometimes entire passages, in Latin and – in Jung's case – Greek. White, who omits Greek from his list of reliable languages,[20] uses it only sparingly in this correspondence; but his Latin easily matches Jung's. Both make frequent use of German, the language in which White knew many of Jung's writings. Their letters are also sprinkled with French, Italian and Spanish.

Themes to which they turn their attention are not limited to academic theology and psychology. They also address practical problems with analysands and colleagues, cultural movements, the philosophy of science, the meaning of faith, and biting existential issues, such as how to stay the course in the midst of unbearable inner and outer conflict. Their unresolved struggle over the nature and origin of evil, which eventually drove them apart, was

19 I want to thank both the Jung Heirs and the publishers at Princeton University Press for their permission to publish this version of Jung's letters to White. Ulrich Hoerni, representing the C.G. Jung Estate, gave his *placet* for this edition of Jung's letters to White, in a written communication to Princeton University Press on 23 November 2004. Permission to republish Jung's previously published English-language letters in a version which reverts to original texts was kindly granted by Princeton University Press on receipt of Mr. Hoerni's letter.

20 "I can read fairly easily French, German, Spanish, Italian, Latin" (White, 9 Oct. 1945, p. 12).

grounded in their mutual desire to find a shared symbolic language about God and the Self – the same goal which first drew them together. Mutual dedication to such ultimate matters is part of what gives their dialogue its poignancy.

As it is important to honor Jung and White in their struggle with inner shadows, it has also seemed right to let their written shadows stand. Textual rough edges and annotations about them may strike some readers as awkward; if so, I take the blame. I have made exceptions, however, to spare the reader unnecessary distraction. If a detail is unbearably petty, or to avoid cluttering the footnote apparatus beyond reason, a few typing errors have been silently corrected, and a few Greek accents quietly moved. In the end, even if one looks under every stone and tracks down every connection, the letters of Jung and White remain full of mystery. What they mean is far more than the words.

Ann Lammers, Ph.D.
Easter 2005

1945

Figure 1.1 Blackfriars, St Giles, Oxford.

Blackfriars[1]
Oxford
Telephone 3607[2]

3rd August 1945[3]

Dear Professor Jung,

Although I have never had the honour to meet you (outside of my dreams!), I am taking the very great liberty of sending to you some of my writings concerning your psychology, written from a Catholic point of view.[4] I doubt, of course, whether you will have time or inclination to read them, let alone to comment upon them; but should you ever do so, it would be a great help to me & any future work I am able to do if I could be shown any points on which I have positively misunderstood you.

I might mention that there is great & growing interest in this country among Catholics (as well as many others) in the theory & practice of Analytical Psychology; & that I personally am one of very many who owe to you & your disciples in England an immense debt of gratitude.

May I be permitted to convey my belated congratulations on your recent birthday, & express my thankfulness for your recovery.

Yours very obediently, gratefully, FR. VICTOR WHITE, O.P.

1 English Dominican priory, located on St Giles in the city of Oxford (cf. photographs, Figure 1.1, p. 2). The house was founded in 1921 by then Provincial, Bede Jarrett, O.P. In September 1929 (the church having been consecrated in May) the officers of the English Dominican studium moved to the new priory. Dominican schooling consists of three years in philosophy, followed by four in theology. The theological studium has been located at Oxford Blackfriars since 1929, and later the philosophical studium was also moved there, with the closing of the Hawkesyard priory (cf. White, 14 Oct. 1945, p. 13 and note; also Appendix 2, "Victor White, a Memoir," p. 310). [AC] (Cf. also Lammers, *IGS*, pp. 43f.)

2 Full information in each writer's letterhead (address, phone number, etc.) is reproduced only in the letters of the first year. Thereafter, when a letter shows the usual letterhead, sender's address is minimized.

3 Handwritten on both sides of a half-sheet of Blackfriars letterhead. On the second side White added a postscript in the left margin, perpendicular to the body of the letter.

4 With this letter White enclosed offprints of four of his recent essays on Jung's psychology: "The Frontiers of Theology and Psychology" (Oxford: The Guild of Pastoral Psychology, Lecture 19, October 1942); "St. Thomas Aquinas and Jung's Psychology" (*Blackfriars*, Vol. XXV, June 1944); "Psychotherapy and Ethics" (Ibid., Vol. XXVI, August 1945), and a "Postscript" to the latter (Ibid., Vol. XXVI, October 1945). "Psychotherapy and Ethics" had recently been reprinted by the Newman Association, subtitled "A Tribute to C.G. Jung on his 70th birthday"; White enclosed this copy. Apart from the one on Aquinas, all these foundational essays become chapters in White's first book, *God and the Unconscious* (London: Harvill Press, 1952; revised edition, Dallas, TX: Spring Publications, 1982). (Hereafter, *God & Unc.*)

P.S. I have also just finished a short article concerning the criticisms of your attitude to religion in J.C. Flugel's "Man, Morals & Society"[5] – which I will also take the liberty of sending to you.

Prof. Dr. C.G. Jung
Küsnacht-Zürich
Seestrasse 228[6]

September 26th, 1945[7]

The Rev. Father Victor White, O.P.
Blackfriars,
Oxford

Dear Father,[8]

It has been a great pleasure and surprise to me to receive your interesting articles about my psychology. Owing to the fact that I celebrated my 70th birthday[9] this summer I have still not emerged from the floods of correspondence that have invaded me. Thus I can only thank you to-day for your kindness and to beg your pardon that I am so late in answering your letter.

I'm highly interested in the point of view the church takes with reference to my work. I had many discussions with catholic priests in this country too and it is on my instigation that catholic scholars have been invited to the Eranos lectures[10] of which you presumably have heard. We enjoy now

5 J.C. Flugel, *Man, Morals, and Society: A Psycho-analytical Study* (London: Duckworth, 1945). White reviewed Flugel's Freudian critique of Jung's ideas in "Psychotherapy and Ethics: Postscript" (op. cit.).

6 Address of the large house on Lake Zurich, in the village of Küsnacht (southeast of Zurich – cf. map of Lake Zurich area, Figure 5.1, p. 137), which C.G. and Emma Jung built in 1909 and where they raised their five children. Jung had an office on the second floor where he saw patients and did much of his writing and professional business.

7 Typewritten by secretary, from holograph, on Jung's letterhead.

8 In *C. G. Jung Letters*: "Dear Father White" (*Letters I*, p. 381).

9 Jung was born 26 July 1875.

10 Annual interdisciplinary gatherings held at a lakeside villa, Eranos, in Porto Ronco near Ascona in the canton of Tessin (Ticino), Switzerland. Jung and other invited lecturers took turns presenting papers. Here Jung gave his most important papers from the inception of the Eranos Tagungen (meetings), in 1933, until the early 1950s, when poor health and old age forced his withdrawal from active public engagements. (Cf. William McGuire, *Bollingen, an Adventure in Collecting the Past* (PUP, 1982).) White first attended an Eranos gathering in 1946.

the collaboration of an extremely competent scholar of the patristic literature, professor Hugo Rahner S.J.[11] of Innsbruck University. Quite a number of catholic publications have been occupied with my psychology in this country too and there are some among them, which are really very understanding. I must say that I never would have expected so much appreciation and real understanding from the theological quarter. Owing to rather obvious reasons the protestant theology is rather reticent and they don't know yet whether I should be condemned as an heretic or depreciated as a mystic. As you know, mysticism and hereticism enjoy about the same bad reputation in protestantism. So there is not much hope for me left from that side.

I shall certainly read your articles with greatest interest and then I will avail myself of the pleasure to write to you again in order to tell you what my reactions were. For the time being I can only thank you for your kindness.

Yours sincerely, [C.G. JUNG] (unsigned carbon copy)

Prof. Dr. C.G. Jung
Küsnacht-Zürich
Seestrasse 228

Oct. 5th, 1945[12]

My dear Father White,

In the meantime I have finished reading the pamphlets you kindly have sent to me. My first reaction was: what a pity, that you live in England and that I have you not at my elbow, when I am blundering in the wide field of theological knowledge. You must grant me though attenuating circumstances: beside all the other things I had to learn I arrived only very late at the treasurehouse of patristic wisdom, so late in fact, that my limited powers didn't suffice any more to acquire all which would be needed to elucidate and explain the perplexities of modern psychological experience. Excuse the

11 Hugo Rahner, S.J. (1900–1968): Theologian, church historian and archeologist, at this time professor at the theological faculty, University of Innsbruck, Austria. His books include *Ignatius the Theologian* (1961), *Church and State in Early Christianity* (1962), and *Greek Myths and Christian Mystery* (1963). The latter contains his Eranos lectures of 1943 and 1944, as well as his contribution to the Festschrift for Jung's seventieth birthday (*EJ XII*, 1945). He was the older brother of Karl Rahner (1904–1984).

12 Typewritten on letterhead. The holograph is dated "Oct. 1st." It was customary for the secretary to redate Jung's typed letters as of the date of typing.

irreverential pun: You are to me a white raven[13] inasmuch as you are the only theologian I know of who has really understood something of what the problem of psychology in our present world means. You have seen its enormous implications. I cannot tell you how glad I am that I know a man, a theologian, who is conscientious enough to weigh my opinions on the basis of a careful study of my writings! This is a really rare occasion.[14]

My temperamental empiricism has its reasons. I began my career with repudiating everything that smelt of belief. That explains my critical attitude in my "Psychology of the Unconscious".[15] You should know, that this book has been written by a psychiatrist with the purpose to submit the necessary material to his psychiatric colleagues, a material, which should demonstrate to them the importance of religious symbolism. My audience then was a thoroughly materialistic crowd, and I would have defeated my own ends, if I had set out with a definite creed or with definite metaphysical assertions. I was not and I did not want to be anything else but one of them. My principle was always not to seek the place where I might do something useful, but to do it there where I actually was. I was impressed with their utter lack of knowledge in matters of symbolism and I wanted to do my best to provide it for them. Only too late I have discovered that it weren't my colleagues at all but very different people who became interested in my work. I have tried to accommodate myself to the psychiatric and medical mind, hardened and often made cynical through the relentless onslaught of brutal and cruel facts and the depravity of mankind.

13 The usual association to ravens, portending death, does not fit this context. A familiar German idiom, "*ein weisser Rabe*" refers to a great rarity. In addition, there is a play on White's name, and possibly a reference to the biblical story (I Kings 17.1–6), where Elijah, in danger of starving, is fed by ravens.

14 In Jung's holograph the first paragraph continues. These sentences were marked for deletion and omitted by the typist: "Prof. Emil Brunner living with me in the same town is typical for the other kind of theologian who in the manner of the grand seigneur wipes me off the slate. Whoever cannot acknowledge the truth of 'gratia perficit naturam' *[grace perfects nature]* proves by this attitude, that he never experienced it. That is the kind of theologian which I always knew, and there is one of the reasons, why I prefer experience to belief."

15 C.G. Jung, *The Psychology of the Unconscious. A Study of the Transformation and Symbolisms of the Libido. A Contribution to the History of the Evolution of Thought*. Translated by Beatrice M. Hinkle from *Wandlungen und Symbole der Libido: Beiträge zur Entwicklungsgeschichte des Denkens* (Leipzig and Vienna: Franz Deuticke, 1912). This translation, generally regarded as a poor one, appeared first in North America (New York: Moffat, Yard, 1916, 1919), then in England (London: Kegan Paul, Trench, Trubner, 1917, 1921). Jung's groundbreaking early work, which precipitated his break with Freud, was later much revised and given a new title. Completed in 1952, it became Volume 5 in Collected Works (hereafter, CW): *Symbols of Transformation: An Analysis of the Prelude to a Case of Schizophrenia*, (1956/1974). In German, Gesammelte Werke (hereafter, GW): *Symbole der Wandlung: Analyse des Vorspiels zu einer Schizophrenie* (1973). White's review of the revised version appeared in *Blackfriars* Vol. XXXVIII, Oct. 1957.

Thus, when I said, that God is a complex, I meant to say: whatever He[16] is, he is *at least* a very tangible complex. You can say, He is an illusion, but He is at least a psychological fact. I surely never intended to say: He is *nothing else* but a complex. Naturally, when my book got into the hands of readers outside my psychiatric sphere, they read it with very different eyes. Hence many mistakes! My book has been originally nothing but a reprint from a psychiatric periodical, which was supposed to be read by doctors chiefly. Concerning my gnoseological standpoint at that time compare please note 42 p.307 Engl. Edit. of the "Psychology of the Unc".[17]

You have rendered justice to my empirical and practical standpoint throughout. I consider this as a very meritorious act, since most of my philosophically or theologically minded readers overlook my empiricism completely. I never allow myself to make statements about the divine entity, since such would be a transgression beyond the limit of science. It would therefore be unfair to criticize my opinions as if they were a philosophical system. My personal view in this matter is, that Man's vital energy or libido is the divine pneuma alright and it was this conviction which it was my secret purpose to bring into the vicinity of my colleagues' understanding. When you want to talk to scientists you cannot start with a religious creed. You have to show the facts and let them draw their own conclusions. You also cannot say, that Man's goal is actually realised in God, but you must again show facts demonstrating in what the goal is realised. What you can show in this respect is the symbol of the self, a well defined psychological phenomenon, which anybody may call God, but the scientist cannot prove it to be God. As a scientist I must give a wide berth to anything dogmatic or metaphysical, since it is not the scientist's task to preach the Gospel. But it is precisely what the theologian has to say, namely that the dogma is the hitherto most perfect answer to and formulation of the most relevant items in the objective psyche and that God has worked all these things in Man's soul. The scientist however can not prove such an assertion, he only can try his best in his limited sphere.

I sympathise fully with you, when you say: "The task before us is gigantic

16 Jung's treatment of the divine pronoun is interestingly inconsistent. Holographs show that he habitually capitalized. In later letters to White (cf. Jung, 24 Nov. 1953) he often went over the draft changing He/His/Him to he/his/him (never the reverse). In earlier letters, as we see here, he might use capital and lower-case pronouns within a single sentence. His secretary at the time – Marie-Jeanne Schmid, who had worked for Jung since 1932 – did not presume to correct this usage.

17 Jung owned the second New York edition of *The Psychology of the Unconscious* (1919; Kegan Paul, 1921), a volume still in his library. The "gnoseological note" attaches to a sentence in Part II, Ch.V, "Symbolism of the Mother and of Rebirth." (It is reprinted here as Appendix 3, pp. 333f.)

indeed".[18] It is enormous and I marvel at the intellectual pachydermia of those who ought to know better and who don't take notice apparently or worse – who try to get rid of the octopus by the most futile arguments. I have frequent discussions with catholic as well as protestant theologians. As a rule they are astonishingly innocent of actual psychological experience and often they seem to have forgotten the wisdom of the Fathers. It is all very well to have it summarized most beautifully by S. Thomas Aquinas, but when it comes to the interpretation of Man's living soul you need actual knowledge. It is far from me to depreciate concepts and formulas. On the contrary I envy you and all enjoying the full possession of scholastic philosophy and I would be surely among the first to welcome an explicit attempt at integrating the fruits of psychology into the ecclesiastic doctrine. I am sure I should draw the greatest benefit from it. I am grateful for every hint you dropped in your papers. I was f.i.[19] most interested in what you said about the problem of the Third Person.[20] I wish you would elucidate me about this subject a bit more. Could you tell me about the sources, where I can find more enlightenment? You can perhaps imagine my feelings of inadequacy when I have to tackle such a problem at short notice. It is usually so, that I keep quiet for years about such intricate matters as f.i. the Trinity. But all of a sudden the subject comes up in a discussion or in a lecture and somebody deals with it in a really inadequate way, then I feel somebody ought to say something more to the point and I am launched utterly unprepared, only supported by my experience with practically nothing on the other, theological side. There I would need some solid theological help. I realise that it can come only from the catholic side, as the sola fide standpoint of the protestant has lost the Tradition of the doctrine too much to be useful in disentangling the knots in the empirical material. This collaboration has been realised to a certain extent as I enjoy the most valuable help of Prof. Hugo Rahner S.J.[21] at Innsbruck University. He is an authority on the ἑρμενευτική[22] of the Fathers. But I see him only rarely and it is most difficult to find out how far his psychological understanding reaches. I think

18 "Psychotherapy and Ethics" (cf. White, 3 Aug. 1945, p. 3 and note) outlines the collaboration he believes must occur between Jung's psychology and Catholic theology, concluding: "The task before us is gigantic indeed." On the same theme, cf. Jung to Pastor Werner Niederer, 23 June 1947, Appendix 1, p. 293).

19 for instance.

20 Third Person of the Trinity, i.e., the Holy Spirit. (Cf. White, 23 Oct. 1945.)

21 Cf. Jung, 26 Sept. 1945, p. 5 and note.

22 (for ἑρμηνευτική) hermeneutics. Because the surface characteristics of these letters, such as errors in typing or spelling, are given importance by the two writers, their spellings and grammatical usages are generally allowed to stand uncorrected. Misspellings in foreign languages are annotated. Silent corrections are made, however, where an annotation would cause unnecessary distraction. (For example, in his "Moses quaternio" – 21 May 1948, p. 121 – Jung accents the name Ἀδάμ incorrectly once, and correctly twice. To avoid confusion, in that case the error is silently corrected.)

he is too careful.[23] Do you know the *Eranos Jahrbücher*?[24] Do you read German? There is stuff for you. If you read German, I should like to send you my book on "Psychology and Alchemy",[25] much better than the badly translated "Integration of Personality",[26] which has been forced out of my hands by the thrift and "pep" of an American publisher. There will be an English edition of it within the next year.

I owe you a special gratitude for kindly remembering my seventieth birthday. The Eranos circle has dedicated a Festschrift[27] in which you find a brilliant paper by Rahner about Moly and Mandragoras[28] and an equally remarkable essay by Layard[29] on the subject of primitive marriage classes and the virginity archetype.[30]

You accuse me of repudiating the divine Transcendence altogether. That is not quite correct. I merely omit it, since I am unable to prove it. I don't preach, I try to establish psychological facts. I can confirm and prove the interrelation of the God image with other parts of the psyche, but I can not go further without committing the error of a metaphysical assertion which is far beyond my scope. I am not a theologian and I have nothing to say about the nature of God. There is no place for subjective confessions in science. Whatever I say about "God" is said about the image expressis verbis.[31] And the image *is* relative, as you yourself have stated.

It is again a matter of to-whom-you-talk. My public does not consist of theologians but of utterly worldly educated people of our day. When you talk of God, they don't know of *what* you talk, since such ideas have been

23 Jung's published letters to Hugo Rahner shed light on this comment. See his letter of 4 August 1945 on the applicability of scholastic language (*Letters I*, pp. 374f).

24 Hardbound annuals, edited by Olga Fröbe-Kapteyn, containing the previous year's Eranos lectures. White was familiar with the *Eranos-Jahrbücher* (hereafter, *EJ*). (Cf. White, 23 Oct. 1945, p. 20 and note, quoting from Jung's 1940 lecture.)

25 C.G. Jung, *Psychologie und Alchemie* (Psychologische Abhandlung 5. Zürich: Rascher Verlag, 1944). Revised, with an additional foreword, it was later republished in German (1952) and appears in English as CW 12 (1953). (Hereafter, *Psych. & Alch.*)

26 C.G. Jung, *The Integration of the Personality* (Trans. Stanley Dell. New York: Farrar & Rinehart, 1939). A compilation and translation of various papers from 1934–37, plus a chapter written for this volume in English. (Hereafter, *Integration.*)

27 *EJ XII: Studien zum Problem des Archetypischen: Festgabe für C.G. Jung zum siebzigsten Geburtstag, 26.Juli 1945* [Studies on the Problem of the Archetypal, Special edition, in honor of C.G. Jung's 70th birthday]. Herausgegeben von Olga Fröbe-Kapteyn. Zürich: Rhein-Verlag, 1945.

28 Hugo Rahner, "Die Seelenheilende Blume, Moly und Mandragora in antiker und christlicher Mystik" ("The Soul-Healing Flower: Moly and mandragora in ancient and Christian mysticism"), *EJ XII* (1945). (Cf. Jung, 26 Sept. 1945, p. 5 and note.)

29 John Willoughby Layard, M.D. (1891–1975), anthropologist and Jungian analyst, then living in Oxford. (Cf. White, 9 Oct. 1945, p. 12 and note.)

30 John Layard, "The Incest Taboo and the Virgin Archetype," *EJ XII* (1945).

31 In the narrow sense, explicitly.

dismissed long ago as nebulous phantasies. I show facts to them and not metaphysical assertions which they can not grasp. If I were talking to peasants I certainly would talk about God, since I know, that they know of what I am talking. It is of *the highest importance* that the educated and "enlightened" public should know religious truth as a thing living in the human soul and not as an abstruse and unreasonable relic of the past. People must be taught to see, where they come in, otherwise you never bridge the gulf between the educated mind and the world of dogmatic ideas, which they comprehend nowhere and which moreover offend their reason. If the Reformers f.i. had ever understood what the Holy Mass is or for what the ritus in general stands, they would certainly not have abandoned it. The appalling lack of understanding threatens the christian religion with complete oblivion. You can not preach to a man who does not understand your language. To shout and to repeat makes no sense. But you feel as I do, that the theologian ought to learn a new language. What if S. Paul had talked on the ἀγορά[32] as if he were in a synagogue? Understanding begins with the individual mind and this means psychology. It is a gigantic task indeed to create a new approach to an old truth. More than once I have put the question to my theological friends: what about new wine in old skins? The old way of interpreting has itself to be interpreted, this time with the help of science. This method can reach the modern mind as I have seen in many cases. I do not combat the christian truth, I am only arguing with the modern mind. We know since long and sufficiently well how things ought to be, but we do not know how to bring them about. This is my main concern. People are not to be lured any more by the promises of Heaven and Hell, they want to understand. I cannot "tell" my patient, I have to seek him and must learn his language and think his thoughts, until he knows that I understand him correctly. Then only he is ready to understand me and at the same time the strange language of the unconscious, that tells him of eternal truths, and incidentally he will discover that he has heard similar things before. That's the practical way. But to get there you have to avoid "suggestions".

Well – a long letter! Not my style at all. "It" has made an exception in your case, my dear Father, because "it" has appreciated your conscientious and far-sighted work.

Yours sincerely, C.G. JUNG.

32 marketplace.

Blackfriars,
Oxford

Telephone Oxford 3607

9th October 1945[33]

Herr Professor Dr. C.G. Jung
Küsnacht-Zürich.

Dear Professor Jung,

I was immensely honoured and gratified to receive your very kind letter of September 26th. I had little thought that my impudence in writing to you would elicit any response at all, especially in view of the immense demands which must be made upon your time and patience. I had supposed that I should have to remain for ever content with a dream of some months ago in which I was one of half-a-dozen recipients of a medal from your hands! I need hardly say that any criticism you are ever able to offer will be much more gratefully received than this very agreeable piece of wish-fulfilment!

There is certainly a very considerable and growing interest among Catholics – and others – in this country. Over a hundred people, including several quite distinguished doctors and psychiatrists, as well as clergy, scientists, teachers and laypeople, turned up for a quite strenuous study-weekend I recently conducted in London on the psychologies of St. Thomas Aquinas and C.G. Jung! Unfortunately, especially in the therapeutic field, the demand far exceeds the supply. But the interest among Catholics is not, I need hardly say, unaccompanied by a certain amount of misgiving and distrust. My own small writings have been mainly directed to meeting some of the more "intellectual" of these misgivings. I cannot expect you, dear Professor Jung, to wade through all these writings; but it would truly be a very great help to know whether I do or do not misrepresent your position in the matter of the relation of your psychology to "Religion" – or, more precisely, to "God". I have in fact epitomised my interpretation of this in my review of Flugel's new book,[34] a copy of which I have ventured to enclose. I have marked the relevant passage (pp. 384ff.)[35]

33 Typewritten, with handwritten corrections.

34 Cf. White, 3 Aug. 1945, postscript, p. 4 and note.

35 White's marked copy has been lost. His review of Flugel's book comprises the last part of Chapter VIII in his *God & Unc.*, which includes the following statement: "The emergence of a 'transcendent' or 'reconciling' function, a *tertium quid*, such as has been observed by Jung as the vehicle of solution, integration and healing (or its recognition should it emerge) is precluded *a priori* by a psychology whose whole preoccupation is with historical

I am very interested indeed to hear that Catholic writers on the Continent are similarly interested; and I should be very glad indeed to hear of any books etc. they have written on the subject. (I can read fairly easily French, German, Spanish, Italian, Latin.)

In common with many others, I am very much hoping that you may be able to visit England before long. My good friend Dr. Gerhard Adler[36] has kindly offered to introduce me to you in that happy event. I am also in close and friendly contact with Dr John Layard[37] and Mrs Sussman![38] I am very much impressed by the variety and catholicity to be found among your disciples, though a Papist sometimes finds the note of unity less easy to detect!

Yours very gratefully and sincerely, VICTOR WHITE, O.P.[39]

causation, which belittles 'intuition' as unscientific . . . and which disregards the functional and teleological aspects of psychological phenomena" (*God & Unc.*, Spring, 1982, p. 162).

36 Gerhard Adler, Ph.D. (1904–1988): a "lay" (non-medical) analyst who had studied with Jung in 1931–34. Living and working in Berlin until 1936, Adler and his family fled Germany to settle in London and then, during the Blitz, moved to Oxford. Adler's interest in philosophy and theology made him a natural conversation partner for White, who went to Adler for analysis after leaving John Layard (Jung/Layard correspondence, ETH Library archive). It was Adler who encouraged White to write to Jung when the war ended (Gerhard Adler, private correspondence, 3 June 1986).

37 (Cf. Jung, 5 Oct. 1945, p. 9 and note.) White had been in analysis with John Layard for four months in 1940 and belonged to a scholarly Jungian society, founded by Layard in 1942, for clergy, professors, doctors and lay analysts, among them Gerhard Adler. White had a profound influence on Layard in turn. In a letter to Jung in late 1945, Layard writes that his positive acquaintance with Catholicism and his connection with the priesthood are due to Victor White, who is the first priest he analyzed in Oxford. He adds that White is "reputed to be the finest Thomist in England" (John Layard, 30 Oct. 1945, Jung/Layard correspondence, ETH Library archive). In the 1940s both Layard and his wife, Doris, took formal instruction to become Catholic.

38 Toni Fanny Sussmann (1883–1967): German analyst and trainer of analysts, then living in England. The spelling of her last name is often rendered, in this correspondence, as 'Sussman'. She retained the German spelling, however: '–mann'. A Jewish convert to Catholicism, she analyzed and studied with Jung starting in 1916, then practiced and taught in Berlin. She had a deep and abiding interest in combining Eastern with Western religious practices, and with Jung's psychology. Early in the 1930s she began writing to Jung about Hitler's anti-Jewish policies, asking his help to find work elsewhere (Jung/Sussmann correspondence, ETH Library archive). She moved to England in early 1938 and settled in Oxford, where White was briefly her pupil in analytic training and occasionally referred others to her. (Cf. letters between White and Schmid in 1946, esp. White, 18 Sept. 1946, pp. 41f and notes; also Appendix 2, "Victor White, a Memoir," p. 313.)

39 Beginning with this letter and in most that follow (until 1955 when his friendship with Jung was broken), White added a flourish to his signature: a line slanting upwards left to right, with two dots below it.

Blackfriars
Oxford
Telephone, 3607

14.10.45[40]

My dear Professor Jung,

I had hardly thanked you for your first letter when your second letter arrived. It has quite *staggered* me. It will unfortunately be some days before I have an opportunity to reply to it. This brief note is just to thank you *with all my heart*.

Meanwhile, "It" simply *insists* that I send you an unadorned record of my January dream which I have already mentioned. Of course I do not expect you to analyse it, but I think it may interest & amuse you, & perhaps tell you much more than "ego" can about me.

I look forward very much to writing to you later in the week.

Yours very sincerely & gratefully, VICTOR WHITE, O.P.

Dream of January 22nd (?) 1945.[41]

PART 1. A group of elderly and ill-looking Dominicans are sitting on my right: it seems to be at Hawkesyard.[42] One of them says that he is eight times worse in health than anybody else!

PART 2. I am in the bathroom. A very rubicund and robust young Irish or Irish-American priest comes in: his name is "Father Bendit". He says he has just been analysed by C.G. Jung: it was very good as far as it went, but he is now going off to look for another analyst. I am surprised that he can think he can find a better analyst than Jung himself, that an Irish priest is so unsuspicious of psychologists, and that so very healthy and matter-of-fact a man can possibly *need* analysis.

PART 3. I am in Jung's garden at Zürich. The war is over. Jung is sitting in a deck chair, wearing (I think) a panama hat, and looking very peaceful and benign. He beckons me to him and tells me he wants to give me a medal for all that I have done to spread and develop his work during the war when he could not get out of Switzerland. He says there are very few who have really understood him correctly and seen the wider implications of his work as well. He reaches to the ground where there is a small oval box; inside the box are about six or seven oval plaques fitting the box closely like hosts in an

40 Handwritten on half-sheet letterhead.

41 The dream text is typewritten.

42 English Dominican priory located in Rugeley, Staffordshire, where White studied philosophy for the requisite three years after his novitiate. Hawkesyard remained as a study house for students in their early years for several decades after the opening of Oxford Blackfriars in 1929 (cf. White, 3 Aug. 1945, p. 3 and note). [AC]

altar-bread box. I know that these are for the "few"; I do not know who the others are, except that Toni Sussman is NOT one and that I must tell her about it when I get back to London! Jung takes one of the plaques and presses it warmly in my hand. It is mostly of some white substance, but the border is somehow inlaid with a green and yellow pattern; in the centre are three nude female figures: one full face in the middle and the others flanking her and facing left and right (outwards). I wake glowing with pleasure and gratitude, and a feeling of assurance.

Notes.

PART 1. Elderly, frustrated and hypochondriac priests are regular shadow-figures of mine! Hawkesyard is the place where I received the earlier part of my Dominican training, and doubtless developed many of the "complications" from which analysis from J. Layard, Toni Sussman – and a good deal of subsequent attempts at self-analysis – have (I hope) pretty thoroughly delivered me. I cannot imagine why this particular (but unknown) Dominican was so emphatic that he was EIGHT times worse than anybody else! But he is evidently a caricature of self-pity at other people's expense.

PART 2. Bathrooms seem to be usually places of psychological cleansing in my dreams. I incline to envy the generality of Irish priests for the fact that Catholicism is in their blood and so seldom presents problems or complications arising from heredity or upbringing (I am myself a convert,[43] and have in the past had many such), but I incline also to resent and despise them for the same fact, and also for what seems to me their frequent complacence and narrowness. I know nobody called "Father Bendit", but I know the book of DR. Bendit on "Paranormal Cognition".[44] I disagree with his plea for a fifth "Psi-Function" in addition to Jung's Four (I don't think he understands what Jung means by a Function), and I think he is very mistaken in thinking that alleged psi-phenomena upset the principles of therapy (it seems to me that what is important therapeutically is not so much where the material comes from, but what the unconscious does with it – though psi-dreams do seem often to prove to be particularly important ones.) But I *do* think that psi-phenomena raise important *theoretical* questions. They seem to me to give *empirical* ground for asking whether we can limit the "unconscious" to the "personal unconscious" and the "collective unconscious" if we are to understand the latter *only* as the product of "inherited brain-structure". Bendit's psi-phenomena, if empirically established, indicate unconscious contents originating outside the historical-causal time-sequence altogether, and will

43 Born 21 October 1902 and baptized Gordon Henry, White was the son of an Anglican priest, vicar of a parish in Croydon, Surrey (now a borough of London). White joined the Dominican Order at 19. For more on White's early life, conversion to Catholicism and later career, see Appendix 2, "Victor White, a Memoir," pp. 307–34. [with AC]

44 Cf. Jung to Dr. Laurence J. Bendit, 12 Nov. 1945 (*Letters I*, p. 389).

postulate *either* a re-definition of Jung's "Collective Unconscious" as an *absolute* "Grenzbegriff"[45] with no causal limitations whatever, *or* the addition of an "Absolute" unconscious to the "Personal" of Freud and the "Collective" of Jung. If this be admitted, the synthesis of empirical psychology with theology and metaphysics will be enormously facilitated: indeed we shall be *compelled* to recognize extra-personal and even extra-temporal agency in the production of dreams, etc. in the manner of (for instance) Aristotle, St. Thomas and (for matter of that) the Bible. Perhaps it may also help to obviate some of the "inflation" complications which are liable to arise in analysis.

PART 3. The War was not in fact over at the time of the dream; but it probably refers to the solution (which the dream helped me to reach) of a problem which was engaging me at the time. I suppose the oval box and medal, with the three Graces (?) is an Anima symbol which Jung gives me. Since his last letter to me, his words in the dream seem to have elements of "psi" themselves! The problem that was engaging me was in fact concerned with Toni Sussmann.[46]

VICTOR WHITE O.P.

Blackfriars,
Oxford

23.10.45[47]

My Dear Professor Jung,

It is over a week since your letter of October 5th reached me, but this is the very first opportunity I have had even to begin to answer it. My life is so full and busy these days that it is seldom I can get an hour without interruption; so please forgive my delay and the disjointedness of what may follow!

It is quite impossible for me to express my gratitude to you for your letter or to tell you how much it has meant to me. For some time past I have found myself ploughing a rather lonely furrow, painfully aware of the inadequacy of my experience on the psychological side, and of my need for expert and understanding guidance – at least to the extent of some reassurance that I was not positively on the *wrong* lines from the psychological standpoint.[48] The matter is one that has come to affect the whole of my life and work

45 boundary concept. 46 Cf. White to Schmid, 18 Sept. 1946, p. 41f.

47 Typewritten on ordinary paper.

48 A penciled line in the left margin, likely made by Jung, highlights this whole paragraph.

profoundly. My principal job in life is that of professor of Dogmatic Theology in this Dominican House of studies (also open to other theological students), and, since reading your books, and still more since my own analysis,[49] I have found myself more and more compelled to expound the "Summa"[50] of St.Thomas Aquinas in psychological terms and with constant reference to its vast psychological relevance and implications. But besides my daily theological lectures here, I have to do a good deal of more popular lecturing, both here in Oxford, in London and in other parts of the country; and latterly I have been receiving an increasing number of invitations to address various societies – clerical (non-Catholic even more than Catholic!) lay, and even medical – on some subject or other connected with "Psychology and Religion".

In addition to this I have somehow accumulated an increasing amount of more personal work: I do not know whether to describe it as Seelsorge[51] or Psychotherapie! It is usually a concoction of both, varying greatly in proportion according to circumstances. I have not sought this work – quite the contrary. But I too have learned (though it took a lot of learning!) to try to make it my principle "not to seek the place where I might do something useful, but to do it where I actually was". So far as possible I have tried to limit my activities to that of liaison between needy souls and professional psychotherapists: introducing them, when possible, to suitable analysts, or "taking over" from analysts when they want "religion". But it has not always been possible so to limit my activities, and circumstances have often arisen when I have felt obliged to take on the whole job myself. Of course I well understand that approval of the general drift of my writings does not imply approval of my practical methods; but your assurance that I have in the main "understood" your work aright is a greater relief and comfort to me than I can possibly say. Nor is it possible for me to express how great is my appreciation and gratitude that you should have written to me at such length and with such candour. Need I say how *entirely* I agree and sympathise with your point of view throughout?

I sympathise particularly with you in the difficulties which you have encountered with the theologians – and philosophers! I have, of course, met

49 Cf. White, 9 Oct. 1945, p. 12, notes 37, 38.

50 *Summa Theologiae* (hereafter *ST*), the last and greatest work of medieval Dominican theologian Thomas Aquinas, O.P., remains hugely influential in some schools of Catholic theology. The work was left incomplete at Aquinas's death in 1274. Victor White was among the English Dominican scholars who worked on a new, annotated translation in the mid-twentieth century: *Summa Theologiae: Latin Text and English Translation* (London & New York: Blackfriars, in conjunction with Eyre & Spottiswode and McGraw-Hill, 1964). A tribute to White, written by Thomas Gilby, O.P., appears on the title page of Volume I.

51 Cure of souls, care of souls: A priest's intimate spiritual conversation with individual believers, which may include sacramental confession and absolution.

with plenty of the same difficulty myself.[52] Despite the lip-service paid to St. Thomas Aquinas, his magnificent conception (so much, I think, akin to your own) of the relative autonomy of the various sciences, each differentiated by its particular methods and "rationes cognoscibiles",[53] seems to be largely forgotten in our day. The results are, in my opinion, quite deplorable. Religion tends to become an escape-mechanism, and Catholic psychologists are often more "materialistic" than the "materialists".

But, small as they are, there are developments among English Catholics which would I think interest and perhaps astonish you. Among my own colleagues in the Dominican Order in England there are now several who are keenly interested in your work. I can at least guarantee that all the students for the priesthood who attend my lectures are acutely aware of the psychological implications of dogmatic theology! My colleague, the Professor of Holy Scripture,[54] has a quite extraordinary insight into the interplay of archetypal motifs in the Bible and its psychological relevance; he too is lecturing in London and elsewhere and drawing extraordinary numbers of people to his present series on the Apocalypse! Fr. Gerald Vann's widely read book, "The Heart of Man",[55] owes much to your work. Another of our priests, my first analysant,[56] is doing fine work in Newcastle-upon-Tyne.

But I think the most influential book has been "Catholic Thought and Modern Psychology" by a simple and unsophisticated country parish-priest, Father Witcutt.[57] It is a quite extraordinary phenomenon, as the author had never met a psychologist in his life when he wrote it, with no other background whatever except your own books! It is, in my opinion, a very naive

52 This and the next two paragraphs are highlighted with a penciled line in the left margin, apparently drawn by Jung.

53 "characteristic forms of reasoning."

54 Richard Kehoe, O.P. (1905–1981): English Dominican, scripture scholar and professor at Blackfriars, Oxford. Kehoe entered the Order in 1919, two years before White. He effectively withdrew from the Order in 1955.

55 Gerald Vann, O.P. (1906–1963): English Dominican, theologian, widely known for his numerous works on spirituality. *The Heart of Man* was published in 1944.

56 Although he writes sometimes in these letters of performing "analysis" or working with an "analysant," White knew himself to be less than fully trained as a Jungian analyst. Certainly his preparation would not qualify him under the present sense of the term. A senior analyst, who knew White well, judged him (in this regard) a "dilettante" (Gerhard Adler, private correspondence, 3 June 1986). But in this period the definitions were not fixed, and Jung also sometimes refers to White's "analysants" (Jung, 24 Nov. 1953, p. 221), and to his "being an analyst" (Jung, 10 April 1954, p. 240).

57 William Percell Witcutt: English Catholic priest, author of *Catholic Thought and Modern Psychology* (London: Burns, Oates and Washbourne, Ltd., 1943) and *Blake: A Psychological Study* (1946). Witcutt lectured to the Guild of Pastoral Psychology (cf. Wolff, 18 July 1946, p. 36 and note) on "The Child in Paradise" (GPP Lecture #29). In *Return to Reality* (London: SPCK, 1954) he describes his disenchantment with scholasticism and his return to Anglicanism. [with AC]

book, which skims too easily over most of the problems, and tends to take a far too static and "semiotic" view of symbolism. But it was just the kind of book needed to break down much suspicion and prejudice, and it has already, I believe, been reprinted two or three times, and is being translated into Spanish and Portuguese! Fr. Witcutt has a quite extraordinary knowledge of English folklore and fiction, and I am expecting very valuable work from him. I wonder if you have seen this book? If not, I will certainly write to ask him to send you a copy. I did not know him at all when he wrote it, and it quite astonishes me that he suddenly produced it from his little country presbytery without any help or collaboration whatsoever! It might also interest you that a Benedictine monk[58] is engaged on a comparative study of traditional "spiritual direction" (especially as represented by Father Augustine Baker[59] in the 17th century) with modern analytical methods.

All this is, indeed, but a grain of mustard seed: the demand (especially the therapeutic demand) far exceeds the supply. But I think you may be interested to hear of these distant, and perhaps quite unexpected, results of your own work!

Your letter is so full of stimulating things that I hardly know where to start – or stop! I have re-read, with renewed interest, your "gnoseological" note in "Psych. of the Unconscious".[60] It is not very easy reading, at least in the English translation, but I think I agree in many respects. Yet I wonder how far the Kantian dichotomy is not itself cause and symptom of the neurosis of Modern Man? Do not the "two realities" themselves imply a deep split in the psyche; and when "God" has been banished from "Pure Reason"[61] and wholly divorced from the field of Sensation, is He not bound to slip into unconsciousness and become, first a purely irrational, then an anti-rational and even pathological function? My little experience in psychology itself has taught me to appreciate the *therapeutic* value of (for instance) St. Thomas Aquinas in contrast with Kant and the post-Kantians. For him, "quod omnes dicunt Deum",[62] while remaining super- (or, if you prefer, extra-) rational is necessarily implied (Summa, I.ii.3) and immanent (I.viii) in "quod sensu constat",[63] besides being expressible only in symbol (I.i.8) and analogy (I.xiii), and being the actual (though not necessarily the conscious) object of all Love and Desire. I do not suggest that Modern Man can retrace the identical "Viae"[64] of Aquinas; but it seems to me that the initial Kantian dichotomy

58 Oswald Sumner, OSB (cf. White, 18 May 1950, p. 155 and note).

59 Augustine Baker, OSB (1575–1641): English Benedictine writer on ascetical theology and history, whose *Sancta Sophia, or Holy Wisdom* (1657), is his most famous work.

60 Cf. Jung, 5 Oct. 1945, p. 7 and note.

61 i.e., Kant's *Critique of Pure Reason* (1781). Cf. White, 20 April 1952, p. 189 and note.

62 "that which all call God." 63 "that which is known by the senses."

64 "Ways": White later published a major essay on Aquinas's *Quinque Viae* (five ways of demonstrating that belief in God's existence is reasonable), titled "The Prolegomena to the Five Ways" (*Dominican Studies: An Annual Review*, Vol. V. Blackfriars Publications, 1952).

must somehow be overcome, and your own psychological work would seem to confirm that the transcending bridge can never be built from one side only. I think that you yourself have wonderfully stated the essential problem for us to-day in your essay on "Psychic Energy"[65] – in terms, that is to say, of the relation of "psychical" and "physical" energy.[66] Obviously it was not your job to solve this knotty problem; but equally certainly its solution must condition our understanding of psychological language itself. You yourself have made every possible "caveat" to the effect that words like Psyche, Unconscious, Introversion, Extraversion etc. are not to be given an ontological or gnoseological meaning. Yet I think it is not only the theologians and philosophers who have failed to appreciate your rigid and stern empiricism. I thoroughly agree for instance that Layard's essay in your Festschrift[67] is magnificent – but I wonder if you would agree that "the maxim that nothing exists outwardly that did not previously exist internally is fundamental to Jung's teaching" (p.264)?[68] Setting aside the question as to what meaning spatial language about "outward" and "inward" can have with respect to the psyche (which, as you say, "can be *regarded* as a *relatively* closed system" – "Contributions," p.6)[69] – is there any possible empirical warrant for such an assertion about *existence*? It seems to me that there neither is nor can be . . .

But I must resist the temptation to bore you by riding this hobby horse any

65 Jung's essay, "Über die Energetik der Seele" ["On Psychic Energy"], was the opening chapter in a collection of four essays, *Über die Energetik der Seele und andere psychologische Abhandlungen* [On the Energetics of the Psyche and other Psychological Treatises] (Zürich: Rascher Verlag, 1928; hereafter, *Energetik* 1928). The other chapters in the book are titled, "Allgemeine Gesichtspunkte zur Psychologie des Traumes" ["General Observations on the Psychology of the Dream"], "Instinkt und Unbewusstes" ["Instinct and the Unconscious"], and "Die psychologischen Grundlagen des Geisterglaubens" ["The Psychological Basis of a Belief in Spirits"]. An English translation by H.G. and Cary F. Baynes appeared the same year, titled *Contributions to Analytical Psychology* (New York: Harcourt Brace; London: Kegan Paul, Trench, Trubner, 1928). (Hereafter, *Contributions*.)

Jung's personal copy of the 1928 Swiss edition (224 pages in large print) served 20 years later as the rough copy for his expanded and revised work, *Über psychische Energetik und das Wesen der Träume* [On Psychic Energy and the Nature of Dreams] (Zürich: Rascher Verlag, 1948, hereafter, *Energetik* 1948). Never published in English as a whole, parts of this work appear in various volumes of the CW, e.g., "On Psychic Energy," Part I of CW 8, *The Structure and Dynamics of the Psyche*, 1960/1968, hereafter, *Structure & Dynamics*).

66 Jung's discussion of psychical and physical energy begins in Part I of *Energetik* 1928, "Die Möglichkeit der psychologischen Quantitätsbestimmung" ["The Possibility of Quantitative Measurement in Psychology"] and is developed in Part II, section a, "Der psychologische Energiebegriff" ["The Psychological Concept of Energy"]. (Cf. CW 8, *Structure & Dynamics*, §6ff and §28–33.)

67 Cf. Jung, 5 Oct. 1945, p. 9 and note.

68 The whole paragraph is highlighted with a pencil line in the left margin, presumably added by Jung. This sentence is marked by a double line.

69 Discussion of the psyche as a "relatively closed system" appears in *Energetik* 1928, pp. 15f.

further; though it seems to me a question of the uttermost importance, not only from the theological and philosophical standpoint, but also from the therapeutic . . .

I feel most truly penitent at having accused you of rejecting the "transcendence" of God altogether. I fully realize that that is not so, though readers are apt to gain that impression from one or two passages in "Ps. Types"[70] and "Ps. and Religion".[71] My "Frontiers" essay was written some two or three years ago when my ideas on the subject were somewhat more fluid. But I realise that the statement was libellous, and I shall certainly see that it is changed if there is another edition. Unfortunately there has already been a second impression, but I was given no opportunity to revise the proofs.

You will find the idea that the Holy Spirit (unlike the Father and the Son) "non habet nomen proprium"[72] developed by St. Thomas in "Summa" I.xxxvi sqq. The point would seem to be that whereas the First and Second Person can be represented by proper logical concepts (though of course only analogically), the Third Person can not, but can only be conceived or named by concepts or words which belong *also* to Father and Son. ("Father" is NOT "Son" nor "Son" "Father"; "Begotten" *not* "Unbegotten" etc. etc. But "Father" and "Son" are ALSO "Holy", "Spirit", "Love", "Gift" and every other concept or name we *can* give to the Third Person.) The point may seem a bit recondite, but was it quite fantastic of me to feel that you had sensed the same truth when you wrote: "Der Hl. Geist als Leben ist . . . ein Begriff, der keineswegs aus der Identität von Vater u. Sohn logisch abgeleitet werden kann, sondern vielmehr eine psychologische Idee, d.h. eine auf einer irrationaler Uranschauung beruhende Gegebenheit darstellt"?[73] At all events, the doctrine

70 C.G. Jung, *Psychological Types*. (Trans. H.G. Baynes. London: Routledge & Kegan Paul, 1923, hereafter, *Types*). Later revised, republished as CW 6. White may be referring to passages such as that found in CW 6, *Types*, §421, p. 247.

71 C.G. Jung, *Psychology and Religion*, (New Haven & London: Yale University Press, 1938), originally delivered in English as the Terry Lectures, Yale University, 1937. Later revised, republished in CW 11, *Psychology and Religion: West and East* (hereafter, *Psych & Rel.*). Passages referred to may be found, for example, in the original edition on pp. 99, 106; or CW 11, *Psych. & Rel.*, §139 (p. 82), §157 (p. 96).

72 "has no proper name."

73 "The Holy Spirit as Life is . . . a concept that by no means can be logically deduced from the identity of Father and Son; rather it represents much more a psychological idea, that is, a given, resting on an irrational primal orientation" (trans. ACL). The sentence appears in Jung's 1940 Eranos lecture, "Zur Psychologie der Trinitätsidee" (*EJ 1940/1941*, p. 37). (White added the ellipsis for emphasis. His quotation includes a grammatical error, *irrationaler* for *irrationalen.*) Cf. "A Psychological Approach to the Dogma of the Trinity," CW 11, *Psych & Rel.*, §169–295 (pp. 109–200), which is an expanded version of Jung's lecture. This crucial lecture also contains what may have been Jung's first public polemic against the Catholic treatment of evil as a privation of good *(privatio boni)* (*EJ 1941*, p. 53), a point of contention which became central to the debate between Jung and White (cf. Jung, 31 Dec. 1949, pp. 140f and notes). (Cf. also *IGS*, ch. 6, "Theodicy.")

seems to be an interesting confirmation of the "irrationality" of the "transcendent function".

I read German moderately well, and of course should love to have a copy of your new book on Alchemy.[74] So far as I know there is only one copy in England as yet, and that is being devoured by members of the London A.P. Club,[75] so I have not yet been able to see it. I wish you could meet my friend Dr. Sherwood Taylor,[76] custodian of the Old Ashmolean Science Museum, a chemist and historian of some distinction, who has somehow found his way from "materialism" through his study of alchemy to Tao and Catholicism! He was at one time an editor of "Ambix"[77] – a periodical which you may have met with, devoted to the history of alchemy. I think he still has a number of offprints of some of the alchemical texts he has edited – Zosimos, Stephanos, etc. If you would like to have any that are available, I am sure he would be delighted and honoured to send them to you. He is in the main agreed with your thesis in "Integration of the Personality",[78] but considers that the earlier alchemy was in the main "extraverted" and produced undoubtedly "real" chemical transmutations. Both of us incline to wonder if the Mass-idea and the Alchemy-idea can be so sharply opposed as is suggested on pp.232–233.[79] For many of the Alchemists, it would seem that the "opus" was primarily an "opus" of God and of Grace; while the idea that in the Mass "man . . . leaves the work of salvation to the autonomous divine figure" sounds rather like reading Protestant "sola fide" and "extrinsic imputation" into a Catholic context. (For a Catholic, while the "opus" of the

74 Cf. Jung, 5 Oct. 1945, p. 9 and note.

75 The Analytical Psychology Club (hereafter, APC) of London was founded in 1922 and continues to the present. For an overview of the early development of the London APC and various schools of Jungian thought in the UK, see Thomas B. Kirsch, *The Jungians: A Comparative and Historical Perspective* (London & Philadelphia: Routledge, 2000), pp. 36ff. (Hereafter, *Jungians*.)

76 Sherwood Taylor (1875–1956): historian of science, author of many works on scientific thought and the philosophy of science. His works on alchemy include the posthumously published *Alchemists, Founders of Modern Chemistry* (1958), and *Alchemists* (1970). Cf. White, 31 Aug. 1946, pp. 39, 41.

77 *Ambix: The Journal of the Society for the Study of Alchemy and Early Chemistry* (London: Taylor & Francis), first published in 1937, now published by Black Bean Press, Ltd., Cambridge, UK. Jung's "The Bologna Enigma" appeared in *Ambix*, Vol. 2, 1938. (Cf. CW 14, *Mysterium*, Chap. II, sec. 3.)

78 Cf. Jung, 5 Oct. 1945, p. 9 and note.

79 "Now, since all these mythical pictures present a human drama on the yonder side of consciousness, we see that man is the one to be redeemed, as well as the redeemer. The first formulation is the Christian one, the second the alchemistic. In the first case man ascribes to himself the need of salvation and leaves the work of salvation (the actual ἆθλον or opus) to the autonomous divine figure; in the last case man takes upon himself the duty of carrying out the work of redemption . . ." (trans. Dell, *Integration*, pp. 232f). (Cf. CW 12, *Psych. & Alch.*, Part III, §414ff, pp. 306ff.)

Mass is indeed Christ's, it is only efficacious by reason of the soul's participation in and with Him).[80] At any rate, it is difficult to find any trace of any opposition to alchemy as such on the part of the Church, or any difficulty on the part of good Catholics to performing the alchemical "opus".[81] I gather that quite a number of my own Dominican colleagues in the past were noted from their proficiency in the Art!

I see that I began this letter on the 23rd of October, it is now the 29th. – so many have been the interruptions that have prevented me from getting on with it. But it is already so long that I am afraid you will hardly have the patience to read so far, and I must bring it to an end. How very much do I also wish that I could indeed be "at your elbow", though very much aware that the benefit would be far greater on my side. I am afraid however that that is impossible and that I must continue to try to "be useful where I actually am". But perhaps I may have the boldness to say that nothing on earth could please or profit me more than to be able to visit you – if only for two or three days. In term-time that is impossible, but perhaps, if you were willing, it might be possible during the Easter or Summer vacation. I certainly cannot feel that I have any such claim on your time and attention as you are so generous as to accord me, but there is very much indeed that I should love to talk over with you.

Thanking you once again for your enormous help and encouragement,

Yours very sincerely, FR. VICTOR WHITE, O.P.

P.S. In a separate envelope I am taking the liberty of sending you one or two other of my pamphlets – external circumstances and interior inhibitions alike seem to conspire to prevent my getting down to a sustained and serious book! The pamphlet on "Scholasticism"[82] was written many years ago and long before I knew anything about psychology, but may be of some interest. That on Hilton[83] may be of some interest as a "popular" exposition of a native "spiritual writer" of the Middle Ages in terms of your psychology; it was intended for a mainly non-Catholic audience. I have kept formal psychology in the background of the "De Modo Studendi",[84] but it may be of some interest as illustrating the fashion in which I have found your psychology to illuminate my understanding of St. Thomas Aquinas.

80 A faint question mark is penciled in the left margin next to this sentence.

81 Later White admits that he has found a series of ordinations in the thirteenth and fourteenth centuries, forbidding Dominicans the practice of alchemy (cf. White, 13 Oct. 1946, p. 45).

82 Victor White, "Scholasticism." Pamphlet No. R 126. London: Catholic Truth Society, 1934.

83 Victor White, "Walter Hilton: An English Spiritual Guide." Guild of Pastoral Psychology, Lecture 31. London: Guild of Pastoral Psychology, 1944.

84 Victor White, "The Letter of St. Thomas Aquinas to Brother John, De Modo Studendi [How to Study]: Latin Text with Translation and Exposition by Victor White, O.P. A Lecture Read at the Inauguration of Studies for the Year 1944–45 in the Dominican Priories of Hawkesyard and Blackfriars, Oxford" (*The Life of the Spirit*, Dec. 1944, Vol. I, No. 10, pp. 163–80).

Blackfriars
Oxford
Telephone. 3607

16.11.45[85]

Dear Professor Jung,

The wonderful gift of your *Psychologie u. Alchemie* arrived safely this morning. I really do not know how to thank you sufficiently. It will always occupy a most important place among my most valued & proudest possessions.

I confess that I had not anticipated a work of anything approaching its size & thoroughness. So far I have been able to do no more than skim over the first pages of the "Einleitung"[86] (of which, of course, I very thoroughly approve!) & to glance at the magnificent collection of Abbildungen.[87] They alone will provide me with life-long matter for contemplation, & recall to the "materia prima"[88] from which so much in my very busied & rather harrassed existence is apt to distract me!

A few days ago I received a very interesting letter from a Spanish Jesuit, by name Pedro Meseguer,[89] who is writing an *Exposicion y Critica de la Psicologia de C.G. Jung*,[90] & is also editing a series of volumes on *Psicologia y Pastoral*.[91] He also sends a review by himself of a book by a German Catholic, Dr. Josef Goldbrunner,[92] called *Die Tiefenpsychologie von C.G. Jung u. christliche Lebensgestaltung*[93] (published by M. Lassleben, Kallmünz

85 Handwritten. 86 "Introduction." 87 illustrations.

88 "prime (first) matter."

89 Pedro Meseguer, S.J. (1904–1963): Spanish Jesuit with Ph.D. in psychology; professor at the Colegio del Sagrado Corazon, Barcelona (Schola Media); editor of the review *Razon Y Fe* ["Reason and Faith"] beginning in 1940.

90 "Exposition and Critique of the Psychology of C.G. Jung." This exact title does not appear in Fr. Meseguer's official bibliography. His many articles in *Razon Y Fe* include discussions of Jung's psychology such as, "Empirismo tradicional y 'Psicologia Profunda' " ["Traditional Empiricism and 'Depth Psychology' "] (1946); "Criticas recientes del Psicoanalisis" ["Recent Critiques of Psychoanalysis"] (1948); and "La aceptacion de la 'Sombra', segun C.G. Jung, y so paralelo cristiano" ["The acceptance of the 'Shadow' according to C.G. Jung, and its Christian parallel"] (1952). His book *The Secret of Dreams* (London: Burns & Oates, 1960) approvingly quotes White's *God & Unc.*

91 Psychology and Pastoral Care.

92 Josef Goldbrunner (b. 1910): German Catholic layman with doctorates in both philosophy and theology, who taught in Berlin, Saarbrücken, and Regensburg (1968–1977), and as guest professor emeritus at the University of Notre Dame (USA).

93 "The Depth Psychology of C.G. Jung and the Christian Form of Life." Later appeared in English with the title, *Individuation: A Study of the Depth Psychology of C.G. Jung* (Trans. Stanley Godman. London: Hollis & Carter, 1955. Republished by the University of Notre Dame Press, 1964).

über Regensburg, 1942). I wonder if you know this book, & whether it is satisfactory. I am extremely interested to find that during the war years, Catholic writers in Spain, Germany & England have been inspired by your work to write quite independently of one another on what seem to be similar lines – though I detect a certain difference of emphasis (such as might indeed be expected) between the approach of the Spanish Jesuit, & that of the English Dominican!

Thanking you once again, dear Dr. Jung, for the very great deal that I (& so many others) owe to you & your work, & for your very great generosity in sending me your book,

I am
Yours very sincerely, FR. VICTOR WHITE, O.P.

1946

Küsnacht-Zürich

Febr. 13th 1946[1]

My dear Father White,

My answer to your kind letter comes very late indeed! I have a bad conscience. There are certain reasons however, that may excuse my long silence. For a number of weeks I felt very low on account of a grippe in the head and in the intestines and beside this ailment I was caught in the grips of a book that eats me alive if I don't write it.[2] As I must still see certain patients, give consultations, write letters, etc., my time for work is very short.

This evening I shall give a report about the way you conceive of my psychology before a group of doctors, who regularly come to my house every fortnight.[3] Once I mentioned a parallel you draw between Thomas' philosophy and my psychology, which remark met with great interest. They asked me to give them fuller details. At this occasion I went through your pamphlets again and found a point, which I forgot to mention in my previous letter. It is in your article "St. Th. Aq. and J's psych".[4] Blackfriars XXV, 216: "J's substitution of indetermined 'libido' for Freud's determined 'sexuality' was a challenge" etc. (9th l. from the bottom). Your statement as to the transformability of instinct is correct in the main, yet it could give cause to criticism from biological quarters. Instinct as seen from a biological standpoint is something *extremely conservative*, so much so that it seems to be almost unalterable. This is a fact, one should not overlook in talking to a scientist. It is a regular fact in the animal kingdom. It is only Man that shows a certain unreliability concerning the functioning of his instincts, and it is only civilized Man, who is capable of losing sight of his instincts to a certain extent and under certain conditions. If he is nothing but instinctive he collides with his civilization, and if he gets a bit too far away from his instinctive basis, he gets neurotic. There is a certain optimum between the two extremes.

1 Typed from holograph.

2 Adler guesses (*Letters I*, p. 413n) that this is *Aion* (CW 9.ii) or *Mysterium Coniunctionis* (CW 14). Both seem unlikely, however, since Jung began work on *Aion* the end of the next year (cf. Jung, 19 Dec. 1947, p. 103), and *Mysterium* first appeared in 1955. The book referred to is probably *Die Psychologie der Übertragung* [The Psychology of the Transference], which Jung sent to the printer a month later (cf. Jung, 23 March 1946, p. 29 and note).

3 Between 1940 and 1948 members of Jung's professional circle gathered periodically at his house for informal discussion of contemporary issues. No contemporaneous records were kept on these informal gatherings. Based on an interview several decades later, the group may have included at various times Medard Boss, Gustav Bally, Hans Trüb, Kurt Binswanger, Eric Katzenstein, Hans Bänziger, Alphons Maeder, and for a brief time C.A. Meier. Dr. Meier recalled these names in conversation with Deirdre Bair, as reported by Bair in *Jung: A Biography* (Boston: Little, Brown & Co., 2003, p. 538).

4 Victor White, "St.Thomas Aquinas and Jung's Psychology," *Blackfriars* XXV, June 1944.

Transformation of instinct therefore can only concern a certain small part of it and it takes untold thousands of years until a noticeable change is effectuated. This is the transformation envisaged by the biologist. But the kind of transformation, which the psychologist has in mind, is something else and cannot be compared to the biological effect, inasmuch as it is not a "real" change such as one understood by a natural scientist. It is rather a "psychological" change, namely a change brought about by a psychological superstructure: a relatively small amount of instinctive energy (i.e. energy of the instinct) is led over into another form i.e. a thought – or feeling – form (idea and value) upon the basis and with the help of a preexisting archetype. This is done f.i. by the ritual anamnesis of an archetypal figure. You can observe this proceedure in nearly all renewal or rebirth mysteries: there is an invocation and dramatic representation of the (spiritual) ancestor and his deeds. This δεικνύμενον[5] and δρώμενον[6] "constellates" (or stimulates) the latent analogous archetype in the μύσται[7] and its inherent fascination causes the instinctive energy ("libido") to deviate from its original, biological course and to adhere to its spiritual counterpart. Cp. f.i.[8] the hermeneutic conception of the Cantic. Cant.[9] where XP[10] corresponds to the "spiritual ancestor" or archetype of Man (as "Adam secundus"), while the fundamental instinctive basis is represented through an indubitable erotic situation.

I am most grateful to you for the information about S. Thomas and for the interesting news. I had no idea, that my work should find so much attention.

March 23rd, 1946[11]

A small book, "Aufsätze zur Zeitgeschichte"[12] is about to appear and

5 thing that is shown. 6 thing that is acted. 7 initiates.

8 Compare, for instance. 9 Canticum Canticorum: Song of Songs.

10 Chi Rho = abbreviation for Christ, based on capitalized initial letters of the word in Greek.

11 This addendum to Jung's letter of 13 Feb. 1946 bears no salutation in either the draft or the typed version. Jung's handwritten draft began with what must have been his standard opening in the spring of 1946: "I am sorry to be so late in answering your kind letter. I had a grippe in the meantime and I was often interrupted in my attempt to write to you. Moreover I am busy with a new book which devours all my spare time." He crossed out these lines, however, which closely echo the opening of his letter from four weeks earlier. Jung's draft, beginning just below the end of the earlier letter, is dated "March 17th '46." The secretary's copy bears the date of typing.

12 C.G. Jung, *Aufsätze zur Zeitgeschichte* (Zurich: Rascher Verlag, 1946), published a year later in English, *Essays on Contemporary Events* (London: Kegan Paul, Trench, Trubner, 1947). The composition of these essays, on Hitler's rise to power and the impact of German nationalism, spans almost ten years: "Wotan" in 1936; "Psychotherapie und Weltanschauung" ["Psychotherapy and a Philosophy of Life"] in 1943; "Die Psychotherapie in der Gegenwart" ["Psychotherapy Today"] and "Nach der Katastrophe" ["After the Catastrophe"] both 1945. Each essay has its own history of translation and publication. (Cf. CW 10, *Civilization in Transition* (1964), Part III, §371–487; CW 18, *The Symbolic Life*, §1360–83.)

another book, "Psychologie der Übertragung"[13] is with the printer. In this book I try to demonstrate the influence of spiritual i.e. archetypal influences on transference to doctors and psychologists. It is difficult and will be certainly misunderstood, as the lack of education is appalling in our days. I recently discovered the interesting fact, that not only communists, but also socialists begin to growl against my insistence on the spiritual value of the individual. They are now handing on the rumour that I am a Nazi.[14] As a matter of fact this endeavour to suppress the individual in favour of mass psychology and of "étatisme"[15] is Nazidom, which thrives now on the left wing. I am also accused of "conversations with Jesuits". In a future socialistic or even communistic state Psychotherapy will be a subversive movement, if it is going to last at all. It will share the fate of Christianity, inasmuch as it is a development on the basis of and within Christianity. I was reading a good deal of Origenes[16] lately and I was deeply impressed with the profound similarity between certain of his views and some fundamental concepts of my psychology.

Two lectures, which I gave at the Eranos meeting 1945 are now printed. The title is: Zur Psychologie des Geistes.[17] As soon as I get reprints I will send you one.

Hoping you are always in good health

I remain yours sincerely C.G. JUNG

13 C.G. Jung, *Die Psychologie der Übertragung. Erläutert anhand einer alchemistischen Bilderserie. Für Ärzte und praktische Psychologen* (Zürich: Rascher Verlag, 1946). Cf. "The Psychology of the Transference. Interpreted in Conjunction with a Set of Alchemical Illustrations. For physicians and practical psychologists," ch. 13 in CW 16, *The Practice of Psychotherapy. Essays on the Psychology of the Transference and Other Subjects* (hereafter, *Transference*).

14 Jung had recently learned he was accused of visiting Hitler at Berchtesgaden and of being responsible for the deaths of 600 Jews (cf. Jung to J.H. van der Hoop, 14 Jan. 1946, *Letters I*, pp. 404ff and 405n). Accusations of anti-semitism and Nazism began to be made against Jung in the 1930s and again at the end of the Second World War, and there were intense debates between Jung's detractors and defenders on the subject. Such accusations were called outrageous by many of his Jewish disciples, including James and Hilde Kirsch, Gerhard Adler, Max Zeller, Aniela Jaffé. (Cf. Kirsch, *Jungians*, pp. 124–35. Also Aryeh Maidenbaum and Stephen A. Martin, *Lingering Shadows: Jungians, Freudians and Anti-Semitism*. Boston & London: Shambhala, 1991.)

15 "statism."

16 Origen (c. 185–c. 254): early Christian theologian, scriptural exegete and ascetic, deeply influenced by Platonism. For Jung's discussions of Origen's psychology, cf. CW 6, *Types*, §21ff (pp. 14ff) and CW 9.ii, *Aion*, §336 (pp. 214ff) (*Letters I*, p. 416n). Cf. also Jung, 31 Dec. 1949, p. 142 and note.

17 C.G. Jung, "Zur Psychologie des Geistes" ["On the Psychology of the Spirit"] *EJ 1945* (Zürich: Rhein Verlag, 1946), two-part lecture. An English translation was published in 1948 for private circulation by the New York APC. Later expanded and revised, titled "Zur Phänomenologie des Geistes im Märchen" ["On the Phenomenology of the Spirit in Fairy Tales"], this essay became the first chapter of Jung's *Symbolik des Geistes: Studien über psychische Phänomenologie* [Symbolism of the Spirit: Studies in Psychic Phenomenology]

Blackfriars, Oxford

1st. April 1946[18]

Dear Professor Jung,

I am most grateful to you for your very kind letter. It fills me with envious admiration and astonishment to learn that you have written two books since your last letter, and with very much joy to know that you have so much vigour. I am particularly thrilled to know that one of the books concerns transference, and I look forward enormously to reading it. I was very much impressed by what you wrote on the subject in the early pages of "Psych. u. Alchemie", and I had been very much hoping that you would develop that particular theme. It presents, I venture to think, even more of a problem to the clergy than to the physician ("protected" as he usually is by a consulting room, consultation hours, a receptionist – and fees!), and we somehow seem largely to have lost the sense of being able either to "resolve" or "carry" it – with results most deleterious both to ourselves and our "flocks".

Thank you so very much for drawing my attention to the point concerning "instinct" in the Blackfriars article. I understand perfectly what you say, and only marvel that I could have written in so slipshop [sic] a fashion. It is rather ironic that I should have written so carelessly on that particular point, for I have not seldom criticised others who would seem to imply that all instinct can be readily "transformed" and even "spiritualized". My own experience – let alone St. Paul or St. Thomas – should have saved me from making that mistake! But it has been a "felix culpa"[19] to have drawn from you so very lucid an exposition.

"Psychologie u. Alchemie" has been a tremendous experience and has given rise to more reflections than I can even begin to enumerate. It is quite enormously illuminating; and of course the whole question it raises of the compatibility of the "process of individuation" (whether the method be alchemical or analytical) with the Catholic pattern is a vital one to myself

(Zurich: Rascher Verlag, 1948; hereafter, *Symbolik*). Parts of this work are mentioned repeatedly in these letters (cf. Jung, 27 March 1947, 23 April 1947; White, 20 April 1947).

Symbolik never appeared as a whole in English. The essays by Jung appear in various volumes of the CW: "On the Phenomenology of the Spirit in Fairy Tales" (CW 9.i); "The Spirit Mercurius" (CW 13); "A Psychological Approach to the Dogma of the Trinity" and "On the Psychology of Eastern Meditation" (CW 11). "On the Phenomenology of the Spirit in Fairy Tales" is also Part I of *Spirit and Nature: Papers from the Eranos Yearbooks* (New York: Pantheon, 1954. London: Routledge and Kegan Paul, 1955).

18 Typewritten except for closing and second postscript.

19 "happy fault." Saint Augustine's characterization of the original act of disobedience, which sets the scene for the story of redemption.

and to my friends. How dearly I wish that I could discuss this with you – and many other cognate things.

I have been very much wondering whether you would be able to spare me any time if I were able to come to Zürich (or elsewhere) for a few days during the summer vacation (i.e. between the second week of July and mid-September.) Now that the ban has been raised on taking English currency to Switzerland, this might be quite practical with the help of friends. Of course I would not take up any more of your time than you could conveniently spare, and I would attire myself in a disguise which would forestall any unseemly comments from the Totalitarian Left![20] But (much as I should like to revisit Switzerland for its own sake), I would rather not undertake the journey if there would be no opportunity of seeing you at all. As it would take some time to arrange (there seems to be a great demand in England for passages to Switzerland and only limited accommodation), I should be most grateful if you would be so very good as to send me a postcard just to say "Yes" or "No". If the answer should be Yes, perhaps you would also be so good as to say what dates during that period would suit you best, and perhaps also indicate where I might apply for fairly inexpensive accommodation in Zürich?

I do very much hope that this suggestion will not appear over-presumptuous; but it is impossible for me to say how much I should appreciate the opportunity to talk to you. But of course I shall quite understand if you feel that you would not be able to spare the time.

The pressure of work forbids that I should write a longer letter now; but if I am not able to see you (which I should much prefer), I should like to send you when time permits one or two of my reflections on some passages in "Psych. u. Alchemie".

Thanking you once again, dear Professor Jung, for all your kindness and most encouraging interest,

I remain,

Yours sincerely, VICTOR WHITE, O.P.

P.S. I wonder if you have seen an extremely interesting article on Square Stones ("Homo lapidi quadrato comparatur")[21] in the July 1945 number of the "Harvard Theological Review"? It is extremely erudite, and seems to me to throw much light on the "Trinitas-Quaternitas"[22] in a fashion which I had already vaguely suspected. Unfortunately the Review is unobtainable

20 Jung complained of being criticized by communists and socialists who objected to his insistence on the value of the individual (cf. Jung, 23 March 1946, p. 29).

21 "Man is likened to a square stone." Arnold Ehrhardt, "Vir Bonus Quadrato Lapidi Comparatur" (*Harvard Theological Review* 38:3, 1945, pp. 177–93).

22 "Trinity-Quaternity": referring to Jung's interest in the archetypal problem of three and four.

here, but I am trying to get a copy from U.S.A. The author, a German ex-Lutheran pastor, knows little of psychotherapy, and indeed is positively hostile to it. He tells me that some analyst analysed his best friend for cancer . . . so you can understand how he feels about it!

P.P.S. Thank you, yet again, for the promise of the "Eranos" offprints. I am ashamed to say I have written nothing for months, but must set to work on a paper on *"God" & The Unconscious* I have rashly promised!

Küsnacht-Zürich

April 13th, 1946[23]

to the Rev. Father Victor White,
Blackfriars,
Oxford.

Dear Father White,

I have been very pleased with your letter and I hasten to answer it at once. It is a nice idea of yours, that you want to come out to Switzerland between July and September. The time that would suit me best would be between the 12th and 27th of August. I should like you to consider yourself as my guest during your stay here. I shall be in the country, on the upper part of the lake of Zürich, where I have a little country place.[24] If you are a friend of the simple life you will have all the comfort you need. If your tastes should be too fastidious you would find it a bit rough. To give you an idea: I do my own cooking and chop my own wood and raise my own potatoes. But you have a decent bed and a roof over your head and we shall have plenty of time to discuss anything under the sun. As to clerical garments, you need no disguise

23 Typewritten.

24 The tower, Jung's lakeside retreat at Bollingen, built in stages over decades of his life. Starting in 1923, assisted by his son and local workmen but relying also on his own skill in stonework, Jung created a secluded refuge for himself in the vicinity of a small farming village on the north shore of the Obersee (Upper Lake Zurich), Canton Sankt Gallen (see map, Figure 5.1, p. 137). Other buildings were later attached to the round, two-story stone tower that was his first construction. The Tower was comfortable though primitive, lacking electrical power and running water. For a more detailed description of the architecture and its symbolic meaning for Jung, see ch. VIII of *Memories, Dreams, Reflections* (Recorded and edited by Aniela Jaffé. Trans. Richard and Clara Winston. New York: Vintage Books, 1961; hereafter, *MDR*). Among the inner circle of Jung's followers, it was considered a great honor and privilege to be invited to spend time with Jung at Bollingen. [with MS]

whatever,[25] since we shall be in a catholic country, not very far from the famous monastery of Einsiedeln.[26] But I warn you to bring something old and disreputable with you so that you spare your good clothes, and a pair of light shoes for occasional sailing on the lake.[27]

In alchemy you find many references to the homo quadratus[28] which is always an allusion to the mercurius quadratus, i.e. the hermai.[29] The quadratura[30] is a symbol for the totality.

Yours sincerely C.G. JUNG

Blackfriars, Oxford

Easter Sunday '46[31]

Dear Dr. Jung,

Thank you so *very* much. It all sounds like my idea of heaven, & I am at once setting about to put passports, permits & tickets in order.

My only misgiving is that I am the world's worst cook; & I see myself torn by the horrible dilemma of giving you indigestion or the humiliation of letting you cook my meal! I suppose the humiliation would be better for us both, but I am certainly going to try & get some lessons in cooking before August. . . .

Before long I hope to send you a few notes on one or two points of detail in "Psych. u. Alchemie"[32] which perhaps may interest you.

With very kindest regards,

Yours very sincerely & gratefully, FR. VICTOR WHITE, O.P.

25 Cf. Jung, 23 March 1946, p. 29; White, 1 April 1946, p. 31.

26 Benedictine monastery, founded in the tenth century. A glorious example of Baroque church architecture at the center of the town of Einsiedeln (cf. map, p. 137).

27 "Sailing on the lake with Jung" would become a theme in White's dreams (cf. White, 13 Oct. 1946, pp. 44f; and 5 May 1949, pp. 136f).

28 Four-sided man: Gnostic symbol, depicted as a cross or four-sided figure, of the union of four directions, four elements, etc., that create the original human totality. The Olympian god Hermes (Mercury) is also called four-sided in ancient writings. (Cf. CW 12, *Psych. & Alch.*, §172 and Pl. 63, p. 132.)

29 Herms: four-sided stone or metal pillars, erected at crossroads to represent Hermes (Mercury), the god of journeys (*Letters I*, p. 420n).

30 Four-sided figure.

31 Handwritten on a half-sheet of Blackfriars letterhead.

32 White's "few notes" were enclosed in his next letter. Cf. Appendix 4, "Some Notes on *Psychologie und Alchemie*," pp. 337ff.

Blackfriars, Oxford

23.6.46[33]

Dear Professor Jung,

I am venturing to enclose a few hasty jottings which I have made regarding some points in your grand book, "Psychologie und Alchemie".[34] I am afraid that some of them are hardly disinterested, being a plea for my own alchemical propensities against the imputation of heresy! But there are others which may perhaps be of some interest to you in preparing a second edition. They are only a few of the very many things I hope to be able to talk to you and ask you about in August.

I am looking forward immensely to my visit. My present plan is to spend a day or two on the way sightseeing in Zürich, and I also toy with the idea of visiting Einsiedeln for the Mariähimmelfahrt[35] celebrations. If it would be convenient to you, I would come to you on the afternoon of August 15th., arriving at Bollingen at 14.40. I should be very grateful if you would let me know if this is *not* a convenient day and time.

In a previous letter you told me that the English volume, *The Integration of the Personality* was "badly translated" and "was forced out of your hands by the thrift and 'pep' of an American publisher". Naturally I understand that this information was not intended for publication, but I am wondering if I might be allowed to publish the statement that the collection and translation of the essays in *The Integration of the Personality* was not authorised or approved by you – and without running any risk of courting a libel-action from the publisher?

The reason I ask is that there has recently appeared a book called *The Mind and Heart of Love* (!) by Father M. C. D'Arcy, S.J.[36] which contains a chapter which very severely, and very uncomprehendingly, criticises you and your psychology. Fr. D'Arcy bases his attack almost entirely on the

33 Typed on Blackfriars letterhead.

34 Four pages of single-spaced typewritten comments by White were handed over to Barbara Hannah and Marie-Louise von Franz, whose point-by-point responses were written to help Jung incorporate White's critique, when he revised *Psych. & Alch.* for its second edition. (Cf. Appendix 4, "Some Notes on *Psychologie und Alchemie*, with responses from Barbara Hannah and Marie-Louise von Franz," pp. 337ff.)

35 The Assumption of the Blessed Virgin Mary, celebrated 15 August. This doctrine was formally defined in 1950. (Cf. Jung, 25 Nov. 1950, pp. 157ff and notes; White, 3 Dec. 1950, pp. 160ff and notes.)

36 Martin Cyril D'Arcy (1888–1976): Jesuit priest and scholar. The full title of his book: *The Mind and Heart of Love, Lion and Unicorn; A Study in Eros and Agape* (1947). Despite his criticisms of Jung's thought, D'Arcy was later invited by Jung to speak at Eranos. (Cf. White, 30 March 1952, p. 180; 10 Nov. 1952, p. 208; Jung, 31 Oct. 1952, p. 207; 14 Nov. 1952, p. 210.)

Integration of the Personality – indeed, apart from some parts of *Psychology of the Unconscious*, this seems to be the only book of yours he has read! A considerable number of people have been asking me to write a "reply" to this attack. I confess I find the idea thoroughly boring and distasteful; I don't think it unfair to say that his criticism is for the most part extremely shallow and unworthy; but Fr. D'Arcy has a great reputation over here as a philosopher and theologian, and it is thought that his criticisms may do a great deal of harm. He is now, in fact, the Head of the English Jesuits, and it is rumoured that he may shortly be elected as "Black Pope", head of the whole Jesuit Order! Although it would not be essential to mention that *The Integration of the Personality* was unauthorised, it might indeed be helpful if I could be allowed to mention the fact – if I can find the time and inspiration to get down to the job at all.[37]

Priestley's broadcast[38] seems to have made a great impression; I thought he did it extraordinarily well considering all the difficulties of popular broadcasting. Miss Wolff's visit,[39] too, was greatly appreciated.

Hoping you are in the very best of health, dear Professor Jung,

Yours very sincerely, FR. VICTOR WHITE, O.P.

as from Bollingen

July 17th 1946[40]

Dear Father White,

Thank you very much for your long letter. Unfortunately I'm unable to answer it fully now, but I'm very glad indeed to have your valuable critique

37 Gerhard Adler wrote to Jung in July 1946 that he hoped White would be willing to review D'Arcy's book, with an eye particularly to clearing up the writer's misunderstandings of Jung's *Psychology of the Unconscious* (Jung/Adler correspondence, ETH Library archive).

38 J.B. Priestley (1894–1984): English journalist, novelist and playwright. His BBC broadcast, titled "Jung," was a positive assessment of Jung's views on psychology and religion, broadcast live by the Home Service on 18 June 1946.

39 In spring 1946 Toni Wolff visited England, giving a lecture, "Christianity Within," to the Guild of Pastoral Psychology (Lecture 42. London: GPP, 1946) (cf. Wolff, 18 July 1946, p. 36 and note). The original version of her lecture, "Christentum nach Innen," appears in her collected writings, *Studien zu Jungs Psychologie* (Zürich: Rhein-Verlag, 1959), pp. 319ff. While in England she also met with several Jungian analysts and students, including Gerhard Adler, Vera von der Heydt, Toni Sussmann and Victor White. (Cf. Wolff, 18 July 1946, p. 38 and note.)

40 Typewritten. Letter previously unpublished.

and I'm looking forward to our discussion of these matters when you turn up in Switzerland.

I only want to tell you that August 15th suits me very well and I hope to be able to meet you at the station at 14.40. I'm amazed that you found out even your arrival at this most insignificant place.

Concerning the "Integration of the Personality"[41] I must say it was all rushed and I had no chance to verify the translations thoroughly. I just could glance at them but had no time to go carefully over them. Afterwards I was shocked to find so many mistakes. I cannot say, though, that the edition is unauthorised, but it was rushed to such an extent that I couldn't keep up with it. As the translator had done good work before I thought that it would be good again, but it wasn't. As "Psychology and Alchemy" is really a new edition of these papers which were mere lectures to begin with, I hope that this new translation will be better and that there will be no more grave mistakes.

Sincerely yours, C.G. JUNG

From Toni Wolff

Freiestrasse 9
Zürich 7

July 18th 1946[42]

Dear Father White,

Many thanks for your letter of July 10th and particularly for the kind thought of the committee of the Guild of Pastoral Psychology[43] about your bringing out a present to me. I shall look forward very much to having it and to seeing you. I regret to say that I shall not be in Zürich between August 11th and 14th. I am very much in need of a vacation and shall leave

41 The book *Integration* contains two poorly translated essays, "Dream Symbols of the Process of Individuation" (*EJ* 1935) and "The Idea of Redemption in Alchemy" (*EJ* 1936). Later expanded and retranslated, they became Parts II and III of CW 12, *Psych. & Alch.* It is generally considered that Hull's translation is a good one. (Cf. Jung, 5 Oct. 1945, p. 9 and note.) [MS]

42 Typewritten.

43 Wolff had recently lectured to the Guild (cf. White, 23 June 1946, p. 35 and note). The Guild of Pastoral Psychology (hereafter, GPP) was launched in London in 1937, originally as a Jungian training group for clergy and others, predominantly Christian, who ministered to distressed personalities. On 5 April 1939 Jung delivered a seminar talk to GPP members, titled "The Symbolic Life" (cf. CW 18, *The Symbolic Life*, Part III), and became the official patron of the Guild. Starting in the 1950s Oxford became the location for the annual conference of the GPP.

at the end of this month. I shall however be staying with Dr. and Mrs. Jung[44] at Bollingen for a time and shall see you there. So please keep the present for that time, as my house will be closed and I should not like a valuable thing left in my letter box for long.

The name and address of the Benedictine priest and psychotherapist whom I mentioned to you is

Dr. Gallus Jud[45]
Zollikerstrasse 19
Zürich 8.

I tried to ring him up to find out if he will be in Zürich when you will be here. Unfortunately it is vacation time now and I got no response. However, the telephone office told me that he is out of town until the middle of August. So the best thing for you to do will be to write him at the above address and ask him when is the best time for you to see him. I am sure you could do so on your way back. But as he is very busy indeed, I am certain he will be glad to know beforehand.

The reference to dogma which I quoted is in the book "Die Gnosis des Christentums"[46] by Georg Koepgen, Verlag Otto Müller, Salzburg 1939. It is a very fine book indeed. I regret to say that, according to Dr. Jud, if I remember correctly, it was put onto the Index[47] later on. But there are several people here who have a copy. I shall remember to take mine along to Bollingen so that you can read it.

When you are at Einsiedeln you will meet Pater Ildefons Betschard,[48] professor of philosophy. Dr. Jung knows him and so do I. He is very

44 Cf. Emma Jung to White, 18 Dec. 1946, p. 59 and note.

45 Gallus Jud, O.S.B. (1900–1988): a Swiss Catholic priest, for many years a psychotherapist in Zurich. He read and corrected the first two sections of Jung's "Transformation Symbolism in the Mass" (CW 11, p. 203n). In Jung's wry portrait, "I often have interviews now with a Catholic priest, an intelligent and scholarly man, who gives me a chance to get thoroughly acquainted with the Catholic mind. It is wonderful to see medieaeval mentality still at its best" (Jung to Baynes, 27 May 1941, *Letters I*, p. 300).

46 "The Gnosis of Christianity."

47 *Index Librorum Prohibitorum* [List of Prohibited Books], "the Index": a list of books compiled by the Holy Office in Rome, on complaint, which Catholics are forbidden to read because they are contrary to faith or morals. Preventive censorship of books by Catholic theologians goes back to the early church. The first Index was issued by the Congregation of the Inquisition in 1557 under Paul IV. Leo XIII, in "Officiorum ac Munerum," 1897, assigned the duties of censorship to diocesan bishops. In response to the modernist crisis, in 1907 Pius X ordered all bishops to appoint as censors qualified theologians. The Index was suppressed in 1966, after the Second Vatican Council (*ODCC*, p. 697). (Cf. White, 5 April 1952, p. 182 and note.) [with AC]

48 Dr. P. Ildefons Betschart, O.S.B. (1904–1959): a Swiss Benedictine priest, author of a respected biography of Paracelsus. He taught Metaphysics, Psychology and Modern Historical Philosophy at the Lyceum of the Einsiedeln Monastery, and served for many years as Secretary of the Swiss Paracelsus Society.

interested in psychology and a member of a society of doctors and psychologists in Zürich.

My visit to England did me a lot of good in many ways. I do hope the same will be the case with your visit to Switzerland.

Sincerely yours, TONI WOLFF[49]

Bellinzona

27.8.46[50]

My dear Professor & Mrs Jung,

Here I am at the parting of the ways, a little uncertain whether tomorrow will take me left in search of a quiet spot for a few days on the Lago di Lugano, or right to Locarno. It has been a magnificent journey, & I am most grateful to you for planning it for me. Weesen,[51] Bad Ragaz, Chur, Dommat-Ems, Ilanz, Dissentis, Andermatt have been my principal stopping places & I do not think I have missed much at any of them. The journey over St. Gotthard, after walking in rain & fog to Hospenthal & in brilliant sunshine to the Teufelsbrücke was an unforgettable conclusion. But I was particularly entranced by the Upper Rhine valley & the Oberalp Pass.

49 Antonia (Toni) Wolff (1888–1953), analytical psychologist and teacher, was for over 40 years a member of Jung's closest circle. Born into a distinguished Zurich family, after her father's death in 1910 her mother sent her to C.G. Jung, a young psychiatrist, for treatment. Her aptitude for psychology was immediately evident, and she quickly became a leading exponent of Jung's thought. From the time of Jung's break with Freud in 1912, she was a trusted confidante and co-worker with Jung, occupying an important place in his life. In his letters of 1947 and 1948, White often includes Toni Wolff in his closing greetings.

Wolff became President of the Zurich Psychological Club for a brief time after its founding in 1916. She then held the presidency, with short breaks, from 1926 until she retired in 1952. From 1948 until her death she taught at the Jung Institute, on whose founding committee she served with Jung and C.A. Meier. At the founding of the Institute, April 1948, Jung singled out her essay, "Einführung in die Grundlagen der komplexen Psychologie" ["Introduction to the Foundations of Complex Psychology"] as "a work distinguished for its philosphical clarity" (CW 18, §1134, p. 474). Wolff's collected papers, *Die kulturelle Bedeutung der Komplexen Psychologie* [The Cultural Meaning of Complex Psychology] (1935), were republished after her death as *Studien zu C.G. Jungs Psychologie* [Studies in Jungian Psychology] (Zürich: Rascher-Verlag, 1959). Jung's Foreword to the latter edition appears in CW 10, *Civilization in Transition* (§887–902, pp. 469ff).

50 Handwritten on lined half-sheets.

51 White's spelling of place-names has been left unchanged throughout, whether accurate (here) or variant (below, Hospenthal for Hospental).

The principal purpose of this note is to thank you both for your wonderful hospitality & generosity to me – but I really do not know where to begin or end. My visit has meant more to me than I can possibly say, & I only wish I knew how I could reciprocate all your many kindnesses. Anything I can say seems all too banal, so I must abandon any further attempt to express my gratitude on the *conscious* level at all . . .

I look forward very much to seeing you again at Eranos in the next few days. I intend in any case to come to your lecture next Sunday, but I hope to come over before that if I can find a satisfactory hide-out in the neighbourhood. I intend to return to Zürich on Monday 2nd (when my ticket expires) & to go to Basel after seeing the Club on the following day.

I hope your own journey was not too tiring & that the Eranos Tagung[52] is being successful. I fear that the lectures which, apart from your own, would interest me most will be over by now.

With renewed gratitude & very kindest regards,

Yours sincerely, VICTOR WHITE, O.P.

P.S. At Ilanz I had a dream about a 'plane crashing in your garden & your cook (masc.) throwing earth over it. The odd thing is that I was woken by the sound of a circular saw, & several months ago I *dreamt* I was talking with you to the sound of such a saw . . . I can make no 'sense' of it.

Pension Mimosa
Porto Ronco[53]

31.8.46[54]

My dear Professor Jung,

As I understood you to say that it is proposed that the next "Eranos" Tagung should take Naturwissenschaft[55] for its subject, I wonder if I might presume to make one or two suggestions?

It occurs to me that what might be described as the non-Kantian view of the history of natural science & its function in human life at least deserves a hearing, & that Dr. Sherwood Taylor[56] might profitably be invited for the purpose. He has made very special study of the subject & written several books about it, & may be particularly interesting as he has paid special

52 Cf. Jung, 26 Sept. 1945, p. 4 and note.

53 The actual location of Eranos, a small village just west of Ascona.

54 Handwritten. 55 natural science. 56 Cf. White, 23 Oct. 1945, p. 21 and note.

attention to the case of Galileo & to the little known *alchemical* letters of Newton. As Curator of the Ashmolean Natural Science Museum I feel he would be of sufficient distinction to claim the attention of your audience. He is also much preoccupied with the practical relationship of Geist & Wissenschaft.[57]

My other suggestion concerns rather my own Peripatetic Hobby-Horse! Since (very understandably) it seems impossible to leave Aristotle alone, would not a lecture on him be welcome from someone who can read him without Kantian Voraussetzungen?[58] I feel there is a real danger in too uncritical acceptance of the general "Teutonic" interpretation, & that (as I have ventured to suggest in a previous letter) the "Transcendentalist" split which is read back into him & his medieval followers, is both cause & symptom of much of the modern "schism" between "Geist" & "Wissenschaft". Once his identification of νους[59] & νοητον[60] is understood it would (for instance) be impossible to suppose that his "categories" were "ontological" & "objective" in the modern sense (or non-sense), even if it were not notorious that the "Categories" were part of the "Organon" & were classes of *predicates*. This may seem a very technical & academic point, but it suggests that the alleged discontinuity of modern scientific method with *authentic* Greek & Medieval thought is by no means so marked as the holders of the "mythe scientiste" love to maintain!

At least I dare to suggest that there *is* another side to this story than that of H. G. Wells & Co.! Profs. Maritain[61] & Gilson[62] are specialists in the subject, & I wonder if one or other might be invited. They are both excellent lecturers in very different ways. I fear that now Maritain is an Ambassador he may not be available, but probably Gilson's approach would anyway be more *sympathique*. (Do you know his "God & Philosophy"? A tiny, but superb, work).

I hope I may be forgiven the impertinence of these suggestions. But perhaps next year's meetings may be all the more creative & "enantidromic"[63] if the audience be given the opportunity of realising that here also is a case of "Audi alterem partem"![64]

57 spirit and science.

58 assumptions.

59 (for νοῦς) the mind.

60 (for νοητόν) the intelligible, knowable.

61 Jacques Maritain (1882–1973): French Catholic philosopher and theologian. During his career he was professor at the Lycée Stanislaus, l'Institut Catholique de Paris, and then in the United States, at the universities of Princeton, Columbia, Notre Dame, and Chicago. In 1948 White met Maritain at least once while in the U.S. [with AC]

62 Etienne Gilson (1884–1978): French Catholic theologian and prolific writer, he was professor at the University of Strasbourg, the Sorbonne, l'Ecole pratique des Hautes, and the University of Toronto. His *God and Philosophy* was first published in 1941.

63 A created word, from "enantiodromia" (cf. p. 171, note 14), here meaning "two-sided" or "balanced."

64 "Listen to the other side."

I am having a quite marvellous time, & I look forward immensely to hearing your lecture tomorrow. I hope I shall have another opportunity of seeing you before I leave.

My kindest regards to Mrs. Jung.

And, once again, a thousand thanks for everything,

Yours very sincerely, FR. VICTOR WHITE, O.P.

P.S. I am not sure that Sherwood Taylor could lecture in German. His address is The Old Ashmolean (Science) Museum, Oxford.

Son Excellence M. le Prof. J. Maritain is at l'Ambassade de la Rép. Française auprès de Saint-Siège, Città del Vaticano. Prof. Gilson will be either at the Sorbonne or at the University of Toronto, Canada. He spends six months at each.

Blackfriars, Oxford

18th September 1946[65]

Dear Miss Schmid,[66]

Thanks so very much for your letter.[67] I am afraid that the French translation of my "Frontiers"[68] is only now being begun, and it will be a considerable time before I expect it in print. Please tell Dr. Jud that I shall not fail to send him a copy so soon as it is available.

I wonder if I could ask your help concerning a rather delicate matter. I have been rather exercised for some time owing to the fact that a number of worthy young people in London are undergoing "Psychotherapeutic Training" from Toni Sussman[69] in the belief that this will enable them to receive at Zürich a diploma[70] qualifying them to analyse. Our conversation at Ronco

65 Typewritten.

66 Marie-Jeanne Schmid (later Frau Boller-Schmid): daughter of Hans Schmid, MD, a pupil and friend of Jung's, became Jung's private secretary in 1932 and served in that capacity until her marriage in 1952. Working in close cooperation with Jung for 20 years, she was entrusted with confidential matters of all sorts. Miss Schmid's personality and the scope of her discretion are often evident in her letters to White, whom she also came to know socially, for example at Eranos (cf. White, 16 Oct. 1946, p. 50).

67 Schmid's first letter to White has not been preserved.

68 "Frontiers of Theology and Psychology," originally published by the GPP (London, 1942), one of four papers White sent to Jung with his first letter (cf. White, 3 Aug. 1945, p. 3 and note).

69 Cf. White, 9 Oct. 1945, p. 12 and note.

70 The first diplomas were awarded after the C.G. Jung Institute was founded in 1948.

has made me wonder more than ever, if these people, for one or two of whom I have a certain responsibility, are not being taken up the garden path. T.S. herself told me that her trainees have never been refused this qualification, and she rather implies that what she says concerning their abilities will "go" with Professor Jung and the Zürich Club.

I cannot help wondering whether this is just another symptom of that disease with the long name that I have still forgotten. If so, no blame can attach to T.S., but it is a very bad show for the trainees.

I do not want to bother C.G. with this matter. And I have professional as well as personal reasons for not wanting to be involved myself in any rumpus with T.S. But if these people are being duped I feel it my duty tactfully to give them some idea of the situation. Do you know of any such arrangement?[71] Or is discipleship of T.S. more likely to *dis*qualify them at Zürich than otherwise? I myself (prompted chiefly by C.G.'s "certificate")[72] once sent a girl to T.S. for "training". It was over that I had the famous dream![73]

I leave it entirely to your discretion whether or not to say anything about this to Professor Jung. Please greet him and Mrs. Jung warmly from me. I hope to begin a letter to him before long, but have so much I want to say

71 This sentence and the rest of this paragraph added by hand. White's anxiety about the legitimacy of Toni Sussmann's claims seems to have resolved in the following years. There is evidence that he continued to meet with her in professional settings. (Cf. Telegram, 4 Jan. 1954, p. 227, signed by a group of Jungian Catholics including White and Sussmann.)

72 Seeking to flee Germany in the 1930s, Toni Sussmann had asked Jung to vouch for her as a therapist, since viability in the workplace was a condition for resettlement abroad. Three times, in 1933, 1937 and 1942 (Jung/Sussmann correspondence, ETH Library archive), Jung sent signed statements attesting to her training with him and vouching for her as a therapist and *Erzieherin*. (The word was apparently chosen with care. Literally "governess"; a more likely translation may be "child guidance counselor.")

Jung's "Attest" of 1933 reads: "Hiermit bestätige ich, dass ich Frau TONI SUSSMANN von Charlottenburg-Berlin schon seit 1916 kenne. Sie hat im Laufe der Jahre mehrfach bei mir gearbeitet und hat sich als eine ebenso tüchtige wie gewissenhafte Therapeutin und Erzieherin erwiesen. Sie ist in meiner Psychologie theoretisch und praktisch völlig ausgebildet und hat gerade der Einführung meiner Psychologie in Deutschland unschätzbare Dienste erwiesen. Sie arbeitet in meinem Namen und Auftrag. gez. Dr. C.G. Jung, Küsnacht-Zürich, den 4. Dezember 1933." [Herewith I testify that I have known Mrs. Toni Sussmann since 1916. Over the years she has worked with me several times and has proven herself to be a competent and careful therapist and children's counselor. She is completely trained in the theoretical and practical aspects of my psychology and has done inestimable service to the introduction of my psychology to Germany. She works in my name and at my direction. Signed, Dr. C.G. Jung, Küsnacht-Zürich, 4 December 1933.] (Jung/Sussmann correspondence, ETH Library archive.)

73 In part three of this dream he is in Jung's garden, where Jung hands him an oval plaque signifying that White is one of the few who have understood the implications of Jung's work. Similar plaques are to be given to others, but in the dream White realizes that Sussmann is not one of them, and that he must tell her so. (Cf. White, 14 Oct. 1945, pp. 14ff.)

and so little time to say it in, that I am sure he will not expect to hear from me until all is ready.

I hope that you, as well as he, are now reposing after those strenuous times.

With greetings to all my friends,

Yours sincerely, VICTOR WHITE, O.P.

Küsnacht-Zürich

September 26th 1946[74]

Dear Father White,

Thank you very much for your letter. I'm sorry I had forgotten all about Mrs. Sussman when I wrote to you last. But I now have taken the matter up and also discussed it with Dr. Jung.

First I've dug out the two certificates Dr. Jung wrote for her.[75] The first was written when she wanted to get out of Germany and Dr. Jung was rather more positive than he felt because he wanted to give her a chance to settle down somewhere else. Dr. Jung said I could send them to you to read them, but he would like to have them back of course. Now the trouble is, that one cannot be 100% certain that there wasn't another certificate written, although it is very unlikely, but sometimes copies get lost or Dr. Jung writes them by long-hand and has no copy.

Now as to the "Psychotherapeutic Training" there is no such thing as a diploma given in Zürich. Up to the present time Dr. Jung has considered as his pupils only people who have worked with him personally and to some of those only did he give a letter or certificate stating that he personally considered them qualified to work as analysts. As a rule it didn't matter at all with whom they had worked before they came to Zürich as only their personal value and aptitude was considered. So whatever Mrs. Sussman says about her pupils does not really matter as neither Prof. Jung nor his pupils here will take anything for granted.

As far as I'm aware of Dr. Jung's feelings in the matter (unfortunately I couldn't have a long talk about it with him) I should say that his attitude towards Mrs. Sussman has changed in the last years simply because what he heard from her directly and indirectly made him feel that caution was indicated. So, as far as I remember he has not sent a single patient or pupil to her ever since she is in England. On the other hand I am certain that he does

74 Typewritten. 75 Cf. White, 18 Sept. 1946, p. 42 and note.

not want to disavow her, simply because he has seen again and again that even pupils whose work is not wholly to their credit can give people what they want and need.

As to the feeling of the people here apart from Dr. Jung it is hard to say as except Frl. Wolff and myself I do not think that many remember her well enough or had any dealings with her to judge her.

But I'm telling you this quite confidentially, just to give you an idea of the situation. Officially one could say (and you can broadcast this as coming from Dr. Jung) that Mrs. S. is or can claim to be Dr. Jung's pupil but *not* his representative. The training she gives is *her* training and people trained by her cannot claim to be Dr. Jung's pupils. But that is the case with Dr. Jung's other pupils too, especially the ones abroad.

If there is any point left which is still not clear to you or on which you want further elucidation, please let me know.

Unfortunately I'm far from reposing, as there was much too much work to catch up with and Dr. Jung is starting his practical work next week. I just shall have to get used to the fact that life is very hard work indeed.

My best wishes to you,

Yours sincerely, [MARIE-JEANNE SCHMID]
(unsigned carbon copy)

Blackfriars, Oxford

13.10.46[76]

My dear Professor Jung,

I do not know what you can be thinking of me and my failure to write you one single line since my return to England. It has not been for want of trying, or even of starting; but every effort I have made so far has been interrupted and frustrated in one way or another. Since my return it has just been "one dam thing after another"; very interesting things, many of them: things I should dearly like to tell you and talk to you about.

Bollingen, Zürich, Ronco – sometimes they seem like a remote paradise in never-never land. I cannot tell you how much I enjoyed them, and how grateful I am to you and Mrs Jung for them.

A few nights ago I dreamed that I was in a largish sailing-boat sailing from (for some reason I have not yet discovered) Norway to England. I was roaming carefree all over the boat. You were the captain at the wheel. After

76 Typewritten.

a while I noticed that we were scudding along in a southerly direction at considerable speed and amid perilous rocks and shoals; but we always missed them. I "knew" there was no danger, not so much because you were at the wheel, but because the *Wind* was taking care of us and would never wreck the pair of us. Presently I found that we were speeding along very close to the shore (on our left), but still we always missed it and its many promontories. After a while we reached a small (?Danish) coastal town; the boat, with you calmly at the wheel and smoking your pipe, imperceptibly mounted the shore and sailed down the streets dexterously missing all the buildings and the traffic. She was amphibious!

I hope this is "all right", and not inflation. Certainly I do seem to have gained much more confidence than hitherto, and my various works – both in Seelsorge and Psychotherapie – seem to be going very much more easily. You said something very important when you told me not to pretend to less "consciousness" than I've got. I only hope I am not overdoing it.

I have been seeing a good deal of John Layard lately, and I feel we really may be getting somewhere.[77] What you said about his treatment of my "kowtowing to the Archbishop" dream has proved to be a most important clue; and it has become more and more clear that his spell of trouble over the past few years had its origins then. He had already gone a good way with the Exeter people[78] (from whom, doubtless, you have lately heard more), but brought from Exeter to Oxford a dream which clearly showed that his "priest-riddenness" was getting in the way of further progress there. I think that we have now pretty satisfactorily disposed of that. But our dear John is certainly a problem; though I think a very worthwhile one.

In common honesty[79] I must tell you that I have lately come across a whole series of ordinations of Dominican General Chapters of the 13th and 14th centuries forbidding Dominicans the practice of alchemy and the possession of alchemical books under the direst penalties! I derive only

77 White was evidently serving as his former analyst's spiritual director, a role reversal which would not have been so startling during this historical period. It is worth noting that White was originally introduced to John and Doris Layard not in a clinical context but by a mutual friend in academic and church circles (Fergus Kerr, O.P., "Remembering Donald MacKinnon," *New Blackfriars*, 2004).

78 A Jungian therapeutic community in Exeter, Withymead, founded in 1941 by Gilbert Champernowne and his wife, Irene, a Jungian analyst. Using group therapy, the community treated disturbed adults. Among the analysts at Withymead were S.H. Foulkes and Eve Lewis (cf. Telegram, 4 Jan. 1954; White, 18 March 1960, p. 283 and note), who jointly authored a paper, "Analysis Studies in the treatment of groups on Psycho-Analytical lines" (1944). The community closed in 1954, having treated 240 people. (Malcolm Pines, "Forgotten Pioneers: The Unwritten History of the Therapeutic Community Movement." *Therapeutic Communities: The International Journal for Therapeutic and Supportive Organizations*, Vol. 20:1, 1999.)

79 Cf. White, 23 Oct. 1945, p. 22 and note.

the slightest satisfaction from the reflection that these prohibitions are no longer in force and that the very frequency of their repetition, progressively increasing in severity, indicates that not much notice was taken of them. It is true that the practice of medicine was also forbidden to the friars, but in nothing like such unqualified terms. If you would like to see these documents I could doubtless have copies of them made.

Such inquiries as I have been able to make so far from specialist friends regarding the origin of the "Aurora Consurgens"[80] have as yet yielded no results, although they have vaguely heard of the work. I am still very much hoping to be able to receive a copy, not only to submit to their expert attention, but also to read for my own profit and delight.

My own more studious activities have had a very thin time of it lately, in spite of the fact that I am resolutely keeping two days per week free from all concern with other people's souls – a resolve I find most necessary for their own weal as well as my own. But of writing I have done practically none. My prospective publishers want me to double the length of my " 'God' and 'The Unconscious" ' essay;[81] it is certainly far too condensed as it is. I was thrilled and amazed when I heard your magnificent Eranos lecture[82] to find you seemed to be *saying* so exactly what in my essay I had been trying to say you *meant*, and even (though with so different an object) following so similar a plan as I had been trying to work out. I do not know when I shall be able to settle down to the necessary revising and rewriting. But I should be extremely grateful if I might send you a typewritten copy when it is done. I wonder if also I might dare ask at the same time for a few words of

80 "Rising Dawn." A medieval alchemical treatise, of special interest to Jung because it was attributed by legend to Thomas Aquinas (cf. Jung, 23 Jan. 1947, p. 70 and note). Marie-Louise von Franz (1915–1998): for many years Jung's assistant in his alchemical research, she wrote an extensive commentary on this work, concluding that the author was not an alchemist but used alchemical symbols to express experiences of a numinous nature. (Cf. Jung, 6 Nov. 1946, p. 54 and note.) [with MS]

Her commentary, *Aurora Consurgens, ein dem Thomas von Aquin zugeschriebenes Dokument der alchemistischen Gegensatzproblematik*, was published as the third volume of GW 14, *Mysterium Coniunctionis* (cf. Jung, early April 1952, p. 185 and note). (Hereafter, *Mysterium*.) The English CW 14 lacks this supplemental volume, which was later published separately: M.-L. von Franz, ed., *Aurora Consurgens. A Document Attributed to Thomas Aquinas on the Problem of Opposites in Alchemy* (Trans. R.F.C. Hull and S.B. Glover. London: Routledge & Kegan Paul, 1966).

81 The essay was later expanded and included in White's first book, *God & Unc.* (1952).

82 "Der Geist der Psychologie" (*EJ 1946*, pp. 385–490). Revised, as "Theoretische Überlegungen zum Wesen des Psychischen" ["Theoretical Reflections on the Nature of the Psyche"] in *Von den Wurzeln des Bewusstseins: Studien über den Archetypus* [The Roots of Consciousness: Studies on the Archetype] (Zürich: Rascher Verlag, 1954). In translation, "The Spirit of Psychology," Jung's lecture appears in *Spirit and Nature* (1954). His revised, expanded version, under the title, "On the Nature of the Psyche," appears in both CW 8, *Structure & Dynamics*, and *On the Nature of the Psyche* (1969).

preface[83] – even in spite of the fact that on one or two points I am a trifle critical? But sufficient unto the day . . .

There are one or two points of "business" I should add to this letter. But I shall be writing to Miss Schmid in a few days, and I think they are matters which she will be able to deal with without my bothering you personally.

I do hope and pray that you are now having a more restful time after your many congresses; and that both you and Mrs Jung are well. Please remember me to her very kindly. Also to Miss Wolff; I hope her "cure" was successful. I have not seen Dr. Bennet[84] since his return; but I heard Dr. Crichton Miller's[85] address to the Guild the other day, which was very good indeed (although we got lost in a rather futile argument about the meaning of "dogma") and much more openly "Jungian" than I had anticipated. To-morrow I am expecting a visit from Dr. Rivkah Schaerf,[86] so hope for more recent news from Zürich.

Please forgive this rather messy and incoherent letter; it is but a few scraps from the multitude of things I should like to write or talk about. I enclose also a few snapshots Zur fröhliche Errinerung.[87]

Yours ever most gratefully & sincerely, FR. VICTOR WHITE, O.P.

83 Jung agreed to this request (cf. Jung, 6 Nov. 1946, p. 53). His "Vorrede" ["Foreword"] for *God & Unc.* was translated originally by Elizabeth Welsh (cf. Schmid, 23 May 1952, p. 194 and note). In Hull's later translation it appears in CW 11, *Psych. & Rel.*, §449–67, pp. 299ff, and in the Spring edition of *God & Unc.*

84 E.A. Bennet, English psychiatrist and analytical psychologist. Author of *C.G. Jung* (1961) and *What Jung Really Said* (1966).

85 Hugh Crichton-Miller (1877–1959): pioneering English psychiatrist. In 1920 he founded London's Tavistock Clinic, and he chaired the gathering of doctors when Jung delivered five lectures there in 1935 (cf. "The Tavistock Lectures," CW 18, *The Symbolic Life*, §1–415, pp. 3–182). From 1933 to 1938 Crichton-Miller served, at Jung's request, as British representative on the board of the International Medical Society for Psychotherapy, while Jung struggled to maintain the organization against Nazi pressure. At the founding of the C.G. Jung Institute in 1948, the three English patrons of the Institute were Crichton-Miller, Herbert Read and Victor White (cf. Jung, 27 Dec. 1947, pp. 104ff). In 1960 Jung wrote the Foreword to Crichton-Miller's memoir, expressing special thanks for his friend's courageous help during the pre-war years ("Foreword," *Hugh Crichton-Miller, 1877–1959: A Personal Memoir by his Friends and Family*, Dorchester: Longmans Ltd., 1961, pp. 1f. Cf. CW 18, *The Symbolic Life*, §1462–65, pp. 639ff).

86 Rivkah Schärf [Schaerf] (1907–1987): Jungian analyst and teacher, later known by her married name, Schärf-Kluger. She recorded in shorthand many of Jung's lectures at the ETH. Her doctoral dissertation, "Die Gestalt des Satans im Alten Testament," first appeared as part of Jung's *Symbolik*. (Cf. Jung, 23 March 1946, p. 29 and note; White, 29 Oct. 1946, pp. 52f and note.)

87 (for *zur fröhlichen Erinnerung*) a reminder of happy times. (Not an idiomatic expression in German.)

Figure 2.1 White's snapshot of Jung at the tiller of his small sailboat, on Upper Lake Zurich.

Blackfriars, Oxford

16th October, 1946[88]

Dear Miss Schmid,

I am most grateful to you for your kind letter and information and for the enclosures which I return herewith. You may be sure that I will use the information you give me with the utmost discretion. Needless to say, there will be no question at all of wanting Dr. Jung to disavow T.S. I merely wanted one or two of her disciples for whom I am in some measure responsible to mind their step.

I do hope that now you are having a more restful time for I am afraid I have one or two more requests to make from you. I am a little uncertain whether I should address them direct to Dr. Jung, but I do not want to bother him with business unnecessarily, and I think these are matters which you would in any case be asked to deal with.

88 Typewritten.

(i) Dr. R.G. McInnes,[89] who is head of the Warneford Mental Hospital here, is being given three or four months leave in the Spring and Summer of next year for combined rest and the opportunity to acquaint himself with psychotherapeutic work in other countries. He is very keen to know and study more of Jungian Psychology, and also to acquaint himself with psychiatric work in Switzerland generally. He has asked me to enquire whether it would be possible for him to be given facilities for this purpose in Zürich, and I have promised him that I would enquire. I imagine that this would involve the possibility of some interviews with Dr. Jung and/or his colleagues, Assistants at lectures and seminars, some use of the Club, and possibly introductions to some Clinics etc. He is a very worth-while person, a disciple of Henderson,[90] and occupying an important position. He is somewhat dissatisfied with "orthodox" psychiatry, and I think that any help that could be given to him in Zürich, would be very beneficial both to him and his patients, as well as to Psychiatry in England generally.

(ii) Can you tell me if there are any Jungian, or near-Jungian, practitioners in Sweden, preferably in Stockholm? I ask on behalf of a very understanding young lady psychiatric worker from Stockholm University[91] who has been visiting me lately and who is likewise dissatisfied with "orthodox" psychiatry, and has much difficulty in reconciling it with religion.

(iii) To descend from the sublime to the ridiculous, might I ask you when next you happen to be shopping in Zürich, to see if you could buy one or two rubber washers to fit a "Mobil" Trockenrasier?[92] Please do not trouble about this if it should be difficult, but I think they would be easy to get from the Parfumerie Schindler, Bahnhofstrasse 90, which is where I bought the razor. The said washer is a small square piece of rubber which fits the pin on top of the razor inside the cutting edge. There is no hurry for this at all, and do not bother if they should be un-obtainable.

89 Dr. Robert Gow McInnis had been Medical Superintendant of the Warneford and Park Hospitals in Oxford since 1938.

90 Sir David Kennedy Henderson, MD (1884–1965): Scottish psychiatrist, perhaps the most eminent U.K. psychiatrist between the First and Second World Wars. After his education in Edinburgh and eight years' post-graduate study in Munich, New York, and London, he taught for three years at Johns Hopkins University, Baltimore. In 1915 he began service as a psychiatric specialist with the RAMC in France, and in 1921 became physician superintendant to the Glasgow Royal Asylum. From 1932 to his retirement in 1954, he was physician superintendant to the Royal Edinburgh Hospital for Nervous and Mental Disorders, and professor of psychiatry at Edinburgh University. While at Glasgow Henderson published, with R.D. Gillespie, his *Textbook of Psychiatry* (1927), which won international acclaim and played a crucial role in raising the medical status of psychiatry. His publications included an article in *Psychiatry for Practitioners* (1936), a monograph titled *Psychopathic States* (1939), and the Morrison Lectures on society and criminal conduct (1955). Henderson was knighted in 1947. [with AC]

91 Killiki Palmquist (cf. Appendix 2, "Victor White, a Memoir," p. 326).

92 (for *Trockenrasierer*) dry razor. White's purchase of a razor in Zurich, and his urgent request for extra washers to fit it, reflect the scarcity of such items in post-war England.

(iv) I am still hoping that it may be possible to obtain a copy of Dr. Jung's Eranos Lecture.[93] I know that the Vermouth and Nostrano were flowing when you made this most welcome suggestion, and so, of course, I shall not hold it against you if it should not be possible. But there was so much in the lecture which affects the rewriting of my essay for publication that I should like to read and study the lecture long before it is likely to be printed in the Jahrbuch.

I had a most welcome visit on Monday from Dr. Rivkah Schaerf. I have just written to Dr. Jung, but please greet him from me, also Miss Hannah[94] when you see her again.

I am so sorry to give you so much trouble: I hope that people over here will soon cease to regard me as a sort of unofficial agent for Zürich!

Every best wish to yourself.

Yours sincerely, VICTOR WHITE

Küsnacht-Zürich

October 24th 1946[95]

The Rev. Father Victor White,
Blackfriars,
Oxford

Dear Father White,

Thank you very much for your letter. Your two letters to Dr. Jung have also safely arrived. He is rather overcrowded at the moment and so cannot answer immediately but he asked me to thank you very much for your kind letter and also for the delightful photographs. Mrs. Jung also sends you her kindest regards.

It is a very good plan indeed to address all business matters directly to me,

93 Cf. White, 13 Oct. 1946, p. 46 and note.

94 Juliet Barbara Hannah (1891–1986): English Jungian analyst and writer. She lived most of her adult life in Switzerland, where she studied and analyzed with Jung. She also transcribed his lectures at the ETH: "Modern Psychology" in 1933–34, and "Process of Individuation: Exercitia spiritualia of St. Ignatius of Loyola" in 1939–40. Sharing a house and many intellectual interests with Marie-Louise von Franz, Hannah's published works include *Striving Towards Wholeness* (1971, 1973, 1987); *Jung: His Life and Work* (1976, 1977, 1981); and *Encounters with the Soul: Active Imagination as Developed by C.G. Jung* (1981). (Cf. Appendix 4, Part II, pp. 344ff.)

95 Typewritten.

as I can answer most of your questions without bothering him and you have a better chance to have a reply within reasonable delay. And I shall always be delighted to help you in any way I can. So now to your questions:

Ad 1.[96] There seem to be two sides to Dr. McInnes's plan. For the Jungian side I think it would be best if he worked with Dr. Meier,[97] but I'm sure that Dr. Jung would also see him occasionally. So the best thing would be if he wrote sometime in the early spring both to Dr. Jung and Dr. Meier (Steinwiesstrasse 37, Zürich), to ask them to reserve time for him. The term for the Jungians begins about April 15th and goes on to the beginning of July. As to the psychiatric side (which in Zürich or anywhere in Switzerland has hardly anything to do with Jungian psychology), he had best apply directly to the head of the Psychiatric Clinic, Prof. M. Bleuler,[98] who will also be able to tell him about lectures at the University. Working with Dr. Meier, Dr. McInnes will have the opportunity to use the Club, but whether there will be any seminars is uncertain until it is known how many Anglosaxons will be here next summer.

Ad 2. There is no Jungian in Sweden. The only person known to Dr. Jung is Dr. Paul Bjerre,[99] Varstavi, *Tumba*, a very nice old gentleman, president of the Swedish group of the International Federation of Psychotherapists. I do not know whether he knows very much about Jungian ideas, but one might try him.

Ad 3. Unfortunately I had some difficulty about your rubber washers, i.e. could not get them immediately. But I finally discovered a kind lady who promised to get some for me in about a week. I shall send them along as soon as I can get hold of them.

Ad 4. You are quite right in suspecting the Vermouth and the Nostrano. It had completely slipped my mind that I promised to send you a copy of

96 To 1. The Latin "ad," normal usage in German-language business letters, may have entertained White, as it also recalls the headings used by Aquinas in the *ST:* "Ad 1," "Ad 2" (Reply to 1, Reply to 2), etc.

97 Carl Alfred Meier, M.D. (1905–1995): Swiss psychiatrist and analyst, professor of psychology at the ETH, whose published works include *Jung's Analytical Psychology and Religion* (1959, 1977); *The Meaning and Significance of Dreams* (1987, 1990); *A Testament to the Wilderness* (1985) and *Atom and Archetype: The Pauli/Jung Letters 1932–1958*, which he edited at the end of his life. For decades a close friend and confidant to Jung, with whom he had analyzed in the late 1920s, Meier was the first vice-president of the Zurich Jung Institute and worked closely with Jung in many major undertakings (*Jungians*, pp. 9ff). (Cf. Jung, 27 Dec. 1947, p. 104).

98 Manfred Bleuler, M.D.: professor of psychiatry at the University of Zurich; from 1942 to 1970 director of the Burghölzli Clinic. Son of Eugen Bleuler (1857–1939), former director of the Burghölzli Clinic, with whom Jung had studied as a young man.

99 Paul Carl Bjerre (1876–1964): Swedish psychotherapist and author of *From Psychoanalysis to Psychosynthesis* (1923) and other works.

Dr. Jung's lecture.[100] I'm doing so now, but I want you to know that Dr. Jung is considerably enlarging it for publication. He has not finished yet and could only copy some pages of it so far, but I'll let you have a copy as soon as it's finished which, however, will not be very soon, I'm afraid.

Rivkah Schärf gave me a short but very enthusiastic report on her visit to Oxford. Elle m'a mis l'eau à la bouche![101] as the French say.

With all my best wishes,

Yours sincerely, [MARIE-JEANNE SCHMID]
(unsigned carbon copy)

Blackfriars, Oxford

October 29th 1946[102]

Dear Miss Schmid,

Thanks awfully for your letter and for so very kindly sending me a copy of the Eranos lecture. Thank you so much too for all the information. I am so sorry to give you so much trouble especially about the washers. Please thank the kind lady also for her collaboration.

Please tell Dr. Jung that I expect no reply to my letter unless he feels like it. I would, however, be grateful if you would draw his attention to an extremely interesting and important article on the problem of Evil[103] – or rather the Evil One – in early Christianity by a Père Bouyer,[104] in a review called "Dieu-Vivant"[105] number 6. I have found it most illuminating and I feel sure it would interest Dr. Jung very much.

With all best wishes to yourself,

Yours sincerely, VICTOR WHITE

P.S. If you should be seeing Dr. Rivkah Schärf again, please tell her that her

100 Cf. White, 13 Oct. 1946, p. 46 and note.

101 She whetted my appetite!

102 Typewritten, except for postscript.

103 P. Louis Bouyer, "Le problème du mal dans le christianisme antique," *Dieu Vivant*, No. 6, 1946, pp. 17–42.

104 Louis Bouyer, SJ (b. 1913): French Jesuit, prolific writer and lecturer on the history of spirituality, liturgy, and church history.

105 *Dieu Vivant: Perspectives Religieuses et Philosophiques*. Paris: Editions du Seuil. This periodical started publishing in 1945, becoming the medium for a heated debate about worker priests in the early 1950s. It ceased publishing in 1955.

Ms. has arrived[106] & that Fr Richard[107] & I are finding it immensely interesting. I hope she will not mind if we have copies made of it – of course not for publication. Would she also drop me a postcard giving the address to which I am to return it.

I hope it will not be long before *you* visit Oxford!

Küsnacht-Zürich

November 6th 1946[108]

The Rev. Father Victor White,
Blackfriars,
Oxford

Dear Father White,

Your dream[109] is very much to the point! I had all sorts of feelings or "hunches" about you and the risks you are running. We are indeed on an adventurous and dangerous journey! But the guiding principle is the "wind" i.e. the πνεῦμα.[110] Norway is the northern country, i.e. the intuitive sector of the mandala.

I have heard nothing about J. Layard from the Exeter People.[111] They had problems of their own. I am glad, that he is getting on.

If you could get me just one or two specimens of the ordinations against Alchemy,[112] I should be most obliged.

I am most interested in what you are going to write and I shall certainly write a preface,[113] if you wish me to do so.

After the congresses[114] I had to spend about 5 days participating in the

106 I.e., Schärf's dissertation (cf. White, 13 Oct. 1946, p. 47 and note). In White's first book, in a chapter titled "Devils and Complexes," he summarizes Schärf's discussion of the biblical image of Satan (*God & Unc.*, 1982, p. 178).

107 Fr. Richard Kehoe, O.P. (cf. White, 23 Oct. 1945, p. 17 and note).

108 Typewritten. 109 Cf. White, 13 Oct. 1946, pp. 44f.

110 wind, spirit; Holy Spirit. 111 Cf. White, 13 Oct. 1946, p. 45 and note.

112 White had written Jung about evidence that the Dominican General Chapters of the thirteenth and fourteenth centuries repeatedly forbade the practice of alchemy (White, 13 Oct. 1946). His response to Jung's question has not been preserved. J.R. Partington, "Albertus Magnus on Alchemy" (*Ambix*, Vol. 1, No. 1, London, 1937), documents repeated papal ordinances against the Franciscans between 1272 and 1313 (*Letters I*, p. 448n).

113 Cf. White, 13 Oct. 1946, pp. 46f and note. It took Jung several years to fulfill this promise. His "Vorrede" was finished in mid-1952 (cf. Schmid, 23 May 1952).

114 On the 8/9 September 1946, a joint congress of the Zurich Society of Natural Scientists and the Swiss Society of Natural Scientists took place in Zurich. The latter organization included a "Section for Practical Psychology."

reception of Mr. Churchill[115] in Berne as well as in Zürich. At the last dinner I even had the seat beside him. He was very tired, more than I was. Afterwards I had to settle down to a careful overhauling of my Eranos Lectures.[116] I have just given them the last touch. They have grown in size, as I have inserted rather extensive material illustrating the multiple "luminosities" of the unconscious, representing the "consciouslike" nuclei of volitional acts (presumably identical with archetypes.) I hope this is not too chinese. I have included St. Ignatius of Loyola's vision of the serpent with the many eyes as a most unorthodox piece of evidence.

Thank you for the photos! They are very good and a pleasant souvenir of your visit to Switzerland. I hope, your next one will not be postponed too far! I wish I could travel more easily. But I am kept down through too many things. Presently I must make up my mind to tackle my dangerous paper about the psychology of the H. Trinity.[117]

The Latin text of the Aurora Consurgens is in the British Museum.[118] A rare print of 1624.[119] The title of the volume is: Harmoniae Imperscrutabilis[120] etc.

Hoping you are always in good health and in good spirit

I remain yours C.G. JUNG

115 Winston Churchill was on holiday in Switzerland, 23 August to 16 September 1946, and visited Bern and Zurich. In Bern the Swiss government arranged a reception, and in Zurich the University, where Churchill gave an address, arranged a dinner. On both occasions Jung was present, and in Zurich he was seated next to Churchill (*Letters I*, p. 442n).

116 These Eranos lectures of 1946 are published in CW8, *Structure and Dynamics*, under the title, "On the Nature of the Psyche." See especially §388–96 (pp. 190–99), containing the "rather extensive material" and the vision of St. Ignatius (§395). (*Letters I*, p. 449nn.).

117 Jung's important Eranos lecture of 1940, "Zur Psychologie der Trinitätsidee" (*EJ 1940/1941*), was undergoing revision for *Symbolik*, where it would appear as "Versuch zu einer psychologischen Deutung des Trinitätsdogmas" ["Toward a Psychological Interpretation of the Dogma of the Trinity"]. A later version, further revised, appears in CW 11: A Psychological Approach to the Dogma of the Trinity" (CW 11, *Psych. & Rel.*, §169–295, pp. 107–200). (For a detailed discussion of this work, cf. *IGS*, pp. 155ff.)

118 Several texts of Aurora Consurgens are listed in the British Library, which now includes the collection of the British Museum. (Cf. White, 13 Oct. 1946, p. 46 and note.)

119 In the British Library this work is indexed under the title: "Aurora sive Aurea hora," Decas II, pp. 175–242.

120 "The Harmonies of the Inscrutable": the British Library holds an example of the Latin text. The author is listed as Hermannus Condeesyanus (Johannes Grasseus). Full title: *Harmoniae imperscrutabilis chymico-philosophicae decades duae*. Frankfurt: Lucas Jennis, 1617. (Date wrongly given as 1625 in *Letters I*, p. 449 and *Briefe II*, p. 64.)

Küsnacht-Zürich

November 7th 1946[121]

Dear Father White,

May I just join my note to Dr. Jung's letter. Enclosed – and I hope they'll pass through this way – the little rubber things[122] – and I *do* hope they are the right ones, if not please let me know! –

I've given your message to Frl. Dr. Schärf who will write or has already written to you directly.

Dr. Jung was very much interested in the article by Père Bouyer you mention in your letter to me. Do you know where this review "Dieu Vivant" appears. Is it in Switzerland or France? If the former I think I could get hold of it through Dr. Jud. But I should be very grateful for a hint in this respect.

In all haste with all good wishes,

yours sincerely, MARIE-JEANNE SCHMID

Küsnacht-Zürich

November 16th 1946[123]

Dear Father White,

Thank you very much for your lovely postcard.[124]

I'm terribly sorry, but I have to give you very bad news of Dr. Jung. He fell ill last Sunday and at first it didn't look very serious but then he got worse and finally the doctors established the fact that it must have been another "infarct" in the heart (I do not know the proper English expression, but it's one of the things he had during his last illness). Of course the situation is very serious, but I'm glad to say that the doctor is much more hopeful to-day so that without being too optimistic I think one could almost say that the worst is over.

I'm sorry if I'm wrong in writing you this letter but somehow I thought you would like to know at once.

In all haste,

yours sincerely, MARIE-JEANNE SCHMID

121 Typewritten.

122 White had asked Miss Schmid to send washers to fit the razor he had bought in Zurich (cf. White, 16 Oct. 1946, p. 49 and note).

123 Typewritten, except for postscript.

124 Postcard now apparently lost.

P.S. I'll write again as soon as possible – meanwhile no news will be good news.

Küsnacht-Zürich

November 26th 1946[125]

Dear Father White,

Well, I've got slightly better news today. Although Professor Jung is not out of the wood yet, he certainly feels better since about two days and the doctor reports that the heart has a slight tendency to be less erratic. So we all hope that there will be further progress in this direction. But there will be a lot of patience needed all round. Fortunately Prof. Jung himself is in very good spirits, he sleeps well and has a very good appetite and he has even begun to read a little, mostly newspapers so far.

I've just heard that John Layard has arrived in Zürich, which surprised me very much, as he apparently knew that Prof. Jung is ill. Have you any idea whether there's anything the matter?

Mrs. Jung just asked me to thank you very much indeed for your kind letter.[126] She hasn't time to write herself, of course, but is feeling reasonably well again. We gave Prof. Jung your messages and he sends you his greetings.

But I have rather a lot of letters to write, and must stop now. I'll keep you au courant.

Yours sincerely, MARIE-JEANNE SCHMID

Blackfriars, Oxford

11th December 1946[127]

Dear Miss Schmid,

Thanks awfully for your letter and for keeping me au courant. I am so thankful to hear there is some progress, but it must mean an awful lot of anxiety for you all. I am sending Dr. Jung a letter by the same post.

Yes of course I had heard of John Layard's going to Zürich; he had

125 Typewritten.
126 White's letter to Emma Jung has not been preserved.
127 Typewritten.

booked his passage on the plane before hearing of C.G.'s illness. He is in a pretty poor way I am afraid, though I don't think so bad as a few months ago. I am glad to hear that Dr. Meyer has taken him on. I hope to goodness he finds some occupation while the analysis is going on.

If you should be writing again, I would be most grateful if you would send the name and address of the American Publishers of the Bollingen Series.[128]

Every very best wish to you and to all.

VICTOR WHITE

Blackfriars, Oxford

11th December 1946[129]

Dear Dr. Jung,

I am extremely thankful to hear from Miss Schmid that you are now able to read. I venture therefore to send you a few lines but refrain from saying all that I should like to do. I need hardly tell you that you are very much in my thoughts and prayers at present, and, as I know, in those of very many other people in England too.

I have not yet thanked you for your very cheery and cheering letter of November 6th. I was on the point of writing when I heard of your illness.

How I wish I could have been under the table at your meeting with Churchill.

I am enclosing, as you asked, the fulminations about Alchemy, though I hardly imagine you will want such dismal reading at present. I should like to know more about what the Alchemy was that was practised in our Order at that time. I have a horrid idea it was mostly a way of making cheap money and still cheaper Schnapps.

128 The Bollingen Series, which supported the publication of Jung's Collected Works, the *C.G. Jung Letters*, etc., was sponsored by the Bollingen Foundation. Founded in 1945, the concept for the foundation and the series had been formed as early as 1941 by Mary Mellon (cf. Schmid, 16 Dec. 1946, p. 58 and note). At first the series was intended only to publish a collected edition of Jung's writings in English, together with selected Eranos lectures. Later it included works by other writers furthering related areas of humanistic scholarship (cf. *Letters I*, p. 283n). The Bollingen Foundation began to wind down in about 1967. It ceased activity in 1969, after making a grant for ongoing projects to Princeton University Press, which continued the Bollingen Series almost 30 more years before declaring Jung's part of the series closed. For an insider's personal view of the series, cf. William McGuire, *Bollingen, an Adventure in Collecting the Past* (PUP, 1982).

129 Typewritten.

I will not trouble you with more now. I am very well and in good spirits and hope that the πνεῦμα will continue to blow and keep us both off the rocks. Any way, He knows best and it's best to leave it to Him.

Ever yours sincerely, VICTOR WHITE, O.P.

Küsnacht-Zürich

December 16th 1946[130]

Dear Father White,

Thank you for your letter to which I want to reply at once so that it won't get snowed under. I gave your letter for Professor Jung to Mrs. Jung who'll choose a good moment to give it to him. It is rather difficult just now as he is inclined to get too excited about things (even quite small matters) and on the other hand he ought to be kept interested and amused, as he is rather depressed these days. Objectively there is still some progress, but there are always bad nights and bad days alternating with good ones. It certainly is a very anxious time for us all – and if I think of my own tiredness – I just marvel at the way Mrs. Jung bears it all. She asked me to send you her greetings, by the way.

I've met John Layard once. He certainly is a problem. But I was particularly glad to notice that he seems to get on well with Dr. Meier. So let's hope for the best in his case too.

The editor of the Bollingen Series is Mr. Barrett.[131] At least I suppose that he is chief editor now that Mrs. Mellon[132] has died. In any case he will be the man to give you any information you require. His address (i.e. the address of the B.S.) is: Bollingen Series, 41 Washington Square South, New York 12, N.Y. (His name is John D. Barrett.)

In case I should not have time to write again before Christmas I just want

130 Typewritten.

131 John D. Barrett: President until 1969 of the Bollingen Foundation (cf. White to Schmid, 11 Dec. 1946, p. 57 and note).

132 Mary Conover Mellon (1904–1946): first wife of Paul Mellon, an American philanthropist and art collector. While in Zurich in 1939–40 the Mellons formed a close friendship with Jung. Mary Mellon oversaw the establishment of the Bollingen Foundation and was the first Editor-in-Chief of the Series but died unexpectedly a year after its founding.

to send you all my best wishes for a "light" Christmas and a good beginning of the new year.

Yours sincerely, MARIE-JEANNE SCHMID

From Emma Jung

Küsnacht-Zürich

Dec. 18th 1946[133]

Dear Father White!

I want to thank you for your nice letter, which was very comforting indeed in this difficult time. It was a great blow to all of us, that my husband fell ill again; he was feeling so well and it came so unexpectedly. Now he is a little better, but still very sensitive (the heart), and weak; however we hope that the recovery will make steady progress and that with the turning of the Sun, his health will return and his spirits, which are at times rather low, will also rise again.

With my best wishes for a happy Xmas and New Year,

Yours very sincerely EMMA JUNG.[134]

Küsnacht-Zürich

Dec. 18th 1946[135]

Dear Father White,

Thank you for your dear letter. It is a great consolation to know that one is included in the prayers of fellow beings. The aspectus mortis[136] is a mighty

133 Handwritten. Letter previously unpublished.

134 Emma Jung-Rauschenbach (1882–1955): wife of C.G. Jung and herself a practicing analyst, was born to a wealthy industrialist family in Schaffhausen, Switzerland. She and Jung were married in 1903 and raised five children. Emma underwent analysis with Jung in the early years of their marriage, and became thoroughly committed to his psychology. In 1941 she published a long monograph, *Animus und Anima* (*Animus and Anima*, New York, 1957). Her study of the Arthurian epic formed her greatest work, still unfinished at her death. (See also Jung, 6 May 1955, p. 265 and note.) *The Grail Legend* was completed by Marie-Louise von Franz: Emma Jung & Marie-Louise von Franz, *Die Graalslegende in psychologischer Sicht* [The Grail legend in psychological perspective] (Zürich und Stuttgart: Rascher Verlag, 1960). (*The Grail Legend*. Trans. Andrea Dykes. PUP, 2nd ed., 1998.)

135 Handwritten.

136 the face of death.

lonely thing, when you are stripped of everything in the presence of God. One's haleness[137] is tested mercilessly. An accumulation of drugs however necessary has made a complete rag of myself. I had to climb out of that mess and I am now hale[138] again. Yesterday I had a marvellous dream: One bluish diamondlike star high in heaven, reflected in a round, quiet pool – heaven above, heaven below –.[139] The imago Dei in the darkness of the Earth, this is myself. The dream meant a great consolation. I am no more a black and endless sea of misery and suffering but a certain amount thereof contained in a divine vessel. I am very weak. The situation dubious. Death does not seem imminent, although an embolism can occur any time again. I confess to be afraid of a long drawn-out suffering. It seems to me as if I were ready to die, although – as it looks to me – some powerful thoughts are still flickering like lightenings in a summer night. Yet they are not mine, they belong to God, as everything else which bears mentioning.

Please write again to me. You have a purity of purpose which is beneficial. Thank you for the records, quite interesting! I don't know whether I can answer your next letter again. But let us hope –

Gratefully yours, C.G. JUNG

Blackfriars, Oxford

31.12.46[140]

Dear Dr Jung,

These can be only a very few brief lines to thank you enormously for the letter you wrote to me from your bed. It moved me very much indeed, & I am exceedingly grateful.

This Christmas time has been very busy indeed, & tomorrow I must go for several days to London. I hope for more tranquillity to write more when I return, though I fear there is not very much of interest to relate. Meanwhile

137 Jung wrote this letter in bed with a shaky hand, and the handwriting is poorly formed. His word here, as read by the editors and confirmed by members of Jung's family, is "haleness." In the previously published version of this letter it was changed, either by Gerhard Adler or by R. F. C. Hull, to "wholeness" (cf. *Letters I*, p. 450).

138 Word changed to "whole" in the Adler/PUP edition (Ibid.).

139 From a seventeenth-century alchemical poem quoted in "The Psychology of the Transference": "Heaven above / Heaven below / Stars above / Stars below / All that is above / Also is below / Grasp this / And rejoice" (CW 16, *Transference*, §384, p. 189).

140 Handwritten.

this short note tells you that you are as always still very much in my thoughts & prayers, & brings you my very best wishes for the New Year. I am very much hoping that I shall see you again, & in the very best of health, in 1947. Of course I am thrilled with my invitation to lecture at Eranos in the summer, & am much hoping that you will indeed be spared the long period of suffering, & will be able to attend.

Yours ever sincerely, FR. VICTOR WHITE, O.P.

P.S. My kindest regards & best New Year wishes to Mrs. Jung, & very many thanks for her letter.

1947

Blackfriars, Oxford

9th January 1947[1]

Dear Miss Schmid,

Thanks awfully for your last letter. I do hope you had a more restful Christmas and that things will be easier for you all during 1947.

I am afraid I have to bother you again, because I do not know to whom else I should apply. A friend of mine, of the name of Edward Thornton,[2] is very keen to go to Zürich for analysis. He is a very interesting and worthy person who would like, and I personally am inclined to think with good reason, to take up psychotherapeutic work. He has worked with several people in England, but I also feel that it would be much better if he could go to Zürich now. He would come with a completely open mind and be ready to accept the judgement of people there as to his suitability for the job. He has had a very varied and interesting career, ranging from the Wool-trade, through Shakespearian acting (he is one of the founders of the well known Repertory Theatre at Bradford) to some rather important "hush-hush" work during the War. He speaks a number of languages, including German, but would prefer an Analyst who speaks English; and I am inclined to agree with him that a male would be preferable at this stage.

He is now free from his military work, and has already established his business and handed its management to others. He would be ready to go to Zürich almost immediately if anyone would be ready to take him on. Of course, he would also like to attend Seminars and Club meetings, etc. etc.

Would it be possible for you to let me know with whom he should get in touch, and perhaps prepare the ground for him at the Zürich end? Would you reply either to me or directly to him at 63 Cromwell Road, London S.W.7.?

I do hope that Professor Jung is better. I was immensely grateful for the little note he sent me. I hope to be writing to him again before long.

With every best wish to yourself.

Yours sincerely, VICTOR WHITE

1 Typewritten.

2 Edward Thornton (b. 1907): English businessman and writer. His book, *The Diary of a Mystic* (London: Allen & Unwin, 1967), has an account of his meetings with Jung and an introduction by his analyst, C.A. Meier.

Küsnacht-Zürich

January 13th 1947[3]

Dear Father White,

Thank you for your letter. As you've probably heard in the meantime, Captain Thornton had already got in touch with me and with Dr. Meier.[4] I had a sort of "hunch" when he wrote, that Meier would be the right person for him and from what you tell me about him and his plans I should say that the "hunch" was right. – I've just phoned up Meier who tells me that he has written to Captain Thornton already, so I hope that things will work out alright. I shall be glad, of course, to help in whatever way I can, but if he is working with Meier he will know through him about Club Evenings, possible Seminars, people to meet and so on. But please tell Captain Thornton, that he can always apply to me for anything he wants or wants to know. – I've passed on your information to Dr. Meier – I hope you don't mind! and he was very glad to have this very good "picture". So the ground should be well prepared.

Professor Jung is still getting on nicely, very slowly but – we hope – surely. A funny thing happened about your last letter to him. He asked me whether there hadn't been any letter from you – and the next day it came. He is still not doing any work whatever – just reading and writing a few personal letters now and then.

Times are certainly less hectic for me now – but rather more difficult in another way, because, as you may guess, everything is even more irrational and – how I wish to have a better feeling function! So I just trundle along and hope for the best!

My best wishes to you!

Yours sincerely, [MARIE-JEANNE SCHMID] (unsigned carbon copy)

Blackfriars, Oxford

19 January 1947[5]

My dear Professor Jung,

I can hardly say how great a joy it is to hear from Miss Schmid that you are, as it seems, so very much better, and that you are, as she puts it,

3 Typewritten. 4 Cf. Schmid, 24 Oct. 1946, p. 51 and note. 5 Typewritten.

"learning to walk again".[6] But I can well imagine that it is a rather particularly trying time for yourself. It is one thing to be thoroughly ill and to feel ill; quite another to feel comparatively well and active, and yet be condemned to relative inactivity and compelled to "learn again" the simplest operations of life.

I wish I could feel that I had any news likely to be of the slightest interest to you. I have seen little or nothing of the Club people lately or any other of our mutual acquaintances in England. I hear *about* some of them from time to time (and rather odd things they sometimes are that one hears); but I have been so tied down by my work here that I am seldom in London and with time to spare. John Layard, as you know, is in Zürich, and, it seems, settling down there for some time and doing excellently with Dr. Meier. You have, Doris[7] tells me, undertaken to see him when you are well enough. I hope you may also one day be able to see Edward Thornton who is shortly coming to Zürich to work with Dr. Meier. He is a very agreeable and unusual person; I don't honestly know quite what to make of him or his potentialities as an analyst, though he certainly seems to have many valuable gifts in that direction. Anyway, since he asked my advice on the subject I thought it much better to go out to Zürich than to play around in England any longer.

For myself, I am in pretty good form; though I must confess I am apt to get rather tired and overwhelmed by the quantity – and still more the variety – of work that comes my way. I am still finding the problem of writing a very big one; it is due partly to the number of distractions and other occupations, but I am afraid not wholly so. There is the daily theological lecture, a weekly lecture for outsiders, the daily round of community services and meals, three regular "cases" (one of which I find particularly taxing), and a highly irregular stream of "occasionals" who ask for appointments on this matter or that. Then, there is always an extra of some sort or another: the University wants an examiner for a D.Phil or B.Litt on some subject of "Religion and Psychology"; a new Scottish review sends a man to interview me on the same subject, etc. etc. etc. And I find it quite essential to do my best (not always very successfully – and seldom very easily) to try and "work" on my own dreams etc. So perhaps it is not altogether surprising that I don't find I am able to do much serious writing, or even have much inclination for it. I am hoping, however, to be able to get the next academic year free from teaching, and to be able to retire into the country to read and write, have a garden to look after – and a small parish. It will be a great blessing, I think, if I can pull it off.

All this notwithstanding, I have somehow to produce by the beginning of

6 This phrase does not appear in the surviving carbon copy of Schmid's letter. It may have been part of a handwritten postscript.

7 Doris Layard (1892–1973): English psychotherapist and Catholic convert, married to John Layard. She was a lifelong friend of Victor White.

March a learned lecture on St. Thomas's conception of Revelation.[8] It is a most fascinating subject from the point of view of analytical psychology, and it is quite extraordinary how it has been neglected even by so-called Thomists.[9] I am afraid the truth of the matter is that St. Thomas's emphasis on the role of dream and phantasy, on such factors in the production of revelation as biological processes at one end and of personal agencies (angels and demons) and of impersonal agencies (the movements and influences of stars and planets) at the other, is a good deal more than most modern theologians can take. And I am afraid that they must find particularly distasteful St. Thomas's repeated assertion that to be a good recipient of Revelation what is needed is "not good morals, but a good imagination"![10] But what I find so refreshing is St. Thomas's rationality about the irrational. I wish I felt I could do the subject justice. I am thinking of incorporating it somewhat into my Eranos paper (though it takes one rather beyond *anthropologia naturalis*);[11] and I hope to expand the whole matter more fully if I can find more peace and quiet next year.

However, taken all round I am in pretty good spirits, although (or perhaps because) I have experienced lately more than ever before what you have called "to stand between a day-world of exploded ideals and values and a night-world of apparent senseless phantasms" . . .[12]

But there are many consolations. One day I hope to tell you more of the remarkable self-analysis of a married woman friend of mine.[13] It's a long and

8 White completed "St. Thomas's Conception of Revelation" on 5 March 1947 and sent it to Jung at once (cf. White, 8 March 1947, p. 78 and note). The essay appeared in the inaugural edition of *Dominican Studies* (Oxford: Blackfriars, Vol. 1, Jan. 1948), an academic annual founded by White and two colleagues, Daniel Callus and Richard Kehoe. The journal ran to less than ten volumes. [with AC]

9 The expression ("so-called") conveys White's response to certain schools of Thomistic teaching, both within the Dominican Order and in the wider community of Catholic scholarship. His own interpretation of Aquinas, shaped by the study of history and linguistics, and most of all his interest in psychological and mythical dimensions of theology, set him at odds with some colleagues and superiors. (Cf. White, 4 March 1954, pp. 228ff) Cf. also *IGS*, ch. 2, pp. 40ff.

10 Referring to a passage in White's essay: "More shocking still perhaps to sweet reasonableness is St Thomas's emphasis that prophetic revelation is as such independent of good morals – let alone of personal sanctity (*De Ver.* 12.5; I–II. 172.4). For prophecy is required, he says tersely, not 'bonitas morum' but 'bonitas imaginationis' " ("St. Thomas's Conception of Revelation," *Dominican Studies*, Vol. I, No. 1. Oxford: Blackfriars, Jan. 1948, p. 8). This essay became Part II of White's 1947 lecture at Eranos, "The Aristotelian-Thomistic Conception of Man" (*EJ 1947*, p. 348).

11 natural anthropology.

12 Quoting from the 1928 English edition of *Two Essays on Analytical Psychology* (trans. Cary & H.G. Baynes. NY & London, 1928): cf. CW 7, *Two Essays on Analytical Psychology*, "Individuation," ch. 2, "Anima and Animus," §325, p. 203. (Hereafter, *Two Essays*.)

13 Barbara Robb (1913–1975), Catholic laywoman living in London, whose interests, aside from Jung's psychology, led her to found AEGIS (Aid to the Elderly in Government Institutions)

intricate and sometimes squalid story, all the details of which I do not know myself. But it all ended (in so far as anything can be said to end) with some remarkable dreams about yourself (whom she has never seen) just before Christmas [. . .]. She seems to have made very good friends with you in her dreams. I had told her about your Xmas letter to me, and she now writes: "I am glad Jung likes being prayed for, because recently my whole life seems to have taken the form of a sort of prayer for him." (I might mention she is no dévote;[14] but a young and gay and smart ex-ballet-dancer.) "Everything that I do, good, bad and indifferent goes into it, and the prayer is THAT HE MAY BE ALL HE CAN BE. I never thought of doing it but just found it happening. It's something to do with having got to know him so well in that dream." It's curious that in this dream, which was a very long one, you were ill in bed in her parental home, and asked her only to fix an electric-fire plug in the wall, which at once produced a luminous blue diamond. The outcome (for some reason beyond my understanding) was a complete change of attitude towards her husband [. . .]; and the next day – defying all advice, entreaties and threats of Doctors and psychologists urging her to be "kind", "patient" and "considerate" etc. etc. – she gave him two hefty socks on the jaw! Since when he has been functioning perfectly; and they show every sign of living happily for ever after! Whatever you may think about it, I somehow feel you might like to know about it; if only as one example of the unknown friends you have all over the globe!

Now I must bring this meandering letter to a close, and get back to some work. Of course I expect no reply; and you will know, on your side, that it is not forgetfulness if I do not write again for some while. I am much hoping and praying that the convalescence will progress without mishap, and will not be unduly prolonged. Evidently you will have to take very great care of yourself, even when you are quite recovered; but I am much hoping that you will be well enough for me to be able to see you when I am in Switzerland in August. I am looking forward very much to the visit, and to seeing the friends I have made there. Please give my kindest regards to Mrs Jung: I do hope she is keeping well. I hope too that Miss Wolff is very much better these days; please remember me to her too when you see her.

And all very best wishes, dear Dr. Jung, to yourself,

Yours very sincerely, VICTOR WHITE, O.P.

and to edit a collection of articles, *Sans Everything: A Case to Answer* (London: Thomas Nelson & Sons, 1967), about society's responsibility toward residents in psychiatric and geriatic institutions. [with AC]

14 an especially devout woman.

Küsnacht-Zürich

Jan. 23rd 1947[15]

Dear Father White,[16]

(Excuse me! My feebleness plays tricks to me! I drop into old Saxon)

Don't even dream of answering this letter! I merely got time to write to you, while you are busy. I must tell you how much your letter has interested me. St Thomas is really remarkable and it seems more and more possible, that he has written the Aurora Consurgens.[17] His psychology of revelation notwithstanding its highly mediaeval terminology coincides with the facts as we see them now. The archetype (the substance of the Collective Unconscious) has two aspects or modos agendi:[18] a) the biological pattern of behaviour, b) the mythological archetype. a = instinctual man; b = "spiritual" man. a is the collective, b idem. The collective U. contains the sphere of personal psychology and its characteristic contents portray themselves in the personal Subconscious in the form of relatively autonomous (fragmentary) personalities, which correspond to angels and demons. That's the reason, why angels are occasionally objectionable. The impersonal character of the Coll.U. however has been aptly expressed by the gods i.e. planets and constellations[19] which Paracelsus has called the "firmament within" or the "Olympus".[20]

Imaginatio with the alchemists meant more than with us. It was a sort of cognition or even creation without the body.[21]

How does your soror mystica[22] know of me? Please tell her, that from whatever she has read or heard of me, she has understood my innermost tendency which I assume is, whether I know it or not, whether I agree with it

15 Handwritten on half-sheets. Letter previously unpublished.

16 Jung first wrote, "Dear Father Wight." Noticing the error, he crossed it out and wrote White's name correctly above it. White may have been amused by the old-fashioned term, which carries a mildly pitying connotation, "poor wight!" [with AC]

17 Cf. White, 13 Oct. 1946, p. 46 and note. Jung repeatedly sought solid evidence for this connection, but without success (cf. Jung, 21 Sept. 1951, p. 169 and note). Today most scholars dismiss the idea.

18 ways of acting.

19 The dual nature of the archetypes is given full theoretical expression in Jung's paper, "On the Nature of the Psyche" (CW 8, *Structure and Dynamics*, §343–442). [MS]

20 Cf. Jung, "Paracelsus as a Spiritual Phenomenon" (CW 13, §145–238, pp. 109–32). [MS]

21 In CW 12, *Psych. & Alch.*, under "Meditation and Imagination" (§390ff, pp. 274ff), Jung defines "imaginatio" in the context of alchemy as "the act of imagining . . . a physical activity that could be fitted into the cycle of material changes, that brought these about and was brought about by them in turn" (CW 12, *Psych. & Alch.*, §394, p. 278). [MS]

22 mystical sister. (Female partner of an alchemist or philosopher.) The symbolism of male–female pairing plays a major role in Jung's archetypal theory (cf. CW 16, *Transference*, §421ff.) [with MS]

or not, the divine cause of my existence. This divine will wills it, that everyone should be all he can be. I have unconsciously conveyed that message to her, and it works as if I had personally urged and helped her, to be all she can be. It is conforming to the divine will, which is all man can do to invite the χάρισμα.[23] Conforming to the divine will I live for mankind, not only for myself,[24] and whoever understands this message contained in and conveyed by my writing will also live for me. Individuation i.e. the integration of the unconscious into consciousness leads to a higher level of existence, where the distinctness of the ego as well as of time and space vanishes to a certain extent, so that a peculiar nearness of otherwise perfect strangers appears. This nearness expresses itself often through synchronistic phenomena, as f.i. parallel dreams and other experiences as f.i. analogous external events.[25] Individuation means something like relativity of ego, Time and space or an increase of the self, an approximation to eternity and a contractible space. Peculiarly enough our psychological reasoning coincides here with the explanatory principles applied to subatomic phaenomena.[26] Thus one could say, that the psychological development gradually transfers the "parties supérieures"[27] of your friend's psychical functions into a space and a time identical with mine and into an indistinctness of ego-personality (upon that higher level only) i.e. a confluence of Self,[28] clearly expressed through her words: "I never thought of doing it, but just found it happening" (viz. her peculiar kind of prayer). "It's something to do *with having got to know him so well* in that dream." I hope she won't be tempted to identify herself with that greater personality[29] owing to which she knows myself.

Please excuse this rather abstruse letter, but I thought this case to be a good opportunity of demonstrating certain fundamental psychological concepts, which show the coincidence of so-called "psychic mysticism" with subatomic phaenomena. Psyche being an *energic* phaenomenon[30] possesses

23 gift of grace.

24 For a full exposition of this perspective, cf. *MDR*, ch. VI, "Confrontation with the Unconscious." [MS]

25 Cf. Jung's essay, "Synchronicity: An Acausal Connecting Principle" (CW 8, *Structure & Dynamics*, §816–997). [MS]

26 Jung worked out many details of the parallels between depth psychology and modern physics in his correspondence with the Nobel prize winning physicist Wolfgang Pauli. (Cf. Jung, 27 Dec. 1947, p. 105 and note.) [MS]

27 higher parts. A term borrowed from the French psychiatrist Pierre Janet, which Jung often uses to indicate higher levels of consciousness. [MS]

28 In Jung's psychological theory the term "Self" refers to a transcendent reality and is not to be confused with ego-consciousness. (Cf. CW 9.ii, *Aion*, §1, p. 3; §43ff, pp. 23ff.) [MS]

29 Identification with the Self leads to inflation and dangerous self-aggrandizement, i.e., grandiosity. For a full discussion of this problem, cf., e.g., CW 7, *Two Essays*, "The Mana Personality," §374–406 (pp. 227ff). [MS]

30 White knew these concepts from Jung's *Energetik* 1928 (cf. White, 23 Oct. 1945, p. 19 and note). Cf. Jung, "On Psychic Energy," CW 8, *Structure & Dynamics*, §1–130.

mass, presumably a very small amount of it, but obviously enough to establish a reflex of subatomic conditions, which needs must be explained by a 4-dimensional continuum. That is also the reason, why you discover synchronistic phaenomena when you begin to integrate the unconscious.

I am feeling a bit stronger. In the meantime I had a hellish attack of cholecystitis and hepatitis. There was a suspicion of my old tropical dystentery, but thank Heaven – there were no amoebas!

Cordially yours C.G. JUNG

Blackfriars, Oxford

4.2.47[31]

My dear Professor Jung,

These few hurried lines can be no sort of answer to your intensely interesting & thought-provoking letter. All I am at present able to do is to scribble a few lines of most hearty thanks. Your letter will provide food for my contemplation for some time to come. It brings together conceptions which I have so far been quite unable to co-relate in my own mind; though I realise how important it is to be able to do so. I fear that at the moment I am more than ever lacking the tranquillity & "leisure" which might enable me to do so. I shall, I fear, have to browse on your letter for a very long time before I can reach your level of understanding. I still find this business of co-relating – or even differentiating – "physical" & "psychic" energy appallingly difficult, & still more so this (to me quite new) idea of attributing mass to psyche, let alone of such sort as will establish a reflex of subatomic conditions. But I can assure you that this thought-provoking suggestion will be very much on my mind – a dreadfully mediaeval mind which finds it particularly difficult to think 4-dimensionally rather than non-dimensionally!

It is very curious that the "soror mystica"[32] (how she will laugh at this description!) has long been trying to tell me that atomic structure plus relativity holds the key to psi-phenomena (I don't know if you use this cipher for paranormal cognition in Switzerland), & has been reading & writing furiously on the subject for the past two years! I confess I had not hitherto taken these efforts of hers very seriously . . .

I have of course sent your message to her, & hope to see her shortly (she lives in London). You may rest assured that I do not think I know anyone

31 Handwritten on half-sheets.

32 I.e., Barbara Robb. (Cf. Jung, 23 Jan. 1947, p. 70 and note.)

less likely to become "identified with that greater Personality". Her quite remarkable γνωσις[33] is balanced by a deeply humble & simple πιστις[34] – as well as by a very earthy common-sense & gaity – all of which I greatly envy.

I am terribly sorry, dear Dr. Jung, to hear of the "hellish attacks". I do hope you are taking the very greatest care of yourself. It is wonderful indeed to know that you can be so mentally active & alive as your letter shows you to be; but I do hope to goodness that you are not overdoing it.

I admire your proficiency in Anglo-Saxon![35] Still, if ever you should care to write again, I should like it very much if you were to drop both WHITE & WIGHT & just call me Victor – even though, I believe it is customary in Switzerland to be much more formal about titles & surnames than it is nowadays in England.

My warmest greetings both to your good self & to Mrs Jung.

Yours very gratefully & cordially, VICTOR WHITE

Blackfriars, Oxford

7.2.47[36]

Dear Professor Jung,

Something tells me that I should send to you the accompanying communication from the "soror mystica" (she seems to be very much more YOUR "soror mystica"!) to make of what you may . . .

I am afraid that unavoidably some of her allusions must escape you; in any case I fear they are beyond my powers of "explanation". What she calls her "working model of God"[37] is a diagram produced by her active imagination on the diamond light in the electric power-plug which, in a dream, you had pointed out to her from your bed in her house. The earlier dream to which she refers was one in which you and she and Gerhard Adler (who had been analysing her husband) and I were each sitting at one side of a square table, and in which you more or less took charge of the situation, or rather (if I remember rightly) showed that she herself was to do so. The subsequent dream about Pablo Casals was one in which, as she says, she was learning about the circulation of atomic energy from Casals' cello playing (she is no

33 (for γνῶσις) knowledge. 34 (for πίστις) faith.

35 I.e., Jung's accidental use of "Wight" ("person") in his salutation on 23 Jan. 1947, p. 70.

36 Typewritten on Blackfriars half-sheets. White mistyped the date, "7.2.46." From context, however, it belongs to the following year. (E.g., first reference to the "soror mystica," Barbara Robb, is in White's letter of 19 Jan. 1947, p. 68.)

37 Barbara Robb's "working model of God" is mentioned in her letter to White, enclosed (p. 76), and at greater length in her "Vision of March 31st" (cf. White, 16 June 1947 (pp. 88ff).

musician, and has never met or heard Casals). The "lesson" took place in a square concert hall in the centre of which were sixteen prie-dieu chairs, arranged four square, of which only twelve had to be occupied – of which twelve she is one who wins Casals' special approval, seemingly for understanding that her piece of furniture was not only a chair to be sat on but also a prie-dieu to be knelt on, and also for having it in some kind of "circular" alignment within the square.

These are the merest footnotes designed to make the enclosed perhaps a trifle less unintelligible in its allusions! In case you should be moved to more direct communications by the more regular channels of Space, Time and Postage Stamps, I add that the name and address is: Mrs B. Robb, 10 Hampstead Grove, London, N.W.3.[38]

I do hope and pray that you are now free from relapses and are well on the mend.

Ever cordially yours, VICTOR WHITE, O.P.

COPY (Extract) – from letter of Barbara Robb to Victor White.[39]

Many thanks for your letter and for the extract from Dr. Jung's. . . .

The *atoms did* take me by surprise. I don't yet know nearly enough about them to know whether there could be no such analogy as that noticeable between the atom and the psyche unless the latter possessed mass. I have thought it might be so (in which case it would presumably have to be, oh, so very small so far as the measurements we use in this world go), but could not think of anything the Lord God had ever said to the effect that it definitely was not so, and would like very much one of these days to have time and opportunity to look further into the matter.

When Jung says that, conforming to the Divine Will, he lives for mankind, I suppose he means the same thing that I do when I say that I live for the Lord God who is Himself "at the service" of mankind, and it is only in so far as I am "orientated" to Him that I myself am able to serve mankind. My life is dedicated to mankind because it has first been dedicated to Him; and in the gloriously impossible event of His turning against mankind, it seems to me that I would automatically be turned against it too! During these "solid" days and nights of prayer, I was "living for Jung", sure enough, but I was living for Jung *for God.*

It seems to me that I had better write down some more about that particular experience. *You* will be interested anyway, I dare say, and you might even think it might be of "scientific" interest some time. . . . .

38 This house, has since passed out of the hands of the Robb family.

39 White typed this extract of Robb's letter on the same typewriter as his letter of 7 Feb. 1947. Cited here with permission of Robb's estate. The annotation, "from letter of Barbara Robb to Victor White," is in White's handwriting.

I feel it worth noting that I did not, as Jung suggests, pick up the idea that "one must be all one can be" from what I had learned of him. I came upon it as a small child when, as you may remember, I discovered that, spiritually speaking, I might turn out to be either a thimble or a bucket, and it didn't matter in the least bit which; all that mattered was that I should become *full to the brim.* Years later I recognised the same "theme" in Jungian psychology, of course, but so far as I'm concerned it didn't *start* there. When it came upon me that I was required to pray for Jung in that particular "all-in" way, I had an astonishingly strong feeling that this was something the Lord Christ *particularly* wanted done, and that it was even possible it couldn't ever quite be carried out if I failed to do my part. Which idea was most unwelcome; I had no difficulty at all in believing that Jung was all that much important to the Lord Christ, but you will understand that I just could not believe I was not getting above myself in daring to entertain for a single moment the thought that I could be useful in such a way. So down I went on my knees and kissed the ground (I think you know I always start the day like that, and it was only a few moments since I had done it but it seemed most advisable to repeat the act), and then told myself I had merely picked up telepathically a desire of Jung's. (After all, there was great likelihood of all the conditions required for telepathy, as described by Whately Carrington,[40] being present). The earlier and apparently so presumptuous idea refused to go away, none the less, and in the end I arrived at a fairly comfortable sort of compromise to the effect that it *probably* was "just telepathy", but it would be wrong to rule out the other idea altogether because, after all, with God *all* things are possible; and anyway, even if it *was* "the other idea", there was no need to feel so "conspicuous" and uncomfortable, because no doubt there were various other people involved in the praying campaign too.

Whereupon I had a "vision" of Jung lying in bed with twelve people (of whom I was one; the rest were unknown to me) kneeling around him in the position of the twelve hours of the clock; each one was praying intently, in his or her own particular way, and without the efforts of any single one of them, the circle or mandala of prayer would have been incomplete, and though good would undoubtedly have been done, THE good would not have been achieved. (Do you remember that in my first dream about Jung, when he and you and Adler and I all sat at a table together, and I felt shy of having to be so much "in the limelight", and thought I would be

40 W. Whateley Carington: English physicist and philosopher of paranormal phenomena. In 1934 Carington applied quantitative testing to the problem, "Are trance personalities real, autonomous individuals, or are they merely phases of the medium's own personality?" Author of *Telepathy* (London: Methuen, 1945); *Thought Transference: An Outline of Facts, Theory and Implications of Telepathy* (New York: Creative Age Press, 1946); and *Matter, Mind and Meaning* (London: Methuen, 1949).

less conspicuous if only there could be twelve of us, but Jung wouldn't hear of such a thing?)

Then, in church on the Sunday, when I was rejoicing at having such a lovely thing as a whole Mass to include in my prayer for Jung, the feeling that it really *was* "the other idea" came over me so strongly that there was no escaping it that time. It seemed utterly ridiculous – perhaps it *was* ridiculous – but there was no question of taking the risk of treating it as ridiculous, and, if you can understand what I mean, at that moment *I had to face up to it fully*; which I believe was very important and necessary. (This may seem double Dutch to you now, but when I see you I think I shall be able to explain with the aid of my "working model of God"[41] and another dream I have had.)

I hold no brief for the power of my own prayers as compared with the prayers of others, but I understood then that the value of this particular prayer was that, whether a thimble prayer or a bucket prayer, it was "full to the brim" by reason of being made up of *everything* that was taking place in my life. I saw it as a Mighty Atom – charged with *so much* energy. (I rather think the dream I mentioned about Pablo Casals will explain this better than I have done here.)

The experience of "living for Jung" brought with it an extraordinary sense of living with a tremendous increase of intensity. I would not be surprised if I were told that I had lived ten years' worth of life in those few days! From the first, I was sure it would not last very long, because although it was indescribably "good" for one for a while, too much of it would surely be "bad". I had no doubt at all that when *the time* came, "it" would stop: and *so it happened*, in my sleep. I woke one morning *having so much forgotten all about it* that for quite a long time I didn't realise that it *had* stopped; I gave not a single thought to what had become of such a habit with me during the previous few days. I liked very much that undramatic ending.

It was amusing to think that I had started off with so much zeal to "help" Jung, being so happy to have a chance of repaying, all unknown to him, something of what he, all unknowing had done for me; only to find, after the first few moments that in "helping" him I was myself being "helped" so much that I had increased my indebtedness to a quite ludicrous extent!!

41 Cf. White, 7 Feb. 1947, p. 73 and note.

Blackfriars, Oxford

26.2.47[42]

Dear Miss Schmid,

As I expect you are still nobly acting as Dr. Jung's shock-absorber, I think I had better warn you that I am afraid the fat is in the fire again about Toni Sussman; for I am afraid repercussions will reach you at Zürich – if they have not already done so.

It would take more hours and pages than I can spare to relate the whole complicated and unsavoury story; and anyway I think and hope there is no need. But if there is anything you or Dr. Jung should want to know about, I am of course at your service so far as I am able.

Of course I entirely see that it is quite impossible and most undesirable for Dr. Jung to disavow T.S. But I should like to say that, in my opinion, if anybody (including T.S. herself) should write to him on the subject, it might be a very big help if you could reply with a categorical statement that Dr. Jung cannot be responsible for psychological methods other than those that he has himself advocated in his books, no matter whether practised by his own pupils or not. And perhaps it might be added that in those books he has described the relationship which should exist between analyst and patient, and also his views on the inadvisability of "Eastern" methods of meditation etc. for most Westerners.[43] A word from Zürich to such effect would carry much more weight than anything anybody over here can say.

Of course I well realise how true it is, as you said in a previous letter, that T.S. can benefit certain people – especially at certain stages. Thornton is one, and I myself am another – which is what makes all this so very disagreeable. But I think Dr. Jung would be amazed if he knew how much human misery was sometimes caused in his name! And how his psychology is thereby brought into disrepute. And, as Dr. Jung has said, this "pseudologia phantastica"[44] is so convincing.

42 Typed on Blackfriars half-sheets.

43 In several passages that would have been familiar to White, Jung discusses the psychological importance of "autochthonous" religious symbols (i.e., rooted in native soil), e.g., in Part II of his Terry Lectures, "Dogma and Natural Symbols" (CW 11, *Psych. & Rel.*, §88, p.50), and the psychological danger associated with the naive adoption, by Westerners, of Eastern religious practices. Cf. especially, "Yoga and the West" (CW 11, §859–76, pp. 529ff); "Foreword to Suzuki's 'Introduction to Zen Buddhism' " (Ibid., §877–907, pp. 538ff).

44 Psychiatric term, meaning "a compulsion to invent stories and believe them oneself." White could have encountered this term in Jung's 1945 essay, "Randglossen zur Zeitgeschichte" ["Marginalia on Contemporary Events"], where the condition is also described as a " 'genius' of irresponsible promises" (CW 18, *The Symbolic Life*, §1368, p. 596).

But enough of that; except to say that I am awfully sorry if any seeming indiscretions of mine should be giving you any trouble or anxiety or just perplexity at Zürich. It just couldn't be helped; and maybe it will blow over anyway.

I do hope that Dr. Jung's improvement continues, and that there have been no more relapses. I hope to be sending him a copy of my Ms. on "Revelation"[45] next week; also much overdue reviews of his books. As you have probably heard, we are having a perfectly frightful breakdown of light, power and heat in England, and at the same time the longest and coldest cold spell since decades. It looks as if the economic repercussions are likely to be very bad for us for a long time to come. I shudder to think what it can be like in Germany. But I am thoroughly looking forward to some good Swiss meals in the summer!

I do hope you too are keeping well. Also Mrs Jung, to whom please give my kindest regards. And if you should see Miss Wolff, please reciprocate the kind messages I have received from her through Mrs Allenby.[46]

Yours very sincerely, VICTOR WHITE

Blackfriars, Oxford

8.3.47[47]

Dear Professor Jung,

The first twelve pages of this[48] are mostly concerned with some preliminary domestic sparrings with some fellow theologians; but in the later pages I hope you may find matters of wider interest.

Hoping very much that your recovery proceeds apace,

Ever yours sincerely, VICTOR WHITE

45 Cf. White, 19 Jan. 1947, p. 68 and note.

46 Amy I. Allenby, analytical psychologist in Oxford, for whose Oxford dissertation, "A Psychological Study of the Origins of Monotheism," Jung wrote a Foreword (cf. CW 18, *The Symbolic Life*, §1486–96, pp. 656ff). The dissertation was not published. Jung's Foreword is dated May 1950. She later published several papers in *Harvest*, including "The nature of personality" (Vol. 2, 1955), "The gas company" (Vol. 3, 1956), "The life of the spirit and the life of to-day" (Vol. 13, 1967), and "Encounter with archetypes" (Vol. 20, 1974).

47 Handwritten on Blackfriars half-sheet.

48 White enclosed the typescript of his just-completed essay, "St Thomas's Conception of Revelation" (cf. White, 19 Jan. 1947, p. 68 and note).

Küsnacht-Zürich

March 11th 1947[49]

To the Rev. Father Victor White,
Blackfriars,
Oxford.

Dear Father White,

Thank you for your warning letter. I'm really sorry that T.S. is causing you so much trouble. The only hint we had over here of this new complication was a letter which came some time before yours, written by a Mrs. Pannell[50] (if it really had to do with what you have in mind.) By some stroke of luck (or misfortune) Professor Jung got hold of this letter and wanted to reply to it himself. But he just rather curtly told the lady that it was a mistake in any case to advise a homosexual to marry. Nothing else was heard here since. But I told Dr. Jung of your letter so that he is au courant too.

Dr. Jung is getting on well. He still takes things very slowly but he can go for small walks even outside the garden and he has dug himself in to a more extensive study of the "Trinity", i.e. more or less rewriting his Eranos-Lecture on this subject.[51] He is enjoying himself very much apparently – but all other business suffers consequently. I'm glad of it for his sake but rather sorry for the pile of unanswered letters. He and Mrs. Jung are planning to go to Locarno at the end of next week and I'm glad especially for Mrs. Jung who certainly needs a change and a rest too. And if I'm lucky I shall be able to go off for a few days over Easter too.

We have been thinking of all our friends in England a lot lately, reading of snow- and other storms, of shortages etc. But we hope – for our sakes too – that Spring is coming for good now.

I'm sorry if this sounds all rather grumpy – I have not quite recovered yet from a slight but long drawn out and tedious "flu" – and I *do* feel grumpy.

My very best wishes to you,

Yours very sincerely, [MARIE-JEANNE SCHMID]
(unsigned carbon copy)

P.S. I have just heard from Frl. Dr. Schärf who is rather wondering what

49 Typewritten. 50 Reference unidentified.

51 Since Jung delivered his "Trinity" lecture at Eranos in 1940 ex tempore, the version printed in *EJ 1947* had been reconstructed from the notes of his listeners (cf. *IGS*, p. 156). In 1947 he revised and expanded it for republication. (Cf. Jung, 6 Nov. 1946, p. 54 note 117.)

became of her manuscript.[52] She doesn't want to make a nuisance of herself, but would be rather glad to have it back in not too far a future as there is a great demand for it over here. I told her that I would drop a hint.

Hôtel du Parc
Locarno, until 10th April

27.III 1947[53]

My dear Victor,

As you see I avail myself of your kind permission to call you by your first name. I hope you will reciprocate by calling me *C.G.* which is the current designation of my unworthy "paucity". Well – I have to apologize for not having answered your interesting letters. The reason is: I have been completely swamped by an article, which I had to elaborate for a new edition. It is that risky thing about the holy Trinity.[54] My efficiency is still very restricted and thus I have to drop everything else, when I have to do something that really demands attention. I have finished the paper now. It is going to appear in a book called "Symbolik des Geistes".[55] The book will include Dr. Schärf's essay on "Satan"[56] and two other papers of mine, "Psychologie des Geistes"[57] and "Der Geist Mercurius".[58] In the meantime I have read your paper about Revelation[59] with greatest interest. I must say it gave me a new light on S. Thomas. His views are really astonishing. It looks now very much more possible that he is the author of the "Aurora Consurgens". I thank you very much, that you let me have your paper. With your kind permission I should like to quote something of it in my paper on the Trinity. I think, his Angels and Demons are simply wonderful. I am most obliged for letting me have the letter of your or my "soror mystica". Whatever the explanation of this relation is, the case in itself is remarkable. She is indeed on the right track in suspecting subatomic physics to be in a secret league with psychology. I am hovering over that point too and keep my mind busy with digesting physical

52 Schärf visited White in Oxford in mid-October (cf. White, 13 Oct. 1946, p. 47) and then sent him the manuscript of her dissertation, which he studied enthusiastically with his scriptural colleague, Richard Kehoe (cf. White, 29 Oct. 1946, pp. 52f). White had asked for a return address but so far received no answer (cf. Schmid, 7 Nov. 1946, p. 55).

53 Handwritten on half-sheets.

54 Cf. Jung, 6 Nov. 1946, p. 54 and note.

55 For complete contents and bibliography, cf. Jung, 23 March 1946, p. 29 and note.

56 Cf. p. 47, note 86.

57 Cf. Jung, 23 March 1946, p. 29 and note.

58 Jung's revised version of "Der Geist Mercurius" ["The Spirit Mercury"], his 1942 Eranos lecture, first published in *Symbolik*, then in CW 13, *Alchemical Studies*.

59 Cf. White, 19 Jan. 1947, p. 68 and note.

facts and theories. As soon as I get back to Zürich, I will read your paper once more looking up the thing I want to quote. It is of course that excellent point, that revelation has more to do with good imagination than with good morals.[60] I should even say that there is only a good prophet, when the devil has caught hold of one of his legs. I beg your pardon! I suppose you had to be mighty tactful in your paper: there are some pretty vertiginous corners. That is of course, because S.Thomas is really a great man apart from his saintliness.

I am looking forward to the summer. The weather is here execrable. Since 10 days it is just pouring and no sunshine whatever. It even has snowed down to the 900 m. level. In Zürich the weather is much better. It has helped my concentration on my work. I shall not lecture in Ascona. Working out my last lecture has given me no end of trouble. It has gone into print. But no proofsheets yet. I have not seen *Layard* yet, since I avoid patients.

Hoping to see you in Ascona!

Yours cordially, C.G.

Blackfriars, Oxford

20.4.47[61]

Dear C.G.,

This is the very first opportunity I have had to thank you for your most welcome letter of March 27th. I have been particularly busy over Easter, & only now have a little time before term begins again to-morrow.

Thank you so much for allowing me to address you by your initials.

I am overjoyed to know you are so much better & able to work so much. I look forward very much to the appearance of "Symbolik des Geistes". Of course I shall be most proud to be quoted in it. I look forward especially to your revision of "Psychologie des Geistes".[62] I have re-read the copy you so kindly sent me several times lately. It is most illuminating; though there are several points in it which much perplex me. I wish I could understand on what grounds you say "Das Unbewusste ist nicht . . . das schlechthin

60 Ibid. 61 Handwritten on Blackfriars half-sheets.

62 White has confused two lectures with similar titles: "Zur Psychologie des Geistes" ["The Psychology of the Spirit"] *(EJ 1945)* and "Der Geist der Psychologie" ["The Spirit of Psychology"] *(EJ 1946)*. His confusion is understandable, since Jung had apparently sent him both offprints at once. "Der Geist der Psychologie," from which White quotes here, was later revised and retitled "Theoretische Überlegungen zum Wesen des Psychischen" ["Theoretical Reflections on the Nature of the Psyche"] (CW 8, *Structure & Dynamics*, §343–442).

Unbekannte, sondern das *unbekannte Psychische*",[63] & just what "Psychische" means to you here if not "Ich-bezogen".[64] (Of course, I quite agree it does not mean "Ich-bezogen", but I find it difficult to discover what the qualification "psychisch" means to you.)

I have been wondering whether there was any *special* subject you had in mind that you wanted me to talk about at Eranos: "Der Mensch"[65] is rather a big one! I have not yet begun to write my paper, & it is difficult to know when I shall be able to do so amid the many interruptions here at Oxford. My present idea is to say something about Aristotle's conception of ψυχη[66] & its relevance (as I think) to the problems you raised in your paper last year; his conception of its relation to Νοῦς;[67] his somewhat contradictory conception of human destiny & happiness & its solution in St. Thomas's conception of Revelation. Even that is perhaps covering too much ground! But I should be very grateful for any hints you care to give me.

The "soror mystica"[68] has had several more dreams about you, & a most remarkable "vision" she had when reading one of your books in which you & she were doing a most interesting "balancing trick".[69] It was pretty clear what it meant for her own psychology, & I don't know what further reference it all may have. But it is remarkable that, though she has seen only a snapshot of you, she describes your appearance & manner with extraordinary accuracy. I cannot remember all the details of all the dreams, but I am sure she would be glad to make a copy of her records if they would interest you.

I have a very busy term in front of me. Among other engagements I have next week to lead a discussion with the analysts of the London Club on "The Problem of the Catholic Patient"! I am much hoping that my superiors will release me from teaching next year so that I can spend the whole year writing & "incubating". I am not yet sure where I shall go to do it, but there is some small chance that I may go to U.S.A., where a millionairess offers me a sinecure chaplaincy![70] I should not be sorry to take a year away from the "austerities" of impoverished England!

Such news as I hear of Layard seems excellent; he seems to be doing fine with Dr. Meier, though I fear at his wife's expense! However, that problem

63 From "Der Geist der Psychologie" (*EJ 1946* p. 421). In Hull's translation, "The unconscious is not simply the unknown, it is rather the *unknown psychic*" (CW 8, *Structure & Dynamics*, §382).

64 ego-related. Jung wrote, "Wir kommen nun zu der Frage: in welchem Zustand befinden sich psychische Inhalte, wenn sie nicht auf das bewusste Ich bezogen sind?" (*EJ 1946*, p. 422); which Hull translates: "We now come to the question: in what state do psychic contents find themselves when not related to the conscious ego?" (CW 8, *Structure & Dynamics*, §383).

65 "The Human Being." 66 (for ψυχή) soul. 67 mind.

68 Cf. Jung, 23 Jan. 1947, p. 70 and note.

69 Cf. White, 16 June 1947, with transcription of Robb's "Vision," pp. 87ff.

70 White spent late 1947 and early 1948 in Stone Ridge, New York. The invitation came from Mrs. Frances Leggatt. [AC]

seems insoluble. You have heard, I think, that Toni Sussman has been giving us some dreadful headaches lately. I wish I knew what could be done for the old thing.

I look forward hugely to seeing you at Ascona. I hope to be through Zürich some while before, & hope I may take the liberty to telephone on the off-chance you may be feeling well enough – & free enough – for me to call on you there.

Please give my best regards to Mrs Jung. I do hope Miss Wolff is better; my good wishes to her, Miss Schmid & all my other friends in Zürich,

Yours ever sincerely, VICTOR

Küsnacht-Zürich

April 23rd 1947[71]

My dear Victor,

You are a more conscientious letter writer than I am. I had been eaten up by work. But now there is a lull – most welcome indeed. I have just finished the ms of "Symbolik des Geistes".[72] From now on it will take quite a while until it is printed. I had to revise my paper "Geist der Psychologie"[73] ("Geist" meaning the same as f.i. in "Esprit des lois")[74] completely. It has increased in size considerably. I quite understand, that it is very difficult to catch my meaning from the very sketchy first form of the paper. I think we agree that the unconscious is psychical i.e. a sort of mind. Yet it is unc. since it is not associated to Ego-consciousness, which is precisely the reason, why it is "unconscious". Though it might be conscious to another subject, an alter Ego, it is at all events severed from the Ego. Yet it has according to its effects a psychical nature or at least we assume it has. I have covered these points in the new edition. The paper is now going into print and I will send you a reprint, as soon as copies are available.

I have made a great effort to explain, what I mean by "psychical": I call those biological phenomena "psychical", which show at least traces of a *will, that interferes with the regular and automatic functioning of instincts*. This formulation raises a mountain of problems, f.i. who is the subject of this will? What

71 Handwritten on both sides of Jung's letterhead.

72 Cf. Jung, 23 March 1946, p. 29 and note.

73 Cf. White, 20 April 1947, pp. 81ff and note.

74 "the spirit of laws" (i.e., the nature of laws, or jurisprudence), in reference to Montesquieu's work of this title. In addition to emphasizing that this essay leans toward metapsychology, Jung also perhaps points to its title to help White distinguish between it and "Zur Psychologie des Geistes."

is the "knowing" coupled with every volitional act? etc. I have dealt with these questions to the best of my ability in the enlarged paper. So you better wait for it. I have gone once more through your splendid essay on "De Revelatione". I think, if you would give a short survey on *The Psychology of S. Thomas* at the Eranos meeting you would fulfill our expectations. You must realize that your public appreciates the demonstration of a mediaeval psychology, which is strange to our ears. We are not used to it as your colleagues are. Moreover a genius like S.Thomas who takes into consideration the action of angels and demons will be accepted with the greatest attention, because it gives us a chance to understand, how a mediaeval mind tackled the modern problem of the collective unconscious. Thus a part of your essay on S.Thomas, if you arrange it a bit for the occasion, would do. The psychological conception of *Aristoteles* has already been dealt with.[75] Since S. Thomas has been influenced by *Avicenna*,[76] the latter's views might deserve some attention.

I should like to have at least one or the other of the dreams of the "soror", but please no bulky mss. They give me a shiver.

Layard is still torn asunder by the opposites inside a dense cloud of inflation. But his is a big problem. I am no more strong enough to tackle it myself. I have seen him. I can only hope that by the grace of God some light will dawn upon him. I know what's wrong, but how can I bring it home to him. He won't lap it up. No cause for optimism in his case!

Toni Sussman – yes I think she would be giving headaches right and left. I got them too, as long as she was on the premises. "God protect me against my friends," said Bismarck. So do I. But I have heard nothing of what she is up to recently.[77]

When you come to Zürich before Eranos, I hope you will give us the pleasure to put you up in the style of last year.

Yours cordially, C.G.

P.S. Mrs. Jung's best regards.
Miss T. Wolff is curious, whether you have written to Koepgen[78] or not.

75 Probably the lecture by Walter Wili, "Problems Connected with the Aristotelian Theory of the Soul" (*EJ XII*, 1945). [AC]

76 Avicenna (Abu 'Ali al Hosain ibn 'Abdullah ibn Sina) (980–1037): Persian doctor and philosopher. His philosophy, primarily Aristotelian but with Neoplatonic aspects, profoundly influenced St. Albert the Great, St. Thomas Aquinas and other early Scholastics.

77 Sussmann visited Jung in Switzerland in March 1936, and she discussed theory with him when he visited England in 1938. In the early 1940s she wrote to Jung repeatedly, trying without success to persuade him to lend his name to the academy she hoped to found in New York (Jung/Sussmann correspondence, ETH Library archive).

78 Cf. Wolff, 18 July 1946, p. 37.

Blackfriars, Oxford

2.5.47[79]

Dear C.G.

This is no "answer" to your letter – "conscientious" or otherwise. Just a line of very warm thanks for your most interesting letter.

Of course I should be thrilled & delighted to stay with you "in the style of last year" if you are really well enough. Please let me know if any dates in August would be more convenient to you than any other. (Perhaps Miss Schmid, to whom I must write shortly, would send a message to save your writing again.)

I have just heard from London that the "soror mystica" has developed cholecystitis . . . I feel this is carrying "coincidence" a bit far![80] I hope to be able to investigate (if nothing more) next week.

I hope also to write more expansively later on.

Very best wishes to you & all,

Ever cordially, VICTOR

P.S. No; I haven't yet got into touch with Koepgen,[81] or know what has become of him.

Küsnacht-Zürich

May 7th 1947[82]

The Rev. Father Victor White,
Blackfriars,
Oxford.

Dear Victor,

It would suit me best if you came here in the week before Eranos[83] – either to Küsnacht[84] or to Bollingen.[85] Though I'm recovering slowly, I hope to stand Bollingen after a while once more.

79 Handwritten.
80 In early 1947 Jung also had cholecystitis (Jung, 23 Jan. 1947, p. 72).
81 Cf. Wolff, 18 July 1946; Jung, 7 May 1947.
82 Typewritten. Letter previously unpublished.
83 Cf. Jung, 26 Sept. 1945, p. 4 and note.
84 Jung's family home and ordinary business setting (Ibid).
85 Jung's Tower, on Upper Lake Zurich (cf. Jung, 13 April 1946, p. 32 and note).

It interested me very much to hear that the lady in question has developed cholecystitis. Mine wasn't exactly the same, it was a hepathitis, but equally painful and so just as good as hers. It's curious: there has been some spook[86] lately here and my thoughts went to the soror, because I thought there might be something the matter with her. Please give her my sincerest sympathy.

With many a sigh and some sweating I have finished my paper about Trinity.[87] It is well-meant but difficult!

Yours cordially, [C.G.] (unsigned carbon copy)

Blackfriars, Oxford

2nd June 1947[88]

Dear C.G.,

Thanks awfully for your letter. I think my best plan, if it suits you, would be to come about August 9th or 10th and leave you to have about 2 or 3 days rest and solitude before the rigours of Ascona. I will come to Küsnacht or to Bollingen as you tell me.

I think you would be very interested in a lecture to be given by Kathleen Raine[89] in Zürich on June 19th or 20th. I do not know where the lecture is to be, or the precise date or time, but it is under the auspices of the British Council and will doubtless be advertised. Her title is "William Blake", but I believe the real subject is the interpretation of Blake in the light of your psychology; she is a very able poet and critic, fairly well known in England.

I am looking forward enormously to my visit and hope I shall find you well. I have much to tell and to ask you, but am so very busy now that I think it better to leave it all until we meet. I was extremely interested in what you

86 In 1950 Jung wrote a Foreword to Fanny Moser's *Ghost: False Belief or True?* and actually contributes a story of his own, in which he recounts the experience of a haunted house in England in 1920 (CW 18, *The Symbolic Life*, §764–89). He tells of similar ghostly events in his own home (*MDR*, pp. 189ff). [MS]

87 Cf. Jung, 6 Nov. 1946, p. 54 and note.

88 Typewritten, except for closing, postscript, and some handwritten corrections, on the same machine used to transcribe Barbara Robb's "Vision of March 31st."

89 Kathleen Raine (1908–2003): English poet and literary scholar, expert on William Blake and W.B. Yeats, founder of the journal *Temenos*. In July 1957 she lectured to the Guild of Pastoral Psychology on "Poetry in Relation to Traditional Wisdom" (Guild lecture no. 97. London: GPP, 1958). *The Collected Poems of Kathleen Raine* were recently published (Washington: Counterpoint, 2001).

said in your letter about the line you are taking in the new edition of *Geist der Psychologie*.[90]

I was awfully grateful for your hints about what to say at Ascona. I'm afraid I shall not be able to think of writing the lecture until term is over at the end of the month.

Every very best wish to you and to Mrs. Jung. Will you please thank Miss Schmid for the information she so kindly sent?

Every yours cordially, VICTOR WHITE

P.S. The S.M.[91] is recovering, & is most grateful for your help at the time of the "haunting".[92] There has been a most interesting sequel to the "balancing" vision.[93] A brief account will follow from her so soon as she is well enough to copy it.

Blackfriars, Oxford

16.6.47[94]

Dear C.G.,

At last I am able to send you this series of "visions" & dreams of the "soror". I am afraid they are somewhat longer than I had anticipated (though really only a small selection of all the material in which you have played a part), but she tells me that "They" (="It") would not allow her to send any of this sequence until it had all been worked through. Her health has improved enormously now.

"Spooky" events continue – especially in her garden. A "Christmas rose" started to flower last summer, & was still flowering early *this* summer after being buried under deep frozen snow for nearly two months. A rose bush which last year produced white roses, this year first produced a pink one (*after* the "vision" of your cheeks),[95] & has subsequently produced a deep scarlet one. I am assured this is botanically impossible, but I have seen all these with my own eyes, & without a drop to drink!

Anyway, I send these documents without prejudice or comment. I, as well

90 Cf. White, 20 April 1947, p. 81 and note; Jung, 23 April 1947, p. 83 and note.

91 Soror Mystica.

92 Cf. Jung, 7 May 1947 (p. 86), referring to the "spook" that inspired Jung to think about and send his sympathy to Robb. [AC]

93 Cf. Barbara Robb's "Vision of March 31st," White, 16 June 1947, pp. 88ff.

94 Handwritten on two Blackfriars half-sheets, with typed enclosure.

95 Cf. Robb's "Vision of March 31st," enclosed with this letter, p. 89.

as "They" have had rather a tussle to get her to "presume" to send them. She's much better physically since she decided to do so.

I am looking forward enormously to seeing you in August. I still have not had an opportunity to start my Eranos paper, but hope to do so when term ends. To-morrow evening I have to go to attend a meeting of a group of undergraduates who have been studying your works with the chaplain of Trinity College,[96] & have formed the suspicion that you want to "debunk God"! They have called me in to remove their doubts, which I trust I shall effectively do!

Every warmest wish to you, dear C.G., to Frau Jung & all my friends.

Ever cordially, VICTOR

P.S. The "soror's" name & address is:
Mrs Barbara Robb
10 Hampstead Grove
London
N.W.3
– should you wish to communicate non-telepathically!
She does NOT expect you to do so, but of course would value it enormously – *whatever* you say.

PRIVATE[97]

"Vision" March 31st.

(Which happened while I was reading Jung's essay on "Woman in Europe".[98] I had the idea that – perhaps because Jung had been describing his own anima and not women in general – there was something "missing". I set to work to try and find out what it was, and there came a strong feeling that Jung was standing close behind my left shoulder, looking at the book with me and helping me to puzzle it out. It was as if he and I were working together in an earnest and happy endeavour to advance Analytical Psychology another step forward. There this vision started:)

I was in the middle of a huge, square green sports arena, entirely surrounded by grandstands from which "all the world and his wife" were looking on. Jung was with me, and we were each holding one end of a white rope (I nearly wrote "*vivid white*", because it seemed bright with life, being made, I realised, of ectoplasm). Jung was wearing a white sports shirt, open at the throat, white trousers, and white, rubber-soled tennis shoes. He had silver hair, but

96 Austin Farrer (1904–1968): theologian, chaplain of Trinity College, Oxford, 1939–60. [AC]

97 White typed Robb's vision, etc., single-spaced on medium-sized sheets of onionskin, apparently using the same typewriter on which he had typed his letter of 2 June 1947.

98 C.G. Jung, "Woman in Europe," originally published in *Contributions*, op. cit. (Cf. CW 10, *Civilization in Transition*, ch. 6, §236–75.)

was upright, strong and vigorous as a man in the prime of life (which means to me that, psychologically speaking, he had kept all the advantages of youth and gained the "silver crown of wisdom" which is the advantage of maturer years). His face was glowing with health; the rosy pink of his cheeks I knew to have been especially acquired for this occasion – or, more correctly, perhaps, *on account* of it. They mean to me the same thing as the red cloak on the statue of the Sacred Heart: integration of the anima. He looked tremendously muscular and powerful.

I was wearing a white silk sports dress, and I had bare legs and the bare feet that have played an important part in my dreams of late. ("One can grip the ground best if one's feet are bare")

Exactly half way between us was a flint-stone, set horizontally into the ground and shaped like this:

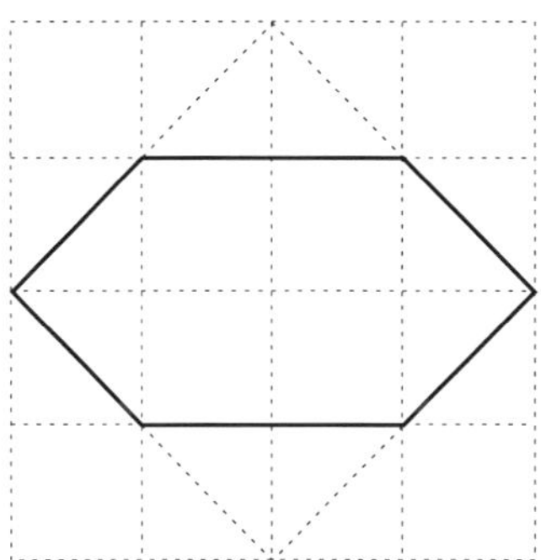

(Sorry this copy of the diagram is cock-eyed. VW)

Figure 3.1

(The ink-line represents the stone. I have left in the pencil lines which seemed to have to be made in order to draw it properly. It is connected with Jung's "blue diamond in a round pool",[99] and also with the "Working model of God" vision[100] which I had when I heard Jung's description of that dream.)

The outside of this stone was chalk-white. The inside, no doubt, would be grey. This represents to me a very hard stone from which fire may be struck with the aid of steel. (Jung's steely muscles, and my own tendency, in my dreams, to be "strong as steel because supple as steel"?). The stone recalls David Gascoyne's[101] poem about the need to find

99 Cf. Jung, 18 Dec. 1946, p. 60 and note. 100 Cf. White, 7 Feb. 1947, p. 73 and note.

101 David Gascoyne (1916–2001): British poet, first known in the 1930s for his surrealist poems, he later emerged, with *Poems 1937–42* (1943), as a religious poet. The two lines, slightly misquoted by Robb, conclude Gascoyne's poem 'Ex Nihilo', part of a sequence called 'Misere' (cf. *Collected Poems*, ed. Robin Skelton, London: Oxford University Press, 1965, p. 43). Thanks to Martin Golding, who located this citation. [AC]

"The hardest stone on which to build
Altar and shelter for eternity".

And Christ's words:

"Thou art Peter, and upon this rock I will build My Church".[102]

Jung and I wound our respective ends of the rope around our waists and over our right shoulders in the professional manner (which recalls the way swords are worn, and "girding on the sword of the spirit"). The task in hand was not the usual tug-of-war business of struggling against one another and trying to pull one another over the centre-stone. Our job was to find out how to balance each other exactly by each pulling on the rope with a precisely even tension, the heaviest one having to adjust his or her weight to the lightest in order that the maximum tension should be attained. The general idea seemed to be that this was a very difficult thing to do – hence the presence of "all the world and his wife" to watch us make the attempt. Much depended, for them, on whether we could bring it off on not.

I took one look at the mighty Jung, thought of my own physical slightness, and decided it was up to me to pull away for all I was worth and leave it to Jung to balance himself against the full measure of my weight. I set about this with a will, but before I was using more than perhaps a quarter of my strength I found to my amazement – almost to my horror – that I was pulling Jung off his feet. I had hastily to reverse my tactics. Jung now threw all his weight onto the rope and then, with a speed which astonished me, my "instincts" immediately found the right tension for my own pull, without trial or error.

As we thus hung in perfect balance on the rope, a tremendous energy swept through each of us simultaneously. It seemed to radiate from the tension on the rope. We "enjoyed" it for a moment; then, when any more of such "intensity" would have seemed too much for us, we let go of the rope, and rushed to the centre-mark, across which we fell into each other's arms, in an embrace which was a somewhat more enthusiastic version of the "kiss of peace" as given in the Mass. Meanwhile the onlookers had burst into a great cheering and waving of flags, and it was evident that the energy which produced this demonstration was "part and parcel" of the energy we had released from the rope. The arena by now had become ROUND in shape; the alteration probably took place at the moment of balancing. It occurs to me that, seen from an aeroplane flying high above, the arena would at this moment have looked like a flower.

ACTIVE IMAGINATION. (some weeks later)

My surprising strength in this vision seemed to come through my contact with the earth via my BARE FEET. This recalls the myth about Antaeus, giant son of Ge,[103] who was stronger even than Herakles so long as he had

102 Mathew 16.18.

103 In Greek myth, Earth (Ge, or Gaia).

contact with his mother. Jung has before now appeared as a Herakles-like figure in my dreams, and it seemed to me that in order to get him to balance me I must persuade him to take off his shoes.

I made the suggestion to him, and he looked extremely surprised. Nevertheless, after thinking it over for a second or two, he stooped down and took them off. His feet were much whiter and more tender-looking than mine (he was a "tender-foot", in fact) because not used to exposure. He shifted his weight from one foot to the other a few times, with a charming comical-rueful expression on his face, and I thought he was afraid of being hurt by little pebbles in the grass. Then he stood on both feet and wriggled his toes in the grass, and he seemed to like that. I noticed that his toes were just as flexible and "prehensile" as my own are in real life. Then he said:

"Come on; let's have another shot at it".

He picked up his end of the rope and wound it round him again. I did the same with mine, and we took up our positions and pulled. This time we were EXACTLY MATCHED IN STRENGTH and there was no difficulty at all in finding the balance; all we had to do was to each put all we had into pulling and it worked out right. This was much more satisfactory for me, because one doesn't want to be using only a bit of oneself.

Because we were pulling harder on the rope than last time there was a greater tension and more energy was released. The result was pretty terrific. A GREAT ROUND SPARK OF LIGHT came out of the rope at the very middle, where it crossed the flint. At this point on the rope, of course, Jung's "pull" was divided from my "pull", there being between these two "pulls" an infinitesimal point of "nothingness" corresponding to the "nothingness" at the centre of the atom. The "nothingness" is the quiet place in the centre of all the tension, like the quiet place at the centre of an explosion, where the spark can be born as a result of Jung and me pulling against one another in order to balance one another FOR it.

This spark spreads in a circle outwards, like the ripple on a pond when you drop a pebble in.*[104] It travels with the speed of lightening. I must leave it for a moment, and come back to it later.

Jung and I, after experiencing ENERGY as we did before (only more intensely so), walked quite calmly to the centre instead of rushing as we did before. We put our arms around one another, and we loved one another so much that we found ourselves right at the very heart of love, where, in the middle of ecstasy, there is another "centre of nothingness" which is PERFECT PEACE.

104 An asterisk at the bottom of the typed page directs, "See note at end." Robb's end-note reads: "[1]'King Lear', 'The Brothers Karamazov', Beethoven's 7th Symphony and Rembrandt's painting of Christ's first meeting with St. Mary Magdalene have recently played important parts in my dreams."

To return to the spark: it reached "all the world and his wife", encircling the round arena, simultaneously, as a matter of course. Immediately, it *entered into them* and was "absorbed" by them, and it became a song which they all began to sing at once. The song was the "Hallelujah" chorus from Handel's "Messiah".

Thus, the spark does not spread outwards any further, but is diverted towards "God in highest heaven" (that is, God I, as seen in the vision of the "Working Model of God").[105] This means, I think, that God II (that is, God *in* the earth and *in* all material things because He is *in* the atom) is being given by the spectators to God I.

The next thing is that by the time the Song reaches Highest Heaven it has turned into billions and billions of bright pink roses which are exactly the same colour as the "roses" in Jung's cheeks in the vision.

These roses all belong to God I, but it is His pleasure to hand them round to all the angels and saints and to the deliciously smiling Blessed Virgin, who is the lover of sinners. Everyone in heaven gets a rose, and the Lord God keeps just one for Himself.

The Lord God and the Blessed Virgin change over their roses; He takes hers and she takes His.

The angels and saints hold their roses close between both hands, and so get something out of them; and at the same time, in some paradoxical way, something else is put in.

Now the angels and saints are going to throw their roses back to earth. The Blessed Virgin is going to throw hers, too; but the Lord God is going to keep His. One rose, it seems, has to stay in Heaven. The Lord God is not exactly ungenerous in keeping this rose, for all the roses belonged to Him in the first place.

The billions of roses are all thrown back to earth at the same time.

I am reminded of St. Therese's prophecy:

"After my death I will let fall a shower of roses".

NOTES

(1) THE PHRASE: "*All the World and his wife*" seems to me typical of a world in which, because animas have not been integrated, women, almost without being noticed by anyone, are treated as man's inferiors. "All the world" is there so long as all the men are there; the wives are implied as being an unnecessary extra.

In a recent dream the "Triumphal March" from Beethoven's 7th Symphony represented "the explanation of my life-long poor health". It was associated with the "March of Triumphant Youth" in the ballet which Massiné wrote to the 7th Symphony, in which the dwarf's dance was the most "triumphant" of all because, through the suffering he had undergone on account of his mis-

105 Refers to Robb's dream, above. (Cf. Jung, 18 Dec. 1946, p. 60; White, 7 Feb. 1947, p. 76.)

shapen body, he had acquired an intensity of feeling, an insight, and a beauty of soul unknown to his more "fortunate" brethren. This seemed to mean that God made me ill in order that I might have all the advantages which suffering brings if accepted.

The next time I turned the radio on in real life, almost immediately an orchestra began to play Beethoven's 7th Symphony. I felt that it was intended to be used by me as a "hymn of praise", to thank the Lord God for all He has done to "help me to help myself". As the music proceeded, it seemed as if the whole story of my life were being "played through again", triumphantly, by that orchestra, and that *this* was my "hymn of praise".

On and on swept the music, each phrase developing out of and explaining the reason for the one which had gone before it. Never a note was without its point – its important place in the whole. The "keynote" of this symphony seems to me to be a perfect economy – a complete absence of waste without there being anything that is unnecessary – which is the result of an absolute abandon to *what is right for it*. An abandon, in fact, to the Divine Will, which is the perfection of freedom. When I have stopped doing anything, then EVERYTHING will be done.

At last came the moment when the "Triumphal March" theme is introduced; and then I had this vision:

I saw twelve priests at twelve different altars which were arranged in a circle like the figures on the face of the clock. They were all saying Mass at the same time. (Which represents the Catholic "superstition" that there is always a Mass being said somewhere in the world. Notice that the Masses, although all being said at the same time from my point of view, are also being said *at twelve different times on the clock-face*). All the priests wore white and gold vestments, such as are reserved for major feast days.

As soon as the vision started, they all simultaneously reached the moment of the Elevation of the Host. (When God is offered to God, to His own glory and in atonement for our sins; which is redemption).

As I saw the twelve Sacred Hosts raised in the priests' hands, the voice of "They" told me that because I had so much longed to do God's will, I was become one with Him to the extent that I MYSELF WAS IN EACH OF THOSE HOSTS. I saw that I must accept the fact that in every past, present and future Host, there was, is and for ever will be an infinitesimal pin-point speck that was, is, and will be me. For God is indivisible, and, as emphasised in this vision by the fact that the twelve priests are saying Mass at the same time, and yet at twelve different times on the clock-face, the God of today must inevitably be at the same time the God of yesterday and the God of tomorrow.

This means that when God first manifested Himself in the creation of the four elements, I was there in Him. I was there when Christ lay in the manger, and I was there when He died upon the Cross. I may be said to be with God in heaven now. Etcetera.

This vision was plainly a further development of the one in which I saw myself praying for Jung "all around the clock".[106]

When I was listening to the playing of the 7th Symphony, there was an extraordinary sense of Beethoven's having been in the service of God's will when he composed it, and of God's will having even then been that, among other things, it should one day be "useful" to me. Also that the Dutch orchestra who were broadcasting were thereby doing God's will, and that part of His purpose in having it played was that it should be for me.

That night I had the following dream:

I was searching for something at my old family home. Mrs. B. had come to help me. In the drawing-room, near the place where in an earlier dream I found Jung waiting for me, I unearthed from among some dust and rubbish on the floor a flat, white, diamond-shaped stone measuring perhaps eight inches from point to point. (It could have been a square, but in the dream it never occurred to me that it was anything but a diamond). As I picked it up and showed it to Mrs. B. a voice cried:

"You've got it now; this is the answer to EVERYTHING".

The stone was plainly related to Jung's blue diamond.[107] The diamond in the "Working Model of God", and the "Centre-Stone" in the tug of war. It is the white stone mentioned in the Apocalypse (Ch.2. v.17.) "To him that overcometh will I give a white stone, and in the stone a new name written, which no man knoweth save he that receiveth it".

Mrs. B. is a Methodist parson's wife who acts as cook for me, and gets satisfaction out of doing it because she feels she is thereby contributing to my work, in which she takes a lively and helpful interest. She's convinced I have what she calls "a great work" to do.

Finding the stone where I had previously found Jung. Finding Jung in the earlier dream was the beginning of a great "development" in me. I had to learn to appreciate *what I can be with the aid of "Him who helpeth me"*. It is as if the "development" had consisted of a "circle of events" which is now completed and so ends where it began. Jung and I have had to help each other to be "all that we can be". But in order to be what we can be it is necessary to "*have bare feet*". I must try to explain what this means.

Having bare feet means to me having direct contact with the ground – the earth. It means freedom, and it is associated with pilgrimage. The vision of the "Working Model of God" pointed out that after "leaving the hands" of "God I" (that is, God-in-Highest-Heaven, Who made me), in my early childhood I found it easiest to love "God II" – God as Christ, God *on* the earth,

106 Cf. White, 7 Feb. 1947, pp. 76ff.

107 Cf. Jung, 18 Dec. 1946, p. 60; White, 19 Jan. 1947, p. 69; Robb's "Vision," p. 89.

God made man as a historical fact, God-for-man's extraversion, God as the introverts must know Him if they are to achieve "balance".

Presumably because I am an extravert, this was the way to God for me. Loving the God Who had walked upon the earth, I became interested in the earth itself. This addition to my interests – for it was an addition and not a switch-over – took place, I think, during the time of my First Communion. I was already learning ballet-dancing, and the "usefulness" of the ground to my dancing was very apparent. Pushing against it, I strengthened my muscles; pushing against it, I could leap in the air. I loved the ground, and had the "absurd" impression that the ground loved me in return, and enjoyed playing its part in my dancing. To "fly" through the air was lovely; one exerted oneself to go as high or as far as one could, and one stayed in the air as long as one could; but just as lovely was the return to the dear, welcoming earth. (That the air loved one and welcomed one too is perhaps another story).

The ground became a most important thing in my life. I began to start the day by kissing it, because I felt that the way to find humility was to stay close to the ground and to love it. God being everywhere, I knew He must be in the earth, and I loved Him there and saluted Him there. I felt that he was there of His divine humility, and I wanted so much to learn something of the secret of humility. I found that however "low" and "little" I might be, He was still there with me. I found that there is no need to be afraid of inferiority, because He is right in the middle of all my inferiority, sharing it with me. In admitting my inferiority, I cannot help at the same time admitting Him into myself. My inferiority is part of ME as He made me; in accepting myself as He made me, I get Him. I cry aloud to the whole world: "I am inferior in all these ways", and as I do so I feel that all the riches of the universe are showered about me.

It seems to me that only by experiencing this could I understand the meaning of humility. In the end, humility is not a matter of feeling myself to be a miserable creature, but in discovering how inestimably rich I am. The only thing I have is Him, and so I have everything.

For the whole earth is mine; the sun and the moon and the stars are mine and Heaven is mine. Every beautiful or valuable thing that ever was, that is, and that ever will be is mine. For me, Shakespeare wrote his plays and Dostoievski his novels, Beethoven wrote his music and Rembrandt painted his pictures. For me are the great discoveries of science, and the wonders and the delights of the future will for ever be for me. For me, every priest says Mass, and will do so for ever. For me is all love. For me Christ was born.

I gave myself to Him, and in return He has given me Himself and everything that belongs to Him. I am a woman, but God was made man, and so men, thinking of themselves as God-like, have called women less than themselves. But what can any man have that has not been given to me?

Later.

The above two paragraphs seemed to come pouring out like a hymn. Behind the words there was music; it was once again the "Triumphal March" from Beethoven's 7th Symphony. When I was thinking this over afterwards, voice of "They" said "That was your 'Magnificat'. Once again He has regarded the humility of His handmaid".

It was the understanding and acceptance of this "Magnificat" that was symbolised by Jung's "taking off the shoes from his feet". Then, like Moses, he could approach the burning bush in safety – then it was safe for the Spark to come.

So this is where Jung's "blue diamond" dream and his "mistake" in the essay on "Woman in Europe"[108] have led me. Throughout the whole "circle of events" I have been aware of him helping me; but particularly since I appealed to him for help when my recent illness started and I felt that there was hard work to be done which was to be *for him and for me*. The white stone belongs to us both, and through us it is to be for EVERYONE.

And still later.

A while ago I had a dream about the "Brothers Karamazof", and so began to read the book. Tonight I came to these passages: "The silence of the earth seemed to melt into the silence of the heavens. The mystery of the earth was one with the mystery of the stars. Alyosha stood, gazed, and suddenly flung himself down on the earth. He did not know why he embraced it; he could not have told why he longed so irresistibly to kiss it, to kiss it all. But he kissed it weeping, sobbing and watering it with his tears, and vowed passionately to love it for ever and ever . . . He had fallen on the earth a weak boy, but he rose up a resolute champion, and he knew it and felt it suddenly at the moment of his ecstacy."

Bollingen. Ct.St.Gallen[109]

July 6th 1947[110]

Dear Victor!

Thank you for sending the Soror's vision. It is pure alchemy! Are the white roses innoculated on a "red" stem? One should ask a gardener, so that we are sure we have not to deal with too many miracles. Please give my best regards

108 Robb thinks that in this essay (cf. her "Vision," p. 88 and note), Jung has confused his own anima with the psychology of European women.

109 Sankt Gallen is the canton, or governmental region, where Bollingen is located. (Cf. map of the Lake Zurich area, Figure 5.1, p. 137). In Swiss style of the period, Jung underlined the town's name.

110 Handwritten. Letter previously unpublished.

to the Soror. I have to postpone writing to her personally on account of an excès de travail[111] and of a corresponding fatigue. My recent ailment was a grippe of the stomach and a wisdom tooth with *4* roots of course. I had to undergo a partial resection of the bone. Otherwise I am pretty well together. 3 days ago a favorable wind blew my boat up to the tower. I sailed it with my son.[112] The trip has done some good to me. I am slowly recovering here from my extreme fatigue, which is chiefly due to the accustomed accumulation of all sorts of embêtements[113] just before my vacations. I am now in the blessed peace of the tower with my wife. *You are welcome here any time after Aug. 5th and you can stay as long as you please*, i.e. until we leave for Ascona. My new book "Symbolik des Geistes"[114] has gone to the publisher, also a new edition of "Energetik der Seele"[115] revised and augmented.

I hope your Eranos lecture does not cause you too much headache.[116] Don't forget his angels and their hierarchies. They are very interesting to us. A survey of his life and his most remarkable Psychology (subjective!) would be welcome.

When you arrive in Zürich you must jump into the train for Rapperswyl-Bollingen, since we shall be up in the tower and nobody at home in Küsnacht.

Hoping you will have a good trip through or over this lamentable French country.

I remain yours, Cordially C.G.

Cunard White Star
R.M.S. "Queen Elizabeth"

14.9.47[117]

Personal

My dear C.G.,

At last I have some leisure – in fact, almost too much of it. Here I am, much sooner than I expected, in mid-Atlantic in this preposterous but definitely

111 overwork.

112 Franz Jung (1908–1996), an architect and, like his father, a skilled sailor. To preserve his solitude at the Tower (and because he preferred not to drive), Jung often made arrangements, as here, to be dropped off there and later picked up by car or boat.

113 obstacles.

114 Cf. Jung, 23 March 1946, p. 29 note; 27 March 1947, p. 80 note.

115 Cf. White, 23 Oct. 1945, p. 19 and note.

116 White had expressed uncertainty about his lecture for Eranos, given the broad theme of the Tagung, "der Mensch" ["the human being"]. Cf. White, 20 April 1947, p. 82.

117 Handwritten on small sheets of grey ship's stationery.

lovable monster. We are now rather more than half-way to New York in the middle of a rather dirty patch of weather. There is every conceivable luxury, the cuisine beggars description, & one is being waited on hand & foot. I am feeling faintly incredulous that I am really here & have a year's freedom from teaching & Seelsorge[118] in front of me. I cannot however believe that every Sorge[119] is left behind me in England, & dreams seem to indicate that I am to find in U.S.A. much of what I have left behind. Perhaps myself!

The twelve days I spent in England were very rushed. I had not expected to leave for U.S.A. until after Sept. 20th. But my Reisebüro[120] suddenly sprung on me that I could get a passage on this sailing, & that perhaps I should not be able to get another before the new D. visa-restrictions[121] come into force. So I packed up furiously; & with less misgiving as I found that my few "patients" were doing almost miraculously well without me, & I felt that maybe they would find they weren't if I hung around too long!

I cannot say how much I enjoyed my stay with you in Switzerland, & how grateful I am for all you have done for me – above all for your friendship & confidence. On my last night in Ascona I had a remarkable & most refreshing dream. I could not & cannot recall the details at all, but in it I seemed to go through a kind of tunnel in which I relived every day & moment I had had at Bollingen & Ascona; but as seen from underneath – i.e. from the standpoint of the Unconscious. It was somehow extraordinarily satisfying & satisfactory. And as, the next day, I travelled on the train up the Ticino valley I had a sense of oneness with the earth such as I have never experienced before.

I have been wondering much how things have been faring with my dear C.G. I hope you have been having a thoroughly good rest at Bollingen, & getting your shoes off & well earthed![122] It is *most* important that you don't get pulled off your feet by "Woman in Europe". Barbara Robb's saga about this has been continuing, & really seems to hit both your problems & mine on the head. Seriously, I think that girl is being shown things of first importance for the future of psychology. I hope she will be persuaded to send the latest batch of dreams & visions to you; at the moment she is reluctant, having a hunch that both you & I are more interested in the "paranormality" of her communications than in what they are trying to say!

I have been wondering whether your own dreams & active imagination has been developing the theme of the two churches on your Zürich hill[123] – whether you have seen anything more of the *other* Catholic church, & whether the top-left & top-right of the one you *do* see are in any better alignment. I am terribly interested to hear about that if ever you have time to tell me.

118 cure (care) of souls. 119 care, trouble. 120 travel office.
121 Reference unidentified.
122 Cf. Robb's visions and active imaginations (White, 16 June 1947, pp. 91ff).
123 Reference to an unidentified dream of Jung's.

But I must not further encroach on your time to read more – let alone to ask you to write more! You know I shall love to hear from you if ever you have the inclination. My address will be –

Ridgely Manor
Stone Ridge,
Ulster Co.,
N.Y.
U.S.A.

Please give my warmest & most grateful remembrances to Mrs Jung & to all my friends. I feel sometimes quite homesick for you all! I enjoyed the Tagung[124] too – much better (I confess) than I had anticipated.

Now I must bid you au revoir, go to the bar for a highball, & plough on to the tantalizing Unknown that awaits me in U.S.A.

Ever most cordially & gratefully, VICTOR

Please attribute 2/3rds of this shocking handwriting to (1) a "Biro" pen; (2) the swayings & vibrations of the Queen Elizabeth in a heavy sea.

Rigi-Staffel[125]

22.IX.1947[126]

My dear Victor,

While you were at Sea, I went up 5000 feet and stuck my head into the clouds.[127] Eranos was rather a strain. For 3 days after I felt a sort of revulsion. You are quite right about women – they are just devouring, if one lets them. – Insatiata, insatiabilis[128] – as a mediaeval cleric said. I must get you that verse. It is the profound sigh of a directeur d'âmes[129] in the XII or XIII

124 At the 1947 Eranos conference, 18–26 August, White had delivered his long, two-part paper, "The Aristotelian-Thomist Conception of Man" (cf. White, 19 Jan. 1947, p. 68 and note).

125 A restaurant near the top of the Rigi, a low mountain (1798 meters above sea level) within easy distance of Zürich.

126 Handwritten, hastily, on plain white stationery. This letter previously unpublished.

127 The Rigi was a favorite hiking area of Jung's. Many people from Zurich take the train to the summit on foggy and cloudy days, hoping to catch a glimpse of the sun. A comfortable hotel and restaurant greet visitors as they disembark from the train. On this occasion, apparently, the Rigi was completely covered in clouds. [with MS]

128 "unsatisfied, insatiable."

129 spiritual director.

Cent. Yet – God has made them to disturb man's self-complacency. Moreover I found that in an exclusive masculine society certain members take it upon themselves to play the rôle of intriguing, insinuating, greedy women, by inclination as well as by environmental suggestion.[130] No escape! The female dominates in our very intestines. Here again a quotation from the famous humanist Aldrovandus,[131] but hélas – my memory! But I assure you, it's a good one.

I make a heroic effort, to keep them at arm's length, sometimes literally so. But I am resigned to the fact, that Man must be plagued with something, why not with women? They are the next in kin.

Ah yes, that reminds me of the great Woman in coelentibus,[132] the Ecclesia,[133] persecuted by the dragon.[134] (This persecution is rather unfortunate). My dreams have not pointed to this problem anymore. Only once, a priest turned up, obviously a Jesuit or a Jesuit pupil, belonging to an archbishop's "capitulum".[135] He was a shockingly intellectual type: he has thought about everything and has put everything into its place. He was even suspected [of] being an adept in Existentialism. I was just discussing the difficult case of a man patient, who used everything he learned to increase his neurosis, with a colleague. The priest, uninvited, suddenly interfered and said, that we were quite wrong – presumably we had not the right philosophy according to his view.

Since the priest had nothing about him I know (except his forehead and his spectacles, which belong to a schizophrenic doctor I used to know) – I can't place him. Perhaps he represents catholic philosophy, with which we don't

130 A humorous reference to Jung's own anima theory, which states that men have a feminine side, with all of its positive and negative attributes. [MS]

131 Ulysses Aldrovandus (Ulisse Aldrovandi, 1522–1605): Italian naturalist and physician, professor at the University of Bologna. His great work was a natural history in 14 volumes. Jung's 1950 essay, "Über Wiedergeburt" ["Concerning Rebirth"], quotes the passage to which he is probably referring here: "Cf. the apt description of the anima in Aldrovandous, *Dendrologiae libri duo* (1668, p.211): 'She appeared both very soft and very hard at the same time, and while for some two thousand years she had made a show of inconstant looks like a Proteus, she bedevilled the love of Lucius Agatho Priscus, then a citizen of Bologna, with anxious cares and sorrows, which assuredly were conjured up from chaos, or from what Plato calls Agathonian confusion' " (CW 9.i, *The Archetypes and the Collective Unconscious*, §223, p. 124n).

132 in heaven. In the biblical passage: "And a great portent appeared in heaven, a woman clothed with the sun . . . she was with child and she cried out in her pangs of birth." A great red dragon threatened to devour her child, but "her child was caught up to God and to his throne" (Revelation 12).

133 Church.

134 Cf. Revelation 12.3. This is an image upon which Jung comments more extensively in *Answer to Job* (CW 11, *Psych. & Rel.*, §698–717). [MS]

135 "chapter." In church usage, the regularly scheduled meeting of members of a religious order, of priests under a bishop, canons under a dean, etc.

interfere, as you know, not being philosophers, but factridden scientists. But that philosophic standpoint might very well interfere with us, assuming that we start from philosophic assumptions. He may represent a Temptation to lay down the law, which seems to be the favorite inclination of old men feeling helpless in the unending rush of life. I feel sometimes like that, but I have Freud's warning example before my eyes.[136] Why after all should one hinder a man to be neurotic, if he likes it?

The theme of the two churches is too tempting, that I would dare to speculate about it. If there is something serious behind it, it will come back with some more material.

I think I have picked up some more health up here. The point is whether I am reasonable enough not to spoil it later on. I really should have learned my lesson. You easily might have an interesting time in USA. When this reaches you, you are already right in it. When you have a chance to see Philip Wylie[137] (Rushford, N.Y.) you might find him rather interesting, but a bit lost, I suspect.

My best wishes,

Yours cordially, C.G.

Ridgely Manor
Stone Ridge, NY

23.10.47[138]

My dear C.G.,

This scrap of paper is no "answer" to your most welcome letter; & of course it calls for none. It is just to thank you for your own letter (which has taken a full month on its journey) & to say I am looking forward to being able to write you more at length later. I am just off to New York for some

136 Jung recounts how Freud asserted his "authority" at a crucial moment in their relationship, which convinced Jung that their days of scientific collaboration were numbered (*MDR*, p. 158). Their struggle around authority is also vividly portrayed in *FJL*, their published corresondence. [MS]

137 Philip Gordon Wylie (1902–1971): American novelist and essayist, author of more than 40 books, on the founding staff of *The New Yorker*. Jung had met Wylie in the United States in 1936 and visited him again in 1937. In *An Essay on Morals* (1947) Wylie defended Jung against the charge of Nazism. He continued his defense in published correspondence ("Letters to the Editor," *Saturday Review of Literature*, 6 Sept. 1947, pp. 21f). Cf. Jung, 19 Dec. 1947, p. 102. Also Jung to Wylie, 19 Feb. 1947 (*Letters II*, "Addenda," pp. xxxviif), 22 Dec. 1957 (ibid., pp. 404f, and notes).

138 Handwritten on a U.S. Postal Service airletter.

days. The visit will include a dinner & meeting at the Club (your kind letter of introduction has proved an almost embarrassingly hospitable Open Sesame – though possibly the rarity-value of a pair of trousers – sorry, I mean *pants* – has something to do with it too!). I hope to have more to relate, & more time to relate it, on my return.

I do hope & pray that your 5000 foot assent has indeed been fruitful for your health; & leave you better able to cope with whatever awaits you in the valleys.

For myself, I have never felt better in my life. The avalanche of new impressions from this strange but fascinating New World has given me plenty to cope with; & the libido, liberated from the daily round & concern with other people's lives & problems, is keeping me very busy too. An undoubtedly necessary & salutary "putrefactio" – or maybe "solutio".[139]

Warmest greetings to you, dear C.G., to Mrs Jung, Miss Wolff, Miss Schmid – & indeed everybody.

VICTOR

Bollingen for a few days.

Dec. 19th 1947[140]

Dear Victor,

Our letters seem to feel that they have to cover a great distance! I have expected your letter with considerable curiosity and it confirms what I thought would be your immediate reaction. It's all very bewildering. Wylie's book,[141] I find, is a most remarkable picture of the things a European has great difficulty to understand. Certainly such a book would be utterly impossible in Europe, because it kills itself. Yet to my idea nobody can foretell the effect it may have upon the average American. Don't forget, that "Mom" has not turned into a monster from a lovely girl on account of nothing but maturation.[142] The animus of women is an answer to the spirit which rules the man. It has its origin from father's mind and shows what the girl has received from the lovely, kind and incompetent father. His family weakness on the other hand he owes to the animus of his mother and thus the evil is

139 Stages in alchemical process (cf. CW12, *Psych. & Alch.*, §334, pp. 230ff).

140 Handwritten.

141 *Generation of Vipers* (with Edwin Balmer, 1942). Adler calls the book "a virulent criticism of the American scene" (*Letters I*, p. 479n). (Cf. Jung, 22 Sept. 1947, p. 101 and note.)

142 In a chapter titled "Common Women," Wylie "discussed the phenomenon of the American 'Mom', the 'destroying Mother' " (*Letters I*, p. 479n). He later published *Sons and Daughters of Mom* (1971).

handed on from generation to generation. I don't think that Wylie's book defeats its own ends in America. The general hide is enormously thick. W. is ethical, but he does not – not yet – understand religion. That is the reason, why his outlook on a further moral development is so peculiarly hazy and so incredibly shallow. But that is decidedly no reason, why it should not appeal to the American appetite, which ever so often prefers sawdust instead of decent food.

You remember my unsympathetic dream figure of the dry Jesuit logician?[143] Not very long after I have written to you, I simply had to write a new essay I did not know about what. It occurred to me I could discuss some of the finer points about Anima, Animus, Shadow and last not least the Self.[144] I was against it, because I wanted to rest my head. Lately I had suffered from severe sleeplessness and I wanted to keep away from all mental exertions. In spite of all I felt forced to write on blindly, not seeing at all, what I was driving at. Only after I had written about 25 pages in folio, it began to dawn on me, that Christ – not the man but the divine being – was my secret goal. It came to me as a shock, as I felt utterly unequal to such a task. A dream told me, that my small fisherboat had been sunk and that a giant (whom I know from a dream about 30 years ago)[145] had provided me with a new, beautiful seagoing craft about twice the size of my former boat. Then I knew – nothing doing! I had to go on. My further writing led me to the archetype of the Godman and to the phenomenon of synchronicity which adheres to the archetype. Thus I came to discuss the Ἰχθύς[146] and the then new aeon of ♓ 30° (following ♈ 0°), the prophecy of the Antichrist and the development of the latter from 1000 A.D. in Mysticism and Alchemy until the recent developments, which threaten to overthrow the Christian aeon altogether.[147] I have found some beautiful material.

Last night I have dreamt of at least 3 catholic priests, who were quite friendly and one of them had a remarkable library. I was the whole time

143 Jung, 22 Sept. 1947, p. 100. Cf. also Jung, 30 Jan. 1948, p. 116.

144 Jung was working on his first draft of a lecture, "Über das Selbst," to be delivered at the 1948 Eranos meeting. Revised, this lecture became chapters IV and V of GW 9.ii, *Aion: Untersuchungen zur Symbolgeschichte* (1951); CW 9.ii, *Aion: Researches into the Phenomenology of the Self* (1958/1968). (Hereafter, *Aion*.) (Cf. Jung, 21 May 1948, pp. 119ff.)

145 Reference uncertain.

146 (for Ἰχθῦς) fish. Ancient, coded reference to Christ. The Greek letters are for a phrase: "Jesus Christ, Son of God, Savior." (Cf. CW 9.ii, *Aion*, ch. VI, VIII–XI.)

147 Jaffé notes, "A central theme of *Aion* is formed by the archetypal developments in the 'Christian aeon', that is, the first millennium of our calendar, in connection with the astrological sign of Pisces (the Fishes). The Fish was a way to refer, originally probably in secret, to Christ. The second Fish of the astrological sign is interpreted as the Antichrist. Preceding the age of Pisces (♓) was the age of the Ram (♈). See also Jung's letter to Baur, 29 Jan. 1934" (*Briefe II*, p. 101, n. 6, trans. ACL).

under a sort of military order and I had to sleep in the barracks. There was a scarcity of beds, so that two men had to share one bed. My partner had already gone to bed. The bed was very clean, white and fresh and he was a most venerable looking, very old man with white locks and a long flowing white beard. He offered me graciously one half of the bed and I woke up, when I was just slipping into it. I must say, that up to now I have handled the problem of Christ strictly on the level with the dogma, which is the leading thread through the maze of "my" unthought thoughts.

Ad "Neurosis": I mean of course, that it is as a rule better to leave neurotics to themselves *in as much* as they do not suffer and seek health. There is enough of a task for the psychotherapist.

I am glad to hear, that "they" gave you a hearty welcome in New York. Please give them my best regards.

The conditions in England are indeed lamentable. Perhaps it is just as well, that you have more dreams to deal with, than to write. The latter can wait, but what you are meant to be, cannot wait.

My best wishes for Xmas and
New Year

Yours cordially C.G.

Küsnacht-Zürich

Dec. 27th 1947[148]

My dear Victor,

I am so "distrait" by my writing, that I forgot a most important point, about which I should have asked you: There exists a plan, to create an "Institute of Analytical Psychology" ("Institut für complexe Psychologie") in Zürich. A "comité" has been elected, consisting of 5 persons (C.A. Meier,[149] Dr. K. Binswanger,[150] Dr. Jolan Jacobi[151] and Dr. L.

148 Handwritten on letterhead half-sheets.

149 Cf. Schmid, 24 Oct. 1946, p. 51 and note.

150 Kurt Binswanger, Dr.med., Swiss psychiatrist. Son of Ludwig Binswanger (1881–1966), founder of existential analysis, who had served with Jung at the Burghölzli clinic; great-nephew of Otto Binswanger (1852–1929), professor of psychiatry at Jena University, where Nietzsche was a patient (*FJL*, p. 24n).

151 Jolan (Jolande) Jacobi, Dr.phil. (1890–1973): Jungian analyst, born to a prominent Jewish family in Budapest; later a Catholic convert. Living in Vienna from 1918, in 1928 she became Vice-President of the Austrian *Kulturbund*, where Jung also lectured. After traveling frequently to Zurich for analysis with Jung, in 1938 she fled Austria, settled in Zurich and

Frey-Rohn[152] and myself),[153] who are preparing the list of the actual founders. I have been asked to write to you whether you would be inclined to allow us to put your name on that list. You risk no further obligations. We only hope you would add the moral authority of your name to the new enterprise. We have already the names of Gebhard Frei,[154] Prof. of Modern Philosophy at a collegium sacerdotale[155] in Schöneck, Prof. Pauli,[156] physicist and Nobel prize man, Prof. Gonzeth,[157] mathematician, ETH. Rob. de Traz,[158] French-Swiss Novelist of fame, Ad. Vischer[159] of the Curatorium

trained as an analyst. She received her doctoral degree in philosophy and psychology (for which she had to return to Vienna, at great personal risk), then practiced and taught in Zurich. Jacobi wrote several books on analytical psychology, including *The Psychology of C.G. Jung* (London: Kegan Paul, 1943), still in print; and *Komplex, Archetypus, Symbol* (Zürich: Rascher, 1957; PUP/Bollingen, 2nd ed, 1965). One of Jung's trusted colleagues and friends until his death, she is also one of the leading exponents of his work in German.

152 Liliane Frey-Rohn, Dr.phil. (b. 1904): Jungian analyst, one of Jung's closest collaborators, author of several works, including *From Freud to Jung: A Comparative Study of the Psychology of the Unconscious* (Zürich: Rascher Verlag, 1969; New York: G.P. Putnam's Sons for the C.G. Jung Institute for Analytical Psychology, 1974; Boston: Shambhala Publications/ G.G. Jung Foundation/Daimon Book, 1990).

153 With Jung, these four of his students became the first Curatorium of the C.G. Jung Institute, Zurich.

154 Fr. Gebhard Frei, SMB (1905–1968): Catholic priest and scholar, was professor of philosophy and comparative religion at the Theological Seminary of Schöneck, Switzerland (*Letters I*, p. 486n). Frei's important essay, "Zur Psychologie des Unbewussten" ["On Analytical Psychology: The Method and Teaching of C.G. Jung"], was printed as an appendix to the first edition of White's *God & Unc.* (cf. White, 25 March 1952, p. 179 and note). Frei also lectured at the Psychological Club, Zurich (cf. Jung, 15 May 1953, p. 214 and note). [with AC]

155 seminary (lit., priestly college).

156 Wolfgang Pauli (1900–1958): Austrian-born physicist, educated in Munich, Göttingen and Copenhagen. In 1928 he was appointed professor of Theoretical Physics at the ETH, Zurich. Pauli taught in the United States during the Second World War, returning to Zurich in 1945, where he continued to live and work until his death. In 1945 he received the Nobel prize for physics for his formulation of the "exclusion principle" (the "Pauli principle"). For many years he and Jung met for discussions of the relations between nuclear physics and psychology, and in 1952 they jointly authored a book, *Naturerklärung und Psyche* (cf. Schmid, 3 April 1952, p. 180; also Jung to Pauli, 29 Oct. 1934, *Letters I*, p. 174n). They also had an extensive correspondence, now published as *Atom and Archetype: The Pauli/Jung Letters, 1932–1958* (ed. C.A. Meier with C.P. Enz and M. Fierz; trans. David Roscoe. London: Brunner-Routledge, 2001).

157 Ferdinand Gonseth (1890–1975): mathematician and philosopher; professor of higher mathematics at the University of Berne and the ETH, Zurich. Throughout his career he focussed attention on the foundations of mathematics, the philosophy of science, and the theory of knowledge.

158 Robert de Traz (1884–1951): Swiss poet, novelist and literary scholar, author of many books; for some time editor of the *Revue de Genève*.

159 Adolf Lucas Vischer, MD (b. 1884): Swiss physician; lecturer and member of the Curatorium at the University of Basel; his work focussed on old age and aging.

universitatis Basiliensis etc. Your name would be in good society. Personally I should be much obliged to you if you could do us this pleasure. In return you will receive further particulars about the Institute. I have written a longish letter to you, which probably goes by slow mail. So this forgotten item reaches you before the letter, which should have contained it. What I am "distrait" about, is depicted in that letter.[160]

As I am getting on in age and as I am going to be assembled to my ancestors and avatars within a measurable time, the Institute is meant to carry on the work. My former English Seminars are already substituted by a number of lectures and courses about dream psychology, ps.[161] of fairy tales, selected topics from the Old Testament, ps. of the Gilgamesh Epos, ps. of the Renaissance (XV Cent.) etc. They are to be consolidated in the form of an Institute. The Psych. Club spends[162] the rooms, the use of the library and a sum of money.

I am very busy just now, but tomorrow I am going to Bollingen for a fortnight.

Cordially yours C.G.

Ridgely Inn
Stone Ridge
N.Y. U.S.A.

December 27th [1947][163]

My dear C.G.

Your letter, which arrived on Christmas Eve, was the very best of my Christmas presents.[164] I am simply thrilled to hear of your Giant's gift of the new, big & beautiful seagoing craft.[165] I can hardly tell you how I am impatient to read the account of your voyage in her; nor, I hope, do I *need* to tell you how my thoughts & prayers are with you in this journey. I have not

160 Cf. Jung, 19 Dec. 1947, p. 103.

161 psychology.

162 donates (from German, *spenden*).

163 Handwritten. White omitted the year, but internal evidence shows this to be his reply to Jung's letter of 19 Dec. 1947.

164 The previous day White had written to a friend, "My best Xmas present has been very good news from Zurich. God is doing amazing things in the Old Man's dreams! But the battle is not yet over, & it's terrific!" (White to a religious, 26 Dec. 1947, English Province archive). He added that her prayers were playing a part in Jung's spiritual progress and asked her to continue praying. [AC]

165 Cf. Jung, 19 Dec. 1947, p. 103.

forgotten my own "vision" of which I told you:[166] how huge & heavy was the rope you used to haul the Ἰχθύς[167] ashore!

I will not dare to comment on your dream of the priests, the barracks & the bed;[168] but somehow, as I read it, I was at once reminded of a dream of my own of over two years ago; & still more so when you go on to write, "up to now I have handled the problem of Christ strictly on the level with the dogma". Note that this dream belongs to December 1945 – before I had even met you, or been to Zürich. Undoubtedly it had a very important subjective meaning for myself at the time, but (although superficially it has little resemblance to your own) "something" seems to tell me it has to do with your "barracks", & that at least no harm will be done by sending a copy from my records to you. So I enclose it herewith.

Yes; what you say about the American's animus explains a lot. I suppose it is confirmed by what to me is the most flabbergasting (& embarrassing!) phenomenon that I have noticed here: in mixed company, EITHER the sexes segregate – the women in one corner & the men in the other, OR (more often) the women do *all* the talking, treat the men as if they do not exist, while the men grin inanely as if they loved it!

And doubtless Wylie knows his public far better than I do. Next year I hope to travel more, & to come in closer contact with "average Americans".

A thousand thanks for your last words – about "being" & "writing". It's one of those things I "know" – but need to be told again & again.

But latterly the writing has begun to flow a little more easily, & the dreaming a little less insistent. But the dreaming was seldom so perplexing. Constantly I dream that I have returned to England, & in successive dreams I find things alternately *far better* and *far worse* (I mean, more or less disagreeable to me) than I had anticipated. So far I know not what to make of such contradictory dreams. In my waking life the stupidity & smugness of some American criticism of England is making me quite fervidly patriotic; & I am not at all sure that the efforts of our Government & people to combine some social justice with freedom isn't going to succeed. Here so many seem utterly unaware that for very many Americans there is neither. There's much here one loves & admires . . . but I am still far from having it all sorted out!

I met Frau Fröbe[169] in N.Y.C. in a somewhat lost, frustrated & resentful state. Poor old thing – it seems a pity, for I do really think Eranos

166 Reference unidentified. 167 (for Ἰχθῦς) fish (cf. Jung, 19 Dec. 1947, p. 103n.).

168 Cf. Jung, 19 Dec. 1947, p. 104. Although he declined at first to comment on this dream of Jung's, his later responses to it were extensive. Cf. White, 3 Jan. 1948, pp. 113f.)

169 Olga Fröbe-Kapteyn (1881–1962): founded the Eranos Conferences in 1928, building the Casa Eranos near her own villa on Lake Maggiore in the Ticino. She edited the *EJ* for many years. (Cf. Jung, 5 Oct. 1945, p. 9 and note.)

worth while, & getting somewhere. The 1945 Jahrbuch[170] which I have been reading (& trying to review!) is really a most impressive collection. She presses me to come next year: I do very much want to, if only to see you, but there are many complications. When she told me that the "Menschensohn"[171] was a desired subject, I at once thought of my colleague, Fr. Richard Kehoe[172] (of whom I have told you). He is a splendid lecturer, & his psychological-exegesis of Scripture etc. is most exciting. I very much want you & him to meet, & this would be a grand opportunity. And "The Son of Man" in the Bible, Apocalypses & Apocryphas is one of his specialities.

I hope & pray that with the coming of the new Boat & its acceptance the severe sleeplessness has departed, & that you are again in the very best of health.

My warm greetings to Mrs Jung, Frl. Schmid, Frl. Wolff & all my friends.

Yours ever cordially, VICTOR

Dream of December 12th. 1945.[173]

A long dream in the course of which I go to Zürich. The "Zürich" of my dream is quite a small pink town nestling in a fertile green valley. I notice many church spires, but am surprised that I see no lake. I first see it looking down from a neighboring hill. Then I am in "Zürich" itself, among a number of people, among whom is Jung. Conversation is all quite casual and trivial, it does not touch on any deep matters. It seems to be some sort of party; I know I have not been invited, but my presence is taken as a matter of course. It seems I have dropped in almost by accident, and in my dream I am aware that I neither have the money to have got to Zürich (from England), nor have I any money to get home again. But none of these things seem to matter. Jung is on my left-hand side; he is a very jolly old man with a bright scarf round his neck.

Then I am just outside a house by the seashore on the South Coast (of England). It is late afternoon, and many people are batheing in the sea. It seems that my parents are living or staying in the house; there is a raised platform between the sea and the house. "We" (I do not remember who the others are, but friends and companions of some sort) decide to wait until the crowds have left the shore before we go swimming ourselves; as the sun sets, the crowds disperse.

The next thing I remember is that I am back at Zürich. It is a Sunday, and I am there just for the day. As all the public churches in this dream-Zürich

170 *EJ 1945*. Jung's lecture "Zur Psychologie des Geistes" appeared in this volume (cf. Jung, 23 March 1946, p. 29 and note).

171 Son of Man (Messiah).

172 Cf. White, 23 Oct. 1945, p. 17 and note.

173 Typewritten dream text, enclosed with White, 27 Dec. 1947.

are Protestant, I had had to say Mass in a nuns' chapel. I seem now to be inside Jung's house. He is sitting at the top of a table on my right; Mrs Jung is also on my right between him and me; I particularly notice that nobody else is there. At first the conversation is again quite commonplace and trivial. But later I am alone with Jung, and talking with him earnestly face to face. I do not remember exactly what it was we were talking about, but presumably something to do with religion and Catholicism; and I think Jung had been talking about the Spirit as manifested in the Unconscious. For at one point he said, with a vehemence that surprised me, "But the Roman Church is all wrong about the Spirit. The last articles in the Creed don't go deep enough," (i.e. "I believe in the Holy Ghost, the holy catholic Church" etc.). I replied, "But articles don't go anywhere, deep or shallow. It is all a matter of how deeply one goes THROUGH them, or INTO them." I start to tell him about St Thomas Aquinas' teaching about Faith in the Unknown and Unseen "Veritas Prima", and how that, and not the dogma, is the term of Faith (i.e. *Summa* II,II.i.1 and 2. etc.) As I tell him this, Jung's face lightens up in an extraordinary way – a moment before it had been quite taut and worried, as though the "last articles in the Creed" somehow threatened to restrict and imprison him. It is as if a load had fallen off him.

(SOME ASSOCIATIONS AND COMMENTS): The Dream-Zürich: SMALL, perhaps I was underestimating its real size and importance, or possibly romanticising it à la Swiss picture postcard. PINK, redbrick, red-tiled houses had always appealed to me as a child, as contrasted with grey stone and tiles. VALLEY, I had been reading Chinese symbolism of Valleys in "Secret of Golden Flower", p.6. LOOKING DOWN, perhaps ego taking "superior attitude", but this only a flash, like Ignatian "composition of place" or opening scene of a film. CASUAL AND TRIVIAL CONVERSATION, perhaps good and proper enough at beginning and in company of "number of people". NOT INVITED, etc. This contact with Zürich and Jung not intended or willed by me; it just "happens" (ACCIDENT); money and other conscious means not essential.

The South Coast Interlude: SOUTH COAST, Feeling, Warmth, Holidays. OF ENGLAND, it seems I have to go back home to my own origins and parents to be able to meet Zürich and Jung on deeper level. There I see the SEA, which I had failed to see at Zürich. THE PLATFORM, there seems to be some barrier between the parents' "home" (? personal unconscious) and the sea (? undifferentiated collective ditto), but this barrier is also a *way* between them. It is in *this* situation that I must wait for the NUMBER OF PEOPLE to disperse, presumably the same NUMBER OF PEOPLE who had got in the way at Zürich. From the parents' "home", when the sun of consciousness has set, I can plunge into the sea.

After having done this, I can return to Zürich, and on SUNday (new light, resurrection, 8th Day of New Creation). I must sacrifice among the women;[174] because the public churches are all Protestant. I am now INSIDE with Jung, and he is now on my more conscious side (right). But we are at first at oblong table; Mrs Jung (only a name to me at time of dream, and presumably an aspect of Jung's anima – the feminine side of psychology) must first be recognised as between us. I particularly notice that nobody else is there, though I had somehow expected Miss Wolff – presumably another, perhaps Thinking, aspect. "Mrs Jung" seems at first to be both mediator and barrier between Jung and me in first part of dream – rather like the PLATFORM. But then we come face to face without intermediary or barrier. JUNG'S VEHEMENT WORDS suggest (taken subjectively) that the psychology-in-me (represented by Jung) still feels restricted and repressed by dogma, especially regarding the Spirit and the Church. But it seems that ego (if only it will use it) has the means – even the conscious, theological means imparted by St. Thomas – to release this repression, and satisfy the unconscious demands.

174 Nearly illegible, due to White's corrected typing error.

1948

Ridgely Inn
Stone Ridge, N.Y.
U.S.A.

3.1.48[1]

Personal

My dear C.G.,

You will be surprised – I trust not too bored – to have another letter from me so soon. The fact is that, after my last letter to you, I too started to "suffer from severe sleeplessness"! At first I could not understand it at all. Then came a message from the Unconscious – just a "flash", but it was enough. You and I were having a meal together; it was on a Friday, perhaps a Good Friday. You asked me to pass you the fish (the IXΘYS!). I said: "Hell: YOU don't have to eat fish to-day" – meaning, of course, that as a non-Catholic you were not obliged to refrain from meat on a Friday. Then I saw you were looking at me terribly reproachfully and disappointed and ill.

I fairly soon came around to the idea (confirmed, I may say, by the subsequent freedom from insomnia!) that this "flash" – and the previous sleeplessness – had to do with my letter to you.[2] In fact I lied – with the stupid pride of false modesty – when I said I did "not dare to comment" on your dream! The truth is that, directly I read it, I felt myself in a part of Dreamland with which I am familiar; the part where my own problems, conflicts and neuroses have been. I interpret: the Catholic should not hesitate to share his wretched bit of fish with the great psychologist, even though (it) he *may* eat meat; certainly not falsely pretend he "dare" not. Moreover, it's Friday: maybe a matter of Death and Eternity. I add (though it may be a superimposed afterthought) that the meal seemed to be in that upstairs room at Bollingen where once you told me that I should not pretend to less consciousness than I have got. At any rate the psychologist will make allowances for my own purely individual or "Catholic" slant on the dream. So I dare-not not-dare: and here goes –

Of course you will have your own personal associations with BARRACKS. But I expect they must include such things as order, discipline, enclosure, restriction, regularity, obedience; also perhaps comradeship with "ordinary" men, security and the rest. Can this be another aspect of the JESUIT – founded by Loyola to be a MILITIA Christi?[3] From outside it is ONLY negative; dictatorial, interfering, No-saying, schizoid. But now you are within; and within the priests are friendly to you, and you to them. Within, too, is a

1 Typewritten, except the twice-underlined heading, "Personal," and the closing.
2 Cf. White, 27 Dec. 1947, p. 107 and note.
3 Army of Christ.

"remarkable library" belonging to one of them; doubtless its CONTENTS and its POSITION in the barracks are significant to you.

The BED-SHARING with the gracious and venerable old man at first perplexed me; but at the same time gave me a tremendous sense of delight and relief. (I can only tell you how it affected *me*). I could little doubt that in this "clean, white, fresh" and SHARED bed the Unconscious was somehow providing the compensation, perhaps the remedy, for your actual sleeplessness. It chances that since then an Austrian-Jewish priest of my acquaintance in New York has told me that our friend Fr Hugo Rahner has recently written a Dialogue between a Doctor and a Priest on insomnia! I have not read it, but perhaps you have, and it has provided material for your dream.

But only after a while did it dawn on me why this part of your dream brought such delight and relief to *me*. At the risk of seeming to "preach", I should like to tell you. I think perhaps it is the Good Friday fish!

There is one thing you have written which has rather worried me; and more so since I have come to know and love you personally. (Permit me to be quite frank about it). It is where you write of the "Demut"[4] of the Protestant; and "Der Protestant ist Gott allein anheimgegeben. Es gibt für ihn keine Beichte, keine Absolution, usw. Er muss seine Sünde allein verdauen . . ."[5] Oh, it is splendid, magnificent; I too still feel deeply and intensely the fascination of it – whether we call it Protestant, or just Stoic – to live like that, and to die like that. But is it really Demut – or Armut?[6] Is it even truly human? (I recall Aristotle's "The solitary man is either a Beast or a God").

The Catholic also "brought nothing into the world, and it is certain that he can take nothing out". Nothing; not EVEN his sins. For they are really our proudest possessions: the only things (theologians say) that are truly and wholly our own. And God insists on taking them too! It took me long to see and to accept it; but I think there is a terrible hidden HYBRIS in "seine Sünde allein verdauen". "Beichte, Absolution, Ritual" and the rest, I see not just as a matter of "consolation". The Catholic must acknowledge and accept to the very end, especially at the very end, his dependence on the Earth which to the very end supports him – even physically: there is always gravitation! To the end he must submit to the Spirit THROUGH matter: the oil, the bread, the wine, the hands and forgiveness and well-wishing of his fellow men, representing earthly society. Consolation perhaps; but only because first the Demut and the Armut are *absolute*, and because Incarnation means that

4 humility.

5 "The Protestant is consigned to God alone. For him there is no confession, no absolution, no possibility of an expiatory *opus divinum* [divine work] of any kind. He has to digest his sins by himself" (CW 11, *Psych. & Rel.*, §86, p. 48, trans. mod. ACL). From the second of Jung's 1937 Terry Lectures at Yale, collectively titled "Psychology and Religion," originally delivered in English and later published in German. White quotes the German version.

6 poverty.

Grace and Peace come – from Spirit indeed – but THROUGH the fruits of the earth and fellow-mankind, even the Barracks perhaps!

Well; that explains *my* great delight and relief in reading that in your dream you are offered no LONELY bed, but to share it with this gracious old man who is already there; and presumably represents a still older wisdom and experience. A purely personal reaction, doubtless; but though it may be "poor fish" and not meant for you, on the contrary it may be, and you will, I know, understand that I cannot refuse it! I don't like insomnia!

You will have heard of our record snow-storm: the general dislocation of transport and food-supply in New York City wrought by 99,000,000 tons of snow. Nature seems still to find some way of making herself felt amid the asphalt and the skyscrapers; though perhaps this is only a mild beginning. I hope the fuel shortage in Küsnacht is not so severe this year; and I hope and pray that all goes very well with you, with Mrs Jung and all my friends.

Ever cordially, VICTOR

Küsnacht-Zürich

Jan. 30th 1948[7]

Dear Victor,

Many thanks for your personal willingness to contribute to our endeavours![8] I have not yet heard from Rome.[9]

Many thanks also for the other contents of your letters! It took me a while to digest everything properly. I am particularly glad, that you have sent me your dream you have had in a time (1945) when you did not yet know me personally.[10] It is very helpful to me. Your interpretation is quite correct as far as it goes. Of course the dream leads up to our personal discussion, it paves the way to it. Thus I am still left somewhat as the representative of the argument pro S. Spiritu.[11] But the argument started in yourself. It is quite clear, that the Unconscious insists rather vehemently upon the problem of the S. Spiritus, which I can confirm by many of my own dreams, including

7 Handwritten.

8 Cf. Jung, 27 Dec. 1947 (p. 104), inviting White to be a founding patron of the C.G. Jung Institut Zürich. White accepted and became one of the Institute's founders. His letter of acceptence is unfortunately lost.

9 Perhaps, as Adler hypothesizes, White had sought support for the Institute from someone in Rome (*Letters I*, p. 490n); it is also possible that Jung himself had done so.

10 "Dream of December 12th, 1945" (cf. White, 27 Dec. 1947, enclosure, pp. 108ff).

11 for the Holy Spirit.

the one I have sent to you, i.e. the one about the senex venerabilis.[12] In your dream you are separated from and connected with me by an *anima*-figure, as by the *platform*, by which you are either separated from the sea or enabled to reach it. Further on in Zürich you must celebrate Mass *among the women*. The female factor i.e. the anima is the bridge and the conditio sine qua non.[13] The unknowable Veritas Prima[14] solved the problem for the time being.

The emphasis on the anima means of course the totality of man: male plus female = conscious plus unconscious. Whatever the unconscious and whatever the S.Spiritus is, the unconscious realm of the psyche is the place, where the living Spirit, that is more than Man, manifests itself. I should not hesitate to call your dream a manifestation of the S.Spiritus that leads you on to deeper understanding away from the narrowness of formulas and concepts to the living Truth, the prima veritas.

Something similar happened in my dream, of which, unfortunately, I have given you the mere outlines. While I stood before the bed of the Old Man, I thought and felt: Indignus sum Domine.[15] I know Him very well: He was my "guru" more than 30 years ago, a real ghostly guru[16] – but that is a long and – I am afraid – exceedingly strange story. It has been since confirmed to me by an old Hindu.[17] You see, something has taken me out off Europe and the Occident and has opened for me the gates of the East as well, so that I should understand something of the *human* mind.

Soon after this portentous dream, I had another one continuing a subject alluded to in the former dream, viz. the figure of the priest, the head of the library. His carriage and the fact, that he unexpectedly had a short gray beard reminded me strongly of my own father. The second dream[18] is very long and has many scenes, of which I can only relate the last one. In all parts of the dream I was concerned with my father. In the last scene I was in *his house* on the ground floor, very much preoccupied by a peculiar question, which had been raised at the beginning of the dream: "*How is it possible, that my mother celebrates her 70th birthday in this year 1948, while I am reaching my 74th year?*" My father is going to answer it and he takes me up with him

12 venerable old man. (Cf. Jung, 19 Dec. 1947, p. 104.)

13 the indispensable condition.

14 First Truth. In his dream White explains to Jung "St Thomas Aquinas' teaching about Faith in the Unknown and Unseen Veritas Prima" (White, 27 Dec. 1947, p. 109).

15 Lord, I am not worthy.

16 During a dream and a series of powerful visions in 1914, Jung encountered a winged old man with the horns of a bull, holding a bunch of four keys. Jung painted this figure, whom he called Philemon, and in conversations with him learned the objective reality of the psyche (*MDR*, pp. 182f). [MS]

17 Jung had talked once about gurus with a distinguished Indian visitor, who told him, "Most people have living gurus. But there are always some who have a spirit for a teacher" (Ibid., p. 184).

18 Ibid., pp. 217ff.

to the first floor by way of a narrow winding staircase in the wall. Coming out on the 1st floor, we find ourselves on a (circular) gallery, from which a small bridge leads to an isolated cuplike platform in the center of the room. (The room has otherwise no floor, it is open down to the ground floor.) From the platform a narrow staircase, almost a ladder, leads up to a small door high up in the wall. I know this is *his* room. The moment we enter the bridge, I fall on my knees, completely overcome by the sudden understanding, that my father is going to lead me into the "supreme presence". By sympathy he kneels at my side and I try to touch the ground with my forehead. I almost reach it and there I woke up.

The peculiar 1st floor is exactly like the famous *divan-i-khas* (hall of audience) *Akbar's the Great* in Fatehpur-Sikri,[19] where he used to discuss Philosophy and Religion with the representatives of all philosophies and all creeds.

Oh yes, it is my way allright. I don't despise the fish. I am glad you share it with me. I can eat fish on Fridays. I have brethren and sisters in the spirit and when once I felt godforsaken and really lonely, there was my guru. Surely, there is something the matter with the solitary Man; if he is not a beast, he is conscious of S.Paul's words: τοῦ γὰρ καὶ γὲνος ἐσμέν.[20] The Divine Presence is more than anything else. There is more than one way to the rediscovery of the genus divinum[21] in us. This is the only thing that really matters. Was there ever a more solitary man than S.Paul? Even his "evangelium" came to him immediately and he was up against the men in Jerusalem as well as the whole Roman Empire. I wanted the proof of a living Spirit and I got it. Don't ask me at what a price.

When I said, that the Protestant has to digest his sins alone, I really meant: he must carry them, because how can God take him with his sins, if he does not carry them? if he has been relieved from the weight of his burden?

Concerning "barracks" you are quite right; they mean submission and discipline, of which I could tell you a very long story indeed. Whoever has clearly understood, what it means: "Qui fidelis est in minimo",[22] is overwhelmed with the dura necessitas[23] of submission and discipline of a subtler kind than the regula S.Benedicti.[24] I don't want to prescribe a way to other people, because I know that my way has been prescribed to me by a hand far above my reach.

19 Akbar the Great, Jalal ud-Din Mohammed (1542–1605): the greatest of the Mogul emperors of India. Fatehpur-Sikri was one of his capitals (*Letters I*, p. 491n.) Cf. *MDR*, pp. 218ff.

20 "for we are indeed his offspring." In St. Paul's address to the Athenians, the complete verse reads: "for 'in him we live and move and have our being'; as even some of your poets have said; 'For we are indeed his offspring' " (Acts 17.28). Adler notes that the poet to whom Paul refers is the Stoic Aratus of Soli (*Letters I*, p. 492n).

21 divine offspring.

22 "He that is faithful in that which is least" (Luke 16.10).

23 hard necessity.

24 Rule of St. Benedict.

I know it all sounds so damned grand. I am sorry that it does, but I don't mean it. *It* is grand, and I am only trying to be a decent tool and don't feel grand at all.

Happily the cloud of sleeplesness has lifted recently. My brain has been too active. My paper about the ἸΧΘΎΣ has disturbed the tranquillity of my mind in its deepest layers, as you can imagine.

In a catholic journal (published by Routledge and Sons)[25] a somebody "condemns" my Essays on Cont. Hist.[26] because my attitude to Religion and to Rational Philosophy is, as he says, "ambiguous". O sancta simplicitas![27]

I hope that your writing is progressing and that you enjoy your interesting holiday in U.S. I have just read Kravtchenko's book on Russia.[28] Worth reading! you get an idea of the princeps huius mundi[29] and his remarkable works.

Cordially yours C.G.

P.S. My mother = Anima is younger than myself.[30] When I was 3 years old I had my first anima-experience, the woman that was *not* my mother.[31] It means a lot that escapes me for the time being.

Küsnacht-Zürich

Mai 21st 1948[32]

Dear Victor!

Finally I am able to write to you. I thank you very much for your excellent lecture on Gnosticism.[33] I admired much your balanced judgement and your

25 Reference unidentified. Adler notes that the publisher has no record of having ever published a Catholic journal (*Letters I*, p. 493n).

26 *Essays on Contemporary Events* (cf. Jung, 13 Feb. 1946, p. 28 and note.

27 Oh, holy simplicity!

28 Victor Kravchenko (1905–1966): a former Soviet spy, whose book *I Chose Freedom: The Personal and Political Life of a Soviet Official* (New York: C. Scribner's Sons, 1946), about conditions in Russia and Russian espionage, created a sensation.

29 prince of this world (= Satan).

30 In Jung's dream (30 Jan. 1948 above, p. 116), his mother is 70, while he is almost 74.

31 A young woman took care of Jung as a child while his mother was away (*MDR*, p. 8).

32 Handwritten.

33 White delivered his lecture, "Notes on Gnosticism," to the APC of New York on 20 February 1948, and to the GPP, London, on 10 December 1948. In 1949 it was published as Guild Lecture No. 59 and in the journal *Spring*. In revised form it became Chapter XI, "Gnosis, Gnosticism and Faith," in *God & Unc*.

just evaluation of a subject, that has been so often represented in a wrong light and misunderstood by all sorts of comprehensible and incomprehensible prejudices. Your presentation of the Pistis Sophia[34] is excellent. Among the patristic writers about Gnosticism I missed Hippolytos,[35] the most thorough and the most intelligent of all. Epiphanius,[36] who shares the former's lot, doesn't deserve much praise. Your paper has made me think: *Have I faith or a faith or not*? I have always been unable to produce faith and I have tried so hard, that I finally did not know any more, what faith is or means. I owe it to your paper, that I have now apparently an answer: faith or the equivalent of faith with me is what I would call *Respect*. I have respect of the Christian Truth. Thus it seems to come down to an involuntary assumption in me, that there is something to the dogmatic truth, something *indefinable* to begin with. Yet I feel respect for it, although I don't really understand it. But I can say, my lifework is essentially an attempt to understand what others apparently can believe. There must be – so I conclude – a rather strong motive-power connected with the Christian Truth, otherwise it would not be explicable, why it influenced me to such an extent. My respect is – mind you – involuntary; it is a "datum" of irrational nature. This is the nearest I can get to what appears to me as "faith". There is however nothing specific in it, since I feel the same kind of respect for the basic teachings of Buddhism and the fundamental taoistic ideas. In the case of the Christian Truth one would be inclined to explain this a priori-respect through my Christian education. Yet the same cannot be said in the case of Buddhism, Taoism, and certain aspects of Islam. Hindoo theology curiously enough never had the same appeal, although it has gripped my intellect at times quite powerfully.

Gnosticism has renewed its vitality with me recently in as much as I was deeply concerned with the question of how the figure of Christ was received into Hellenistic naturephilosophy and hence into Alchemy. It is just a little book[37] that has grown out of such studies within the last months. It will be, I am afraid, a shocking and difficult book. It has seduced me into a most curious attempt to formulate the progress of symbolism within the last two

34 Trustful Wisdom, title of a Gnostic work in Coptic (*Letters I*, p. 501n).

35 Hippolytus of Rome (*fl.* c. 230 CE): bishop of Portus Romanus, early Christian theologian. His writings, rediscovered in the nineteenth century and attributed at first to Origen, are an indispensable source of Gnostic teachings. His *Philosophumena; or, The Refutation of All Heresies* (trans. 1921) is copiously quoted in Jung's later works under the title *Elenchos* (*Letters I*, p. 501n). For elucidation of the following passage on Self-symbolism, cf. CW 9.ii, *Aion*, ch. XIII–XIV, esp. §338ff.

36 Epiphanius, bishop of Constantia (c.315–402): early Church Father who in his youth was greatly influenced by Gnostic teachings. His main work, *Panarion*, is a treatise on heresies (*Letters I*, p. 501n).

37 The "little book" would become *Aion* (CW 9.ii), in which Jung's 1948 Eranos lecture, "Über das Selbst" ("On the Self"), appears with slight additions as ch. IV–V.

thousand years through the figure of 4 quaternities based upon 2 quaterniones of the Naasenes[38] as mentioned by Hippolytos. The first one is the socalled *Moses-quaternio*:

(a double pyramide)

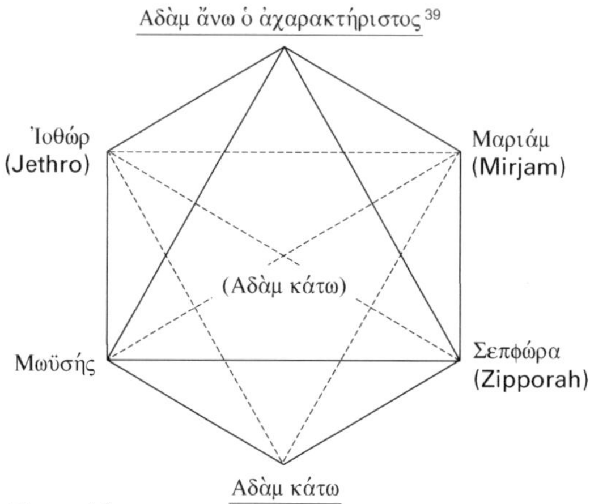

This is a classical *marriage quaternio*, as I have described it in Psych. of Transfer. p.96 ssq.[40]

Figure 4.1

It is of greatest importance, that, according to Hippolytos, this quaternio symbolizes the ἀβασίλευτος γενεά[41] which is synonymous with all their symbolisms of the central figure viz. the redeemer, the yod,[42] the grain of mustard, the "celestial horn of the moon", Jordan, Attis, Korybas etc. They all refer psychologically to the *Self*. This second quaternio (with the same significance) is *Paradise with its 4 rivers*. Well, it is a mad thing, which I cannot

38 A Gnostic sect in which the serpent (*naas* from Hebrew *nachash*) occupied a central place (CW 9.ii, *Aion*, §288ff, 358ff). Discussed in the *Elenchos* (cf. note 35, p. 119, above).

39 Top: "Higher Adam/without characteristics." Center and bottom: "Lower Adam." Left and right: "Jethro . . . Miriam"; "Moses . . . Zipporah." (Cf. CW 9.ii, *Aion*, §359, p. 227.) This entire passage, including Jung's diagram of the "Moses-quaternio" and his larger diagram (Figure 4.2, p. 122) is omitted from the Adler and Jaffé versions of this letter. (Cf. *Letters I*, p. 502; *Briefe II*, p. 126f.)

40 Cf. CW 16, *Transference*, §425ff.

41 a race free from kingly rule. (Cf. CW 9.ii, *Aion*, §402, p. 255.)

42 The smallest Hebrew letter, like a tiny point, which in Kabbalistic thought represents the presence of God in the human being or, in Jung's terms, the Self (cf. Jung, 12 May 1950, postscript, p. 152 and notes). Scarcely legible in Jung's holograph (cf. Figure 4.3, p. 123), this word might also be read as "god." In context, however, grouped with a grain of mustard seed, the reading "yod" is more likely.

explain here; but it seems *hellishly important*, insofar as it winds up with the physical Time–space quaternio.[43] The whole seems to be logically watertight.

I feel reasonably well and I hope you do the same. You must have had an interesting time. A Jesuit, professor of theology at Louvain is coming to see me next week.[44] They begin to sit up. Looking forward to the summer, where I hope to see you again at Bollingen.

Yours cordially, C.G.

Ridgely,
Stone Ridge, N.Y.
U.S.A.

June 1st 1948[45]

My dear C.G.,

I am ashamed to find that I owe you for two letters. For I have never sent you more than a brief acknowledgment for the grand letter[46] you sent me shortly before I left here for my tour to the West.

The tour was a huge success: the West – and especially the Northwest – strikes me as vastly more civilized than the East. I paid my way around mostly by giving a few lectures: these were mostly very elementary introductions to your psychology to various Catholic colleges and institutions! The enthusiastic response was very gratifying; we got some really intelligent questions and discussions going. I also talked to the A.P. Club in San Francisco,[47] where I was given a grand reception. One of the highspots of the trip was meeting your friend Fowler McCormick[48] in Chicago. We seemed to "click" remarkably well, and I was sorry not to have seen more of him.

43 See photograph of Jung's sketch, with translation: Figure 4.2, p. 122. The large, diamond-shaped diagram, with its ascending and descending quaternities, recalls both Hermetic and Kabbalistic diagrams of the Tree of Life. (Cf. "Gnostic Symbols of the Self," CW 9.ii, *Aion*, chaps XIII–XIV.) Thanks to Connie Eichenlaub of the Seattle Jung Society and to Ken Kimmel of the Jung Institute of Seattle, who brought my attention in 2003 to the philosphical and religious ancestries of Jung's diagram.

44 Adler guesses (*Letters I*, p. 503n) the promised visitor may have been Raymond Hostie, SJ (cf. *Letters II*, pp. 244f), then still a seminary student at Louvain.

45 Typewritten.

46 Cf. Jung, 30 Jan. 1948. White's reply is missing.

47 White spoke to the APC of San Francisco on 23 April 1948 at the home of Dr. and Mrs. Joseph Henderson on "The problem of the Catholic analysant" (Minutes of 1947–48, APC of San Francisco library archive).

48 Harold Fowler McCormick (1898–1973): Chicago industrialist, an old friend of Jung, whom he accompanied on journeys to New Mexico (1924–25) and India (1938). In later years in Zurich, he often took Jung and Ruth Bailey (p. 215 and note) on auto excursions (cf *Letters II*, pp. 5f, note).

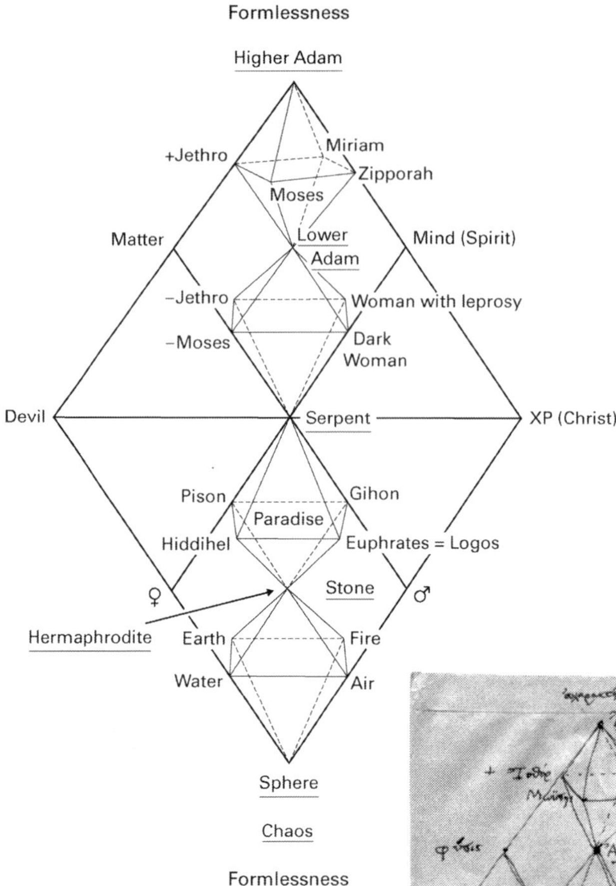

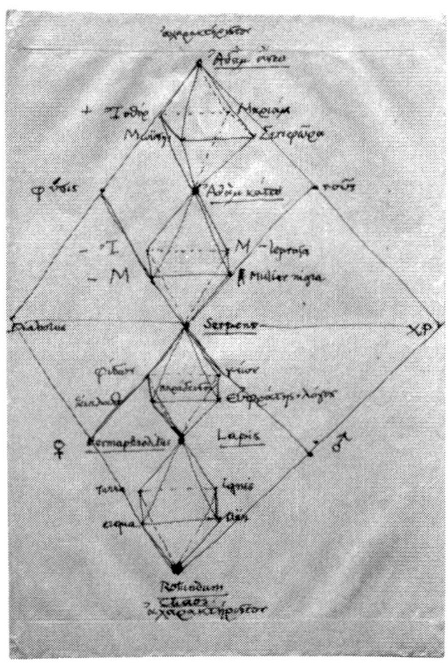

Figure 4.2 In his letter of 21 May 1948, Jung enclosed a sketch of interlocking "quaternios" drawn in pen on the back of a manilla envelope (photograph). (Diagram, upper left, trans. ACL.) Five separate figures from this sketch, the Moses, Anthropos, Shadow, Paradise and Lapis quaternities, were later published (*Aion*, CW 9.ii, pp. 227, 231, 236, 238). Another figure, also derived from this sketch, relates four quaternities hierarchically (Ibid., p. 247). One polarity belonging to "Lapis" in the 1948 sketch (female/male; Stone/Hermaphrodite) is omitted from the published diagrams in *Aion*.

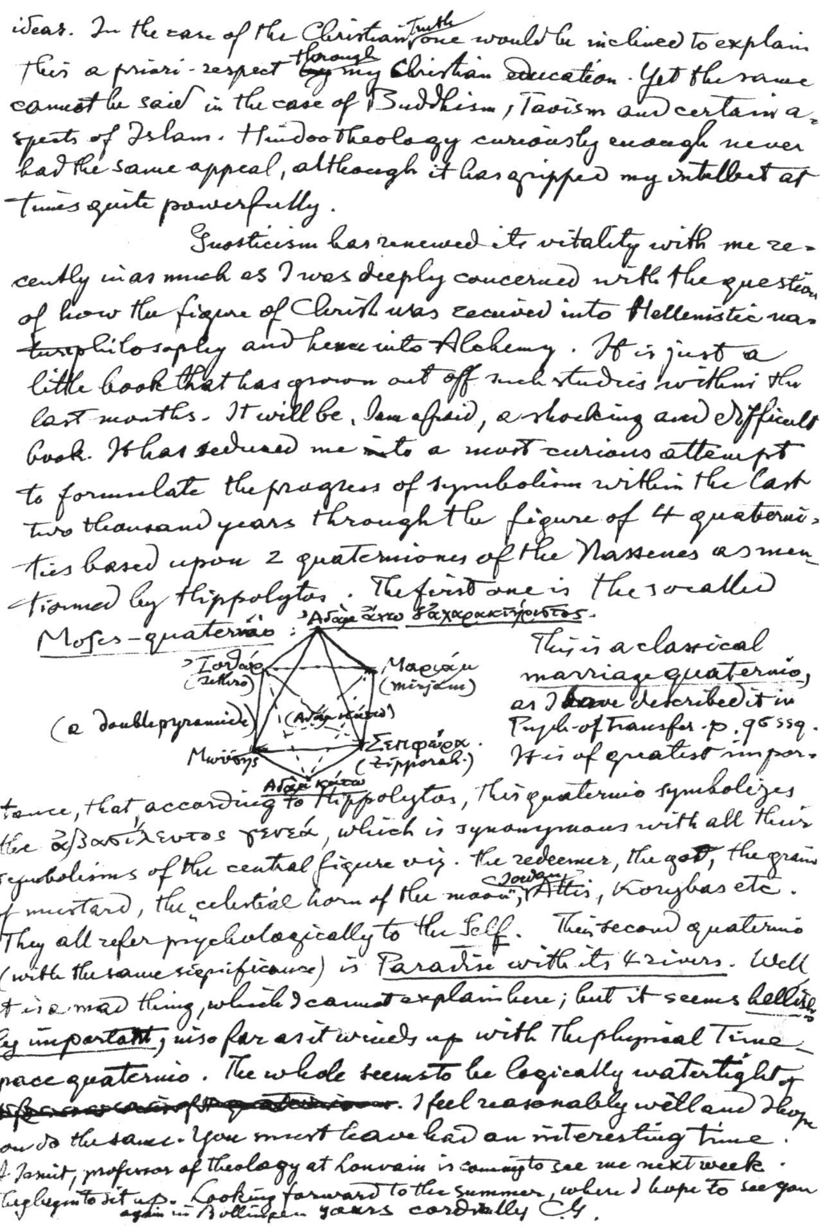

ideas. In the case of the Christian truth one would be inclined to explain this a priori-respect through my Christian education. Yet the same cannot be said in the case of Buddhism, Taoism and certain aspects of Islam. Hindoo theology curiously enough never had the same appeal, although it has gripped my intellect at times quite powerfully.

Gnosticism has renewed its vitality with me recently in as much as I was deeply concerned with the question of how the figure of Christ was received into Hellenistic philosophy and hence into Alchemy. It is just a little book that has grown out of such studies within the last months. It will be, I am afraid, a shocking and difficult book. It has seduced me into a most curious attempt to formulate the progress of symbolism within the last two thousand years through the figure of 4 quaternities based upon 2 quaterniones of the Naassenes as mentioned by Hippolytus. The first one is the so called Moses-quaternio: Ἀδὰμ ἄνω ὁ ἀχαρακτήριστος.

Ἰοθόρ (Jethro)
Μαριάμ (Mirjam)
(a double pyramide)
(Ἀδὰμ κάτω)
Μωϋσῆς
Σεπφώρα (Zipporah)
Ἀδὰμ κάτω

This is a classical marriage quaternio, as I have described it in Psych. of Transfer. p. 95 ssq. It is of greatest importance, that, according to Hippolytus, this quaternio symbolizes the ἀβασίλευτος γενεά, which is synonymous with all their symbolisms of the central figure viz. the redeemer, the god, the grain of mustard, the celestial horn of the moon, Jordan, Attis, Korybas etc. They all refer psychologically to the Self. The second quaternio (with the same significance) is Paradise with its 4 rivers. Well it is a mad thing, which I cannot explain here; but it seems hellishly important, in so far as it winds up with the physical Time-space quaternio. The whole seems to be logically watertight. I feel reasonably well and hope you do the same. You must have had an interesting time. A Jesuit, professor of theology at Louvain is coming to see me next week. They begin to sit up. Looking forward to the summer, when I hope to see you again in Bollingen yours cordially C.G.

Figure 4.3 Final page of Jung's letter of 21 May 1948, containing the "Moses-quaternio."

I was tremendously gratified – and perhaps rather surprised – about what you say of my "Gnosticism" paper; especially about the "Pistis Sophia" part, which was quite a wild hit in the dark. What you tell me of your "history of symbolism" is quite tantalizing: I guess I must await its publication before I "understand" that intriguing "Moses Quaternio". I am sure it is hellish important, but I am as yet very perplexed at *this* disposition of Moses with his relations. I am very struck, however, by the identity of its *shape* with that of the stone in Barbara Robb's tug-of-war with you – a symbol which, by the way, has subsequently developed in a most remarkable and (to me) illuminating way. Incidentally, have you noticed that C.G. Carus[49] seems to have had your marriage-quaternio all set out just as in your own "Ps. der Übertragung"[50] (cf. Bernouli, Die psychologie des C.G. Carus, S.39)?[51]

I should of course simply love to come and see you at Bollingen again this year and discuss these and other things. I am most grateful to you for asking me. But the only time I could possibly come would be in early SEPTEMBER, as I shall not be back in England until late August. *Would this be too late for you?* I am rather afraid that this time would clash with your needed repose after the Eranos Tagung. But if you assure me it would not, I will set about seeing what I can do to get the necessary extension of my leave of absence (which may not be too easy after having had a whole year off!) as well as the dollars! It would certainly be grand to be with you at Bollingen again.

I confess that I am not relishing the idea either of leaving U.S.A. or returning to England and getting back again into harness, and the old routine and responsibilities. I really do like it over here immensely; and by and large I seem to get on very well with the people, though I find that they differ enormously from place to place. But few of them seem to suffer from the frustrations and inhibitions of Europeans; I always feel I know where I am with them, and even their neuroses seem comparatively straightforward and uncomplicated. All this is perhaps largely a projection of the freedom of my own situation over here; but it does not alter the fact that I shall be very, very sorry to leave. Added to this has been a curious recurrence of dreams in which I find myself back in England (usually before I am due there) in a state of acute, claustrophobic anxiety – though the dreams never seem to show anything to be anxious about. I have been able to make very little sense at all of these dreams.

What you say of Faith interests me profoundly: indeed I think it is crucial.

49 Carl Gustav Carus (1798–1869): German artist, scientist, psychologist, and professor in the Department of Gynecology & Obstetrics, School of Medicine, University of Dresden.

50 "Psychology of the Transference."

51 Christoph Bernoulli (b. 1897): German psychologist; taught at the Marbacher Institute. Full title: *Die Psychologie des C.G. Carus und deren geistesgeschichtliche Bedeutung* [The Psychology of C.G. Carus and its Significance in the History of Ideas] (1925).

I am not sure how far my own limited experience and reflection here concurs, and how far it may conflict, with yours. The old medieval analysis of faith into "Credo in Deum", "Credo Deo" and "Credo Deum"[52] might help to sort this out; (it is odd that I was expounding this to you in the dream of long ago which I mentioned in a previous letter!). I too find that the basic teachings of Buddhism and the fundamental Taoistic ideas compel my involuntary respect; but, for my part, I'll be damned if I've much involuntary respect for the Christian creeds! What more eminently sane and sensible and rational than the Middle Way, the Four Aryan Truths, the Eightfold Path? What more respectable – even Hegelian – than the emanation of all from the Nameless opposites? I cannot help respecting it, whether I will to or no; but it conveys to me no mystery. I can put no *faith* in it at all. On the other hand: an all mighty Father-Maker, Jesus his son . . . conceived by the Spirit, born of a virgin, dead, risen, ascended in heaven: I do not understand how one can have any *respect* for a yarn like that, least of all involuntarily. So I am perplexed – or dreadfully lacking in the anima naturaliter christiana.[53]

All this is rather in the air: just my immediate personal reaction to what you say. But what profoundly moves me is your "my lifework is essentially an attempt to understand what others apparently can believe", and I am tempted to comment, "I have not found such great faith in Israel"![54] St Anselm's famous formula, "I do not seek to understand in order that I may believe, I believe in order that I may understand" seems to me alone to be able to co-ordinate Pistis and Gnosis,[55] or – shall we say – "Credo quia impossibile" and "Quaero quod impossibile".[56]

I am intrigued to hear of the visit of the Louvain Jesuit;[57] and I am wondering who he is and how the interview went off. I am thankful to hear you are "reasonably well", and hope the "reasonably" is only a very mild qualification. Please do not bother to reply to this meandering letter; only I would ask you to ask Miss Schmid to send me a line fairly soon to say whether or

52 "I believe in God" . . . "I believe (trust) God" . . . "I believe that God exists." (Thanks to Dr. Arthur Holder for his help with this and several other Latin translations.)

53 naturally Christian soul. A phrase of Tertullian (c.161–c.225), one of the early Fathers of the Church, from his *Apologeticus*. White was familiar with Jung's appreciation of this formula, as pointing to the inherent reality of a religious process in the psyche. (Cf. CW 6, *Types*, §19, §28; also CW 11, *Psych. & Rel.*, §771.)

54 Matthew 8.10; Luke 7.9: Jesus says this of a Roman centurian. White went on to publish this comment in a letter to *The Commonweal*, in which he refuted an attack by H.A. Reinhold on Jung and Jung's life at Bollingen. (Cf. White, 6 Aug. 1948, p. 127 and note.)

55 faith . . . knowledge.

56 "I believe because it is impossible" . . . "I inquire about the impossible." These phrases, from Tertullian's *De carne Christi*, signify the priority of faith over reason when the two are irreconcilable. White was undoubtedly familiar with Jung's description of Tertullian as an introverted thinker, who practiced self-denial by the sacrifice of intellect (CW 6, *Types*, §17f, pp. 12ff).

57 Cf. Jung, 21 May 1948, p. 121 and note.

not early September would be a suitable time for me to come and see you. Please remember me to her (I fear I never thanked her for her very welcome Xmas greetings); and also of course to Mrs Jung and all my friends.

Ever cordially, VICTOR

Küsnacht-Zch.

June 21st 1948[58]

Dear Father White,

Professor Jung asked me to send you his best greetings and many thanks for your letter, and also to let you know that the first part of September would suit him very well. He just has had a week's holiday on the Rigi and consequently feels very well, but unfortunately he got swamped by people and things on his return and so was afraid that you would have to wait too long if he waited to be able to write to you personally. His having too much to do is really getting worse and worse – but fortunately he keeps well by having small holidays in between.

I hope that you are well yourself and that you haven't turned quite "american" yet!

With all best wishes,

yours very sincerely, [Marie-Jeanne Schmid]
(unsigned carbon copy)

Ridgely
Stone Ridge, N.Y.

August 6th 1948[59]

My dear C.G.,

I am not sure whether or not I have told you that I am all fixed up to arrive at Zurich on September 6th. – and to fly back on September 14th. I am looking forward to it immensely.

58 Typewritten.

59 Typewritten on folding "U.S. Postal Service Air Letter."

As it seems to be impossible for me to take any money at all out of England, I shall shortly be sending a few dollars to M.-J. Schmid in the hope that she or somebody will be able to meet me at the airport (where I am due at 11:45 a.m. on the 6th) with enough francs to bring me to Bollingen or Küsnacht – as the case may be.

Under separate cover I am sending you – with blushes – two issues of a weekly called "The Commonweal".[60] I fear you may be justly annoyed with the indiscretions of the idyllic picture of "Bollingen" in my letter in the second of these:[61] my only excuse (and of course it is not really an excuse) is that the cracks about you and Bollingen[62] in the review of Zimmer[63] got me mad – in the American if not in the British sense of the word. I do hope I have not been *too* indiscreet: I am painfully aware that I was altogether too hasty. The article, in the earlier issue,[64] is not worth YOUR reading: but it seems to have caused quite a lot of excitement over here. Americans are very easily pleased!

I do hope and pray you are well, and ready for the rigours of Ascona. I sail

60 *The Commonweal: A Review of Religion, Politics, and Culture*, an independent journal, managed and published since 1924 in New York City by progressive lay Catholics. It is no longer a weekly but publishes 22 issues per year.

61 White's letter responding to Reinhold's review appeared in *Commonweal*, 13 August 1948, followed immediately by Reinhold's reply. White wrote: "Your readers . . . may be surprised to learn that 'Bollingen' is no more than a tiny, rural lakeside cottage which lacks the most elementary of modern conveniences. There for several months of the year live the seventy-two-year-old Dr. Jung and his wife, without servants, electricity, gas, indoor sanitation or any more water than can be pumped and carried with their own hands. . . . I have no wish to publicize these trivial domestic intimacies, of which I happen to have been the witness and sharer; I am painfully aware that such publicity must be distasteful to my hosts. But Father Reinhold's highly imaginative intrusion compels me to record that the holy poverty and simplicity of living that I have found at Bollingen might shame many a cloister or rectory. I am tempted also to add that I have seldom found such faith in Israel" (Victor White, O.P., Stone Ridge, N.Y., "Communications": "The King and the Corpse," *Commonweal*, 13 August 1948, p. 424).

62 The 23 July 1948 *Commonweal* featured a negative review of Zimmer's book by an American Catholic priest, H.A. Reinhold, who used the occasion to issue a personal attack on Jung: "Let us remember the Bollingen Series has its name from Bollingen, the Swiss sanctum of Freud's counterpart, Jung, who once supposedly sympathized with the philosophy of Nazism." His review concludes: "If we ever let the mad Shiva dance in our midst, tired of our effort to see the Creator's face in history . . . then André Gide, Arthur Koestler, Nietzsche, Hitler and Bollingen (financed by tired heirs) will become prophets and then God help us" (*Commonweal*, 23 July 1948, pp. 357f). Called to task by White for repeating unfounded rumors, Reinhold quickly apologized for maligning Jung's character (*Commonweal*, 13 August 1948, p. 425). He pointedly did not retract his warnings about Jung's and Zimmer's false religious teachings.

63 Heinrich Zimmer (1890–1943): German Indologist, friend of Jung, professor at Columbia University. Authored many books, including, posthumously, *The King and the Corpse* (Ed. Joseph Campbell. Bollingen Series XI. New York: Pantheon, 1948).

64 White's earlier essay, "The Analyst and the Confessor" (*Commonweal*, 23 July 1948, pp. 346–49), would become Chapter IX in his *God & Unc*.

for England on the 21st.: somewhat bewildered as to just what it is that America has done to me and what awaits me on the other side!

With every best wish to yourself and to Mrs Jung and everybody,

Ever cordially, VICTOR O.P.

Küsnacht-Zürich

August 12th 1948[65]

Dear Father White,

Professor Jung asked me to reply to your letter of August 6th and above all to send you his cordial greetings.

He also asked me to let you know that if he is at all well enough he would like to meet you at Dübendorf (I suppose it is) on September 6th, 11:45 a.m. himself, as he rather enjoys meeting people on the aerodrome. If for some reason he cannot do so, I shall be there or – in case I should have to be away then, Mr. Müller the old gardener-chauffeur who knows you. In any case you will be met with the necessary funds.

Since I last wrote to you Professor Jung has unfortunately had a relapse and he is back in Küsnacht. He is almost quite well again but under the circumstances he has decided not to go to Ascona, as the strain of it would certainly be too much, and also he needs to have a real holiday very badly. This has nothing to do with your visit to which he is looking forward very much.

I shall be here until the 22nd (when I shall have to go to Ascona to "represent" Professor Jung after a fashion)[66] and shall let you know either to Ridgely or Oxford as soon as the dollars have arrived. As my holidays have been postponed to September I'm not quite sure to be here still on September 6th, but I hope so.

With all good wishes for a pleasant trip to England and a good taking up of things in Oxford,

Yours very sincerely, [Marie-Jeanne] (unsigned on carbon copy)

I'm glad to dropped [sic] the "Miss Schmid"!

65 Typewritten.

66 Jung's health prevented his attending the 1948 Eranos Tagung to present his lecture, "Über das Selbst," on which he had been working with such energy (cf. Jung, 21 May 1948, pp. 119ff).

Bollingen

Sept. 24th 1948[67]

My dear Victor,

Your letter reminds me, that, no sooner you had left,[68] I discovered, nicely stowed away in my mail bag, your article in Commonweal.[69] Sorry! I never opened that bag, because I felt rather rotten in the beginning of my vacations. I am very grateful to you, that you took up the revenging sword in my favour. Reinhold's article[70] is immeasurably stupid and prejudiced. There is such a thing as intellectual responsibility of which R. seems to be unaware. Such people poison the spiritual atmosphere.

In my rather distracted mental state I quite forgot to ask you a question which has been on my mind for a long time: it is the *Anima Christi*.[71] I refer to the meditation on the anima Christi in the Exercitia Spiritualia S.Ignatii.[72] What is the a.XP^{i}?[73] Has XP an "anima"? By which I mean "Soul". XP is God. Has God a Soul? It cannot very well be the human anima rationalis.[74] It would have no place beside God. It seems as if God were His soul. But what does the "Anima XP^{i}" mean then?

I should be much obliged, if you would kindly enlighten me about the Teaching of the Church in this respect.[75] No hurry! You are probably busy enough after your long absence.

67 Handwritten. 68 White had visited Jung at the Tower, 6–14 Sept. 1948.

69 Cf. White, 6 Aug. 1948, p. 127 and note.

70 H.A. Reinhold's review in *Commonweal*. (Ibid).

71 Soul of Christ. A prayer in Catholic tradition, often used as a private Eucharistic devotion, begins: "Soul of Christ, sanctify me, Body of Christ, save me." Attributed to St. Ignatius, who quotes it at the beginning of his *Spiritual Exercises*, it may actually date to the early fourteenth century. (*ODCC*, p. 58.)

72 Spiritual Exercises of St. Ignatius. Ignatius of Loyola (1495–1556), founder of the Jesuit Order, wrote a famous treatise on sanctification, *The Spiritual Exercises*, begun in 1522 and completed over the remainder of his life (*ODCC*, pp. 689f, pp. 1300f). In the 1930s Jung had offered lectures on this treatise at the ETH, which Rivkah Schärf took down in shorthand and Barbara Hannah later transcribed for informal publication under the title, "The Process of Individuation: Exercitia Spiritualia of St. Ignatius of Loyola, Notes on Lectures given at the ETH, Zürich, June 1939–March 1940."

73 Jung's abbreviation (mixing Latin and Greek) for *anima Christi*.

74 rational soul. A term used by Aquinas to distinguish angels and humans from lower creatures, which have lesser forms of soul. Jung's logical question is whether Christ, being God, can be said to have a creaturely soul.

75 It is evident that White answered this question in detail (cf. Jung, 8 Jan. 1949, p. 135). Unfortunately his reply has not survived. To Jung's question, Adler observes: "The Council of Chalcedon, 451, formulated the doctrine of the two natures of Christ as 'at once truly God and truly man of reasonable soul and body'. As God he is pure spirit and thus has no soul; as man he has man's *anima rationalis*" (*Letters I*, p. 506n).

Since a fortnight we have here a real summer. I was so full of pep that I have overdone my wood chopping a bit. I have to keep quiet now, writing letters and doing some scientific work about the Antichrist.[76] You remember the two fishes, Satan discovered swimming on the dark waters?[77] They have perhaps some connection with the two martyrs (testes) in the Apocalypse. A mediaeval text says about them: "Sibylla nuncupat eos duo stellas".[78] This might refer back to the coniunctio of Jupiter and Saturn in XPs nativity. As duo stellae announced the first coming of XP, so they appear to be the praesagium[79] of His second coming. Jupiter and Saturn are a contrast: ♃ is beneficus,[80] ♄ is a typical maleficus,[81] the *sol niger*[82] of the alchemists. It is remarkable that the praesagium consists in either case in a complexio oppositorum.[83] It would point to a secret intention to make a mediator oppositorum[84] of XP, i.e. an incarnation of the archetype of the Self.

By the way: the earliest use of the word "ἀρχέτυπος"[85] I have just found, occurs in *Philo*:[86] de opificio mundi §69,[87] referring to the εἰκὼν τοῦ Θεοῦ = "κατὰ; τὸν τῆς ψυχῆς ἡγεμόνα νοῦν".[88] Hitherto I had believed, that it first occurs in the *Corpus Hermeticum*[89] "θεὸς τὸ ἀρχέτυπον

76 Cf. CW 9.ii, *Aion*, §130, §156, et passim.

77 Ibid., §225–30, pp. 145ff.

78 "The Sibyl names them two stars."

79 harbinger, foreteller.

80 benefactor, doer of good.

81 evil-doer, malefactor.

82 black sun. Adler comments, "Black sun or 'counter-sun' . . ., the shadow of the sun or the sun itself in its negative aspect. It also symbolizes the alchemical states of *nigredo*, blackness . . . and *putrefactio*, both necessary for the achievement of the opus" (*Letters I*, p. 507n). To this Jaffé adds: "Compare *Psychology and Alchemy*, Figure 34, and *Mysterium Coniunctionis I*, §114. The image of the *ignis niger* (black fire) is used in alchemy in the sense of the *ignis gehennalis* (the fire of hell)" (*Briefe I*, p. 400, trans. ACL).

83 complex of opposites.

84 mediator of opposites.

85 (for ἀρχέτυπον?) "archetype." The word should probably be in the neuter, as in the quotation from the *Corpus Hermeticum* below.

86 Philo (c. 20 BC–c. AD 50): Jewish writer and exegete, from an Alexandrian priestly family. "The most important figure among Hellenistic Jews of his age and a fertile author," he made an eclectic combination of Jewish religious and Greek philosophical sources (*ODCC*, pp. 1083f).

87 On the Creation.

88 The image of God = "with reference to Mind, the sovereign element of the soul." From Philo: "Let no one represent the likeness as one to a bodily form; . . . No, it is in respect of the Mind, the sovereign element of the soul, that the word 'image' is used . . ." (*On the Creation* I. Trans. Colson & Whitaker. Cambridge, MA: Harvard University Press, 1929/1949/1956/1962/1971, §69, p. 55).

89 A Neoplatonist work from the third or fourth century AD, to which Jung refers several times in letters and in published works, when discussing historical sources of the word "archetype." Jung first connected the term "archetype" to the *Corpus Hermeticum* in his paper "Instinct and the Unconscious" ("Instinkt und Unbewusstes," trans. by H.G. and Cary Baynes), which he presented at a London symposium of the same name in 1919 (cf. CW 8, *Structure & Dynamics*, Part III, §263, §275). In his 1934 Eranos lecture, "Archetypes of the Collective Unconscious" (known to White as a chapter in *Integration*, but revised in 1954) he refers again to this work but gives historical priority to Philo and Irenaeus (cf. CW 9.i, *The Archetypes and the Collective Unconscious*, §5, p. 4 and notes).

φῶς".[90] *S. Augustinus* does not use "archetypus" as I once erroneously surmised,[91] only the idea, but it occurs in *Dionysius Areopagita*.[92]

Hoping your weather is as fine as ours I remain

Yours cordially C.G.

P.S. The "Symbolik des Geistes"[93] will soon reach you. The details mentioned above might interest your friend the ἐξηγέτης.[94]

Bollingen

Sept. 30th 1948[95]

Dear Victor,

I quite forgot in my last letter to tell you how much I appreciated your article on Confession and Analysis.[96] Its a remarkably clear exposition of the difference between the two methods.[97] I'm very glad to have it.

Cordially yours, C.G. JUNG.

90 "God the archetypal light." The phrase τὸ ἀρχέτυπον φῶς occurs in the second book of *Corpus Hermeticum*, "The Discourse of Hermes Trismegistus to Asclepius" (Scott, *Hermetica*, I, §126, p. 140). (Cf. *Letters I*, p. 360n.)

91 In his 1919 lecture, "Instinct and the Unconscious" (op. cit.), Jung had credited Augustine with the term "archetypus." In its original form, as "Instinkt und Unbewusstes," this lecture was published in *Energetik* 1928. Later, when he revised it for republication in *Energetik* 1948, Jung added a footnote explaining that the idea was Augustine's, but "the actual term 'archetype' . . . is to be found in Dionysius the Areopagite and in the *Corpus Hermeticum*" (CW 8, *Structure & Dynamics*, §275n).

92 Greek Christian writer, also known as Dionysius the Pseudo-Areopagite, who probably lived and wrote in Syria around 500 AD. His writings, mistakenly attributed to the Dionysius baptized by St. Paul (Acts 17.34), deeply influenced medieval Christian theologians (*ODCC*, pp. 405ff). The word ἀρχέτυπον occurs in his *De divinis nominibus*, 2.5; 4.1; and in *De coelesti hierarchia*, 3.3.1; 3.3.7; 4.3.1 (*Letters I*, p. 507n).

93 Cf. Jung, 23 March 1946, p. 29 and note.

94 (for ἐξηγήτης) exegete. I.e., Richard Kehoe (cf. White, 23 Oct. 1945, p. 17 and note; 27 Dec. 1947, p. 108).

95 Plain postcard, typewritten by secretary, signed by Jung. Previously unpublished.

96 Cf. White, 6 Aug. 1948, p. 127 and note.

97 Jung had written of confession as the first stage of analysis in his 1929 article, "Problems of Modern Psychotherapy" (CW 16, *Transference*, §114–74, pp. 53–75). [MS]

Küsnacht-Zürich

Dec. 16th 1948[98]

Dear Victor,

The spirit prompts me to write to you. It is quite a while since I have heard of you and very much longer since I have heard you really. I may be all wrong, but I confess to have a feeling, as if when you were in America a door had been shut, softly but tightly. I don't want to disturb you, but I feel as if I ought to tell you about my phantasy, so that you know my side of the picture at least. I know there are things somewhere too damned difficult to be even mentioned, but they should not cut you off entirely. It is not bad for you to get a breath from the great wind of the world occasionally and from all the dark things "that go bump in the night". That is why I take the liberty to knock at your door. I suppose you are very busy. Don't feel pressed for an answer, please! I am looking for my own peace and that is the reason why I tell you about my qualms. Having done so I recline in my grandfather's chair going on dreaming about Virgilius' "Tityra tu recubans sub Tegmina fagi. . . ."[99]

Light that wants to shine, needs darkness.

Cordially yours, C.G.

98 Handwritten.

99 "Tityrus, thou liest canopied beneath thy spreading beech" (Virgil, *Eclogue* I, 1) (*Letters I*, p. 514).

1949

Bollingen

Jan. 8th 1949[1]

Dear Victor,

Thank you cordially for your nice human letter![2] I know now at least, where you are. I was afraid, America had spirited you away altogether. It is of course just like myself to forget your most helpful and comprehensive letter about the anima XP[i],[3] i.e. to forget to thank you. As a matter of fact I felt particularly grateful to you for having answered my request so thoroughly. Such things happen to me time and again and always have happened, namely that my feelings or a certain kind of them are suddenly no more in sight, especially in that moment, where I should acknowledge them. That's how the inferior function behaves.

I suppose, this Mrs. [. . .] is the one that was in Zürich, doing Analysis with Dr. J. Jacobi. If that is the case I don't envy you for your neighbourhood. She is precisely the person, that should never do analysis. I hope you are not called upon to be interested in her in any way.

Your cryptic remarks about "synchronistic effects" on Dec. 16th[4] arouse my curiosity, since I feel peculiarly innocent as to ulterior motives of my letter. This feeling of innocence may prove the contrary. I am sorry, you can't tell me more about it. On my side it was an inner urge that prompted me to write. I felt a need to hear from you. The effect, America had upon you, looks exactly like something, that went right through to the unconscious, whence it will appear again, after a more or less prolongated incubation, in a new form.

The combination of Priest and Medicine Man is not so impossible as you seem to think.[5] They are based upon a common archetype, which will assert its right, provided your inner development will continue as hitherto. It is true, the "fringe" of new things is always made up by funny figures. I imagine we could have observed very similar lunatics among the early christian followers, f.i. those people, which were cured from possessions. After all England and our old world is your Rhodus, hic salta![6] One's anxiety always points out our

1 Handwritten.

2 Two important letters are missing, written by White in 1948, as Adler notes (cf. *Letters I*, pp. 506n, 516n), the "nice human letter" mentioned here, and the letter containing White's answer to the question, about the "*anima Christi*."

3 Cf. Jung, 24 Sept. 1948, p. 129.

4 Cf. Jung, 16 Dec. 1948, inquiring about White's long silence (p. 132).

5 This paragraph appears to contain Jung's discussion of a personal dilemma, probably posed in a dream described by White in the missing letter.

6 "[Here is] Rhodes, jump here!" In a tale by Aesop, a man boasts of making a huge jump in Rhodes and is challenged to perform the feat where he stands.

task. If you escape it, you have lost a piece of yourself and at that a most problematic piece, with which the Creator of things was going to experiment in His unforseeable ways. They are indeed apt to arouse anxiety! Particularly so, as long as [you] can't see below the surface. The independent mind in you is subject and object of the divine experiment. It needs (in the shape of "True-Man") the Declaration of Independence at Oxford. New libido (= money) is ready for a new attitude (new clothes). If you feel isolated in England, why don't you make one of your fratres into a real brother in the spirit. When I came to Zürich, the most materialistic city of Switzerland, there was nobody ready made for my needs. I then shaped some for me. They were meant for this experience. One could see it from their dreams.

Sorry, this is a long letter again. Don't trouble to answer it.

Yours cordially, C.G.

Blackfriars, Oxford

5.5.49[7]

My dear C.G.

It is now months since I have been waiting the opportunity to write you a real long letter. Even now the opportunity has not come: these few lines can be little more than a brief salutation. But it comes with all my heart.

The difficulty is not only one of time: somehow I am so weary after constant concern with the Ten Thousand Things that it's hard to get into touch with Reality at all – let alone get it onto paper! The Creator of things is doubtless (to quote your last most welcome letter) up to some experiment.

Some while ago I had a curious but refreshing dream – "deep" & correspondingly obscure & untranslatable. I was with you on the Obersee[8] in some strange kind of *motor* boat; on the far side from Bollingen & travelling East(!)wards.[9] At a given point you did something to the engine, which thereby, although still running, became quite silent & somehow "spiritual". There was some ineffable conformity of the silence of the engine with the silence of the environment. As the boat glided silently & speedily, the water rose to make a "channel" for us on either side (cf. the Israelites' passage of the Red Sea!). Then the silence was suddenly broken by a terrific explosion

7 Handwritten.

8 Upper Lake Zurich. Cf. Jung, 13 April 1946, p. 32 and note.

9 White had written "Westwards," then crossed out the first syllable, writing "East(!)" above it.

on the shore – behind us to the left, in the neighborhood of Wormsbach[10] or Jona. Somehow this explosion divided the air in the same way as our boat divided the water.

Now I write it out, it seems hardly even coherent, let alone impressive. But somehow it was – very.

I am quite particularly eager to come & see you this summer, and, if possible, to laze at Bollingen. I am more grateful than ever for your invitation.[11] I think my most likely opportunity will be some time between July 18th & August 2nd. Would some days during this time suit you? If so, & if you could be so good as to let me know which, I will set about trying to fix it up at once. Otherwise, I might be able to get away in the second half of August; but it will be less easy.

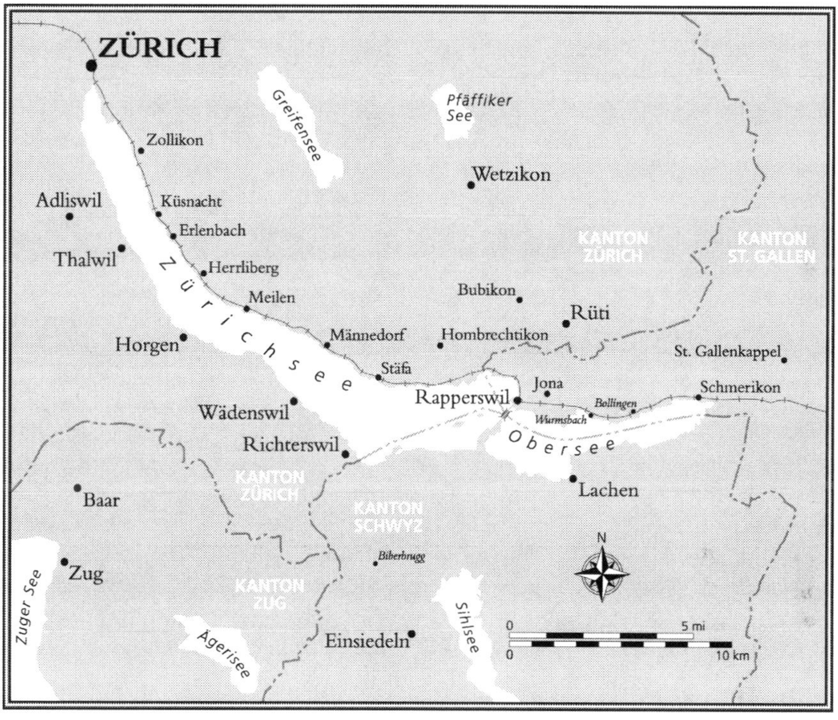

Figure 5.1 The area around Lake Zurich and the Upper Lake, based on a 1948 map of the region.

10 For Wurmsbach: located west of Bollingen on Upper Lake Zurich, near Jona (see Figure 5.1, above): location of a cloister of Cistercian nuns, founded in the Middle Ages.

11 Jung's invitation to White, to visit again in 1949, is missing from the collection.

I have just heard (via Ed. Thornton & Marie-Jeanne) that you've just gone to Bollingen. So I hope this finds you there, & that you, Mrs Jung & all are in very good health & spirits. I am so looking forward to seeing you all again.

Ever cordially, VICTOR

Küsnacht-Zürich

14th of May[12]

Dear Victor!

The time you point out in July would suit me. Your dream[13] is very interesting indeed, but demands more than a few remarks in a letter. It deals with the problem arising when you are not *west*ward bound. This travel motive seems to be part of a peregrinatio spiritualis.[14] Please let me know, when you plan to arrive in Zürich. I am very busy just now; which explains why my letter is so short.

Cordially yours C.G.

Gracedieu
Boar's Hill, Oxford

19.5.49[15]

My dear C.G.,

Thank you so much for your note. I will write you later when I have dates fixed. It will probably be about July 20th.

I have escaped from the City for a couple of days, & finding time to read last year's Eranos Jahrbuch.[16] It is most impressive.

Meanwhile – warmest greetings to you & all.

VICTOR

12 Handwritten, no year given. Based on content, this is Jung's reply to White, 5 May 1949. Letter previously unpublished.

13 Cf. White, 5 May 1949, p. 136f.

14 spiritual pilgrimage.

15 Handwritten note.

16 Refers to *EJ 1947, 1948*. White was preparing to review Jung's 1948 lecture, "Über das Selbst" (cf. Jung, 31 Dec. 1949, pp. 140f and note).

Blackfriars, Oxford

30.5.49[17]

Dear C.G.

I have just read your "Ulysses"[18] for the first time. It's *marvellous*. I only wish I'd known it years ago to tell me what it was the book was doing to me – & others!

Very gratefully, VICTOR

Küsnacht-Zürich

June 13th 1949.[19]

Dear Father White,

I'm sorry your last letter wasn't answered before, but I had to send it on to Bollingen where Dr. Jung spent a short holiday and he has only just come back. He asked me to let you know that it would be quite all right for you to be here on his birthday.[20] So you could come on the 19th or later – just as it suits you best.

I shall probably still be hard at work when you come but I hope that I shall have a glimpse of you at least.

Best wishes till then!

Yours ever, MARIE-JEANNE (unsigned carbon copy)

Blackfriars, Oxford

30.6.49[21]

My dear C.G.

I am looking forward enormously to seeing you. Not now being in possession of a Swiss timetable, I cannot be sure of the exact time of my

17 Handwritten postcard, sent by air.

18 Jung's essay, "Ulysses" (*European Review*, Vol. VIII, 2/9, 1932), was published in English first as "Ulysses, a Monologue" (*Spring 1949*, trans. W. Stanley Dell, for private circulation. New York: Analytical Psychology Club, 1949, pp. 1–20). Later in CW 15, *The Spirit in Man, Art and Literature*.

19 Typewritten from holograph.

20 Jung celebrated his 74th birthday on 26 July 1949.

21 Handwritten.

arrival, but all being well, it will be in the afternoon of Tuesday July 19th. I expect to arrive in Zürich in the morning, where Marie-Jeanne has kindly offered to meet me with some Wherewithal.[22]

I am glad to hear from her that you & Mrs Jung are very well. I too seem to be coming to life again after rather a black year, & am now fighting fit.

I have some very strange alchemical goings-on to relate to you if you are interested. They include an indubitable prediction of the first three horses of the Derby[23] – as well as of the fact that they would be (except for the "photo-finish") neck-and-neck! And all from contemplation of the Pisces – the winning horses were Nimbus (Halo-Cloud), Swallowtail (Ouroboros) and Amour-Drake (Love-Hero).

It makes no "sense" to me, but the chances being one in billions of billions (or so I am told) I've not been able to resist the facts. I will bring the documents with me, in case you would like to see them.

Meanwhile, all best to you & Mrs Jung,

Ever cordially, VICTOR

Küsnacht-Zürich

31 XII 1949[24]

My dear Victor,

Before the old year goes to end, I should like to write to you – a thing, I tried since a while ago, but never found time enough. First we had (in the end of Oct.) a regrettable accident: my wife fell in the corridor (slipping on a carpet) and broke her right arm in the shoulder – a nasty fracture indeed. I had her in the hospital for 2 months. Then I myself was laid up with a gastric grippe and a troublesome liver; then Marie-Jeanne Sch. came down with a similar ailment, knocking her out completely. My correspondence and other obligations could and did go up the chimney i.e. they just dropped into Nirvana. Now I am reasonably well again and can write to you. You have kept me busy for a while with your "correctio fatuorum"[25] in the Dominican Studies![26] I have found it very interesting and illuminating and it has forced

22 It had become customary for White to send money ahead, so it could be exchanged before his arrival.

23 The Derby winners were predicted by Barbara Robb. (Cf. Jung, 21 Sept. 1951, p. 169.)

24 Handwritten.

25 "correction of fools."

26 White's review, "Eranos: 1947, 1948," focusses on Jung's 1948 Eranos lecture, "Über das Selbst" ["On the Self"]. He concludes that in attacking the Catholic definition of evil as a

me, to go as far back as *Basilius Magnus*,[27] who is the perpetrator of "omne malum a homine"[28] (Hom.II in Hex. Migne T.XXIX col.37 sqq.):[29] τῆς ἐν ἑαυτῷ κακίας ἕκαστος ἑαυτὸν ἀρχηγὸν γνωριξέτω.[30] Evil originates out of a "διάθεσις ἐν ψυχῇ"[31] and thus it is "οὐχὶ οὐσία ξῶσα".[32] It merely derives from "τὰ ῥαθυμία",[33] from carelessness and negligence, which are obviously "μὴ ὄν",[34] as they are merely psychological. As it is still so today: reduce something to a whim or an imagination, then it vanishes into μὴ ὄν, i.e. nothingness. I firmly believe however that psyche is an οὐσία.[35] I also took a dive into S.Thomas, but I did not feel refreshed afterwards. All and sundry disregard the fact, that good and evil are the equivalent moieties of a logical

privation of good, Jung has ignorantly fallen into an ancient heresy. White writes: "An elementary study of (for instance) St. Thomas's sections in the *Prima Pars* On the Good, On the Goodness of God, On Evil, and On the Cause of Evil, should suffice to dispel Dr Jung's misunderstandings and misgivings, and to supply a metaphysic which would account for the phenomena which concern him at least as satisfactorily as the quasi-manichaean dualism which he propounds. These somewhat confused and confusing pages might be dismissed as another infelicitous excursion of a great scientist outside his own orbit, were it not that the matter is one which is heavy in its consequences for psychology itself, and more especially for the understanding of the character of the Christian warfare. It is regrettable indeed that, supported only by such naïve philosophizing, the most pregnant movement in contemporary psychology should be burdened with an irrelevant association with gnostic dualism" ("Eranos: 1947, 1948," *Dominican Studies*, Vol. 2, No. 4, Oct. 1949, p. 399).

27 St. Basil the Great (c.330–379), Bishop of Caesarea and one of the Cappadocian Fathers, who had a profound influence on early Christian thought.

28 "all evil from humankind."

29 St. Basil's "Homilia II in Hexaemeron" ["Second Sermon on the Six Days"], *Patrologiae Cursus Completus: Patrologia Graeca*, ed. J.-P.Migne, Vol. XXIX (Paris: D'Amboise, 1837, columns 27–52, Greek text and Latin translation in facing columns). Jung cites from Greek, cols. 37ff.

30 "Each of us should acknowledge that he is the first author of the wickedness in him." Following this exchange with White, Jung added eight new paragraphs to his lecture "Über das Selbst" (cf. CW 9.ii, *Aion*, §81–88, pp. 46f), discussing this and other quotations from St.Basil in greater depth.

31 "condition of the soul."

32 "not a living entity" (Ibid.).

33 Probably for τα ῥάθυμα, "the easy things." Jung mistakenly combined a neuter plural article with a feminine singular noun. Adler silently corrects the error by deleting the plural article, translating the singular noun: "indifference, frivolity" (*Letters I*, p. 540n). The plural article is clear in Jung's holograph, however. As the change from noun to adjective is often signaled in Greek by "ι" (e.g., -ία), Jung's error may have come from a confusion in usage. The plural phrase also seems the best reading when paired with the appositive phrase that follows.

34 "non-being," "that which does not exist." Beginning with this letter Jung often uses the phrase "μὴ ὄν" as shorthand for what he sees as the perverse denial, by Catholic theologians, of the reality of evil. The phrase's likely origin is a related usage in St. Basil's sermon: "τὰ μὴ ὄντα" ("things which are not") (*Hexaemeron*, op. cit, col. 33), which in turn echoes St. Paul (Romans 4.17). In subsequent letters White objects strenuously to Jung's phrase, as linguistically incoherent (cf. White, 5 April 1952, p. 184 and note), a protest which adds heat but no light to their debate.

35 substance, essence; something existing.

judgement. They also omit to discuss at the same time the eternity of the devil, hell and damnation, that are certainly not μὴ ὄν and equally not good (i.e. good only to the heavenly spectators). This privatio boni[36] business is odious to me on account of its dangerous consequences: it causes a negative inflation of Man, who can't help imagining himself – though not as a source of the Good[37] – at least as a great destroyer, capable of devastating God's beautiful creation. This doctrine starts luciferic vanity and it is also greatly responsible for the fatal underrating of the human soul being the original abode of Evil. It gives a monstruous importance to the soul and not a word about upon whose account the presence of the Serpent in Paradise belongs!

The Question of Good and Evil inasmuch as I am concerned with it, has nothing to do with Metaphysics; it is only a concern of psychology. I make no metaphysical assertions and even in my heart I am no Neomanichean;[38] on the contrary I am deeply convinced of the unity of the Self, as demonstrated by the mandala symbolism. But dualism is lurking in the shadows of the Christian Doctrine: the devil will not be redeemed, nor shall come to an end eternal damnation. Origenes optimistically hoping or at least asking, whether the devil might not be redeemed in the end, was not exactly welcomed.[39]

36 privation of good. Term frequently used in the letters of Jung and White to refer to the classic Catholic teaching about evil. With roots in Platonism and Catholic theology, the "privative" theory of evil encapsulates the conclusion (argued by Plato, adopted by Augustine and systematized by Aquinas) that, since God is all-good and all-powerful and has created a good universe, what we call evil cannot be a self-sustaining entity or a natural part of creation. It must have only a parasitic existence, preying on, diminishing and distorting what is good. Jung had begun his polemic against the doctrine of *privatio boni* in his 1940 lecture on the Trinity (*EJ 1940/41*, p. 53). For an overview of Jung's argument, cf. CW 9.ii, *Aion*, esp. §74f, §89f, §98. For White's explication of the Catholic position, cf. *God & Unc.*, p. 75f; *Soul and Psyche*, ch. 9, "The Integration of Evil" (*Letters I*, p. 540n). Analysis of the dispute between Jung and White, concerning the problem of evil, is the topic of ch. VI ("Theodicy"), *IGS*, pp. 197ff.

37 The word "Good" is clear in Jung's handwritten original. Adler, however, in editing *C.G. Jung Letters*, substitutes the word "Evil" (*Letters I*, p. 540). This change is found also in Jaffé's German translation (*Briefe II*, p. 169). Jung's statement, as written, refers to the inflated human craving for divine power, which may take either a positive or a negative form. Perhaps we don't pretend to be the Creator, he says; but it is just as dangerous to ape the Destroyer.

38 Modern believer in the heresy of Manichaeism. Mani (c. 215–277): Babylonian philosopher, taught that the universe is ruled by two principles eternally in conflict – good and evil, light and dark. This teaching was rejected by the early Church as violating the first premise of monotheism, that there is only one God. In his review, "Eranos: 1947, 1948" (cf. p. 141n, above), White suggested that Jung had fallen into a form of this ancient dualism. Jung acknowledges White's criticism in an important footnote: "My learned friend Victor White, O.P. . . . thinks he can detect a Manichaean streak in me" (cf. CW 9.ii, *Aion*, §112, p. 61n).

39 Origen taught that ultimately all souls – of angels, humans and devils – share in the grace of salvation. "Origenist" heresies were condemned by Church councils in 400 and again in 543 (*ODCC*, pp. 1008ff), and many of Origen's writings were destroyed. (Cf. also Jung, 23 March 1946, p. 29 and note.)

As long as Evil is a, μὴ ὄν *nobody will take his own shadow seriously*. Hitler and Stalin go on representing a mere "accidental lack of perfection". *The future of mankind very much depends upon the recognition of the shadow*. Evil is psychologically speaking – *terribly real*. It is a fatal mistake to diminish its power and reality even merely metaphysically. I am sorry, this goes to the very roots of Christianity. Evil verily does not decrease by being hushed up as a non-reality or a mere negligence of Man. It was there before him, when he could not possibly have a hand in it. God is the mystery of all mysteries, a real Tremendum.[40] Good and Evil are psychological relativities and as such quite real, yet one does not know what they are. For this reason they should not be projected upon a transcendent being. Thus you avoid manichean dualism without petitiones principii[41] and other subterfuges. I guess I am a heretic.

You must have had an interesting time in Spain.[42] I had indeed not the faintest idea of what an English College in Valladolid[43] would do.

I know you must criticize me. I am decidedly not on the winning side, but most unpopular right and left. I don't know whether I deserve to be included in your prayer. Yet there is a consolation that has reached me across the gulf of an aeon: καὶ ὅπου εἷς ἔστω μόνσς, λέγω, ἐγώ εἰμι μετ᾽ αὐτοῦ.[44]

With all good wishes for a successful and happy New Year

Yours cordially C.G.

40 that which is awe-inspiring, overwhelming (from Latin root meaning "tremble"). Adler notes, "The German theologian Rudolf Otto (1869–1937), in his book *The Idea of the Holy* (trans. 1926; orig. 1917), defined the *Tremendum* as an aspect of the *numinosum*, "numinosity", which for him was the central characteristic of the Divinity" (*Letters I*, p. 541n).

41 the logical fallacy of appealing to principles to prove the same principles.

42 White evidently visited his "alma mater" in Spain (cf. next note), but this trip is not reported in any of his letters to Jung. Two long gaps in the 1949 correspondence, from January to May and June to December, suggest that one or more letters have been lost. Based on unpublished documents, White's visit to Spain probably occurred in October or November (White to a religious, 7 October 1949, English Province archive). [AC]

43 The English College of St. Alban in Valladolid, Spain, a seminary for English Catholics preparing for ordination, was founded in 1589, during the English Reformation. White studied there in his early twenties, before joining the Dominicans (cf. Appendix 2, "Victor White, a Memoir" p. 309).

44 "and where there is one alone I say I am with him" (James, *The Apocryphal New Testament*, Oxyrhynchus Papyrus I, logion x, p. 27) (*Letters I*, p. 541n).

1950

Blackfriars, Oxford

10.2.50[1]

My dear C.G.,

I was thrilled to get your long letter, but very sorry indeed to hear of your series of misfortunes. I do hope & pray that you & Mrs Jung & Marie-Jeanne are now fully recovered. The disappearance of correspondence & obligations into Nirvana can do no harm. I think you have done your bit as a Bodhisattva, & deserve to be a Buddha now!

Your letter certainly got me working too – it produced a remarkable dream anyway, although I am still far from being quite clear about its purport. Things must simmer a bit, & I must be less pressed by work, before I can present any results or comments. I hope you won't be too bored if I write later about "privatio boni".[2] Anyway, if pages of typescript arrive from me in the next few weeks, you can always put them on the fire. They will (I hope) already have served their autoplastic[3] purpose!

I am being kept fearfully busy. It seems that before the year is out, I shall have to go to Rome for an exam[4] – probably in June or October–November; & I hope very much to look you up on the way. The Oxford University Theology Faculty want me to lecture on Theology & Psychology next term.

You may well wonder what I was doing in Spain![5] Several English Catholic colleges were started there during the reigns of Queen Elizabeth & her successors – the time, of course, of penal laws. The one at Valladolid is still there.

Please pardon the brevity & superficiality of this note. It is a shadow (I fear) of things to come.

All very best wishes to you, dear C.G. Also to Mrs Jung & M.-J.

Ever cordially, VICTOR

Blackfriars, Oxford

4.5.50[6]

My dear C.G.,

This is still not the threatened essay on 'privatio boni'! But I enclose a dream which I had soon after your last letter, which may partly explain my

1 Handwritten. 2 Cf. Jung, 31 Dec. 1949, p. 142 and note. 3 self-reparative.

4 A requirement for the degree of Master of Sacred Theology (STM).

5 Cf. Jung, 31 Dec. 1949, p. 143 and notes.

6 Handwritten on small sheets of letterhead.

reluctance to embark on it – though I am not sure that it shows my motives to be wholly creditable or courageous! The dream seems to say: You & C.G. are looking in opposite directions at something different. What you each see, you see – & argument will not help. You must both *see* that you are at cross purposes (the aeroplane) – then the Kabir[7] can carry on with their work "beyond all differences", & the children can disport themselves. I must admit, however, that the final denouement is less satisfactory!

For the moment I do indeed feel that *that* discussion has reached deadlock. What is so perplexing to me is the fact that it is precisely your psychology which has enabled me to *experience* evil as the "privatio boni"! For my part I can give no meaning at all to psychological terms like "positive-negative", "integration-disintegration" if evil is *not* "privatio boni". Nor can I see any motive for "integrating the shadow" – or any meaning in it either – if the shadow is not a good deprived of good![8]

All this is not an argument: just a statement of what I see & do not see.

This is not the only reason for my failure to write. I am fearfully busy. This term I have been roped in by the Faculty of Theology in the University to give a course of lectures on "Theological Truth & the Psychology of the Unconscious". It is an exacting task! I have yet to learn how to show people the Unconscious without turning it into an artificial construction – as in the dream!

I do hope & pray that things fare well with you, my dear C.G. I trust that Mrs Jung too has now quite recovered, & that Marie-Jeanne is now back in action. My greetings, please, to them all.

My movements this year are still uncertain, but I expect to be going to France in late July and (though with little time to spare) to Rome in October. I hope very much to have a chance of seeing you on one or other occasion.

All very best wishes, my dear C.G.,

Ever cordially VICTOR

P.S. I hope you will not object if I quote in my lectures from your first long letter to me on Psychology & Dogma?[9] I know no better statement.

7 *Cabiri (Kabiroi):* small but powerful divinities of Phrygia. They are described in Goethe's *Faust II* as either four or eight in number (Act 2, vv. 8070–8226). Jung frequently invokes them to illustrate the alchemical riddle of Three and Four. (Cf. CW 5, *Symbols of Transformation*, §183&n, CW 11, *Psych. & Rel.*, §119f; CW 12, *Psych. & Alch.*, §203ff & Plate 77). Since White is familiar with the alchemical riddle, his mention of "Kabir" in this context also evokes the ongoing debate about evil, as "Trinity" vs. "Quaternity."

8 In "Good and Evil," a lecture delivered to the London APC on 21 November 1953 and published posthumously, White elaborates this point from the perspective of his own experience in Jungian analysis (*Harvest*, Vol. 12. London: APC, 1966).

9 Refers to the first substantive letter Jung sent to White, dated 5 Oct. 1945. With permission from the writer (Jung, 12 May 1950, p. 151), White incorporated a long passage from this

Of course I expect no comment on the enclosed dream. I send it only because I think it may be more informative than "ego" could be!

Dream of Jan. 21st. 1950[10]

I am sitting with C.G.J. facing the Lake at Bollingen. But we are sitting on the LEFT hand side of the Tower (not on the right, as usually in fact): indeed we seem somehow to be quite close to the end of the Lake and Schmerikon. The scenery is also slightly different from "fact". A range of mountains rises steeply from the Lake on the other side; and far beyond is a single range of very high Alps.

C.G.J. and I are alternatively talking and meditating in silence. Everything seems very peaceful and harmonious between us. It is evening and dusk is falling fast.

It gets darker. Then, as I am looking silently across the Lake, I see a spot of bluish light dart across the scene: it is very near and very low, between ourselves and the first row of mountains: it is not very bright. I say, "Hullo; is that a meteor?" But C.G. has not seen it: he had been looking behind himself, over his shoulder. He asked what I saw and where, and when I tell him says it could not possibly be a meteor because at so low an altitude the friction with the atmosphere would be too great for it to be lit up. I secretly think this is not at all convincing, and *say to myself* that surely the greater the friction the greater the light? But I decide to say nothing to him, as I don't want to spoil the agreeable harmony between us; nor do I feel too sure of my knowledge of physical science to start an argument about it.

It gets quite dark. Then a huge aeroplane, flying very low, comes from over the mountains (i.e. at right angles to the path of the "meteor"). It has lights on its wingtips, tail and front, forming a cross, and I somehow think of it as the "Southern Cross", and as coming from the South and flying North. C.G. and I both see this.

Then it is completely dark, far into the night. Across the Lake is a quarry[11] or cave where men are working hard burrowing into the mountain; it is brilliantly lit with arc-lights to enable them to work without stopping. Then I

letter into his 1942 essay, "Frontiers of Theology and Psychology." The revised lecture, including the quoted passage (with slight corrections in Jung's English), then became a chapter in *God & Unc.* (cf. White, 25 March 1952, p. 179 and note).

10 Typewritten.

11 A stone-quarry is actually located on the southern shore of Upper Lake Zurich, roughly facing Jung's property at Bollingen. From it the stones for the original tower were brought, including, in 1950, a large, cube-shaped stone, which proved unsuitable for its intended use as the cornerstone of a wall. Jung kept this block, later called "the Stone," and on its surface carved words in Latin and Greek, surrounding an image of a little figure of Telesphoros, companion to Asklepios. (For illustration, cf. Gerhard Wehr, *An Illustrated Biography of C.G. Jung*, trans. Michael H. Kohn, Boston & Shaftesbury: Shambhala, 1989, p. 70.)

hear the noise of children and youngsters bathing and paddling with yelps of pleasure and delight, although it is a cold winter night. I see them come out of the water at the landing-stage at Schmerikon.

Follows a complete change of scene; perhaps "another" dream. I am showing somebody a quarry (in daylight) which has a house built in the centre. I point out how the rock strata give the quarry a "built-up" appearance, as in a Cézanne painting. Then I see that in fact it IS built up, out of artificial blocks.

Back at Bollingen, now broad daylight, but now on the RIGHT side of the Tower near the outdoor fireplace. C.G. is sitting by me, and G.v.H.[12] is sitting on my knee making eager amorous advances. I am a bit unresponsive and embarrassed by this, as I do not know what C.G. will think. I think, "If he'd seen that meteor it[13] would not matter."

Some associations etc.

At the beginning of the dream everything seems to correspond with actual memories of Bollingen, except the position (which suggests a more "unconscious" point of view) and the view, which in the dream is somewhat more formal.

The incident of the "meteor" certainly seems to describe our disagreement about "privatio boni" – but I do not see very clearly why the dream describes it in these images. Until C.G. wrote to me about my "refutatio fatui",[14] I had not been fully conscious that there was, in fact, a certain acerbity in my review.[15] The dream seems to be saying: "The radical difference between you is not one of judgment or argument, but of perception: he does not see what you see in front of you, and you do not see what he sees behind him." The light I see is of course associated with actual meteors seen at Bollingen . . . But am I right not to argue it out? Are my motives right in not wanting to risk disharmony? At least, I seem to be inconsistent with my own view that "the greater the friction the greater the light": and I do feel that this matter of "privatio boni" is of enormous importance. In the dream, at least, no harm seems to come from not discussing it – quite the reverse: unless it be at the very end.

For we both see the Southern Cross and the Quarry. The floodlit quarry or mine is associated with an account a friend had just brought from Germany, relating how Köln is being rebuilt[16] without stopping, the building being done under floodlights at night. My friend had expressed admiration of this zeal, but a German acquaintance had said, "It's mainly to cover it all up as

12 White's typescript gives only initials. The name of the couple that ran the Ridgely Inn in New York, where White stayed in 1948, was von Hildebrand. [AC]

13 Originally "he." White crossed this out by hand and wrote "it" above the line.

14 refutation of a fool. Cf. Jung, 31 Dec. 1949, p. 140 and note.

15 "Eranos: 1947, 1948" (Ibid.).

16 Köln (Cologne) had been devastated by Allied bombing during the Second World War.

quickly as possible and forget it ever happened". The quarry: I recall one of C.G.'s seminars which refer to a mountain whose interior is beyond all differences.[17] It all suggests that there is a far deeper harmony between C.G. and myself, beyond our differences about "privatio boni"!

The built up quarry in daylight suggests the way I see the deeper unconscious from the conscious level: It is TOO artificial and intellectualized.

I am very perplexed about the last incident. G.v.H. was a neighbour in America, but I was never particularly interested in her. She is the Irish wife of a German. I notice however that the incident takes place at the spot where C.G. supervised my geomancy, and discovered with some surprise that I had "Puer" in the VIIth house![18]

Küsnacht-Zürich

May 12th 1950[19]

Dear Victor,[20]

You are welcome to quote anything you like from my letter.[21]

Your dream is very interesting, but too complicated to be fully dealt with in a letter. I can only give you a few hints.

1. "I" should be looked at (on the subjective level)[22] as *the psychologist in yourself*, looking for the unconscious behind, while it is just as much in front of yourself.

2. When we trust somebody with an obvious error, it means the "Jung" in your dream is in reality White II.

3. The difference lies between theological thinking and scientific nominalism.

4. The "meteor" is really the lumen naturae.[23] All the other lights are

17 Cf. Jung, 12 May 1950, p. 152. Also the discussion of *unus mundus*, referring to Abu'l Qasim Muhammad, CW 14, §660, p. 462.

18 White's geomantic chart is reproduced in Figure 6.1 (p. 154). Cf. Jung, 10 April 1954, p. 239.

19 Typewritten. Parts of this letter, Jung's responses to White's dream and the postscript, are previously unpublished.

20 In holograph: "Dear Victor!"

21 Cf. White, 4 May 1950, p. 148 and note; also 25 March 1952, p. 179 and note.

22 Jung interpreted dreams on the "objective" and the "subjective" level. At the subjective level, dream interpretation looks to intrapsychic rather than to interpersonal dynamics. In this case, he points White in the intrapsychic direction. [MS]

23 the light of nature. A term found in alchemical texts, which Jung interprets extensively in his writings on alchemy (cf. CW 12, §356, pp. 242f). [MS]

artificial and manmade, even the quarry, that should lead into the interior of the mountain of no-differences. (This is Abu'l-Qasim's invention!)[24]

5. The Unconscious is the beautiful nature we are beholding. Out of the lake comes young life (though it is "winter" = no libido or warmth in it), and in the end the anima, the archetype of life unmitigated, sits in your lap, stealing the whole show, i.e. filling the horizon with her picture.

I, myself in reality, am looking forwards just as much as backwards, when observing the unconscious.

Your metaphysical thinking "posits", mine doubts, i.e. it is weighing mere names for insufficiently known οὐσίαι.[25] That is presumably the reason, why you are able to integrate a shadow "μὴ ὄν",[26] while I can only assimilate a substance, because for "positing" thinking "non-being" is just as much an "ens" or "ὄν" as "being", i.e. a conceptual existence. You are moving in the universe of the known, I am in the world of the unknown. That is, I suppose, the reason, why the unconscious turns for you into a system of abstract conceptions. Thus the anima puts herself in front of the vista.

Well, since friction in the case of a real meteor (not in the case of the lumen naturae) increases the light, it is advisable, that you should not disregard points of difference. I am fully aware of them.

I hope you can manage to come up to Switzerland, whenever you are in the vicinity.

Yours cordially, C.G.

P.S.[27] The blue spark is archetypal:
It is the, σπινθήρ, ι or י[28] of Monoimos[29] and
the Kabbalists,[30] the imago Dei in homine.[31]
ι = ἡμία κεραία י[32]
י = jod hebr.[33]

24 Cf. White, 4 May 1950, p. 151 and note.
25 beings, natures.
26 Cf. Jung, 31 Dec.1949, p. 141 and note; White, 5 April 1952, p. 184 and note.
27 This postscript, referring to White's dream, concerns self-symbology. Unfortunately, he cannot have grasped much of it. The postscript as it reached him was hard to read. A signed holograph of this letter is stored at the ETH Library archive, together with an unsigned, typed, onionskin copy. In holograph this P.S. occupies five short lines, as printed here. In the typed version which White received, it makes only three lines at the bottom of the page. Jung's lexical definitions, handwritten on separate lines, become a single line of typescript, broken by a comma. Insufficient spaces were left in the typed version, also, for the Greek and Hebrew words. Jung added these in cramped handwriting that is almost illegible.
28 spark, iota or Yod.

Blackfriars, Oxford

May 18th 1950[34]

My dear C.G.,

Although there is little to tell you, & less time in which to tell it, I am prompted to send you a few lines of greeting. You are very often in my thoughts & prayers, & although there is little occasion or opportunity to bother you with letters, I hope you know that you are not long forgotten.

I hope very much that all goes well with you & yours.

For myself I am very well, but very busy – & not a little lonely! Apart from Edward Thornton,[35] whom I see fairly often, I have little contact these days with the psychological world.

Among many other activities I am giving a course of University lectures on "Christian Doctrine & Practice in the light of Analytical Psychology"! They are being very well attended & very well received – & I am getting quite a kick out of them myself. The next one is to be on the Trinity! How I wish I could discuss with you the various points as they arise.

I hope very much to be able to get to Switzerland again some time in late July or early August, & I hope very much to be able to come & see you again if you will permit it. If any time would suit you better than another, I

29 Monoïmos: Arab Gnostic Christian writer of the second century, familiar with Jewish motifs and traditions, who writes about the "little point," the divine spark within the human being. Cf. Jung's essay, "Transformation Symbolism in the Mass," Part 4, where he has a long quotation from Monoïmos, including this admonition: "thou wilt find him in thyself, the One and the Many, like to that little point" (CW 11, §400, pp. 264f).

30 Jung compares the Christian Gnostics of antiquity with the Jewish Kabbalists, whose first published works date from the twelfth and thirteenth centuries, and with these he combines the "modern" (sixteenth-century) Kabbalistic myth. According to this myth, the *pintl Yud* ("tittle of Yod," so the tiniest point of the smallest Hebrew letter) signifies Wisdom, the Divine Spark in exile from the Eternal One, thus the living presence of God within the human being. (Cf. Moshe Idel, *Kabbala: New Perspectives*. New Haven & London: Yale University Press, 1988. Idel discusses Monoïmos, pp. 114f, noting that Monoïmos' "tittle of iota" reflects the Jewish "tittle of Yod," p. 328, n.12.)

31 God-image in the human being. In Jung's thinking, equivalent to an image of the Self in the psyche; not to be confused with biblical-theological language about the image of God. [with MS]

32 half hook. As Jung says, this term refers both to the Greek letter iota (ι) and to the tiny serif at the top of the Hebrew letter Yod (י). In Kabbalistic symbology, the Yod represents God's immanence in the soul; but its extra serif (the "half hook") is the transcendent Godhead itself, beyond human knowing. (My thanks to Steven Joseph, MD, who generously shared with me this bit of insight into the Kabbala and referred me to Moshe Idel's work.)

33 *Jod hebraica:* Hebrew Yod.

34 Handwritten.

35 Cf. White, 9 Jan. 1947, p. 65 and note.

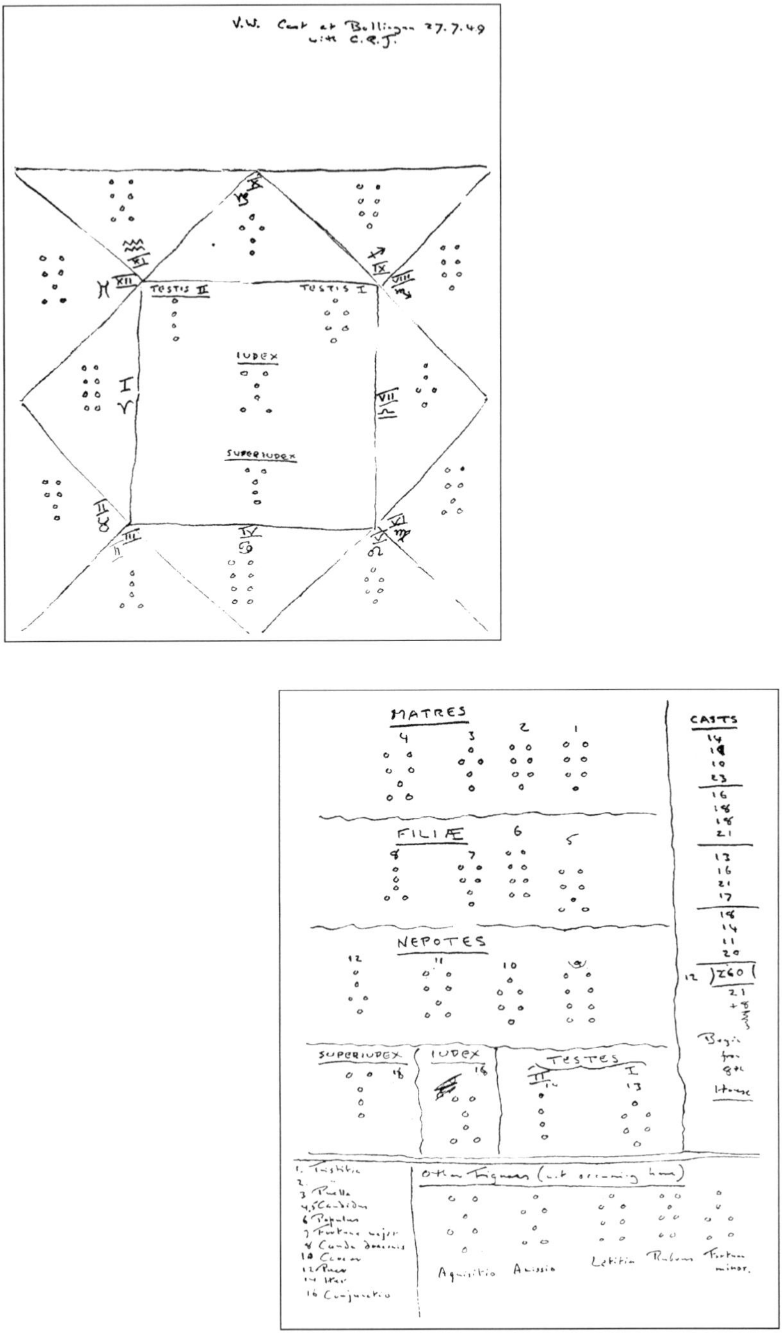

Figure 6.1 White's geomantic diagram, labeled in his handwriting: "V.W. cast at Bollingen 27.7.49 with C.G.J."

should be grateful if you would let me know so that I can make plans accordingly.

I hope you have met, or will meet, Fr. Oswald Sumner[36] of Downside Abbey, who has the good fortune to be working at the Institute this Semester. I am very envious of him.

Please give my greetings to Mrs Jung – I hope that she is now quite well. Also to Marie-Jeanne & all friends.

And all most cordial good wishes to you, my dear C.G.

Ever yours, VICTOR

Blackfriars, Oxford

20.6.50[37]

My dear C.G.,

I am hoping to be able to reach Switzerland, after a rather long itinerary in France, about August 17th. I am very much hoping that this is a time when you will be free and able to see me, as you have so kindly suggested. If it should *not* be so, I should be most grateful if you would let me know as soon as possible. I can hardly suppose you will want me to stay with you again for so long a time as hitherto (I must in any case be back in England about August 24th), but it would be wonderful for me to see you again, even if you can only spare a few hours.

I am simply fascinated by the *I Ching*, whose translation has recently arrived.[38]

With every very best wish to yourself, Mrs Jung, and all, VICTOR

36 Oswald Sumner, OSB (1906–1964): Catholic priest and monk, residing at Downside Abbey, near Bath, England. In addition to serving as parish priest, he was a psychotherapist. He studied under Jung and lectured at the Jung Institute, Zurich, and at the GPP, London. Lectures to the GPP: "St John of the Cross and Modern Psychology" (No. 57) and "St. John Climacus: The Psychology of the Desert Fathers" (No. 63). [AC]

37 Typewritten.

38 Jung had sent White a copy of the newly published *I Ching or The Book of Changes* in Richard Wilhelm's translation, English trans. by Cary F. Baynes, with Foreword by C.G. Jung. (PUP, 1950. Bollingen Series XIX.)

Küsnacht-Zürich

June 24th 1950[39]

Dear Father White,

Professor Jung asked me to write to you as he is not quite feeling up to writing letters yet. He had a bad go of intestinal flu last week, and although he has almost quite recovered he still feels rather tired. He would prefer if you could make it a little earlier than the 17th of August, as he intends to go down to Ascona for the Eranos Meeting which begins on August 21st. So if you could be here about August 14th that would be perfect.

I don't know anything definite about my own holidays yet, but I hope to be here – even if it is only to play reception committee again!

Both Professor and Mrs. Jung send you their herzlichste Grüsse[40]
and I add mine.

Yours [Marie-Jeanne] (unsigned carbon copy)

Blackfriars, Oxford

10.7.50[41]

My dear C.G.

Thank you very much for your message. I was sorry to hear you had been having gastric flu & hope you are now fully recovered.

I am afraid I cannot very easily reach Bollingen (or Küsnacht) earlier than August 15th. I will come straight to you at Bollingen[42] on that day unless I hear to the contrary. I shall be at

St-Hyacinthe
rue du Botzet, 14
Fribourg (Suisse)

on Aug. 14th, so perhaps I could ask you to send a note to me there if there should be any hitch, or if I should go to Küsnacht instead of Bollingen.

I look forward so very much to seeing you.

All best to you & all[43]

Ever cordially, VICTOR

39 Typewritten. 40 most cordial greetings. 41 Handwritten.

42 The name is underlined with a wavy line, not in White's hand.

43 The last two lines are written sideways in the left margin.

Paris VII

20 – 7 1950[44]

Wishing you a splendiscious birthday. I shall be wishing I could be at the Schmerikon party. As it is, I have now to return to England as my father died today.[45] But I hope to see you about Aug 15th.

Cordially always, VICTOR

Prades

5 – 8 1950[46]

My dear C.G.

I am looking forward so very much to seeing you. I hope to arrive towards the evening of Monday 14th, & I shall come straight to Bollingen unless I hear to the contrary at Fribourg (14 rue Botzet).

Meanwhile all very best wishes to all, VICTOR

Küsnacht-Zürich

November 25th 1950[47]

Dear Victor,

I thank you very much indeed for kindly sending me "The Life of the Spirit".[48] I have read your article with the greatest attention and interest. Well

44 Handwritten picture postcard, whose caption reads: "PARIS . . . EN FLANANT / 13 l'Obélisque de la Place de la Concorde / Au fond, la Tour Eiffel." It is addressed to Jung at Bollingen, using his full academic title: Herrn Prof. C.G. Jung.

45 White's father was an Anglican priest. White converted to Catholicism in 1921 (cf. "Victor White, a Memoir", Appendix 2, pp. 308ff).

46 Handwritten picture postcard, addressed to Jung at Bollingen. Its caption reads: "LA DOUCE FRANCE / 600 Environs de PRADES (Pyr.-Or.) / Le Village d'Eus."

47 Typewritten from holograph (dated 24 November).

48 White had sent Jung a copy of his essay, "The Scandal of the Assumption" (*Life of the Spirit: A Blackfriars Review*, Volume V, Nov./Dec. 1950, Nos. 53–54: *The Assumption in the Life of the Christian*. London: Blackfriars Publications, 1950).

you succeeded in putting the petra scandali[49] very much in evidence. Concerning the "universalia",[50] you know, I have not much to say, if I refrain from drawing conclusions and from speculating about the possible psychological consequences of the new dogma. It is a fascinating subject, which is intensely discussed in Zürich. It has released a series of dreams in me, concerned with further developments, i.e., consequences of the new situation. Quite against my expectation the declaration has stirred up something in the unconscious, viz. in the archetypal world. It seems to be the *Hierosgamos*[51]-motive: the cutdown tree has been brought into the cave of the mother. It takes so much space, that the people living in the cave are forced to leave it and to live outside exposed to wind and weather. This motive refers to the night-sea-journey of the Hero in the belly of the great fish = mother.

The "universale", as you so neatly put it, is the interesting aspect of the dogma. The "particulare" on the other side is the thing – as you obviously realize – that takes my breath away.[52] If the miracle of the Assumption is not a living and present spiritual event, but consists of a physical phenomenon, that is reported or only believed to have happened some 2000 years ago, then it has nothing to do with the spirit or just as little as any parapsychological stunt of today. A physical fact never proves the existence and reality of the spirit. It only tries to concretize the spirit in material visibility.[53] Certainly the life and reality of the spirit are in no way demonstrated through the fact, that 2000 years ago a body has disappeared or other miracles have happened.[54]

49 stumbling block; *lit.* stone of stumbling (Isaiah 8.14). White's essay refers to the "many earnest and honest minds" that were "scandalized" by the promulgation of the Assumption of the Blessed Virgin Mary as an official dogma of the Catholic Church, 15 August 1950. Pope Pius XII's *Munificentissimus Deus*, published 1 November 1950, declared the Assumption an article of faith (p. 163 and note).

50 universal things. White's essay consisted of two chapters, "The Scandal of Particularity" and "The Scandal of Universality." Particularity refers to the personal dimension of the dogma, Mary's individual identity, universality to its symbolic dimension.

51 sacred marriage. Jung interprets this dream-image as referring to the Assumption. Cf. Jung, 10 April 1954, p. 236, which explores symbols of the Attis cult. He makes an analogy between the cut-down tree of Attis, carried into the ship (the cave of the Great Mother), with the union of Christ and Mary, accomplished through Mary's bodily assumption into heaven.

52 In holograph: "that takes people's breath away," corrected to read, "my breath." Jung's handwritten draft continues with a crossed-out statement, not included in the typed letter: "All the protestant polemics I have seen, are hypnotized by the concretized historicity of the miracle and are thus carefully led away from any attempt to understand something of the all-important meaning of the dogma. In the significance of the symbol is its real spiritual life, but certainly not in the dead historic fact."

53 In holograph, a crossed-out sentence follows: "It is unadulterated materialism – not 'Ideen-Realismus' [idea-realism], but 'Ideen-Materialismus' [idea-materialism]."

54 In holograph a break occurs here, at the bottom of the second page. The original text becomes unreadable, as Jung has crossed out 20 lines and then pasted a smaller piece of paper, bearing a new paragraph, over the deleted material. The handwriting in the original

Why should one insist upon the historical reality of this particular case of a virgin birth and deny it to all the other mythological traditions? This insistence is particularly curious, because it adds nothing to the significance of the idea; on the contrary it diverts the interest from the all-important spiritual aspect to a very questionable and completely irrelevant physical phenomenon. I only can explain this peculiar tour de force as an attempt to prove the existence of the spirit to a coarse and primitive mind unable to grasp the psychical reality of an idea, a mind needing miracles as an evidence of a spiritual presence. It is more than probable that the idea of the Assumptio has not begun its real life in apostolic times, but considerably later. The miracle of the A. has obviously begun to operate noticeably from the VI. Century onwards only.[55] If the A. means anything, it means a spiritual fact, which can be formulated as the integration of the female principle in the Christian conception of the Godhead. This is certainly the most important religious development since 400 years.

I am enclosing an article that has appeared in the Neue Zürcher Zeitung.[56] It does not insist upon the concretistic historicity of the miracle but rather upon the Christian nature of the idea. I have not seen the text of the "definition"[57] yet. Could you lend me a copy? Please return the article, as I want to keep it. To judge from this article, the "definition" does not insist upon the reality, but rather upon the *belief in the reality* of the A. and thus upon the *reality of the idea*. As you put it, it sounds rather like a blatant materialism, which arouses the strongest objections. If the A. is essentially a concrete historic fact, then it is no more a living spiritual experience. It degenerates to a merely synchronistic effect in the past, just as interesting and curious as the departure of Elias[58] or the sensational disappearance of Henoch.[59] It is a mere sidestepping from the real problem viz. the symbol of the A., whereas the really and only important factor is the living archetype forcing its way into consciousness. When insisting on historicity you risk not only the most awkward and unanswerable questions, but you also help everybody

letter is loose and loping, whereas the substitute text – the paragraph which follows – is in small, tightly spaced handwriting.

55 A sentence follows in holograph, not crossed out but nevertheless omitted by the typist: "Before that time it was there but unrevealed and implicite [sic]."

56 Otto Karrer, SJ, "Das neue Dogma und die Bibel" ("The New Dogma and the Bible"), *Neue Zürcher Zeitung*, 26 November 1950. Otto Karrer, (1888–1976), a German Jesuit theologian, was one of ten writers invited by the *NZZ* to write brief articles about the new dogma. These articles appeared in the paper between 30 October and 26 November 1950.

57 Cf. portion of the Papal Bull defining the dogma of the Assumption, in Latin, attached to White's letter of 3 Dec. 1950 (p. 163 and note).

58 Elijah (Elias) was taken bodily to heaven in a whirlwind (2 Kings 2.1–14).

59 Enoch (Henoch), father of Methuselah, "walked with God; and he was not, for God took him" (Genesis 5.24; Hebrews 11.5).

to turn his eyes away from the essential idea to the realistic crudity of a merely physical phenomenon, as it is only physical phenomena that happen in a distinct place at a distinct time, whereas the spirit is eternal and everywhere. Even the corpus subtile[60] is only relatively within time and space. If we designate the A. as a fact in time and space we ought to add, that it happens really in eternity and everywhere, and what we perceive of it through our senses is corruptible matter, i.e. we don't see it, but we conclude to or believe in the idea. This conclusion took not less than 1900 years to reach its finale. Under these conditions it seems to me preposterous to insist upon concrete historicity. But if you say: I believe that Mary endowed with her corpus glorificationis[61] (i.e. characterized by almost "corporeal" distinctiveness)[62] has attained her place in the vicinity of the Deity, I can agree with you. This seems to be also Mr. Karrer's opinion,[63] and, as he points out, Mary wouldn't be the only one. There seems to be a certain traditional consensus that a life of religious wholeness (i.e. a conscious integration of the essential archetype) justifies the hope for a distinct existence in eternity. The extension of such a consideration to Mary seems to be well within the scope of Christian philosophy.

Yours cordially, C.G. [64]

Blackfriars, Oxford

December 3rd 1950[65]

My dear C.G.,

It was delightful to hear from you. I had been intending to write to you for some time; indeed I had even been hoping to see you for at least a few hours. For I was suddenly hustled off to Rome towards the end of October, and was kept there for nearly three weeks. I had greatly hoped that I could arrange to make my return flight via Zürich, but it was impossible to arrange it with the return ticket I held. It was tantalizing to pass the Alps, and to be so near and yet so far from Zürich.

It was my first visit to Rome, and I found it all rather overpowering: in many ways I was not at all sorry to get away from it! The outcome of it is that I passed

60 subtle body (term used in alchemy).

61 glorified body.

62 In holograph: "distinctness."

63 See above, p. 159 and note.

64 No signature in carbon copy. Holograph also ends with the words, "scope of Christian philosophy."

65 Typewritten on plain paper.

this ridiculous examination[66] (so I must presume that my peculiar "heresies" – which I did not disguise – are tolerable even there), and that means the end of my hopes that I can retire from teaching and the wear and tear of community life and devote my time to quiet reading, writing and Seelsorge![67]

I return, with many thanks, Otto Karrer's article[68] – which interested me very much, especially towards the end; though I think it rather skirts *our* problem. I also enclose a copy of the text of the definition. That brief formula is all that is strictly dogma;[69] but you will not fail to notice the terms *corpore*[70] and *expleto terrestris vitae cursu*;[71] clearly it is not *merely* an extra-temporal "idea" that is envisaged.

Your letter interested me enormously; especially as I too have been collecting a good deal of archetypal stirrings on the subject – some of which I might be able to send you later. I wish I could give you all the reflection to your letter which it deserves, but I must content myself with a few spontaneous jottings as they occur to me – and, as you will see, your letter stimulates in me more questions than answers!

I think there is no softening or disguising of the "scandal". But do we not hold the clue to the problem in the Gegensatzquaternio[72] which you set out in Eranos Jahrbuch 1948? page 314?[73] That diagram, it seems to me, is THE scandal at which the mind reels. But is it naive to think that, once it is grasped that the Einmalig and the Ewig,[74] the Einzigartig and the Allgemein,[75] are to be viewed *functionally* as complementary opposites, of which no one must be overvalued at the expense its opposite, nor any one is intelligible except in function of its opposite, then the other difficulties vanish?

You see, I think I agree with almost everything you say. Indeed, I was at pains to try and say much the same thing, especially on pages 205 and 206 of my article in regard to miracles.[76]

But of course there are differences of standpoint. As you once wrote to me in another context, "it is a matter of to whom one is speaking". I write (usually!) as a Catholic to Catholics. You, for instance, (and rightly enough from a purely empirical and positive standpoint), will see the Assumption as a case (perhaps also an extension) of the Hierosgamos-motive. A Catholic who was

66 Required for the STM, one of the prerequisites for being appointed Regent of Studies. (Cf. White, 4 March 1954, p. 230 and note.)

67 cure of souls.

68 Cf. Jung, 25 Nov. 1950, p. 159 and note.

69 Definition concludes with this formula: "we pronounce, declare and define it to be a divinely revealed dogma: that the Immaculate Mother of God, the ever Virgin Mary, having completed the course of her earthly life, was assumed body and soul into heavenly glory." (Cf. text and translation, p. 163 and note.)

70 with the body; bodily.

71 having completed the course of her earthly life.

72 quaternity of opposites.

73 Cf. CW 9.ii, *Aion*, §115, p. 63.

74 the Singular and the Eternal.

75 the Unique and the Universal.

76 White, "The Scandal of the Assumption," in *Life of the Spirit*, op. cit.

also interested in comparative religion etc. might share that standpoint, but as a Catholic believer he will be much more likely to see Hierosgamos stories and rituals as antetypes, shadows of, or aspirations towards, the Assumption. That is merely an instance of what I think must be taken into account.

I agree entirely that what the definition insists upon is the "belief in the reality", with the proviso that the reality is not *only* ewig and allgemein,[77] but *also* einmalig and einzigartig![78] I agree also that *as* einmalig and einzigartig *alone* the Assumption would be senseless. I was in fact at some pains to *avoid* saying it was "historical" – plainly in almost any recognizable sense of that very ambiguous word it is not! It is precisely (in any case) not a matter of history but a matter of faith, though the matter of faith touches not *only* an eternal idea but *also* a matter of fact in space and time – and I would even suggest that, unless it does so, it can never come effectually into full consciousness or reach the depths as well as the heights of total reality, "spiritual" AND "material".

So I am all with you on "Nothing-But-ism"[79] here as elsewhere. But perhaps there are other differences. I suppose that what one finds most interesting, or to be *the* important point, about the Assumption or anything else will depend largely on one's typology? Will not the introverted intuitive thinker see it differently from (say) the extraverted sensation-feeler? The *Catholica*[80] by definition must try and provide for all, and lead each to "the other side" from where they are, as best she can.

I wonder. Your letter sets me wondering many things. . . . I wonder if we can really flatter ourselves that we have left behind the "coarse and primitive mind" that needs miracles – or have just pushed it into the unconscious – and hinc illae lachrymae?[81] And I wonder sometimes, my beloved C.G., when you write of the "spiritual" and a shade slightingly of the "material" if (in spite of so much that belies it) you are not really a wicked old Manichee[82] at heart, and that a really sound Dominican would not hand you over to the Civil Arm[83] for the good of your soul. . . .

77 eternal and universal. 78 singular and unique.

79 Jung's term, "the Nothing But," is his shorthand reference to the reductive rationalism and concretism of modern materialist thinkers. The term, which Jung adopted from William James, appears in many contexts in Jung's work (cf. e.g., CW 6, *Types*, §315; CW 7, *Two Essays*, §400; CW 10, *Civilization in Transition*, §347, §362, §365, §367, §658). (Cf. Eugene Taylor, "William James and C.G. Jung," *Spring: An Annual of Archetypal Psychology and Jungian Thought*, 1980, p. 165.)

80 Catholic [business; endeavor].

81 hence those tears. Phrase common to Horace (Epistles I.xix.41), Terence (Andria I.i.99:126), Cicero and Vergil.

82 Cf. Jung, 31 Dec. 1949, p. 142 and note.

83 During the Inquisition, friars in the Order of Preachers (Dominicans) were assigned to identify, investigate and try heretics in ecclesiastical courts, turning them over to the civil courts, if found guilty, for punishment.

But I must be frank. The night after I received your letter I dreamed that I was at the airport at Rome in a big four-engined aeroplane, intending to fly to Zürich. The pilot received the signal to take off before he was ready; the aeroplane was heavily overweighted in the starboard wing; there was no time to warm up the engines, and there was no proper runway. The aircraft lumbered along the rough turf, which was strewn with projecting trees, and could never get airborne before I woke up. . . .

I *think* I have corrected all that, but am not at all sure. But if this letter fails to "reach" Zürich, you will know I am still too earthbound at Rome, but hope to be able to make a better take-off later on!

In case that is not before Christmas, please accept now my seasonable greetings to you, Mrs Jung, Marie-Jeanne and ALL,

Ever affectionately, VICTOR

On a separate sheet, enclosed with this letter:

"Quapropter, postquam supplices etiam atque etiam ad Deum admovimus preses, ac Veritatis Spiritus lumen invocavimus, ad Omnipotentis Dei gloriam, qui peculiarem benevolentiam suam Mariae Virgini dilargitus est, ad sui Filii honorem, immortalis saeculorum Regis ac peccati mortisque Victoris, ad eiusdem augustae Matris augendam gloriam et ad totius Ecclesiae gaudium exsultationemque, auctoritate Domini nostri Iesu Christi, Beatorum Apostolorum Petri et Pauli ac Nostra pronuntiamus, declaramus et definimus divinitus revelatum dogma esse: *Immaculatam Deiparam semper Virginem Mariam, expleto terrestris vitae cursu, fuisse corpore et anima ad caelestem gloriam assumptam.*"

(from the Bull "Munificentissimus Deus", copied from *L'Osservatore Romano*, Nov. 2nd.1950).[84]

84 "Munificentissimus Deus," an Apostolic Constitution issued 1 November 1950, defining "ex cathedra" (from the chair of Peter) the dogma of the Assumption of the Blessed Virgin. The English version of this passage (paragraph 44) reads: "For which reason, after we have poured forth prayers of supplication again and again to God, and have invoked the light of the Spirit of Truth, for the glory of Almighty God who has lavished his special affection upon the Virgin Mary, for the honor of her Son, the immortal King of the Ages and the Victor over sin and death, for the increase of the glory of that same august Mother, and for the joy and exultation of the entire Church; by the authority of our Lord Jesus Christ, of the Blessed Apostles Peter and Paul, and by our own authority, we pronounce, declare and define it to be a divinely revealed dogma: that the Immaculate Mother of God, the ever Virgin Mary, having completed the course of her earthly life, was assumed body and soul into heavenly glory."

1951

as from Bollingen

June 19th 1951[1]

Dear Victor,

I'm sorry to be so late with my answer.[2] I have been ill during most of this spring and it isn't long ago since I have recovered.

If you come to Switzerland this summer I shall be pleased to see you. I shall be in Bollingen again after about July 10th and stay on for the greater part of August. Just let me know a few days ahead when you are coming out.

Cordially yours, C.G.

Blackfriars, Oxford

July 17[3]

My very dear C.G.,

I hope very much to be able to come to Switzerland again towards the end of July, & I am extremely keen to see you if the idea would be agreeable to you, & you are not bored to tears with me by now. But this time I have some very remarkable things to tell you about & which I should like to discuss with you.

I am having some difficulty in plotting out my itinerary, but so far as I am able to anticipate, it would suit me best if I could come & see you about July 30th. Or, if this would be inconvenient about August 5th. I should be most grateful if you would tell me if either of these dates would be suitable for you – & would it be convenient for me to stay a few days?

I hope very much in any case to see you, & hope I shall find you, Mrs Jung & all fighting fit.

Ever cordially, VICTOR

1 Typewritten. Letter previously unpublished.

2 After a six-month pause, this is Jung's reply to White's last letter (3 Dec. 1950), deferring discussion of the substantive issues until they can meet in person.

3 Handwritten. No year is given, but this letter logically follows Jung's invitation of 19 June 1951, and other possibilities have been ruled out. (E.g., White's 1953 diary shows appointments in England during late July and early August that year.) [AC]

Blackfriars, Oxford

6.9.51[4]

My dear C.G.,

I expect you will now be back from Eranos, and I am hoping you are not too exhausted as a consequence, and that the meetings were really worthwhile.

Owing to my absence in Edinburgh (at a rather interesting conference of psychologists and clergy) I have only just received a letter from our friend Barbara Robb (the Derby-winner, etc.)[5] to say that she and her husband will be going to Weesen (at the Strandhotel du Lac) for a few days this Saturday. I hope it was no grave indiscretion, but I passed on to her one or two of your comments on her dream, including your remark that it might be a good thing if she could meet you in the flesh. . . . I expect she will be writing (or perhaps already has written) to ask if she could possibly come over and see you during her stay at Weesen. I hate to inflict more visitors on your time and energy; but Something told me it was the thing to do in this instance – and if I was mistaken, the fault is entirely mine. She, at any rate, was as reluctant in fact to impose herself upon you as she was (as you may remember) in her dreams. So if you do hear from her with a request to be allowed to visit you, please put all the blame on me – or Them.

I am here for a few days only, with mountains of work to attend to – mountains which I have not the faith to remove! So please forgive this very brief note.

All very best wishes to you, dear C.G., and please to Mrs Jung also.

Ever cordially & gratefully VICTOR

as from Bollingen

September 21st 1951[6]

Dear Victor,

I have seen Mrs. Barbara Robb, and I assure you, she is quite an eyeful and beyond! We had an interesting conversation and I must admit, she is

4 Typewritten. 5 Cf. White, 30 June 1949, p. 140.

6 Typewritten, except for postscript.

quite remarkable. If ever there was an anima, it is she, and there is no doubt about it.

In such cases one better crosses oneself, because the anima, particularly when she is quintessential as in this case, casts a metaphysical shadow which is long like a Hotel-bill and contains no end of items that sum up in a marvellous way. One cannot label her and put her into a drawer. She decidedly leaves you guessing. I hadn't expected anything like that. At least I understand now why she dreams of the Derby winners: it just belongs to her! She is a synchronistic phenomenon all over, and one can keep up with her as little as with one's own unconscious.

I think you ought to be very grateful to St. Dominicus that he has founded an order of which you are a member. In such cases one appreciates the existence of monasteries. It is just as well that she got all her psychology from books, as she would have busted every decent and competent analyst. I sincerely hope that she is going on dreaming of winners, because such people need money to keep them afloat.

If you see Mrs. Robb, please tell her how much I've enjoyed her visit – but keep quiet about my other expectoration. She must not be frightened too soon.

Don't work too much!

Yours cordially, C.G.

P.S. Please don't forget to tell your Swiss friend and co-frater at the Vatican Library to inquire about unpublished MSS of St. Thomas!!![7]

Oxford

3 Oct. 1951[8]

I loved your letter – how right you are! Except about her getting it all from books, *and* about Dominican monasteries being a protection. (I know nowhere more exposed.)

I wish I knew how *not* to work too much! It is pressure of work that prevents my writing the letter I should like to write!

Ever, VICTOR

7 Jung still urgently seeks evidence to substantiate the attribution of *Aurora Consurgens* to St. Thomas Aquinas. In his footnote to this passage, Adler draws attention to M.-L. von Franz's edition of *Aurora Consurgens* (English trans., 1966, p. 431, n. 130) (*Letters II*, p. 25n).

8 Handwritten postcard, whose caption reads: "XIII Century Dominican Graduale in Blackfriars Library, Oxford / The *Sequence* for the Feast of St. Dominic."

Gracedieu[9] Boar's Hill, Oxford.

7.10.51[10]

My dear C.G.,

You will, I hope, already have received my postcard saying how delighted I was to receive your letter. This is just to say it again!

Barbara certainly is quite a corker, isn't she? For weal or woe I cannot see her very often these days; but it occurs to me to mention that IF you should be moved to offer any hints about how to deal with her when I do, I'd be very grateful. I saw her on Thursday, for the first time since her visit to Switzerland, and I must say I was rather at a loss, and it struck me that she was running one hell of an inflation. Of course I'm awfully aware that that judgment may just be *me*. It doesn't worry me the way it used to; but though I think I *understand* these claims for the infallibility and omnicompetence of introverted intuition, I have not the foggiest notion how to cope with it when I meet it – hinc illae lacrymae[11] with Layard and Sussman also! I know better now than to try to reason with it or appeal to the evidence of commonsense facts; but the only result of that is that I am left speechless and dithering – though not I think now without genuine and sympathetic feeling.

I just mention this, as I guess it's what you may mean by a "metaphysical shadow". And I notice you say, "She must not be frightened TOO SOON", and I've got a hunch that she is heading some place where I may be needed!

No, I haven't had any dreams that seem to bear on it, and anyway the matter is not a major preoccupation with me these days. But it has just occurred to me that you MIGHT have something to say on the subject.

It was the Belgian co-frater[12] whom I had hoped to meet at Bollingen who might have told me about the alleged skeleton in the Vatican Library cupboard[13] – but he did not turn up before I left. I will however make further inquiries – so far I've drawn only blanks!

All very best wishes to you, Mrs Jung, M.-J. and all. I do not know if you are still at Bollingen, so send this to Küsnacht.

Ever gratefully and cordially, VICTOR

9 for Grace Dieu. Grace Dieu had been left to the Dominicans by Bernard Newdigate of the Shakespeare Head Press. It was used as a pleasant retreat from the often taxing Oxford climate. [AC]

10 Typewritten.

11 hence those tears.

12 Reference unidentified (cf. also Jung's reference to this "co-frater" in the following letter).

13 Rumored manuscript of the *Aurora Consurgens* (cf. Jung, 21 Sept. 1951, p. 169).

Küsnacht-Zürich

16th of Oct. 1951[14]

Dear Victor,

It is not yet time to worry about the anima Barbara. I will believe that she has come home as inflated as one can be. I have given her every reason for it by applying Heraklitos' method to her case: "O ye gods let the Ephesians always have gold enough, that their abomination may come to the daylight."[15] Of course it is as bad as all that,[16] but if you remember Layard and Sussman, you get a certain idea of what the trouble is with intuitive introverts: you only can feed them with their own stuff to the bursting point, if they don't sit up once all by themselves and begin to listen. Once they reach the point of saturation and then something snaps. Either they go beyond the human reach (like Layard) or they realize their human misery in all the apparent wealth of their lofty castles. B.R. is not yet there quite. (How old is she by the way?) You know the "metaphysical shadow"[17] is cast by their inflated personality over the heavens so that the light eventually begins to fail and the ground to drop away under their feet. Their case will be taken care of: no tree will ever grow into heaven. But as long as it grows nobody shall hinder it. It would be violence or a superhuman effort towards a doubtful end. You only can tell her, what your conviction is, if the case occurs. If she does not listen, it's her own funeral.

I have seen – I think – your co-frater sitting in the garden near the lake – you know – at my neighbour's house near Bollingen about a fortnight ago, but I was a bit far out in my sailboat.

There is a question, we cannot settle here: We have found that S. Thomas is on the same day with SS. Perpetua et Felicitas in the Acta Sanctorum. The lectio[18] of that day is Sap. VII, 7–14.[19] Curiously enough this text forms also the beginning of the *Aurora consurgens*.

14 Handwritten. Letter previously unpublished.

15 Jung often quotes Heraclitus with reference to the concept of "enantiodromia," a principle stating that extremes turn into their opposites when they reach a critical point. [MS]

16 Given Jung's otherwise genial attitude toward Mrs. Robb, the harshness of this statement is jarring. Possibly he meant, "Of course it is *not* as bad as all that". The handwriting shows that Jung wrote this letter hastily, and it was not transcribed before sending.

17 A quasi-technical term in Jung's theory, "shadow" refers to the repressed contents of the psyche, which are often (but not always) ignoble, inferior, morally corrupt. White and Jung argued endlessly over the question of whether God too has a shadow, i.e., an unloving, destructive, unconscious side. Here Jung seems to be saying that inflated personalities have a depressing, "darkening," unconscious influence on people around them. Their own consciousness is bound to turn dark, as well, when they run into serious obstacles in themselves or in the world. [MS]

18 reading from scripture, selected for liturgical use.

19 Wisdom (Sapientia) 7.7–14. This passage begins, "Therefore I prayed, and understanding was given me; I called upon God, and the spirit of wisdom came to me."

The question is: *When* and *why* has this text been assigned to the 7th of March? Is there any connection with S. Perpetua? or with S. Thomas only? If so, has a former text been substituted for the sake of S. Thomas?

I think you might be able to give me a tip.

Yours cordially C.G.

P.S. Synchronicity[20] and Job[21] are going to the printer.

Blackfriars, Oxford

23.10.51[22]

My dear C.G.,

Thank you immensely for your very helpful letter. It thoroughly confirms what I had come to think myself about B.R. – and introverted intuitives generally; what I had learned from my mistakes! But it is very good to have your confirmation. I suppose B.R. must be around 38 now.[23] One point in which she differs widely from Layard and Sussman lies in the fact that she runs a very vigorous and efficient Sensation life as well. . . .

My inquiries into this matter of March 7th has not yet yielded anything very conclusive. However, I find that the feast of SS. Perpetua and Felicitas was kept on that day until St Thomas Aquinas was canonized. As he had died on that day, his feast displaced theirs, and SS. P.& F. were left with a "memoria" (a second prayer after the principal one) only. They did not have a feast-day of their own again until 1908, when it was fixed for the preceding day, March 6th.

The matter of the "lectio" (Sap.vii, sqq.) is odd. What is particularly odd

20 Jung's major essay, "Synchronizität als ein Prinzip akausaler Zusammenhänge" ("Synchronicity: an Acausal Connecting Principle") appeared, together with an essay by Wolfgang Pauli on the influence of archetypal images on the thinking of Kepler, in *Naturerklärung und Psyche* (Zurich: Rascher Verlag) in May 1952. An English edition appeared three years later, as *The Interpretation of Nature and the Psyche* (London: Routledge and Kegan Paul, 1955).

21 *Answer to Job* (hereafter, *Job*) was available for several years only in the original Swiss edition, *Antwort auf Hiob* (Zürich: Rascher Verlag, 1952: hereafter, *Hiob*). Jung's most controversial work on religion and theology, *Job* became a major source of conflict between Jung and White. White had seen the work in typescript and initially greeted its publication with enthusiasm (cf. White, 23 Oct. 1951, 30 March 1952, 5 April 1952). Later he publicly accused Jung of betraying his Catholic followers by publishing this work (cf. Appendix 6, "Jung on Job," pp. 349ff), and privately chided him for breaking a promise in doing so (cf. White, 17 March 1955, p. 259). [with MS]

22 Typewritten.

23 Barbara Robb, born 15 April 1913, would have been 38.

about it is the fact that the Mass for St Thomas's Day follows the "Commune Doctorum"[24] in all its features, with the single exception of this lectio. It certainly looks as if the compilers went out of their way to choose this lectio for his feast, and had some reason for thinking it particularly apposite. I do not know that this lectio was ever used for SS. P. & F. It seems very unlikely, since it was as martyrs that they were celebrated, and even less likely that their lectio should remain when their feast had been abrogated. Of course it is known that St Thomas was writing what is presumed to be a commentary on Canticles when he died, and it is disputed still which of two extant ones – if either – it was. A chronicler has it: "ut cantando moreretur et moriendo cantaret rogatu monachorum Fossae Novae Cantica Canticorum exponens maioris vi amoris quam morbi ad caelum raptus".[25] But, as you know, the pundits won't have it that it was the Aurora Consurgens, or that it was known till centuries later.

I am thrilled to hear that "Hiob" – especially – has gone to the press. I cannot say how much I am looking forward to being able to read and ponder it again. I am curious to know what the Biblical pundits – let alone the "psychologists" – will have to say.

In a few days I hope to be able to send you a little thing of my own – the script of two talks I am to give next month on the BBC;[26] following on three by Prof. Frankfort[27] on "The Dying God". It has to be something fairly simple and not too esoteric, and time will prevent my saying all I should like to say. But I should be very interested to hear whether or not you think the line is sound – so far as it goes.

I do hope and pray you keep fit this winter. My kindest remembrances, please, to Mrs Jung and all,

Ever cordially VICTOR

24 "Common of Doctors," i.e., the prayers, readings and psalms assigned for mass or the divine office for the celebration of a saint who is a teacher of the faith ("Doctor of the Church").

25 "In order that he might die while singing and sing while dying, it was when he was expounding the Song of Songs at the request of the monks of Fossa Nova that he was taken up to heaven, more by the force of love than of disease" (trans. Holder). Fossa Nova is the Benedictine abbey in Italy where Aquinas died. At the time of death he was reportedly working on a commentary to the Song of Songs.

26 White delivered the final two parts of a five-part radio series, "The Dying God," broadcast by BBC Radio's Third Programme [Radio 3] in October and November. White's lectures were, "The Dying God – Similarities in the Pagan, Psychological and Christian Approach" (10 November 1951) and "The Dying God – Differences in the Pagan, Psychological and Christian Approach" (16 November 1951).

27 Henri Frankfort (1897–1954): archeologist in Egypt and Iraq. Born in the Netherlands, Frankfort became an American citizen in 1944. In 1949 he was appointed director of the Warburg Institute of the University of London. On 24 and 28 October and 1 November 1951 Frankfort delivered three BBC lectures: "The Concept of the Dying God," "The Dying God in Mesopotamia and Egypt," and "The Dying God in Syria and Greece: A Problem of Similarities."

1952

Küsnacht-Zürich

January 28th 1952[1]

Dear Victor,

Thank you for the good wishes you sent me for the new year of 1952. Unfortunately I was unable to hear you on the radio,[2] because I was in Bollingen then.

I'm looking forward to the galley-proofs of your book[3] and I will try to write some words as an introduction.[4]

I have heard about your meeting in London through Frau von der Heydt[5] also. It seems that it has been very successful. I haven't seen Frau Dr. Jacobi[6] yet but shall do so soon.

You remember my letter to you about St. Thomas Aquinas.[7] Dr. von Franz wonders, who the compilator is you mention. We only need the exact title of the book where we can read about the question I asked you. I should be much obliged to you if you could just give me the title in question.

It is indeed most regrettable that you are unable to give your lectures in Zürich. Bennet[8] was here lately and lectured with much success.

Toynbee[9] has been invited by the "Institut für Auslandsforschung" in Zürich and has expressed the wish to see me privately before his lecture.[10]

1 Typewritten. Letter previously unpublished. The ETH Library archive has both the original letter and the onionskin carbon copy. In the original it can be seen that, contrary to his habit when writing to White, Jung signed his name in full.

2 Cf. White, 23 Oct. 1951, p. 173 and note.

3 Cf. Jung, 6 Nov. 1946, p. 53 and note.

4 Jung's "Foreword to White's 'God and the Unconscious' " (CW 11, *Psych & Rel.*, §449–67, pp. 299–310) discusses some of the grave difficulties arising in a dialogue between an empirical psychology and a philosophically grounded theology. [MS]

5 Baroness Vera von der Heydt (1899–1996): friend and follower of Jung, whom she met in Darmstadt in 1922; later a Jungian analyst. Born to a German-Jewish business family, she converted to Catholicism in adulthood and committed herself to Jewish-Christian dialogue. With the Second World War she emigrated to England, where she entered analysis with John Layard. She later analyzed with Jung, remaining in consultation with him until his death. [with MS]

6 Cf. Jung, 27 Dec. 1947, p. 104 and note.

7 Cf. Jung, 16 Oct. 1951, p. 171; White, 23 Oct. 1951, pp. 172ff.

8 E.A. Bennet, prominent London psychiatrist and analyst, friend of Jung, and for some years a member of the Society of Analytical Psychology. He was also the author of *C.G. Jung* (1961) and *What Jung Really Said* (1966). [MS]

9 Arnold Joseph Toynbee (1889–1975): British historian, who lectured worldwide on "world civilization" and "world religion." Author of many works, including the 12-volume *A Study of History* (1934–61).

10 Reference unclear. The Institut für Auslandsforschung (Institute for Foreign Research), Zürich, has no record of any lecture by Toynbee during the 1950s. In 1952–53, however, Toynbee delivered the Gifford Lectures at the University of Edinburgh, later published as *An Historian's Approach to Religion* (1956). [with AC]

I'm trying to avoid work as much as possible, but it is an almost hopeless task.

Hoping you are in good health,

I remain yours cordially C.G. JUNG

Küsnacht-Zürich

February 16th 1952[11]

Dear Victor,

Thank you for your kind answer.[12] Unfortunately we are aware of those books and they don't give us the answer we need, namely, What is the reason that the Lectio on the 7th of March is taken from Sapientia?[13] I just want to know the reason for the fact that the text from Sapientia is used at all. If you could tell me where I could find the answer to this question I should be most grateful.

Cordially yours, [C.G.] (unsigned carbon copy)

Oxford

21–2.52[14]

My dear C.G.,

I am sorry I answered the wrong question! But I am afraid there is no known answer, so far as I can discover, about the reason for the choice of lectio for St Thomas Aquinas' Day, and one can only speculate – as I did in a previous letter.[15]

To my knowledge, there is not a shred of historical evidence on the subject, and it is unlikely that there would be. Dr v. Franz could, however, inquire from the Institutum Historicum/Convento de Santa Sabina/Aventino/Roma – to make sure.

All very best wishes

Ever VICTOR

11 Typewritten. Letter previously unpublished.

12 White's answer is missing from the ETH Libary archive.

13 Cf. Jung, 16 Oct. 1951, pp. 171f and note.

14 Typewritten, except for closing ("Ever").

15 Cf. White, 25 Oct. 1951.

Blackfriars, Oxford

March 25th 1952[16]

My dear C.G.,

Very shortly now you will be receiving from my publishers a typescript copy of my book of collected papers ("God and the Unconscious"),[17] for which you have so generously offered to write a preface. (It will also include a translation of Gebhard Frei's "Zur Psychologie des Unbewussten".)[18]

Much of it you will have read before, and, I'm sure, you will have little inclination to plough through the whole opus. But I should like to draw your attention especially to Sections IV & V,[19] which touch most directly on the points of contact with our[20] psychology, and make most effort at "bridge-building" between theology and psychology: perhaps without too much success, but at least, I trust, with no shirking of the difficulties!

Thanking you again in anticipation for this generous undertaking; I only hope and pray it will not be too burdensome, nor distract you from more important work.

Ever cordially[21] VICTOR

P.T.O.[22]

P.S. And please read also my own short preface. I trust I have done nothing improper in quoting a letter of yours in Chapter V.[23]

16 Typewritten.

17 Cf. Jung, 28 Jan. 1952, p. 177; White, 5 April 1952, p. 181 and note.

18 "On Analytical Psychology." Frei's substantial essay had first been published in a shorter version (*Gloria Dei*, 1947), then at full length in *Annalen der philosophischen Gesellschaft Innenschweiz und Ostschweiz* [Annals of the Philosophical Society of Central and Eastern Switzerland] (1948). In White's translation, it appeared as an appendix to the first edition of *God & Unc.* (cf. Jung, 27 Dec. 1947, p. 105 and note); but this appendix is lacking from the second edition (Spring 1982). [with AC]

19 Chapters 4, "Freud, Jung, and God," and 5, "The Frontiers of Theology and Psychology," are taken, revised and expanded, from White's 1942 essay, "The Frontiers of Theology and Psychology" (cf. White, 3 Aug. 1945, p. 3 and note).

20 White's use of the first person plural ("our"), which is clear in his typed letter, suggests that he identified himself unambiguously, at this point in the correspondence, as a Jungian and perhaps even as a psychologist.

21 The closing and everything below it is handwritten.

22 Please Turn Over.

23 (Cf. White, 4 May 1950, p. 148 and note.) In Chapter V, under the heading, "A letter written to a theologian in 1945," White quotes a long excerpt from Jung's first long letter to him (5 Oct. 1945), beginning, "You have rendered justice to my empirical and practical standpoint throughout" (*God & Unc.*, 1982 ed., pp. 72f).

30–3–52[24]

My dear C.G.,

I am very excited to hear to-day from Michael Fordham[25] that *Das Buch Hiob*,[26] as well as *Synchronizität*,[27] has appeared.

May I make bold to ask if you have a spare copy, and remind you of your assurance that I could *if* it were published?!

I hope (in very poor exchange) to send you some more of my squibs in a few days.

Ever cordially VICTOR

P.S. I am dumbfounded to see that Fr D'Arcy[28] is to speak at Eranos. But it's very broad-minded.

Küsnacht-Zürich

April 3rd 1952[29]

Dear Father White,

The "Antwort auf Hiob" was mailed to you yesterday, and Dr. Jung asked me to write to you and apologize for not having sent it before. He meant to do so, but had flu (nothing very bad fortunately) and everything had to wait. He has now gone down to Locarno with Mrs. Jung and I hope they will have good weather and a real rest, which they both needed. – He also asked me to tell you that he is looking forward to reading the manuscript of your book (which hasn't arrived yet) which he asked me to forward to him immediately.

The paper on Synchronicity hasn't come out yet. It is to be included in a volume together with a paper by Prof. Pauli[30] and this fact delayed the printing. It should come out sometime in May.

24 Handwritten postcard.

25 Michael Scott Montague Fordham (1905–1995): London psychiatrist, analytical psychologist and writer, and prominent member of the Society of Analytical Psychology (SAP). In addition to his full clinical practice, Michael Fordham developed the training programs of the SAP, edited the *Journal of Analytical Psychology* for 15 years, and co-edited the English-language edition of Jung's *Collected Works*. (Cf. White, 4 March 1954, p. 230 and note.) Cf. also Jung to Fordham, Appendix I, pp. 294f.

26 The Book of Job (Rascher Verlag edition of *Hiob*). Cf. Jung, 16 Oct. 1951, p. 172 and note.

27 Cf. Jung, 16 Oct. 1951, p. 172 and note.

28 Cf. White, 23 June 1946, p. 34 and note.

29 Typewritten.

30 Cf. Jung, 27 Dec. 1947, p. 105 and note.

Both Dr. and Mrs. Jung send you their best regards. I'm adding mine together with a lot of good wishes for Easter!

Yours ever, [MARIE-JEANNE] (unsigned carbon copy)

as from Blackfriars, Oxford

5–4–52[31]

My dear C.G.

Thank you a million for "Hiob". Though I have countless other things to do, I can hardly put it down. It is the most exciting and moving book I have read in years: and somehow it arouses tremendous bonds of sympathy between us, and lights up all sorts of dark places both in the Scriptures and in my own psyche. . . . Of course, this is not a considered judgment on all it says! The first impact is too strong for me to dare any such thing.

I am so glad to hear from Marie-Jeanne that you and Mrs Jung are taking a holiday. I hope it is much refreshing you both.

My own MS[32] should shortly reach you, if it has not done so already. By comparison with "Hiob" it is very small beer – and inevitably rather "intellectualist" too. You will realize, I am sure, that this is at least partly deliberate; and that I have exercized a certain *disciplina arcani*.[33] It is no use my trying to sell yet what my public is not ready to buy. The crucial Chapter V[34] is particularly inconclusive and unsatisfactory (I am afraid *you* will find it particularly so): this "Frontiers" job of talking both languages (the psychological and theological) at once, and trying to explain the two parties to one another, quite baffles me. The whole thing has still got to get through the

31 Typewritten, with handwritten corrections and insertions.

32 Manuscript of White's *God and the Unconscious*.

33 "discipline of the secret." A seventeenth-century term referring to the practice in the early Church (third to fifth centuries) of holding some teachings secret from new Christians (those not yet baptized) and from the heathen. It was "a custom intended to shield the doctrines and mysteries of Christianity from ridicule or misconception" (*The New Catholic Dictionary*, 1929, p. 298). *Disciplina* here refers to a specialized teaching; *arcanum* (lit. "secret") here connotes "mystery."

34 Cf. White, 25 March 1952, p. 179. In Chapter V, "The Frontiers of Theology and Psychology," White quotes from Jung's first long letter to him, but also criticizes Jung's essay on the Trinity from a theological as well as a psychological point of view. For example, he argues that Christian believers find psychological meaning, which Jung overlooks, in the traditional symbolism of the Trinity (*God & Unc.*, pp. 74f).

ecclesiastical censorship,[35] which – besides its legitimate and worthy concern not unduly to disturb the more faithful sheep – is apt to be very troublesome sometimes.

All this is not to forestall any criticisms and disagreements you are moved to express in your preface (on the contrary, I shall welcome them heartily), but to explain what may seem an undue cautiousness, and stress on the difficulties.

I have been re-reading "Aion" with greater care, and absorbed interest, lately. I do wish we could somehow resolve this deadlock about *privatio boni*. (For one thing, my colleagues and perhaps many others, will fight shy of your psychology until we do!) At first I inclined to think the difference was unimportant and academic; but now it seems to me it must affect one's value-*judgments* on almost everything (alchemy, gnosticism, Christ and Antichrist, the Second Coming, the whole orientation of psychotherapy), without there being any dispute about the *facts*. You will notice I have not gone into the matter further in my book: only added a footnote to attempt to clarify the traditional position.[36]

Would it (I wonder) help at all if I concede that evil cannot be *per*ceived (sensed or intuited), nor even necessarily *felt*, as *privatio*; while maintaining that it cannot be correctly *con*ceived otherwise? If that is so, perhaps I could begin to find some common ground – which I am extremely eager to do. But I also find common ground in "gut ist das, was von einem gewissen Standpunkt aus als passend, annehmbar oder wertvoll erscheint"[37] (is not this Aristotle's own "id quod omnia appetunt"?),[38] and that "Böse ist das entsprechende Gegenteil."[39] But (I ask), if that is so, must not evil be UNpassend, UNannehmbar, wertLOS?[40] (I.e. precisely privatio boni?) And if that is so, what can be the meaning of "gut ist, was nicht schlecht ist"[41] – the privation of a privation?

But I am asking you questions (not, you will know, to score a dialectical point: but to try to penetrate the veil of unconsciousness which prevents my even understanding your conviction) – before I have answered yours (Aion,

35 Since 1546 members of religious orders had been required to have the approval of a superior's *imprimi potest* (it can be printed). This was in addition to a censor's *nihil obstat quominus imprimatur* (nothing prevents it from being printed), and the bishop's *imprimatur*, confirming the work as free of moral or doctrinal error. Thus in 1952 White's *God & Unc.* received the *imprimi potest* from his prior provincial, Fr. Hilary Carpenter. The *nihil obstat* was issued by Fr. Richard Roche and the *imprimatur* given by the archbishop of Birmingham, in which diocese Oxford is located. [AC]

36 In a long footnote (*God & Unc.*, pp. 75f) White summarizes the traditional position of the Church on the problem of evil. Cf. Appendix 5, p. 347.

37 "good is that which appears from a specific standpoint fitting, acceptable, or valuable."

38 "that which all desire."

39 "evil is the corresponding opposite."

40 UNfitting, UNacceptable, valueLESS.

41 "good is that which is not bad."

pp.96,97)![42] In Catholic theology of course the devil is *not* intrinsically evil (many Fathers consider him the best and noblest of all God's creatures); he is "evil" precisely inasmuch as he has *deprived* himself of his due and connatural relationship to God. The "evil" in hell is likewise the *privation* of the divine vision (and so of man's own entelechy); and so likewise in the damned. (A "privatio boni in subjecto bono"[43] in every case.) Of course these are called "eternal" only in the sense of timeless and endless, not in the sense in which God is eternal ("interminabilis vitae tota simul et perfecta possessio").[44] There is no question of dualism in the sense of some positive existence co-existing with, but other than, the summum bonum[45] which must include all good. Of course a moral, man-made, chosen dualism should be admitted, in the sense that man (and angels) may refuse the unity. But this, so far from involving a permanent and intrinsic evil principle, would mean that even our *dis*order comes from within the divine order: from which standpoint of course hell is good!

Of course, these are only the bare, fleshless bones of answers to your questions: not intended to be convincing! But then, about the last paragraph of your note, I'd want to put a question to you! Is this "Einheit des Selbst",[46] this complexio oppositorum,[47] good or evil? Perhaps you would say, "beyond good and evil"? I should agree it was beyond the *opposites* of goods and evils of our ordinary acquaintance; but certainly not beyond all we can call good – on the contrary, supremely "annehmbar, passend, wertvoll";[48] certainly *not* "das Gegenteil".[49] Indeed, if fully realized, would it not be the summum bonum – not only including the good in all goods, but in all evils as well?

Please forgive me all these questions and arguings: the more so as I fear I may be starting a correspondence I shall not have the leisure to continue. I am sure you will know that I am not just trying to be captious, but feel that something of enormous importance may be involved – certainly something

42 White's page references correspond to portions of chapter V, "Christ, A Symbol of the Self," where Jung argues forcefully against what he understands to be Catholic orthodoxy. In one footnote Jung challenges White directly, demanding answers to several questions that Jung sees as arising from the Catholic description of evil as "privation of good": "My learned friend Victor White thinks he can detect a Manichaean streak in me. I don't go in for metaphysics, but ecclesiastical philosophy undoubtedly does, and for this reason I must ask what are we to make of hell, damnation, and the devil, if these things are eternal? Theoretically they consist of nothing, and how does that square with the dogma of eternal damnation? But if they consist of something, that something can hardly be good. So where is the danger of dualism?" (CW 9.ii, *Aion*, §112–114, pp. 61f, n. 74.)

43 "privation of good in a good subject."

44 "the possession of unending life is complete [total, whole], and at the same time perfect."

45 highest good. (An attribute borrowed from Platonic philosophy, which in Thomistic thought applies only to God.)

46 unity of the Self.

47 complex of opposites.

48 "acceptable, fitting, valuable."

49 the opposite.

you and I both feel rather strongly about, which must suggest some lurking shadows somewhere, which I am eager to penetrate as dispassionately as possible. One can not, I now think, dismiss the matter as a matter of metaphysics with no psychological relevance: for, after all, metaphysical beliefs are themselves psychological facts which must enormously affect a whole Weltanschauung. So I am tapping all this out in an effort at least to try and feel my own way to understanding. I hope I don't bore you too dreadfully! It would help a lot if you should find the distinction of *perceptions* and *conceptions* of good and evil acceptable – or perhaps could give an example of evil that was NOT a privatio boni. Or can it be that there is some confusion of privation (absence) and negation (not-being), of μὴ ὄν and οὐκ ὄν?[50] Sometimes, in reading "Aion", one might suppose that SS. Basil, Thomas, etc. were Christian Scientists denying the **reality**[51] of evil!

However, it IS a fascinating book – and an encouraging one too in these grim, deluded times. Certainly that and "Hiob" have given me an entirely new (or perhaps very old) angle on the Second Coming, and on the dreadful loss to preaching and theology in letting Nazis and Marxists steal our eschatology. For that, and for countless other things, I'll be eternally grateful to you, whatever befall this difficulty with privatio boni! And whithersoever it all leads. . . . How, I sometimes wonder, would Job have wrestled with God as a member of a modern, happy, sheltered, religious community?! And sometimes the complexio oppositorum of those extra Ecclesiam[52] looks childsplay compared with that of some within! Which, I suppose, is what one would expect.

But I must meander on and bore you no more, with all this spilling of ideas.

My renewed thanks, and most cordial greetings to all. Please forgive the length of this letter; it is a little self-compensation for my disappointment and not being able to come to the Institut this summer.

Ever yours[53] VICTOR

50 White points to a grammatical rule in classical Greek, which is actually more complicated than he indicates. Jung's usage, as noted earlier, probably comes from his reading of New Testament and Patristic writers, such as St. Paul and St. Basil (cf. Jung, 31 Dec. 1949, p. 141 and note). White's real objection, however (cf. also White, 9 July 1952, pp. 202f), seems to be that by unfairly caricaturing an ancient philosophical account of evil, Jung ridicules the stance of conscientious Catholics, including White, who continue to hold it.

51 White drew a wavy line under the word. It is a copy-editor's mark for boldface type. Since White edited articles for *Blackfriars* and *Dominican Studies*, he may have developed a habit of using copy-editor's marks for emphasis, even in private writings.

52 outside the church.

53 Handwritten closing.

early April 1952[54]

pro tempore *Locarno*,
Ticino
Parkhotel

Dear Victor,

Thank you very much for your reprints! You have been obviously busy. I have read them all and I think the one about the "Dying God" is particularly good. The one about Freud is clever and remarkably openminded. Your meditation about the way of the Cross contains nothing I could not subscribe to. It is psychologically "correct". This amounts to a sincere compliment. Does the book you are planning contain these articles?

I hope you have received my "Antwort auf Hiob". I had a pretty miserable time throughout March on account of a grippe, from which I am recovering very slowly. I came down here, to pick up again. Although we are in the sun, the air is still pretty cold and windy. I have finished the dreaded last chapter of my "Mysterium Coniunctionis".[55] It has knocked me flat, and my head is tired. Well, I am approaching my 78th year, and complaints are pointless. My next goal seems to be a thorough contemplation of the spiritual life of lizards and similar coldblooded animals. But the world does not let me go so easily. After this letter I have to write another one about understanding and believing to a protestant theologus.[56] I am afraid I cannot conceive of any religious belief, which is less than a violation of my ego-consciousness. Otherwise I would hardly be aware of believing anything at all. If belief does not come to me as a shock, it would not convince me. I don't know whether they are going to like my opinions or not.

54 Handwritten letter, undated. From the evidence it must have been written in early April 1952. On 20 April 1952 White answers both this and Jung's next letter.

55 "mystery of union" or "marriage." An alchemical concept of great importance to Jung, referring to the wholeness created by the union of opposites in the psyche, symbolized by but not limited to the joining of male and female. Jung had just completed what would become, in German, the first volume in a three-volume work (cf. White, 13 Oct. 1946, p. 46 and note). The first volume appeared three years later: *Mysterium Coniunctionis. Untersuchung über die Trennung und Zusammensetzung der seelischen Gegensätze in der Alchemie* ([Psychologische Abhandlungen 10], Zürich: Rascher, 1955). The English edition, CW 14, *Mysterium Coniunctionis: An Inquiry into the Separation and Synthesis of Psychic Opposites in Alchemy*, is a single volume, combining Volumes I and II of GW 14.

56 Reference unclear. See however Jung's letter to a professor in Vienna, who has sent Jung his review of *Aion*. In this letter Jung distinguishes the divergent meanings of *gnosis* (knowledge) in Christian, Gnostic, and scientific discourse (Jung to H. Haberlandt, 23 April 1952, *Letters II*, pp. 53ff).

The Curator of the Museum of the History of Science in Oxford[57] has sent me a rather long series of dreams, which he has unearthed from the Elias Ashmole MSS,[58] the editor of the Theatrum Chemicum Britannicum 1646(?).[59] They extend over about 5 years and contain the remarkable story of an invasion of unconscious contents aiming at a coniunctio with the unconscious. The attempt fails, i.e., is superseded by a return of the former onesided masculine consciousness. It is an unconscious parallel to *Faust*. The attempt culminates in a symbol of the Self: Paradise on the North pole, 4 springs and on a hill the chapel of Our Lady. The series begins with Venus in the IX house = *Sapientia*. It ends with death, fraud and murder. A fine example of an individuation that did not come off.

Hoping to see you in summer again!

Yours cordially C.G.

April 9th until 14th, 1952[60]

Parkhotel
Locarno

Dear Victor,

Thank you for your human letter.[61] It gives me some idea of what is happening inside of you.

The privatio boni does not seem to me such a particular puzzle, but I understand, that it is of greatest importance. It is perhaps best if I set forth my point of view, so that you can see how I look at it. At the same time I shall try to consider your standpoint too.

I think you agree with me, that within our empirical world, Good and Evil

57 C.H. Josten (Conrad Hermann Hubertus Maria Apollinaris Joesten, 1912–1994): German-born historian who actively resisted the Nazis in the 1930s. On a visit to Oxford in 1948 he encountered the writings and alchemical collections of Elias Ashmole, about whom he later published two books. In 1950 Josten succeeded Sherwood Taylor as curator of the Museum of the History of Science, housed in the Old Ashmolean Museum, Oxford University.

58 Elias Ashmole (1617–1692): royalist, antiquarian, astrologer, alchemist and botanist, who published three collections of alchemical writings. His books, historical documents, and Cabinet of Curiosities became the initial source of the Old Ashmolean Museum.

59 *Theatrum Chemicum Britannicum* (London, 1652), compiled by Elias Ashmole, originally published with subtitle: "Containing severall poeticall pieces of our famous English philosophers, who have written the hermetique mysteries in their own ancient language" (New York: Johnson Reprint Corp., 1967).

60 Handwritten on hotel stationery.

61 Cf. White, 5 April 1952, pp. 181ff.

represent the indispensable parts of a logical judgement, like white and black, right–left, above–below, etc.

2.[62] These are equivalent opposites and it is understood that they are always relative to the situation of the one that makes the statement, a person or a law. Empirically we are unable to confirm the existence of anything absolute, i.e. there are no logical means to establish an absolute truth, except a tautology.

Yet we are moved (by archetypal motives) *to make such statements*, viz. religious or metaphysical assertions such as the Trinity, the virgin birth, and other exceedingly improbable and physically impossible things. One of these assertions is the Summum Bonum and its consequence, the privatio boni. The latter is logically as impossible as the Trinity. It is therefore a truly religious statement: "prorsus credibile quia ineptum".[63] Divine favour and daemonic evil or danger are archetypal. Even if you know that your judgement is entirely subjective and relative you are nevertheless forced to make such statements more than a dozen times every day. And when you are religious you talk in terms of impossibilities. I have no arguments against these facts. I only deny, that the privatio boni is a logical statement, but I admit the obvious truth, that it is a "metaphysical truth based upon an archetypal motif".

The way in which opposites are reconciled or united in God, we just don't know. Nor do we understand how they are united in the Self. The Self is transcendental ergo only partially conscious. Empirically it is good and evil, the same as the "acts of God" have decidedly contradictory aspects. This fact however does not justify theological judgement, that God is either good or evil. He is Transcendental just as much as the Self and therefore not subject to human logics.

The supreme powers are assumed to be either indifferent or more often good than evil. There is an archetypal accent upon the good aspect, but only slightly so. This is understandable, because there must be some sort of aequilibrium, otherwise the world could not exist.

The great difficulty seems to consist in the fact, that on the one side we must defend the sanity and logics of the human mind, and that on the other side we have to accept and to welcome the existence of illogical and irrational factors transcending our comprehension. We must deal with them as rationally as we can, even if there is no hope of getting ever on top of them. Inasmuch as we can't deal with them rationally we have to formulate them symbolically. A symbol when taken literally is nearly always impossible. Thus I should say, that the privatio boni is *a symbolic truth*, based on archetypal

62 Jung numbers this paragraph as his second point. The preceding brief paragraph, not numbered, is apparently his first.

63 "absolutely believable because absurd."

motivation, not to be defended rationally as little as the virgin birth. Excuse my bad writing. I am in the garden and there is no table but my knee. Answer not expected! I will try to help you as much as possible.[64]

Yours C.G.

Hawkesyard Priory,
Rugeley, Staffs.
as from Oxford

20.4.52[65]

My dear C.G.

Please pardon my writing to you in green ink, & with a ball-point. I am on a journey in the Midlands and North of England, conducting retreats & lectures, & my ordinary pen has run dry.

I was so very grateful to you for both your letters. I do hope that you have now fully recovered from the grippe, & that the weather got warmer for you at Locarno. I can well believe that the consummation of the "mysterium coniunctionis"[66] exhausted you, but I am very thankful to hear it is done, & greatly look forward to the result.

Your letter to the "Protestant Theologus"[67] would interest me very much. It sounds as if it touches on matters that have much exercized me of late – apart from the fact that I am eager to understand just what *you* mean.

I am very interested that Josten[68] should have written you, & communicated his Ashmole finding. I am also rather pleasantly suprised, as "Jungian psychology" was his bête noir not long ago.

Thank you very much for your most encouraging remarks about my journalistic efforts – they are certainly encouraging. But I think I have been rather *too* busy lately with this rather trivial sort of work. The demand seems to be enormous for that kind of thing.

About the *privatio boni*, we seem to be approaching the same deadlock again of assertion and counter-assertion! I am most eager to penetrate this darkness. For I just don't understand what you see irrational or illogical about it, nor can I think of a single empirical specimen of a real or alleged "evil" in which the "privatio" definition is not verified – any more than I can think of an empirical darkness that is not a "privatio" of light. The validity

64 Apparently referring to White's difficulty in grasping Jung's psychological explanation of the relationship of good and evil (cf. White, 20 April 1952, below).

65 Handwritten on Hawkesyard Priory letterhead. A notation at the upper left corner of the first page, in dark pencil, apparently in Jung's hand: "to file!"

66 Cf. Jung, early April 1952, p. 185 and note.

67 Ibid.

68 Cf. Jung, early April 1952, p. 186.

of any particular *judgment* of value is surely quite another question from the *meaning* of the terms (good or evil) employed. There is surely nothing religious or archetypal in my motivation, nor anything illogical or transcendental when I call an egg "bad" because it *lacks* what I think an egg ought to have – even though a Chinaman may find in that very fact something that makes it "good". Our tastes and standards may differ, but our meaning is the same, surely?

However, perhaps this is a *philosophical* deadlock, & I am not out to convert you to quite different philosophical premisses. But what DOES concern me personally & profoundly is that in the sphere in which I work, it is essential to show that your empirical psychology is not necessarily bound up with *any* particular philosophical system of interpretation, & that the facts & aims of your psychology are at least as amenable of statement in terms of the philosophia perennis as of Kant[69] or any kind of positivism & religious irrationalism. We move in different circles, & our minds have been formed in different philosophical climates. But it is not only Catholics, but many others besides (not least among Anglo-Saxons) whose resistance to your psychology (& so to their own psyches) must be immeasurably reinforced if they think that they must swallow Kant & Schleiermacher[70] along with Jung, & necessarily abandon hard-won convictions of a theological or philosophical character.

Ampleforth Abbey
York

I have moved my address & filled my pen since writing the foregoing. I am here conducting a retreat for the holy monks – so far it is singularly uninspired.

This letter is already much longer than I intended, & I await no *reply*. I should indeed love to come & see you again this summer, & am exceedingly grateful for your invitation. Then perhaps we could *talk* about these things. That would indeed be a great "help" – & I only wish I could offer you some adequate help in return.

My warmest greetings to you, & to Mrs Jung & all.

Ever cordially, VICTOR

69 Immanuel Kant (1724–1804): German philosopher. His moralism and aversion to metaphysics make him uncongenial to many Catholic theologians. Aspects of Kant's thought, especially his epistemology, are foundational for Jung (cf. White, 23 Oct. 1945, p. 18 and note; Appendix 3, pp. 335f). Cf. also Jung to Bernhard Lang, *Letters II*, pp. 375ff.

70 Friedrich Schleiermacher (1768–1834): German Protestant theologian, author of *On Religion: Speeches to its Cultured Despisers* (1799) and *Christian Faith* (1822). His definition of religion as the "feeling of absolute dependence," had a major impact. According to Jung, Schleiermacher converted his paternal grandfather to Protestantism (cf. Jung to Ewald Jung, *Letters II*, p. 528n).

Küsnacht-Zürich

April 30th 1952[71]

Dear Victor,

The *privatio boni* seems to be a puzzle. A few days ago I had an interesting interview with a Jesuit father from Munich (Lotz is his name).[72] He is professor of dogmatics (?) or christian philosophy. He was just in the middle of "Antwort auf Hiob" and under the immediate impact of my argument against the privatio. He admitted that it is a puzzle, but that the modern interpretation would explain "Evil" as a "disintegration" or a "decomposition" of "Good". If you hypostasize – as the Church does – the concept or idea of Good and give to it metaphysical substance (i.e. bonum = esse or having esse),[73] then "decomposition" would be indeed a very suitable formula, also satisfactory from the psychological standpoint, inasmuch as Good is always an effort and a composite achievement, while Evil is easily sliding down or falling asunder. But if you take your simile of the good egg, it would become a bad egg by decomposition. A bad egg is not characterized by a mere decrease of goodness, however, since it produces qualities of its own, that did not belong to the good egg. It develops among other things H_2S, which is a particularly unpleasant substance of its own right. It derives very definitely from the highly complex albumen of the good egg and thus forms a most obvious evidence for the thesis: Evil derives from Good.

Thus the formula of "decomposition" is in so far rather satisfactory, as it acknowledges that Evil is as substantial as Good, because H_2S is as tangibly real as the albumen. In this interpretation Evil is far from being a μὴ ὄν. Pater Lotz therefore had my applause. But what about the privatio boni? Good by definition must be good throughout, even in its smallest particles. You cannot say, that a small good is bad. If then a good thing disintegrates into minute fragments, each of them remains good and therefore eatable like a loaf of bread divided into small particles. But when the bread rots, it oxydizes and changes its original substance. There are no more nourishing carbohydrates, but acids, i.e. from a good substance has come a bad thing. The "decomposition" theory would lead to the ultimate conclusion that the Summum Bonum can disintegrate and produce H_2S, the characteristic smell

71 Typewritten by secretary from holograph.

72 Johannes Baptist Lotz, S.J. (b. 1903): German Jesuit, student of Heidegger; professor of philosophy and theology at the University of Munich and at the Gregorian University in Rome.

73 good = being or having being. Following both Augustine and Aquinas, a basic premise of orthodox Catholic thought is that the creation as such is good, and nothing but what is good has real existence. ("Whatever is, is good," Augustine, *Confessions*, Book 7.) In Platonic and Aristotelian philosophy, evil does not share in the "being" which good possesses.

of Hell. Good then would be corruptible, i.e. it would possess an inherent possibility of decay. This possibility of corruption means nothing less than a tendency inherent to the Good to decay and to transform into Evil. That obviously confirms my heretical views. But I don't even go as far as Pater Lotz: I am quite satisfied with non-hypostasising Good and Evil. I consider them not as substances, but as a merely psychological judgement, since I have no means of establishing them as metaphysical substances. I don't deny the possibility of a belief, that they are substances and that Good prevails against Evil. I even take it into consideration, that there is a large consensus in that respect, for which there must be important reasons (as I have pointed out in AION). But if you try to make something logical or rationalistic out of that belief, you get into a remarkable mess, as the argument with Pater Lotz clearly shows.

You know, I am not only empirical but also practical. In practice you say nothing when you hold that in an evil deed is small Good: there is big Evil and a little bit of Good. In practice you just can't deny the οὐσία[74] of Evil. On the metaphysical plane you are free to declare that what we call "substantially evil" is in metaphysical reality a small Good. But such a statement does not make much sense to me. You call God the Lord over Evil, but if the latter is μὴ ὄν, He is Lord over nothing, not even over the Good, because He is it Himself as the Summum Bonum, that has created but good things which have however a marked tendency to go wrong. Nor does evil or corruption derive from Man, since the Serpent is prior to him, so πόθεν τὸ κακόν???[75]

The necessary answer is: Metaphysically there is no Evil at all; it is only in Man's world and it stems from Man. This statement however contradicts the fact, that paradise was not made by Man. He came last into it, nor has he made the Serpent. If even God's most beautiful angel, Lucifer, has such a desire to get corrupt, his nature must show a considerable defect of moral qualities – like Jahwe, who insists jealously on morality and is himself unjust. No wonder that His creation should have a yellow streak.

Does the Doctrine of the Church admit Jahwe's moral defects? If so, Lucifer merely portrays his creator; if not, what about the 89th Psalm,[76] etc.? Jahwe's immoral behaviour rests on biblical facts. A morally dubious creator cannot be expected to produce a perfectly good world, not even perfectly good angels.

I know theologians always say: one should not overlook the Lord's greatness, majesty and kindness and one shouldn't ask questions anyhow. I don't

74 being; reality. 75 where does evil come from?

76 Psalm 89 rehearses God's promises to David, who laments: "But now thou hast cast off and rejected, thou art full of wrath against thy anointed. Thou hast renounced the covenant with thy servant; thou hast defiled his crown in the dust. . . . Lord, where is thy steadfast love of old, which by thy faithfulness thou didst swear to David?" (vv. 38ff).

overlook God's fearful greatness, but I should consider myself a coward and immoral, if I would allow myself to be deterred from asking questions.

On a practical level the privatio boni doctrine is morally dangerous, because it belittles and irrealizes Evil and thereby weakens the Good, because it deprives it of its necessary opposite: there is no white without black, no right without left, no above without below, no warm without cold, no truth without error, no light without darkness etc. If Evil is an illusion, Good is necessarily illusory too. That is the reason why I hold that the privatio boni is illogical, irrational, and even a nonsense. The moral opposites are an epistemological necessity and, when hypostasized, they produce an amoral Jahwe and a Lucifer and a sinful Man and a suffering creation.

I hope we can continue worrying this bone in Summer!

Cordially yours, C.G.

P.S. Unfortunately I have no copy of the letter to the Prot. theologian. But I will send you an offprint of my answer to Buber,[77] who has called me a Gnostic.[78] He does not understand psychic reality.

Blackfriars, Oxford

13–5–52[79]

My dear C.G.

This is no answer to your long letter. It is just a brief note to thank you for it, very much indeed. I hope to find time to write at length about it before

77 Martin Buber (1878–1965): Austrian political and religious philosopher, born into a family of Jewish scholars, played an important role in almost every aspect of Jewish life in Western Europe and Israel. Buber's mature thought was influenced by Hasidism. His published works include *Paths in Utopia* (1950), *Eclipse of God: Studies in the Relation between Religion and Philosophy* (1952), *Hasidism and Modern Man* (1958), *I and Thou* (1923), and *The Knowledge of Man* (1965). In 1923 Buber lectured at the Psychological Club in Zurich. In 1934 he and Jung both spoke at Eranos.

78 Jung had written a long letter to the editor of a German periodical ("Religion und Psychologie," *Merkur*, Stuttgart, VI:5, May 1952), defending himself against Buber's charge of Gnosticism ("Religion und modernes Denken," *Merkur*, VI:2, Feb. 1952). As in his "Foreword to White's 'God and the Unconscious'," Jung outlines the difficulties of holding a dialogue between philosophically grounded theology and scientifically based psychology. (Cf. "Religion and Psychology: A Reply to Martin Buber." CW 18, §1499–1513.) Buber's rejoinder was published in the same issue of *Merkur*. Both it and the original article were later incorporated in his *Gottesfinsternis: Betrachtungen zur Beziehung zwischen Religion und Philosophie* (Zurich, 1953) (*Eclipse of God*, 1952). (Cf. *Letters II*, p. 43n.)

79 Handwritten.

long – anyway before I see you, which I hope to be able to do in July. I will also write soon to suggest dates for my visit – to which I am much looking forward.

I hear you are at Bollingen, but send this to Küsnacht in case you have returned. I hope you have a very refreshing time there, & that the script of "God & the Unconscious" is not spoiling your holiday!

I have just been reading Professor Onians' "Origins of European Thought".[80] It should not be missed for dream-symbolism etc. Another – very different but remarkable – book is Karl Stern's autobiography, "Pillar of Fire".[81] Unfortunately he skips the details of his "Jungian analysis" which was the turning point of his life.

More anon! And warmest greetings to you, Mrs Jung & all.

Ever cordially VICTOR

Küsnacht-Zürich

May 14th 1952[82]

Dear Victor,

Here is something that might interest you. It is an evidence[83] for that rumour that has been going on lately, that psychoanalysis has been condemned by the Church, which I couldn't believe. – No answer needed!

You might also be interested to see my controversy with Mr. Buber.[84]

Cordially yours, C.G. (unsigned carbon copy)

80 Richard Broxton Onians, *The Origins of European Thought about the Body, the Mind, the Soul, the World, Time and Fate*. Cambridge, England: Cambridge University Press, 1951.

81 Karl Stern (1906–1975): *The Pillar of Fire* (New York: Harcourt Brace, 1951). Stern, a prominent neuropsychiatrist, recounts his struggle to reconcile his Jewish identity with the claims of the Christian faith, starting with his boyhood in the Weimar Republic, through his emigration to England and conversion to Catholicism. White's review of Stern's *The Third Revolution* appeared in *The Commonweal*, March 1954.

82 Typewritten. Letter previously unpublished.

83 No identifying information available.

84 Cf. Jung, 30 April 1952, p. 192 and note.

Oxford

21–5–52[85]

[to Marie-Jeanne Schmid]

My publishers are much wondering if the MS. of my book arrived all right. As C.G. did not mention it in his last letter, I wonder if you would be so good as to send a postcard if it did *not* arrive? It was sent several weeks ago.

Please tell C.G. I have begun a long letter to him about *privatio boni* & the immorality of God, but I do not know when I shall have chance to finish it!

All best to you, VICTOR WHITE

Küsnacht-Zürich

May 23rd 1952[86]

Dear Father White,

I'm terribly ashamed of myself for not having acknowledged receipt of your manuscript either to yourself or to your publishers. It is really quite unpardonable and I apologize humbly. It came not quite two weeks ago and C.G. has already read it and also written a foreword of about 13 pages. But since he finally wrote it in German he would like to give it to Elizabeth Welsh[87] to have it translated. He hopes that you have no objection.

Please let me know whether you'd like to have a copy of the German version too and also where the manuscript should be sent back to: you or your publishers?

Thank you so much for your good wishes! I'm ever so grateful that you will hold thumbs for me as to finding a flat, because it looks rather hopeless so far. However, it would be ungrateful to be pessimistic.

All my best wishes to you!

Yours ever MARIE-JEANNE (unsigned carbon copy)

85 Handwritten postcard. 86 Typewritten.

87 Elizabeth Welsh, an Englishwoman living in Zurich, had translated notes from Jung's lectures and other writings into English since the 1930s. E.g., "Modern Psychology" (notes on lectures given at the ETH, Zürich, October 1933–February 1934). With Barbara Hannah and Mary Briner she translated Jung's 1946 article, *Aufsätze zur Zeitgeschichte*; and with Andrea Dykes, *Der Traum des Descartes* [The Dream of Descartes] by von Franz (Jung-Studien 3, 1952). A few weeks after this letter, Welsh's translation of Jung's "Foreword" was sent to Harvill Press, while White received the original "Vorrede" (cf. Schmid, 29 May 1952, p. 195).

[undated][88]

[to Marie-Jeanne Schmid]

Thank you so much. No apologies necessary at all. I am very eager to see the Preface, but perhaps it would be better if it were sent directly to the publishers (Harvill Press, 23 Lower Belgrave St, London, S.W.1.)

All best wishes, VICTOR WHITE

Küsnacht-Zürich

May 29th 1952[89]

Dear Father White,

Thanks for the Postcard and for being so nice about my shortcomings! I shall send the translation of the Foreword direct to the Harvill Press, but am enclosing a copy of the German original.[90]

You did not tell me where I should send the manuscript of your book. (I suppose my question was not clear enough.) Or is it a copy which is not needed any longer? I'll keep it here until you let me know.

I wonder whether C.G. ever mentioned Dr. Zwi Werblowsky[91] to you, that young Jew who gave him all that valuable material about Jahwe. His book (i.e. his dissertation) "Lucifer and Prometheus"[92] has just come out with Kegan Paul and you might have seen it or heard of it. (C.G. wrote a foreword.) In a letter to C.G. which arrived this morning Dr. Werblowsky asks him to recommend him to you. He would like to look you up during his holidays (of which I don't know when they take place). I wrote him that I'd tell you about it since C.G. has just left for Bollingen and was so fed up with things that I don't want to forward any letters to him at present. I think that

88 Typewritten postcard. Date illegible in postmark. 89 Typewritten.

90 A typescript of Jung's "Vorrede" was preserved with this letter. Elizabeth Welsh's translation, produced in three weeks, appeared in the first edition of White's book (Harvill, 1952). A later translation by Hull, closer in meaning to Jung's original, is printed in CW 11, *Psych. & Rel.*, §449ff (pp. 299ff), and in the 1982 edition of *God & Unc.*

91 R.J. (Raphael Jehudah) Zwi Werblowsky (b. 1924): teaches and writes about the history of Judaism, especially Jewish mystical tradition. In 1956 he co-founded the Department of Comparative Religion at Hebrew University, Jerusalem, where he is now Martin Buber Professor Emeritus of Comparative Religion.

92 R.J. Zwi Werblowsky, *Lucifer and Prometheus: A Study of Milton's Satan* (Introduction by C.G. Jung. London: Kegan Paul, 1952). Cf. White, 25 June 1952, p. 197; 9 July 1952, p. 201; and notes.

you will enjoy meeting Dr. W. who is full of bright and interesting ideas, and I know that C.G. would recommend him to you. So if you have a little time to spare for him, I'm sure you will not regret it. (I forgot to mention that Dr. W. is lecturer for Semitics at Leeds University.)

All my best wishes to you!

Ever yours, MARIE-JEANNE (unsigned carbon copy)

as from Blackfriars, Oxford

6.4.52[93]

Dear Marie-Jeanne,

Thank you so very much for your letter, and for sending me the original of CG's preface. It is fine, and of course I am writing him to thank him.

I have written to my publishers to ask them to let you know direct if they want the script back again or not. I expect they will do so; but if you do not hear from them within a week or so – just burn it!

Of course I should be delighted to meet Dr Werblowsky. But as I get so booked up, and shall be away most of the vacation, it would be well if he would write me well in advance to say when he will be in these parts.

All very best wishes to you, VICTOR WHITE

as from Blackfriars, Oxford.

25.6.52[94]

My dear C.G.,

This is principally to tell you that I have arranged to fly to Zurich on the night of July 16th–17th (it is cheaper to fly by night, but has the disadvantage of arriving at Zurich long before cock-crow!). So, unless I hear from you to the contrary, I should arrive at Bollingen not very late on July 17th. I look forward to it very much, and should love it if you could put up with me for about 10 days with you. It seems we have rather an extra lot to talk about this year: I certainly have!

93 Typewritten. From context the date ("6.4") must be June 4.

94 Typewritten.

I continue to be very delighted with the preface you have written to my book; I (and my poor readers) will always be very grateful.

The proofs are now coming in, together with exam-papers for correction, and a great influx of "souls". So it looks rather as if I shall never finish the famous letter to you which I began many weeks ago. I send you the *opus imperfectum*:[95] many matters about Bad Eggs, Jahwe's morals, Job & Elihu, you & Buber, must wait till we can meet – if you can still bear it.

I also enclose a mimeograph copy of a short article[96] I have done on the Vocatus atque non vocatus Deus.[97] It is straight, simplified, thomist theology for a pious Catholic magazine; but I think it might interest you, possibly even surprise you!

I am just amazed at the amount of writing and correspondence you can do, my dear C.G., with such a variety of people. It chances that I have just seen your correspondence with Josten, and also with Werblowsky. Though I share many of the latter's difficulties, you have my very great sympathy. You must feel rather like the pussy-cat at the animal show who hoped for first prize in the Cat class, and was given the booby prize among the Dogs!

PLEASE do not trouble to answer or acknowledge this, so long as July 17th is a convenient day for me to arrive.

Ever cordially & gratefully VICTOR

P.S. Our friend Barbara seems quite to have won through the difficult patch I wrote to you about,[98] and to be doing quite marvellously.

P.S.[99] You may like to know that "God & the Unconscious" has got both the Bishop's and the Dominican "Imprimatur"[100] without a murmer from either of these!

95 incomplete, imperfect work.

96 Enclosed with this letter was White's typescript of his essay, "The Unknown God," for *The Life of the Spirit*. It later became Chapter 2 in Part I of his second book, *God the Unknown and other Essays* (London: Harvill Press, 1956).

97 The called or uncalled God: words which Jung attributes to a Delphic oracle (cf. Jung to E. Rolfe, 19 Nov. 1960, *Letters II*, p. 611), "*Vocatus atque non vocatus Deus aderit*" ("Called or uncalled, the god will be present"), are chiseled over the front door of Jung's house in Küsnacht and into a wall at the Tower. Jung first encountered the saying when he was 19, in a 1563 edition of Erasmus' *Collectanea Adagorium*, a compilation of Latin and Greek proverbs (*Letters II*, p. 611n).

98 Cf. White, 7 Oct. 1951, p. 170. At this period Jung was also in correspondence with Barbara Robb (Appendix 1, pp. 293f).

99 Handwritten footnote added on back of page.

100 Cf. White, 5 April 1952, p. 182 and note.

Küsnacht-Zürich

June 30th 1952[101]

Dear Victor,

First of all I should like to know, whether the doctrine of privatio boni ranks as a dogma or as a sententia communis.[102] In the latter case it could be a disputable subject, inasmuch as I understand the ways of ecclesiastical thinking. At all events I have started the discussion under this assumption. If on the other hand it should be a defined and declared truth, I will not discuss it any more, but I shall try to understand the deeper reasons for its existence, as I have already tried at least tentatively.

The crux seems to be lying in the contamination of the two incongruous notions of Good and of Being. If you assume, as I do, that Good is a moral judgement and not substantial in itself, then Evil is its opposite and just as nonsubstantial as the first. If however you assume, that Good is Being, then Evil can be nothing else than Non-Being. In my empirical thinking the tertium quid[103] is always the observer, i.e. the one who makes the statement. Your example of light and darkness is a subjective and relative statement, inasmuch as light is equal to motion and darkness equal to rest, that is, more or less frequency or more or less stand-still. Darkness is certainly a decrease of light, as light is a decrease of darkness. Thus it amounts to a play of words to say that only Good is, i.e., has substance and Evil not. Standstill is just as real for an observer as movement.[104] You could not even have a notion of movement, if there were not standstill to compare with.

Things are quite simple, if you only could admit, that Good and Evil are judgements, having nothing to do with the incommensurable concept of Being. It is true, that motion is everything, since all things move, but it is equally true, that certain things are less moving for a certain observer than

101 Typewritten by secretary from Jung's handwritten copy.

102 a commonly accepted (theological) opinion. In his next letter White replies that "privation of good" is not a dogma; it functions as a theological definition and as such is open for discussion. The privative definition of evil, however, is too tightly connected with basic tenets of Catholic faith – the doctrine of Creation and the doctrine of God – to allow for much latitude of interpretation. It soon becomes evident White cannot yield this point. Also, he sees no necessary conflict between the *privatio boni* doctrine and a practical application of Jung's psychology (cf. White, 9 July 1952, pp. 200f).

103 third thing.

104 The concept of movement might carry a special set of meanings for a Thomist. In Aristotelian philosophy, which shaped the theology of Aquinas, a being was only said to have, or be, a *natura* ("nature") if it was capable of independent movement. In this tradition, evil is thought not to have (or be) a "nature," but to be in parasitic relationship with things that do. Against this position, Jung's insistence that "standstill" has its own reality corresponds to his argument for the independent reality of evil.

other things. From this fact you form the notion of standstill, which in itself, as far as we know, does not occur in our empirical world. Thus you can hold, that everything is good, but certain things are less good for a certain observer. But this argument also depends upon an observer and his statement, which is always subjective. What you call *fixed stars* for instance, may move much faster in reality than our sun, and what you call good, may be in other respects a great Evil, that is for another observer.

The whole question may be a case like that of the earth, around which the sun has revolved for the better part of 1900 years.[105] In recent times only it became an admissable truth, that the earth is moving round the sun.

If the privatio boni is merely a doctrine and not a dogma,[106] it can be discussed or is that not so? S. Thomas is not infallible.[107] His views about the Assumptio for instance don't seem to agree with the new dogma.[108]

Whereas Being is obviously a concept of +, Non-Being is one of –. But Evil is as substantial as Good, as the devil and his hell are substantial. If Evil should be a very small Good, it would nevertheless be good, however little, and not at all bad. If I am condemned to hell, I am still nothing but good, in spite of the fact that I have lost 99% of goodness, because Evil is *not*.

Is it quite impossible that a theologian admits the obvious fact of Good and Evil being moral judgments and as such relative to an observer? There is not the faintest evidence for the identity of Good and Being. God is certainly the Being itself and you call Him the Summum Bonum. Thus all Being is good, and even Evil is a minute Good, even Satan's disobedience is still good to a small degree and nothing else. For that small Good he is in hell. Why should Good be thrown into hell? And at which percentage of goodness are

105 As Adler remarks, Jung may be counting from the time of Aristarchus of Samos (born c. 320 BC), who first put forward the view that the planets revolve around the sun. His theory was forgotten until the sixteenth century, when Copernicus rediscovered the heliocentric system. (*Letters II*, p. 72n).

106 Following colloquial usage, Jung assumes that these terms, "doctrine" and "dogma," refer to church teachings at sharply different levels of authority, a doctrine being open to debate, a dogma being an official and final statement of belief. As a professional theologian, White treats these terms with greater differentiation, varying their meaning according to context.

107 White would have no difficulty with this statement. Infallibility can be claimed only by a Pope speaking *ex cathedra* (with full authority).

108 It is hard to know on what authority Jung makes this statement. St. Thomas knew of the Feast of the Assumption, which was celebrated in his lifetime (though not yet defined as a matter of faith); but wrote little about it. What he wrote (*ST* IIIa q.27, a.1; q.83, a.5, ad 8) is consistent with the dogma as formally defined in 1950. (Cf. "Munificentissimus Deus," pp. 163f and note.) Perhaps Jung confused two doctrines about Mary. St. Thomas saw the doctrine of the Assumption as following from the Immaculate Conception; but his ideas about the latter differed from the church's official teaching, as defined in 1854. (Thanks to Fr. Fergus Kerr, O.P. for supplying information on this and other doctrinal and historical points.)

you liable to get condemned? Moreover there is no darkness in God and God is All – where in hell is the absence of light then, where the host of fallen angels, where the "evildoers" (i.e. those having done a little good) and Satan himself? Why should a little good be against God? It is still with God, even Satan is. Whatever he is doing, it is always a little good and nothing else.

That is how the christian doctrine gets out of its inherent dualism, i.e., Manicheism,[109] by denying the existence of Evil. You do deny it by calling Evil a decreasing Good. Absolute Evil is for you a merely neutral condition, in which there is nothing at all, a μὴ ὄν, but in as much as Satan exists, he is nothing but good, because Being = Good.

It reminds me of S. Malo's baptism of the penguins and S. Katharine's advice: Donnez-leur une âme, mais une petite![110]

I'm looking forward to seeing you on the 16th or the 17th VII. I shall be in Bollingen then.

Cordially yours, C.G. (unsigned carbon copy)

Blackfriars, Oxford

9.7.52[111]

My dear C.G.,

I am sorry to have fobbed you off with a postcard![112] I just have been hectically busy lately. I still am; but very briefly, and by way of a preliminary Auseinandersetzung,[113] I would say rather tersely:

1. No; there is no dogma about the privatio boni, any more than there is about the *meaning* of many other words included in dogmas. In any case, they would be quite open to discussion.

2. You say, "The crux seems to be lying in the contamination of the two incongruous notions of Good and of Being." This does indeed seem to be the crux; though I'm not *sure* I understand what you mean. For what is any value-judgment since the world began but a predication-of-value of a subject-of-being? If this is incongruous and contamination, I indeed plead guilty – with the whole adult human race. And I *am* concerned with what Good (and/or) Evil *IS*.

109 Cf. Jung, 31 Dec. 1949, p. 142 and note.

110 "Give them a soul, but a little one!" In *Penguin Island*, a novel by Anatole France (orig. pub. 1908; English trans. 1948, p. 30), St. Catherine of Alexandria proposes this compromise to resolve a dispute in the heavenly council (*Letters II*, p. 73n).

111 Typewritten on large sheets of paper.

112 This postcard has not been preserved.

113 a coming to terms; a thorough sorting-out.

3. "If you assume, as I do, that Good is a moral judgment . . ." But how can I? "Good" is a term, not a judgment. Nor is every predication of "good" (bzw![114] "Evil") moral; neither "This egg is good" nor "Hell is evil" are moral judgments.

4. Of course I agree that what value-judgments are made are conditioned by "position of observer" (which is why this discussion concerns me so much!). I am not discussing the validity of any particular judgment, but the *meaning* of *terms*; and I supposed you were. Or, to take your own example, Ptolemy says the sun goes round the earth, Copernicus that the earth goes round the sun; but they are agreed about what they mean by their terms, "sun", "earth", "go round" – otherwise their assertions are incommensurable, and astronomy would cease to be a science of heavenly bodies, and become a "science" of the positions of Ptolemy and Copernicus.

5. "Things are quite simple if you only could admit that Good and Evil are judgments. . . ." But how can I, when every dictionary or logic book in the world tells me a judgment can never consist in a single noun, let alone, adjective!,[115] but must always contain a verb? I am wondering if this is the crux behind the crux – a contamination of *perception* and *judgment*, and intellectual judgment in particular. (It does rather *read* like it when you complain, prefacing Werblowsky, that the privatio boni is "pale": one does not expect a theorem of Euclid, an equation of Einstein or a High Court judgment to be colourful!) Trying hard as I am to grasp your "observer's position", I begin to think it must be in a confusion of perceptions and judgments that we get stuck; and it seems to me that you and Buber get at cross-purposes at the same point – where he talks of a judgment ("Gott kann nicht losgelöst vom Menschen existieren")[116] you talk of *Bilder*.[117]

6. No, St Thomas (Gott sei Dank)[118] is not infallible. His utterances stand or fall on their own merits.

7. "Evil is as substantial as Good." But neither are in the abstract; doesn't this beg the question?

8. "Is it quite impossible that a theologian admits the obvious fact of Good and Evil being moral judgments? . . ." But why pick on theologians? How (I must ask) is it possible for *any*one who has learned any grammar (let alone logic – or, I should have thought, psychology) to say that single nouns or adjectives can be judgments – or that all judgments of good and evil are moral? This quite baffles me.

9. "There is not the faintest evidence for the identity of Good and Being." But at least as an *empiricist* you must surely acknowledge the *fact* (the *psychological* fact) that we all do it umpteen times every day ("The weather is

114 *beziehungsweise:* by logical connection; by extension.
115 The phrase, "let alone, adjective!", was handwritten by White in the margin.
116 "God cannot exist cut off from humanity." 117 images. 118 thank God.

good"; "The coffee is good"; "Mr X is good" etc.). What are these if not identifications of something which IS with something GOOD? (Of course, the abstract *meanings* of Good and Being are not identical, or such statements would be tautologies.) Similarly we say, "the weather . . . the coffee . . . Mr X is bad or evil." When *I* say that, I do not mean there is NO coffee, weather or Mr X, but I do mean that they have NOT got something they should have – at least in my opinion. Don't you?

10. Until we have got over these "crucial" hurdles together, we can hardly approach more difficult ones like the "Summum Bonum" and Satan! But the position you attack is simply not the Catholic one – nor can I divine where you have met it, for certainly I never have before! *I* do not say that "Evil is a minute Good", on the contrary I say it is not good at all – just as I do not say that blindness is not "minute sight", but no sight at all, an absence of sight: sight which simply does not exist. But blind men *do* exist, and are really blind. A blind man is a Plus (as a man) with a Minus (with regard to sight). Similarly I say Satan is (not a minute good but a very great) good with a (very big) minus. . . .

But I must agree all such talk begs the question (I am only *stating* the position here). Of course I agree entirely that *if* Good and Evil are a "moral judgment" ONLY (or even a purely moral category) then I would say it was positively blasphemous to call God "good" (for he can be no more subject to moral law than to the law of gravitation, though we would say he is the Author of both). Equally, I suppose, *if* evil were NOTHING BUT moral evil, and the devil also NOTHING BUT moral evil – then IF such a devil could exist,[119] evil would exist in its own right too. On the other hand, by the same logic, there would be no hell, no good coffee and no evil smells. But who else, in all the world, restricts Good and Evil to moral judgment? Certainly no theologian of any denomination that I have ever met. And certainly no dictionary, nor the consensus humani generis. . . .[120]

"That is how the christian doctrine gets out of its inherent dualism . . . by denying the existence of evil. You do deny it by calling Evil a decreasing Good. Absolute Evil is for you a merely neutral condition, in which there is nothing at all, a MH ON. . . ."[121]

My dear C.G., I love you and owe you more than I can say. When you write like that it hurts – I feel it is terribly unworthy of you – and I wonder *what makes you do it*. (I leave aside the point that MH ON, at least since

119 Added in White's handwriting, at bottom of page: "i.e., immorality with nobody to be immoral!"

120 consensus (agreement) of humankind.

121 Transliteration of Jung's phrase, starting in his letter of 31 Dec. 1949 (pp. 141ff), for "non-being." (Cf. White, 5 April 1952, p. 184 and note.)

Plato and Aristotle, does *not* mean "nothing at all".)[122] But I am sure that never in my life have I called Evil a decreasing Good – or anything like it. Never have I said Absolute Evil was a neutral condition – on the contrary I have said (I expect) that it is a non-existent abstraction, as Absolute Blindness and Absolute Darkness, or even Absolute Buttercup, are non-existent abstractions. Christian doctrine has never denied the existence of Evils – evil people, things, actions – these are the *real* evils which Christian faith and practice makes one wrestle with daily to an extent that amazes me in my pastoral work, and the like of which I must confess I seldom find elsewhere, least of all (quite frankly) among the members of psychological clubs. Never, certainly, does Christian doctrine encourage us to escape from real, concrete evils, within or without, to reified abstractions. (Indeed, I suspect that Absolute Evil is one of the devil's cleverest inventions: get people bothering about TON KAKON,[123] and they'll trouble no more about TA KAKA!)[124]

Oh, I know *YOU* never escape like that. I suspect that YOU have wrestled with real evils as few others ever have; and certainly in a way that nobody (probably) has ever done before. But WHY in heaven's name level accusations about Christian doctrine which the New Testament, any prayerbook or simple catechism, let alone any of your theologian friends, can tell you – and have told you – is demonstrably untrue? – and lay you open to charges of ignorance and arrogance? (Forgive my being so frank.)

I agree, of course, about the de facto dualism inherent in fallen humanity. I agree that Christianity has immeasurably intensified that dualism; especially for those who have made the "intellectual disavowal", and that this makes a fearsome problem for the psychotherapist. But why project the blame onto the doctrine, asserting that it asserts what it plainly denies, and denies what it asserts? (Because the heightening, or conscious-making, of the dualism comes surely not from Xtianity's affirming the dualism, but from its denial of its ultimate reality.) Or, has Job suffered in vain (and Christ too); and morality again to become the criterion of good and evil, the judge of God and man alike? (Salvation by works alone!)[125]

122 As above (White, 5 April 1952, p. 184 and note), White insists on the distinction in Greek between "μὴ" (absence or lack) and "οὐ" (absolute negation).

123 Literally, "the Evil One." Perhaps this is a typing or grammatical error for TO KAKON (Evil). Either way, White is making the point that by concentrating on a conceptual absolute, an abstraction (Evil), we lose sight of concrete evils and are distracted from the hard work of making moral choices.

124 "evils" (particular actions, events, moral choices, etc.), contrasted with "Evil" (as an abstraction).

125 One of the chief theological disputes at the heart of the Reformation concerns the role of divine grace in salvation, as opposed to the role of human choice and action. Luther had insisted on the primary role of God's action (Grace), opposing the Catholic theology that, he claimed, placed too much emphasis on works.

But I wander. . . . Here, at least, is *some* agenda for dear Bollingen! In a week, I hope and intend, I shall be with you. May good Empathy penetrate all these tiresome walls of paper and typescript! I look forward so much to *being* with you, and reposing a little, too!

Every cordially and gratefully yours, VICTOR

Küsnacht-Zürich

7.VIII.52[126]

Dear Victor!

I forgot to tell you, that I Ching 16 Ist place[127] refers to "putting in music" the problem of priv. boni i.e. to understand it as a *feeling* problem. You would get a more complete picture, if you contemplate such ideas not only from an intellectual but also from a feeling standpoint. In this case you could feel the "contrapunctum"[128] very clearly. You were followed by a letter which I have re-addressed to Blackfriars.

Greetings!

Yours cordially C.G.

126 Handwritten postcard.

127 In the sixteenth hexagram of the I Ching, "Yü / Enthusiasm," the text under The Image reads: "When, at the beginning of summer, thunder – electrical energy – comes rushing forth from the earth again, and the first thunderstorm refreshes nature, a prolonged state of tension is resolved. Joy and relief make themselves felt. So, too, music has the power to ease tension within the heart and to loosen the grip of obscure emotions. The enthusiasm of the heart expresses itself involuntarily in a burst of song, in dance and rhythmic movement of the body" (*The I Ching or Book of Changes*. The Richard Wilhelm Translation rendered into English by Cary F. Baynes. Bollingen Series XIX. PUP, 1950/1977, p. 68). (Hereafter, *I Ching.*)

128 counterpoint. In musical composition, the art of writing two or more independent melodies that harmonize together.

as from Blackfriars, Oxford.

10.8.52[129]

My dear C.G.,

Thank you so much for your postcard, which I found on my return yesterday. Yes; I do agree with you and the I Ching about the FEELING side of the question, and that no answer is complete which neglects that.

Perhaps you may be interested in the dream which I enclose, and which I had on my last night at Bollingen[130] – which, you may remember, was also your birthday and is the feast of St Anne (the "Grandmother of God" as the Easterns call her).

I have now returned, enormously refreshed and revived from my visit to you, followed by much rambling over the mountains of Vaud and Valais.

You will soon be going to Ascona. May all fare well with you there. I should love to be listening under the table when you and Father D'Arcy meet![131]

Much correspondence awaits my attention, and many other chores; so please excuse this brief note.

Ever cordially, VICTOR

P.S. Of course no answer is required, nor any comment on the enclosed – which I send purely as a matter of interest. I think its *subjective* interpretation (understanding "CGJ" as your-psychology-in-me, and allowing for "wishful thinking") is pretty clear. DREAM of 26.7.52 (last night at Bollingen, CGJ's birthday).

I am in a tramcar in High Street, Croydon – about in the centre of the town. CGJ is with me, sitting very close to me, and we are engaged in very close, friendly and intimate conversation. He tells me, to my surprise, that for many years he has been brutally cruel to his wife; it is as if he were making his confession to me, and he is very penitent about it. I embrace him with my left arm, and he lays his head on my shoulder while I try to console him. It then occurs to me that he *is* making his confession, and that I should give him absolution; I tell him that since he is baptized of course I can do so, even though he has not openly been a Catholic. I raise my right arm making the sign of the cross and pronounce the words of absolution. He does not say anything, but seems unspeakably grateful and relieved.

129 Typewritten.

130 White visited Jung in Bollingen from 17 to 27 July 1952. His last night there was 26 July, i.e., Jung's 78th birthday.

131 Cf. White, 30 March 1952, p. 180; Jung, 31 Oct. 1952, p. 207, and notes.

Some associations:

"High Street, Croydon". The central street running through the town where I was born. It occurs often in my dreams, and I have come to think of it as the "spinal cord" of my native condition. In other dreams, I am often at the north or south end, or on one side or another, of it. Here I am in a very central part of it and of my home town.

Tramcars – public vehicles (though in this dream CGJ and I are the only occupants) which (unlike buses) follow "determinate grooves" and draw their power from outside of themselves – from the rails *beneath* and the wires *above*. Thus to me (whose early ambition was to be a tram-driver!) a symbol of the group-vehicle fixed to the determined track, but drawing its power from heaven and earth rather than from within (as with the automobile) and from its very determinations. An apt emblem for the Church, etc., though this is not a Church, but something mobile which, like Kundalini, travels up and down the "spinal column". In THIS situation, CGJ and I are very close together.

"Brutally cruel to his wife". This surprises me very much: I think CGJ even says he regularly beats his wife and hits her over the *head*. But somehow I don't even think he means Mrs Jung; but the "feminine principle" which he has unwillingly tried to dominate. (It is clear from his "confession" that it has all been MOST unwilling.)

"Try to console". At first I take him with my left arm only, and my right arm is inactive; I think he only wants my *human* friendship; only when this seems futile to allay such sorrow, does it occur to me that the occasion demands my right arm and my professional aid as a *priest*. So soon as this occurs to me, the fact that he has undoubtedly been baptized seems quite enough to fulfil the legal requirements for giving him absolution without any formal "reconciliation" with the Church.

Küsnacht-Zürich

October 31st 1952[132]

R.P.[133] Victor White, O.P.,
Blackfriars
Oxford

Dear Victor,

Hurrah! Today your book[134] arrived, the child of many sorrows!

132 Typewritten. Letter previously unpublished.

133 Reverend Father.

134 *God & Unc.*

I am actually in bed, recovering from a most disagreeable attack of Tachycardia, so I have the time to browse through the pages of your work, refreshing many memories of our discussions. Although I am fully conscious of the fact that I am a most awkward Petra Scandali,[135] I cannot help feeling a great satisfaction when I see somebody at grips with the problem of many horns. Just a few days ago I got Upton Sinclair's new book "A Personal Jesus"[136] which he himself sent to me, with the curious enquiry for my opinion. Feeling very much under an obligation to give him an honest answer, I have concocted a long letter which you might be interested to see.[137] The book is in true American style, making something nice and handy and rational of a life of Jesus. As a matter of fact, so smooth and simple that one asks oneself in the end how such a personality could possibly have had such an astounding effect. In his American way he is trying to Bultmannise[138] his Christ and the whole eschatology goes by the board. I should not have bothered about the book if the author had not applied for my judgment.

At the Eranos Tagung this year, which, by the way, was not particularly edifying, we had the occasion to hear Father D'Arcy.[139] It was a flop! The good man was completely at sea and had no idea what kind of audience he was confronted with. He gave a beautiful sermon that was so good in style that I could not help making the remark afterwards that he must have gotten the wrong calendar, namely the one of 1852. It painted everything that was difficult and dubious in the most glowing colours, producing a long string of the most wonderful sentiments which had the effect of dead leaves in the autumn. Moreover, he ought to be mighty careful when coming to such a place inasmuch as certain people got round him and caught hold of his considerable shadow. Well, this is entre nous and not for general circulation, but I think I had better keep you au courant so that you know what to think when you hear certain statements about Eranos, which he might issue. I had no particular discussion with him as there was no occasion for it.

The news is that I have to reduce my work still more and make of myself a confirmed recluse in order to avoid all temptation to overwork. It got me this

135 stumbling block.

136 Upton Sinclair (1878–1968): American novelist, essayist, playwright, and short story writer, whose works reflected socialist views. His new book was *A Personal Jesus: Portrait and Interpretation* (New York: Evans Publishing Co., 1952).

137 *Cf. Letters II*, pp. 87ff.

138 i.e., demythologize. Rudolf Karl Bultmann (1884–1876): German Protestant theologian and New Testament scholar, influenced by existentialist philosophy. He was then Professor of NT at the University of Marburg. Taking Form-criticism to an extreme, Bultmann rejected as mythical large portions of the New Testament. According to Jung, Sinclair likewise oversimplifies, deliberately ignoring all "mythical" features in the scriptural record. [with MS]

139 D'Arcy's Eranos paper was titled, "The Power of Caritas and the Holy Spirit." (Cf. White, 23 June 1946, p. 34 and note.) [with MS]

time good and proper and I do not want to repeat this experience. One is scared, and gets small and ugly, like a solitary crab peeping out of his small shell.

Thank you very much for sending me two copies. I think I will give one to the Club library, where it will find grateful readers.

Hoping you are always in good health, I remain

Yours cordially, C.G. (unsigned carbon copy)

Nov. 4th. A third copy has arrived. This time with your dedication. Many thanks.

Blackfriars, Oxford

10.11.52[140]

My dear C.G.,

I am so very sorry to hear you are poorly again; but am thankful if it is meaning that you are having to relax more, and suspend somewhat your voluminous correspondence. But I do hope and pray the illness is not serious this time; my thoughts and prayers are very much with you.

I am sorry you are being so deluged with copies of "God and Unc."! I did not know the publishers had already sent you *two* copies when I sent one also. However, I hope this superfluity will at least help in lighting the fire.

Yes; the book is out now, and I await with trepidation the reviews – both from the clergy and the psychiatrists.

Of course I am delighted to hear Father D. was a flop . . . (I think I told you he's quite a Shadow of mine!)

I hadn't read Upton Sinclair's book; and it looks like I haven't missed much! It's astounding to me that such books can still be written in 1952. I liked most of your letter to him very much. But I am quite bewildered when in your "third" view you refer to Christ as the *Father*-God.[141] Surely this

140 Typewritten.

141 In his letter to Sinclair Jung had argued for a view of Jesus different from the novelist's, laying out three other stories that might legitimately be read into the scriptural record: "1. Jesus is an idealistic, religious teacher of great wisdom, who knows that His teaching would make the necessary impression only if He were to sacrifice His life for it. . . . 2. Jesus is a highly strung, forceful personality, forever at variance with His surroundings, and possessed of a great will to power. . . . 3. Jesus is an incarnation of the Father-God. As a God-Man He walks the earth drawing to Himself the [chosen] of His Father, announcing the message of universal salvation and being mostly misunderstood" (Jung to Upton Sinclair, 3 Nov. 1952, *Letters II*, p. 89).

Patripassianism[142] is contradicted by all the records, for which he is always the Son, emphasizing his distinction from the Father and talking of him in the second and third person? Can this be (I ask myself) just a slip, or some sinister hangover of the *venenum freudianum*[143] (cf. God and Unc. p. 162!)[144]

I am looking forward hugely to coming out in May, and conversing on these and suchlike things at the Institut.

All very best wishes to you, dear C.G., and to Mrs Jung and all,

Ever cordially, VICTOR

P.S. I hope "Passage to India"[145] reached you, and gave you some entertainment. Of course I expect no reply to this.

November 14th 1952[146]

R.P. Victor White, O.P.,
Blackfriars
Oxford.

Dear Victor,

You take the "Father God" too seriously.[147] It is only an unmannerly and loose way of talking suggested by Sinclair's own American gabbling. There is surely no sinister association with a "repressed Father" in the Freudian sense, but rather a condensation of Father and Son, the One God, and the incarnation idea, and the Son begotten of the Father. I wrote the letter when I was still in a pretty bad mental condition on account of fever and feebleness. I am free of fever now and also my heart is in order again, but I am still a wreck for the time being, yet looking forward to a slow process of resurrection.

142 From the Latin for "father" and "suffer": the teaching (declared heretical during early controversies about the Trinity) that God the Father suffered and died on the Cross.

143 Freudian poison.

144 From Chapter VIII: "Notwithstanding the immense advances which Freudian psychoanalysis is shown to have made in its recognition of the importance of 'super-ego' factors in psychological health and disease, it is still apt to conceive the way of health and happiness to lie in the murder (however 'symbolic') of the Father rather than in reconciliation with the Father through the self-sacrifice of the co-equal Son" (*God & Unc.*, p. 162).

145 E.M. Forster (1879–1970), *A Passage to India* (London: Edward Arnold, 1924).

146 Typewritten. Letter previously unpublished.

147 Cf. previous letter, p. 208 and note. In his letter to Sinclair, which pleads for Jesus' mythological, i.e., more-than-human status, Jung wrote: "Jesus is an incarnation of the Father-God" (*Letters II*, p. 89).

I naturally forgot to thank you for that very wonderful book "Passage to India"[148] which I have read with the greatest appreciation. It is extraordinarily true and excellently absurd.

I had quite forgotten that you gave me a hint[149] as to your feelings about Father D'Arcy. He certainly was a big disappointment.

Yours cordially, C.G. (unsigned carbon copy)

148 Cf. White, 10 Nov. 1952, p. 209. In 1938 Jung had visited India and recorded a number of memorable experiences (*MDR*, ch. IX, pp. 274ff). [MS]

149 Cf. White, 23 June 1946, p. 35.

1953

Blackfriars, Oxford

2.4.53[1]

My Dear C.G.,

Although I write to you so little, you are very often in my thoughts. I must just take occasion of Easter to send you a brief greeting & salutation.

I have been quite shocked to hear of Toni Wolff's sudden death.[2] She must be a great loss to you all, & you have my very great sympathy. I had particularly been looking forward to hearing her this summer,[3] so I am very disappointed, too.

I hope to arrive about May 15th,[4] though I understand I am not to start talking until June, & I propose to make a little tour during the Whitsun holiday. I understand I am to stay at "Hinder Zühnen,"[5] not too far from Küsnacht. So I hope I may come & see you from time to time – especially as I am afraid I shall not be able to return to Bollingen later this year.

I am just off to celebrate the Rites of Spring in Wales[6] – then to lecture in Dublin. So please excuse the brevity of this note.

Wishing you & Mrs Jung a very happy Easter.

Ever cordially, VICTOR

Küsnacht-Zürich

15th of May 1953[7]

Dear Victor,

I should have written to you long ago, but somehow I could not make up my mind; probably I have nourished the vain hope to have you stay with us

1 Handwritten.

2 The death of Toni Wolff, early on 21 March 1953, was completely unexpected (cf. Jung to J. Kirsch, *Letters II*, pp. 117f.).

3 Toni Wolff was a founding member of the Psychological Club and had also been a regular teacher at the C.G. Jung Institute, Zurich, since its founding in 1948.

4 White arrived in Zurich on 19 May 1953 (cf. Jung to Werblowsky, 21 May 1953, *Letters II*, p. 116).

5 Now spelled "Hinder Zünen." The address of Dora Kalff (cf. Jung, 15 May 1953, p. 214 and note).

6 Probably referring to a small religious community where White was both spiritual director and friend. "Rites of Spring" seems to refer to the liturgical celebrations at the end of Holy Week, including Easter, which fell that year on the fifth of April.

7 Handwritten. Letter previously unpublished.

during your time in Zürich. It is only about a week ago that I feel better and that I can go down into my garden. My wife was not well either. She is subject to high blood pressure and has to avoid anything like overactivity. Under those conditions I could not think of inviting you, which I would have liked to do otherwise.

I want to see you as soon as possible. I am planning to go to Father Frei's[8] lecture tomorrow evening in the Club.[9] It will be the first time again since seven months. I hope my condition allows such an adventure. I have to be careful of overwork.

My compliments to Mrs. Kalff![10]

Yours cordially, C.G.

Hintendorfstr. 3
Zollikon/Zch.

22.6.53[11]

My dear C.G.

Alas, I must leave next Monday, & shall probably be away tomorrow and Wednesday. Could I call in for a chat, & to say good-bye, some time next Friday, Saturday or Sunday?

Phew! As I think you already know, I am having *quite* a time! She's nice too – if she didn't think she was a psychologist. Shades of Layard, Sussman, Robb – shall I ever be able to cope with these intuitive ladies of either sex? "Inflating them till they bust"[12] may be right – but what about the innocent public when they are passed off as analysts? Anyway, l'affaire N.[13] won't be packed up in a week, & I can only *hope* not to leave too terrible a mess for you to clear up!

Ever cordially, VICTOR

8 Cf. Jung, 27 Dec. 1947, p. 105 and note.

9 Fr. Gebhard Frei's lecture to the Psychological Club on 16 May 1953 was titled, "Zwei Traumserien von Theologen" ["Two Series of Dreams of Theologians"]. (Cf. White, 8 Nov. 1953, p. 217 and note.)

10 Dora Kalff (1904–1990): a Swiss Jungian therapist, Dora Kalff studied the therapeutic use of sand trays and miniatures with Margaret Lowenfeld in London, before developing her own method, Sandplay Therapy, based on Jung's theories.

11 Handwritten.

12 Cf. Jung, 16 Oct. 1951, p. 171 and note.

13 First name of a young Swiss doctor, later an analyst. At her family's request her name is withheld. (Cf. White, 15 Sept. 1953, p. 215; 4 March 1954, p. 232; Jung, 24 Nov. 1953, p. 223.)

Hawkesyard Priory
Rugeley, Staffs.

15.9.53[14]

My dear C.G.

It is over a week since I left Bollingen, but I have not hitherto had much opportunity to thank you & Mrs Jung for your very kind reception of me. It was very refreshing to be at Bollingen again, & I was particularly grateful to you for listening patiently & helpfully to my own "mild case".

After leaving you I saw N.N.[15] I hope you won't think it a great impertinence if I express the hope that you will be able to find the time & energy – & love – to see her some after your return to Zürich. Your "holding" of her (as she calls it) seems to have been the only *temenos* she has had for years, & although I suppose she is only one of many who must sooner or later find their own, she did not strike me as in any state to be dropped too abruptly. There does not seem to be anybody else in Switzerland who can help her through, &, as you may imagine, I feel rather bad about it myself, & it would be a great favour & relief to me too if you could give her an hour or so soon. Your time is very valuable, I know, but I think you will agree she is worth plenty!

The above is not my permanent address. Ironically, I am conducting a retreat here for my Dominican colleagues. The inevitable difficulties are increased by a poor schiz. who follows me around like a hurt lap-dog, & pops into my room every few minutes. There are times I wish I had never heard of psychology, or anyhow could barricade myself behind a receptionist & a brass plate.

Please pass on my thanks to Mrs Jung, & give her my warm greetings. Also to Miss Bailey[16] if she is still with you. I hope I may have another chance to see you next year, & that this winter will not be so trying to you as the last.

Ever cordially yours, VICTOR

14 Handwritten. 15 Cf. White, 22 June 1953, p. 214 and note.

16 Jung had met Ruth Bailey in Africa in 1925; at his invitation she joined his expedition. Thereafter she sometimes visited him for a few weeks at a time. After Emma Jung's death in 1955, Ruth Bailey lived as a caregiver in Jung's household.

PERSONAL & PRIVATE

Gracedieu[17]
Boars Hill, Oxford

8.11.53[18]

My dear C.G.,

I have just asked the I Ching if I should write and report to you on my present miseries! It replied with "29" – the Abysmal – with 6 in the 1st, 3rd, 4th and 6th places.[19] That did not seem to answer the question I asked, one way or the other, but it is a perfect description of the situation.

The dilemma, reduced to its simplest terms, seems complete and insoluble. If Christ is no longer an adequate and valid symbol of the Self, and in fact very inadequate, one-sided, unintegrated and harmful, then must not one choose – at whatever the cost? Faith in him, it seems to me, must be unconditional; once one "criticizes Christ" one has lost faith in him, and one cannot in honesty preach him any more. And one has lost any sense of oneness that one ever had with one's community, with the Church, with the "cause" that animates them. I have come to realize how many of my friends and "analysants" I have positively helped to get out of the Church! Yet I am paid, I owe my bread and butter, to the alms and gifts of good Christians, who support me in the belief that I am a good Christian priest, labouring to bring all I can into the one Ark of Salvation! Their God simply isn't my God any more; my very clerical clothes have become a lie. I feel acutely that the position has become morally impossible and dishonest – quite different (if I may say so) to your own in the medical profession. And increasingly I find it psychologically and even physically impossible, too.

So I tell myself from time to time that, whatever the cost, I must get out. I don't relish the idea of starting life again at 51 in a "world" for which I am totally unequipped. But – "what shall it profit a man if he gain the whole world and lose his own soul?" and the "pearl of great price" requires "all that a man hath". So I almost decide I must pack up and go; and for a while I feel in peace and tranquillity. I did so two days ago, but (and something of the sort has happened on similar occasions before), I promptly had

17 for Grace Dieu (cf. White, 7 Oct. 1951, p. 170 and note).

18 Typewritten. A crossed-out note at the top, in Jung's handwriting, reads, '*Zu den Pfarrerbriefen'!*' ("For the 'clergy letters'!").

19 The text for the 29th hexagram, "K'an / The Abysmal (Water)," opens with a warning: "The name of the hexagram, because the trigram is doubled, has the additional meaning, 'repetition of danger'." Danger is also emphasized by three of White's four changing lines. One is benign, counselling simplicity in dangerous times (*I Ching*, pp. 114ff).

a nightmarish dream. I was with other chaps in a trench firing guns; an officer on the right hand side is cursing us because we are hitting nothing (apparently firing blanks) and just making the hell of a lot of smoke. I couldn't go to sleep again, developed the deuce of a stomach-ache and a mild temperature; and frankly hoped I was going to be able to retire from the whole conflict into a nice long neurotic illness! But not a bit of it; it soon passed off, except for a general stiffness which seems symptomatic of my general paralysis when it comes to trying to do any sort of work – other than analytical work, in which I feel comparatively happy and (if I may say so) rather successful.

Well, my dear C.G. I won't bother you with any more; anyway, it's all just as simple and (so far as I can see) as insoluble as that. I don't expect an answer (though I cannot pretend I should not like one): I don't think there *is* an answer. But I am just indescribably lonely, and it's some relief to me to tell you.

I do hope, my dear C.G., that this winter will not treat you too harshly; and that all is well with you and Mrs. Jung. I am sorry (for many reasons) that I could not come to Zurich for the presentation to you of the Gnostic papyri.[20] I must confess there are times when I wish to heaven I had never heard of your psychology (and some of your disciples!); and yet I tremble to think what would have happened if I hadn't!

Ever cordially, VICTOR

P.S. You remember my "Jonah" dream? In spite of Fr Frei's[21] satisfaction with Christou,[22] it seems there is something in the story which the Bible does not tell – namely, what happened to poor Jonah?

To return to the I Ching, I suppose it should be encouraging that this "29" changes into "1" – the Creative. Humanly speaking, it seems most unlikely.

20 Cf. Jung, 24 Nov. 1953, p. 223 and note.

21 Fr. Gebhard Frei had lectured at the Analytical Club in May, an event attended by both Jung and White (cf. Jung, 15 May 1953, p. 214 and note).

22 Evangelos Christou (1923–1956): at this time an analytic candidate at the Jung-Institut Zürich. He grew up in Alexandria, Egypt. Before starting his training he lived in England, where he was in analysis with Toni Sussmann (cf. White, 9 Oct. 1945, p. 12 and note). Christou went on to practice as an analyst in Alexandria but died at the age of 33 in a car accident. His thesis for the Institute was later edited for publication by James Hillman (Evangelos Christou, *The Logos of the Soul*, Hillman, ed., Spring, 1977/1987).

Küsnacht-Zürich

Nov. 24, 1953[23]

Dear Victor,

Forget for once dogmatics and listen to what psychology has to say concerning your problem: *Christ as a symbol is far from being invalid*, although he is one side of the Self and the devil the other. This pair of opposites is contained in the creator as his right and left hand, as Clemens Romanus says.[24] From the psychological standpoint the experience of God the creator is[25] the perception of an overpowering impulse issuing from the sphere of the unconscious.[26] We don't know whether this influence or compulsion deserves to be called good or evil although we cannot hinder ourselves to welcome or curse it, to give it a bad or a good name, according to our subjective condition. Thus Jahwe has either aspect[27] because he is essentially the creator (primus motor)[28] and because he is yet unreflected[29] in his whole nature.

With the *incarnation* the picture changes completely, inasmuch as it means that God becomes manifest in the form of Man who is conscious and therefore cannot avoid judgment. He simply has to call the one good and the other evil. It is a historic fact, that the real devil came only into existence together with Christ. Though Christ was being God, as Man he was detached from God and he watched the devil falling out of heaven, removed from God as he (Christ) was separated from God inasmuch as he was human. In his utter helplessness on the cross, he even confessed that God had forsaken him. The Deus Pater would leave him to his fate, as he always "strafes" those whom he has filled before with this[30] abundance by breaking

23 Typewritten, from holograph dated 18 Nov. 1953.

24 St. Clement, Bishop of Rome (Pope Clement I), *fl.* c.96. The concept of Christ as the right hand and the devil as the left hand of God first arises in the Clementine Homilies, a collection of Gnostic-Christian writings from the second or third century, which were credited to Pope Clement I beginning in the Middle Ages (*Letters II*, p. 8, n. 10; CW 9,ii, *Aion*, §99, p. 54; cf. also "Clementine Literature," *ODCC*, p. 304). Jung again discusses Satan as the "left hand" of God in his "Foreword to Werblowsky's *Lucifer and Prometheus*" (CW 11, *Psych. & Rel*, §470, pp. 313f).

25 In holograph, crossed out: "coincides with."

26 Cf. CW 11, *Psych. & Rel.*, §137: "it is always the overwhelming psychic factor that is called God." Similarly, in a letter written at the end of Jung's life: "[God] is the name by which I designate all things which cross my wilful path violently and recklessly, all things which upset my subjective views, plans, and intentions and change the course of my life for better or worse" (Jung to M. Leonard, 5 Dec. 1959, *Letters II*, p. 525).

27 In holograph, crossed out: "Thus Jahwe has either aspect, in the most paradox way."

28 Prime Mover (a term applied to God by Aquinas).

29 In holograph, crossed out: "because he is yet unconscious."

30 In holograph: "His" (typist's error). In writing this letter Jung at first capitalized all the divine pronouns (He, His). Later he crossed out most of those capitalizations, replacing them with

his promise. This is exactly what S. Joannes a cruce[31] describes as the "dark night of the soul". It is the reign of darkness, which is also God, but an ordeal for Man. The Godhead has a double aspect, and as Meister Eckart[32] says: God is not blissful in his mere Godhead, and that is the reason for his incarnation.

But becoming Man, he becomes at the same time a definite being, which is this and not that. Thus the very first thing Christ must do is to sever himself from his shadow and call him devil. (Sorry, but the Gnostics of Irenaeus[33] already knew it!)

When a patient in our days is about to emerge from an unconscious condition, he is instantly confronted with his *shadow* and he has to decide for the good otherwise he goes down the drain. Nolens volens[34] he "imitates" Christ and follows his example. The first step on the way to Individuation consists in the discrimination between himself and the shadow.

In this stage the Good is the goal of individuation, and consequently Christ represents the Self.

The next step is *the problem of the shadow*.[35] In dealing with darkness you have got to cling to the Good, otherwise the devil devours you. You need every bit of your goodness in dealing with Evil and just there. To keep the light alive in the darkness, that's the point, and only there your candle makes sense.

Now tell me how many people you know, who can say with any verisimilitude, that they have finished their dealings with the devil and consequently can chuck the Christian symbol overboard?

lowercase "h". For the most part, the typist was able to follow his corrections. Occasionally, however, Jung failed to make the change. His intended phrase, "His [God's] abundance," was evidently misread by the secretary.

31 St John of the Cross (1542–1591): Spanish mystical Doctor of the Church and joint founder, with St. Teresa of Avila, of the Discalced Carmelites. His writings combine a poet's imagination with the intellect of a theologian trained in Thomistic philosophy.

32 Meister Eckhart (c.1260–1327): German Dominican and mystic. He was investigated as a heretic at the end of his life.

33 In *Aion* Jung elaborates the point as follows: "Irenaeus (*Adversus haereses* II,5,1) records the Gnostic teaching that when Christ, as the demiurgic Logos, created his mother's being, he 'cast her out of the Pleroma – that is, he cut her off from knowledge.' For creation took place outside the pleroma, in the shadow and the void. According to Valentinus (*Adv.haer.* I,11,1), Christ did not spring from the Aeons of the pleroma, but from the mother who was outside it. She bore him, he says, 'not without a kind of shadow.' But he, 'being masculine,' cast off the shadow from himself and returned to the Pleroma . . ., while his mother, 'being left behind in the shadow, and deprived of spiritual substance,' there gave birth to the real 'Demiurge and Pantokrator of the lower world.' But the shadow which lies over the world is, as we know from the Gospels, the *princeps huius mundi*, the devil. Cf. *The Writings of Irenaeus*, I, pp.45f" (CW 9.ii, *Aion*, §75, p. 41n).

34 willy-nilly.

35 In holograph a crossed-out question follows: "What are you going to do about that?"

As a matter of fact, our society has not even begun to face its shadow or to develop those christian virtues so badly needed in dealing with the powers of darkness. Our society cannot afford the luxury to cut itself loose from the imitatio Christi, even if it should know that the *conflict with the shadow*, i.e. Christ versus Satan, is only the first step on the way to the far away goal of the union of the Self in God.

It is true however that the imitatio Christi leads you into your own very real and *christlike conflict* with darkness, and the more you are engaged in this war and in these attempts at peace making helped by the anima,[36] the more you begin to look forward beyond the christian aeon to the *Oneness of the Holy Spirit. He is the pneumatic state the creator attains to through the phase of incarnation.* He is the experience of every individual that has undergone the complete abolition of his ego through the absolute opposition expressed by the symbol Christ versus Satan.[37]

The state of the Holy Spirit[38] means a restitution of the original oneness of the unconscious on the level of consciousness. That is alluded to, as I see it, by Christ's logion: "Ye are gods".[39] This state is not quite understandable yet. It is a mere anticipation.

The later development from the christian aeon to the one of the S. Spiritus has been called the "evangelium aeternum"[40] by Gioacchino da Fiori[41] in a time when the great tearing apart had just begun. Such vision seems to be granted by the divine grace as a sort of "consolamentum"[42] so that Man is not left in a completely hopeless state during the time of darkness.[43] We are actually in the state of darkness viewed from the standpoint of history. We are still within the christian aeon and just beginning to realize the age of darkness where we shall need christian virtues *to the utmost*.

In such a state we could not possibly dismiss Christ as an invalid symbol although we clearly foresee the approach of his opposite. Yet we don't see

36 In holograph: "helped by the anima" is added interlinearly.

37 Jung's usual shorthand for "Christ" is the first two letters of the name in Greek: Chi Rho (XP). Here he uses the Greek Sigma (Σ) as shorthand for Satan, joined to the symbol for Christ by an arrow, and "versus": "XP <--->/versus Σ."

38 In holograph: "S.Spir."

39 Psalms 82.6; John 10.34.

40 "eternal Gospel."

41 Gioacchino da Fiore (Joachim of Fiore, c.1145–1202): Italian theologian and mystic, taught that the history of the world occurred in three eras: the Age of the Law, or the Father; the Age of the Gospel, or the Son; finally the Age of Contemplation, or the Holy Spirit. His teachings were condemned in 1215 by the Fourth Lateran Council (cf. CW 9.ii, *Aion*, §137ff, pp. 82f). (*Letters II*, p. 136, n. 10.)

42 "consolation" (central rite of the Cathars), a baptism by the Spirit. The name *consolamentum* recalls the name "Paraclete" (comforter) given to the Holy Spirit (John 14.16). (Cf. *Letters II*, p. 136, n. 11.)

43 In holograph, crossed out, this sentence continues: "i.e., the [two illegible words]. But one should not assume that one is already there."

and feel the latter as the preliminary step toward the future union of the divine opposites, but rather as a menace against everything that is good, beautiful and holy to us. The adventus diaboli[44] does not invalidate the christian symbol of the Self, on the contrary: it complements it.[45] It is a mysterious transmutation of both.

Since we are living in a society, that is unconscious of this development and far from understanding the importance of the christian symbol, we are called upon to hinder its invalidation, although some of us are granted the vision of a future development. But none of us could safely say that he has accomplished the assimilation and integration of the shadow.

Since the christian Church[46] is the community of all those having surrendered to the principle of the imitatio Christi, this institution (i.e. such mental attitude) is to be maintained until it is clearly understood, what the assimilation of the shadow means.[47] Those that foresee must – as it were – stay behind their vision in order to help and to teach, particularly so, if they belong to the church as her appointed servants.

You should not mind if some of your analysands are helped out of the church. It is their destiny and adventure. Others will stay in it anyhow. It does not matter, whether the ecclesiastical powers in being approve of your vision or not. When the time is fulfilled, a new orientation will irresistibly break through as one has seen in the case of the Conceptio Immaculata[48] and the Assumptio,[49] which both deviate from the time-hallowed principle of apostolic authority, a thing unheard of before.[50] It would be a lack of responsibility and a rather autoerotic attitude if we were to deprive our fellow beings of a vitally necessary symbol before they had a reasonable chance to understand it thoroughly and all this because it is not complete if envisaged from an anticipated stage[51] we ourselves in our individual lives have not yet made real.[52]

Anybody going ahead is alone or thinks he is lonely at times, no matter whether he is in the Church or in the world. Your practical work as directeur de conscience[53] brings to you individuals having something in their character,

44 advent of the devil.

45 In holograph, underlined: "*it complements it.*"

46 In holograph, crossed out: "(or churches)."

47 In holograph: "until it is clearly understood what the symbol of Christ is good for, namely the assimilation of the shadow."

48 The Catholic teaching of the Immaculate Conception of Mary, Mother of Christ, first officially defined in the papal bull, *Ineffabilis Deus* (1854).

49 Assumption. (Cf. White, 3 Dec. 1950, p. 163 and note; Jung, 30 June 1952, p. 199 and note.)

50 I.e., neither of these recently defined dogmas sprang from apostolic or scriptural authority, but derive their authority from centuries of adherence by ordinary believers. Also "new," and politically significant, promulgation of this dogma rested on the idea of papal infallibility. [with AC]

51 In holograph, crossed out: "standpoint."

52 In holograph, crossed out: "not yet really attained to."

53 spiritual director.

that corresponds with certain aspects of your personality (like the many men fitting themselves as stones into the edifice of the tower in the "Shepherd of Hermas").[54]

Whatever your ultimate decision will be, you ought to realize before that staying in the church makes sense[55] as it is important to make people understand what the symbol of Christ means, as such understanding is indispensable to any further development. There is no way round it as little as we can eliminate from our life old age, illness and death, or Buddha's Nidana-chain of evils.[56] The vast majority of people is still in such an unconscious state, that one should almost protect them from the full shock of the real imitatio Christi.[57] Moreover we are still in the christian Aeon, threatened with a complete annihilation of our world.

As there are not only the many but also the few somebody is trusted with the task to look ahead and talk of the things to be. That is partially my job, but I have to be very careful not to destroy the things that are. Nobody will be so foolish to destroy the foundations when he is adding an upper story to his house, and how can he build it really, if the foundations are not yet properly laid? Thus making the statement that Christ is not a complete symbol of the Self, I cannot make it complete by abolishing it. I must keep it therefore in order to build up the symbol of the perfect contradiction in God by adding this[58] darkness to the lumen de lumine.[59] Thus I am approaching the end of the christian Aeon and I am to take up Gioacchino's anticipation and Christ's prediction of the coming of the paraclete. This archetypal drama is at the same time exquisitely psychological and historical. We are actually living in the time of the splitting of the world and the invalidation of Christ.

But an anticipation of a faraway future is no way out of the actual situation. It is a mere "consolamentum" for those despairing at the atrocious possibilities of the present time. Christ is still the valid symbol. Only God himself[60] can "invalidate" him through the Paraclete.

54 An early Christian text ascribed to Hermas, brother of Pope Pius I (c.140–55), containing lessons to be disseminated for the instruction of the Church. Cf. CW 6, *Types*, §381ff, esp. §390, pp. 230f (*Letters II*, p. 137n).

55 This sentence has been considerably worked over. In holograph: "that it makes sense [illegible] somebody stay in the church."

56 The twelve *nidanas* of Buddhism, starting with "ignorance" and ending with "despair," form the *nidana*-chain, the conditions which keep the human being prisoner in *samsara*, the endless chain of rebirth (*Letters II*, p. 137, n.15).

57 In holograph: "the full shock of the christian [illegible word]."

58 In holograph: "His" (mistyped). Cf. note 30, above.

59 light from light. In the Nicene Creed, a designation of Christ.

60 In holograph: "Himself."

Now that is all I can say. It is a long letter and I am tired. If it is not helpful to you, it shows you at least what I think.[61]

I have seen N.N.[62] She is as right as she can be and as she usually is, and just as wrong as her nature permits, altogether as hopeful as a hysterical temperament ever can be.

You have probably heard of the little celebration we had here round the Nag Hammadi Gnostic Codex[63] given to the Institute by a generous donor. There was even a note in the Times.[64] It was a disproportionate affair and neither my doing, nor liking. But I was manoeuvered into saying in the end a few words about the relation between Gnosticism and Psychology.[65]

My best wishes!

Yours cordially, C.G. (unsigned carbon copy and holograph)

Blackfriars, Oxford

29.11.53[66]

My dear C.G.

I am very penitent for having prompted so long & tiring a letter from you. I feel it was very inconsiderate of me thus to add to your labours. But I am *immensely* grateful to you. There is no doubt that it will be a great help, but I must sink into it all more than has yet been possible.

The points that "ring the bell" most immediately are those about the "autoerotic attitude", & about "an anticipation of a faraway future is no way

61 In Jung's handwritten copy a line is drawn across the page here, separating this paragraph from those that follow. Above the line is his scribbled instruction to the typist, "4 Durchschläge" ("four copies"); and below the line, "nur 1 Durchschlag" ("only one copy"). Because of their confidential material, the last two paragraphs went only into White's letter, with a copy for Jung's locked file. The main body of this letter presumably went into Jung's growing collection of "clergy letters," with a copy for the secretary's file.

62 Cf. White, 22 June 1953, p. 214 and note.

63 A Gnostic papyrus in Coptic found in 1945 near the village of Nag-Hammadi in Upper Egypt and acquired in 1952 for the C.G. Jung Institute, Zurich. In total some 52 tractates in 12 books were discovered, the majority being Gnostic in varying degrees, but also including a few Hermetic discourses and a fragment of Plato's Republic. Codex I, now known as the Jung Codex, consists of five parts: "The Prayer of the Apostle Paul"; "The Apocryphon of James"; "The Gospel of Truth" (the longest part, attributed to Valentinus); "The Treatise on the Resurrection"; and "The Tripartite Tractate." All five parts of Codex I have now been published in English.

64 "New Light on a Coptic Codex," *The Times*, 16 November 1953.

65 Cf. CW 18, *The Symbolic Life*, §1514ff, pp. 671f.

66 Handwritten.

out". For those two points I am especially grateful: there are others that need more time for assimilation, but I am for that very reason unspeakably grateful for having them in writing.

Thank you a million, my dear C.G., for this token of your interest and friendship.

Ever cordially, VICTOR

1954

Telegramm – Télégramme – Telegramma[1]
8245 LONDON

Küsnacht (Zürich) 4.1.54

= LT = PROFESSOR JUNG
SEESTRASSE KUESNACHT
ZUERICH SWITZERLAND

= A GROUP OF JUNGIAN CATHOLICS[2] ASSEMBLED AT THEIR ANNUAL MEETING ARE SENDING THEIR BEST GREETINGS AND BEST WISHES FOR A VERY HAPPY NEW YEAR = FATHER WHITE FATHER OMALLEY FATHER SUMNER SUSSMAN SELO LEWIS DOCTOR ELKISCH 91 GLOUCESTER PLACE LONDON W1

Küsnacht-Zürich

Jan. 11, 1954[3]

Dear Father White,

Professor Jung charges me to thank you provisionally for your kind telegram from London. He has been away on holiday since end of December, and also ill (though not seriously) for some days, and this is the reason why he wants me, for the moment, to send you his kindest regards and best wishes.

Sincerely yours, [SECRETARY][4] (unsigned carbon copy)

1 On upper left corner, a secretary's handwritten note: "Bitte, danken Sie Father White für Telegramm – Erklären, weil krank." [Please thank Father White for the telegram – explain, because sick.]

2 An informal association, calling themselves "the Catholic Analysts Group," centered in London. In addition to White, those named are Fr. Francis O'Malley, Dom Oswald Sumner, OSB (cf. White, 18 May 1950, p. 155); Toni Sussmann (cf. White, 9 Oct. 1945, p. 12); Agnes Selo; Eve Lewis (cf.White, 13 Oct. 1946, p. 45 and note; 18 March 1960, p. 283 and note); and Dr. F. Elkisch. [AC]

3 Typewritten.

4 Absent a signature, the secretary's identity is impossible to ascertain. Marie-Jeanne Schmid had left at the end of 1952. Jung subsequently employed several secretaries, including Magda Pestalozzi, from 1952 to 1954 and again briefly in 1957, and Aniela Jaffé (cf. Jaffé, 17 Sept. 1956, p. 275 and note), from 1954 until Jung's death in 1961. Others occasionally filled in. Unlike Miss Schmid, these later secretaries observed a formal courtesy in their letters to White, writing only what Jung dictated.

Personal and Private.

Blackfriars, Oxford

4.3.54[5]

My dear C.G.,

It has long been on my mind to send you greetings, and to send you some news of developments.[6] But there do not seem to have been any clear developments; and I do not want again to provoke you into tiring yourself by feeling that you have to write another long letter. If I now send a few of my confused reflections, please understand that *NO ANSWER IS REQUIRED.* But I think it may interest you a little to know where I have got; anyway it will do me good to try and put it on paper.

I have read and re-read your good letter of November 24th many times. More and more I am convinced that your "view" is, in the main, right. I cannot help sharing it myself. But of course that is just the trouble. As a theologian I don't for the life of me see how this view can be squared with Catholic doctrine: what I am supposed and am under oath to teach, and for teaching which I am provided with my bread and butter!

Take this matter of Christ's shadow. To me it is now obvious that Christ had a shadow AND that he projected it; possibly on the devil, certainly on the Pharisees. Your point that the Incarnation involved being this and not that makes sense of it; and of much subsequent history. But according to Catholic doctrine he could have had no shadow: even with his human mind he knew everything! Truly, this is not defined dogma; but it is quod semper, ubique et ab omnibus.[7] It's Aquinas – which as a Dominican I am obliged to teach (though I've managed to skip that bit for several years now!). And the Roman Holy Office (June 5th, 1918)[8] lays it down that it is a "certa sententia quae statuit animam Christi nihil ignoravisse" and "ab initio cognovisse . . . omnia, praeterita, praesentia et futura . . .".[9] And here am I saying that

5 Typewritten.

6 Concerning White's vocational conflict, cf. also White, 8 Nov. 1953, pp. 216f; Jung, 24 Nov. 1953, pp. 218ff.

7 The "Commonitorium" of St. Vincent of Lérins (d. before 450), defines true Catholic doctrine as *quod ubique, quod semper, quod ab omnibus creditum est* [that which has been believed everywhere, always, and by all] (*ODCC*, p. 1443).

8 On 5 June 1918 the Holy Office issued a Decree, approved by Pope Benedict XV, discussing whether certain propositions are "safe" to teach. White refers especially to this "unsafe" opinion: "Nor can that opinion be called certain which states that the soul of Christ was ignorant of nothing, but that from the beginning He knew in the Word all things, past, present, and future, that is, all things which God knows by the knowledge of vision."

9 "the opinion is certain which states that the soul of Christ was ignorant of nothing . . . he knew everything from the beginning . . . all things, past, present and future. . . ."

Christ had a shadow, AND didn't know it (though I do!) AND projected it. So he is slain by it (the Pharisees anyhow). Then Saul the Pharisee becomes converted (in every sense of the word) from the law-lover into the law-hater, gets into an unholy muddle of love-aggression; and the Church has been progressively rotted by pharisaism ever since – and never more than to-day. All "good Catholics", from the Pope to poor little, scrupulous nuns are law-obsessed. And so with all the enemies of the Church who are treated in the same aggressive-defensive way, whether sex or communism. The poor dears are sex-obsessed and communist-obsessed, and more and more inclined to adopt the police-state mentality of communism while ignoring its merits.

Yes; of course one must cling to the good in dealing with the shadow. But is that way of dealing with the shadow (I mean by projection, defence and aggression) *good*? And (I ask myself) what IS the good? Does not enantiodromia mean that yesterday's good will be tomorrow's evil? I see well enough that the imitatio Christi leads to just this, and is priceless for that reason. I see too that the Catholic Church is an inimitable Durchgang,[10] with treasures which I can never repudiate, and which cannot be found elsewhere; and that many who are in her will and should stay there, and that perhaps many others should take that Durchgang, I do not doubt. That she is what she claims to be, and what as a Catholic I must hold her to be, the one ark of salvation for all till the end of time (due allowances made, of course, for "invincible ignorance"), I just don't believe.

God knows we need the Christian virtues – and that I haven't got them. What troubles me are the Christian vices, and the damage they do. And God knows I have not integrated my shadow very much, or met anyone who has. The conflict is with the darkness all right; but there is all the difference between lightening the darkness and opposing it: between shadow-*casting* and shadow-*integrating*. There is *the* rub; and I feel the whole apparatus of the Church (in clerical circles especially) to be committed to shadow-*casting*. I meet it within me and all around me in the people with whom I have to do. I try – and often succeed – in dissipating the avidya.[11] I cannot, any more, impose a defensive pattern upon them; I must meet them where I find them: see where they *can* go from there – but that is often not at all what is in the moral theology books, and what I am supported by the alms of the faithful to do! They cannot wait for some future aeon to integrate at least a part of their shadows; and I cannot tighten the very armour plating which is suffocating them and bruising their fellows.

But all such ideas are a million miles from the ideas (if such they can be called) of my colleagues – who mostly seem to me to be suffering from the same complaint, and to be less than half alive. I suppose this damned introverted-thinking of mine makes me particularly dependent on a good

10 passage, opening; transition. 11 (Sanskrit) ignorance.

feeling-relationship with my environment; and what you said about the autoeroticism of my attitude rang the bell, though I still don't know the remedy! But I think there is more to it than that. I feel this question of "Can I stay where I am?" as a *moral* issue; and not just one of suffering, loneliness and discomfort. Is it *honest* to go on wearing a persona with which my inner thoughts and much of my outer conduct is in such violent contradiction? In particular, can I again take an oath (as I shall shortly be required to do) that I believe all the Nicene Creed, the Creed of Pius IV,[12] the anti-modernist oath[13] (including the quaint idea "fidem non esse caecum sensum religionis e latebris subconscientiae erumpentem sub pressione cordis et inflexionis voluntatis moraliter informatae"!!!),[14] and "not to teach otherwise than the SOLID doctrine of St Thomas Aquinas and his school"? Ugh. . . .

Well, there are those who maintain (viz. Barbara Robb) that I shouldn't be so finnicky about my conscience, that just that sin of perjury is required of me for the cause, etc. That only rouses the English Protestant within me[15] about these damned double-crossing papists, justifying the means by the end – and anyway I don't know what the end is. Not my idea of karma-yoga and integrity either. But maybe that's narcissism too.

It's quite a corker. But I am not unrelievedly unhappy! I got a lot from old Suzuki[16] (PLUS his secretary) in Zurich, and I can often retire into a Zen "unknowing" very blissfully. And I am carrying on business as usual – on an "als ob"[17] basis – so far as possible. You have heard we had a lively time at the Club with privatio boni[18] – and thanks to M. Fordham[19] quite an

12 White refers, with irony, to the Tridentine Catechism of 1566, which was in standard use until the 1960s. [AC]

13 Cf. Appendix 2, "Victor White, a Memoir," p. 315.

14 "faith is not a blind feeling of religion which breaks out of the darkness of the subconscious under pressure of the heart and the inflexion [turning] of the morally informed will." White quotes a *motu proprio* (document issued by the Pontiff on his own initiative) by Pius X on 1 September 1910, in which this statement appears: "Certissime teneo ac sincere profiteor fidem non esse caecum sensum religionis e latebris subconscientiae . . . erumpetem" ["I maintain as quite certain and sincerely avow that faith is not a blind feeling of religion," etc.]. (Cf. *Letters II*, p. 171n.)

15 Cf. White, 20 July 1950, p. 157 and note; also Appendix 2, pp. 308f.

16 Daisetz Teitaro Suzuki (1870–1966): Japanese philosopher and authority on Zen. Jung's acquaintance with Suzuki dated back at least to 1933 (*Letters I*, pp. 127f).

17 "as if."

18 On 21 November 1953 White delivered a long lecture on "Good and Evil" at the London APC (cf. White, 15 May 1954, p. 245 and note), in which he argued, using illustrations from his own analysis, that no necessary or practical contradiction exists between Jung's psychology and the Catholic (privative) theory of evil.

19 Cf. White, 30 March 1952, p. 180 and note. Fordham had chaired the London APC in the 1930s. He evidently played an active role at White's presentation in November 1953. (Cf. Appendix 1, Jung to Fordham, pp. 294f.)

illuminating one too. Then, a series of seminars at S.A.P.,[20] with Layard (divorced last week) in evidence. More interesting was when I was invited to the Worcestershire asylum to talk to the staff, and (as I found) try to lend a hand with religious-archetypal material which patients were producing under the LSD drug. I wonder if you have met this drug; if not you would be interested in the reports on it which I could get for you. It seems not only to produce both personal and archetypal material in fairly digestible and orderly form, but positively to stimulate ACTIVE imagination in the incubation period after taking it. It was a novelty to me to be asked to collaborate by the psychiatric pundits; and to talk with the patients in their wrestlings with their material. There I felt at home, as I seldom do when I *am* at home!

This is a shockingly egoistical letter; but it's a change to be egoistical sometimes. And you may be interested to know what is going on in my mind, however confused it is. Alas, from the unconscious side little or nothing comes through. There seems to be quite a blockage; maybe I could do with a course of LSD myself. Seriously, I wonder if it is a bad idea?

You will doubtless have heard that I shall be meeting Dr Jacobi[21] at this affair of Caruso's[22] in Brussels this April.[23] I am glad she will be there, as I don't know any of the others and I'm not sure I shall like them – though I much approved of Caruso's own book,[24] for the most part. Goodness knows if I can get to Switzerland this year, or where and what I shall be by the end of the summer.[25] But I should much like a chat or two with you if I can and it is not too exhausting for you.

I do hope, my dear C.G., that this winter has treated you kindly, and that you and Mrs Jung are in the best of health. Please remember me to her. I was

20 Society of Analytical Psychology, London.

21 Cf. Jung, 27 Dec. 1947, p. 104n.

22 Igor Alexander Caruso (1914–1981): Ukrainian psychoanalyst, who lived and worked mainly in Austria. Groundbreaking in his emphasis on the social-psychological aspects of Freudian psychoanalysis, in 1947 he founded the Arbeitskreis für Tiefenpsychologie (workgroup for depth psychology) in Vienna. In 1972 he was named Professor of Psychology at the University of Salzburg.

23 A colloquium on "The Psychology of the Person," sponsored by Caruso's "Arbeitskreis." White attended, as did Jolande Jacobi (cf. White, 15 May 1954, p. 244). Others in attendance included Michael Fordham, Fr. Beinert, SJ, and Jacques Lacan. [with AC]

24 Caruso's first major work, *Religion und Psychoanalyse*, was published in 1948. His later works included *Soziale Aspekte der Psychoanalyse* (1962) and *Trennung der Liebenden* [Separation of Lovers] (1974).

25 White had been proposed by the Master General of the Dominican Order to become the next Regent of Studies for the English Province. He was expected to assume this position at the end of the summer after receiving his STM (Master of Sacred Theology) degree, for which he had successfully taken examinations in 1950 (White, 3 Dec. 1950, p. 160 and note). As the present letter shows, however, he was struggling over whether to again take the anti-modernist oath, another prerequisite for his promotion; hence his uncertainty about his future. (Cf. also White, 25 Sept. 1954, pp. 246ff and notes.) [with AC]

so glad you saw N.N.[26] So far as I am concerned, she has quite vanished, and seemingly curled up in her own cocoon, in strange contrast to last June!

Ever cordially, VICTOR

P.S. Re-reading this letter, I see it gives only one side of the picture. Of course there is another; of which (I must frankly confess) not the least is material security. I don't relish the idea of packing my bags and finding another occupation at my age, and with my training so useless in a hard competitive world! Also, the feeling that I've still got something to do where I am; how often there are things I can do which I could not so if I were not what I am. I couldn't have helped some people out of the Church if I wasn't in it! Whether that is "good" is another matter. . . .

Also I see there are many question marks in the letter. Please understand these are purely rhetorical; and that I do NOT ask you to answer them!

as from Bollingen

April 10th 1954[27]

Dear Victor,

Your letter has been lying on my desk waiting for a suitable time to be answered. In the meantime I was still busy with a preface[28] I had promised to P. Radin[29] and K. Kerényi.[30] They are going to bring out a book together about

26 Cf. White, 22 June 1953, p. 214 and note.

27 Typewritten from a handwritten draft, which reveals extensive rewriting. Jung added material in the margins and scribbled longer interpolations on slips of paper, with careful directions to the typist. An excerpt of this letter was retyped, and copies of it were kept together with a copy of the complete letter. As sent to White, this letter included three formal footnotes, each designated by *1)* in the text. These are printed in the appropriate points in the body of this letter, enclosed in brackets.

28 C.G. Jung, "On the Psychology of the Trickster Figure," Part V of Paul Radin's book *Der göttliche Schelm* (Zürich: Rhein-Verlag, 1954; English edition, *The Trickster*, 1956), also appears in CW 9,i, *The Archetypes and the Collective Unconscious*, §456–88, pp. 255ff.

29 Paul Radin (1883–1959): Polish-born anthropologist, specializing in the study of North American Indian tribes and languages. His many books on ethnography include *Der göttliche Schelm: ein indianischer Mythen-Zyklus* [The Divine Scoundrel: A Cycle of American Indian Myths] (Zürich: Rhein-Verlag, 1954), with commentaries by Karl Kerényi and C.G. Jung. An English edition, *The Trickster: A Study in American Indian Mythology* (London: Routledge and Paul, 1955), was followed by several American editions.

30 Karl Kerényi (1897–1973): Hungarian classicist, who after 1943 lived and worked in Ascona, Switzerland. He lectured extensively at the C.G. Jung Institute, Zurich, and at Eranos meetings in Ascona. (Cf. *Letters I*, p. 284n and *Letters II*, p. 19n.) Kerényi wrote *Introduction to a*

the figure of the *Trickster*. He is the collective shadow. I have finished my preface yesterday. I suppose you know the greek-orthodox priest Dr. Zacharias?[31] He has finished his book representing a reception, or better – an attempt of integrating Jungian psychology into christianity as he sees it.[32] Dr. Rudin S.J.[33] from the Institute of Apologetics did not like it. Professor Gebhard Frei[34] on the other side was very positive about it.

I am puzzled about your conception of Christ and I try to understand it. It looks to me, as if you were mixing up the idea of Christ being human and being divine. Inasmuch as divine he knows, of course, everything, because all things macrocosmic are supposed to be microcosmic as well and can therefore be said to be known by the Self. It is an astonishing fact indeed, that the collective unconscious seems to be in contact with nearly everything. There is of course no empirical evidence for such a generalisation, but plenty of it for its indefinite extension. The sententia, therefore: "animam Christi nihil ignoravisse"[35] etc. is not contradicted by psychological experience. Rebus sic stantibus[36] Christ as the Self can be said "ab initio cognovisse omnia"[37] etc. I should say that Christ knew his shadow – Satan – whom he cut off from himself right at the beginning of his career. The Self is a unit, consisting however of two, i.e. of opposites, otherwise it would not be a totality. Christ has consciously divorced himself from his shadow. Inasmuch as divine, he is the Self, yet only its white half. Inasmuch as human, he never has lost his shadow completely, but seems to have been conscious of it. How could he say otherwise: "Do not call me

Science of Mythology (1951), to which Jung contributed "The Psychology of the Child Archetype" (CW 9.i, *The Archetypes and the Collective Unconscious*, §259–305, pp. 151–81). [with AC]

31 Gerhard P. Zacharias (b. 1923): German Greek-Orthodox priest, later an analytical psychologist. The book to which Jung refers is *Psyche und Mysterium: Die Bedeutung der Psychologie Jungs für die christliche Theologie und Liturgie* [Psyche and Mystery: The Meaning of Jung's Psychology for Christian Theology and Liturgy] (Zürich: Rascher, 1954).

32 After reviewing Zacharias's *Psyche und Mysterium* in manuscript, Jung had responded with faint praise: "I think you have succeeded in assimilating from the theological standpoint the findings of the modern psychology of the unconscious with fair completeness." Jung criticized the author's dependence on Heideggerian phrases and concluded: "Also, you cite my name too often. Pardon!" (*Letters II*, pp. 120f).

33 Josef Rudin, SJ (Dr.phil.): psychotherapist; instructor at the University of Fribourg; after 1957 Professor at the University of Innsbruck. Author of *Psychotherapie und Religion* (1960) and *Fanatismus* (1965). His reviews of Jung's work include "Antwort auf Hiob. Zum gleichnamigen Buch von C.G. Jung" ["Answer to Job: On Jung's book by the same name"] (*Orientierung*, Zürich, 28 Feb. 1953). Cf. Jung to Rudin, especially 14 March 1953 and 30 April 1960 (*Letters II*, p. 110, pp. 253f). Cf. also Jung to Mother Prioress, 19 Oct. 1960 (Appendix 1, p. 305).

34 Cf. Jung, 27 Dec. 1947, p. 105 and note.

35 Cf. White, 4 March 1954, p. 228 and note.

36 as things stand.

37 "he knew all things from the beginning."

good . . ."?[38] It is also reasonable to believe that as human he was not wholly conscious of it, and inasmuch as he was unconscious he projected it indubitably. The split through his Self made him as a human being as good as possible, although he was unable to reach the degree of perfection his white Self already possessed. The Catholic doctrine cannot help to declare, that *Christ even as a human being knew everything*. This is the logical consequence of the perfect union of the duae naturae.[39] Christ as understood by the Church is to me a spiritual, i.e. mythological being; even his humanity is divine inasmuch as it is generated by the celestial Father and exempt of original sin. When I speak of him as a human being, I mean its few traces we can gather from the gospels. It is not enough for the reconstruction of an empirical character. Moreover even if we could reconstruct an individual personality, it would not fulfill the role of redeemer and Godman, who is identical with the "all-knowing" Self. Since the individual human being is characterised by a selection of tendencies and qualities, it is a specification and not a wholeness, i.e. it cannot be individual without incompleteness and restriction, whereas the Christ of the Doctrine is perfect, complete, whole and therefore not individual at all, but a collective mythologema viz. an archetype. He is far more divine than human and far more universal than individual.

Concerning the omniscience it is important to know that *Adam* already was equipped with supernatural knowledge according to Jewish and Christian tradition,[40] all the more so Christ.

I think that the great split[41] in those days was by no means a mistake but a very important collective fact of synchronistic correspondence with the then new Aeon of Pisces. Archetypes, in spite of their conservative nature, are not static but *in a continuous dramatic flux*. Thus the Self being a Monad or continuous unit would be dead. But it lives inasmuch as it splits and unites again. There is no energy without opposites!

38 When Jesus hears himself addressed as "good teacher, he answers: "Why do you call me good? No one is good but God alone" (Mark 10.18).

39 two natures. The union of the divine and human natures in Christ was affirmed by the Council of Chalcedon in 451. The formula adopted at Chalcedon was intended only to set limits on legitimate theological speculation, not to define the mystery of Christ's nature in an exact or final sense (*ODCC*, pp. 262f). Nevertheless, since the document is known as "The Definition of Chalcedon," Jung's argument is understandable. [with AC]

40 In *Mysterium*, under the heading, "Adam as the First Adept," Jung quotes Christian, alchemical, rabbinic and kabbalistic sources, even briefly citing Aquinas, to demonstrate that according to many ancient traditions, Adam was omniscient. "The 'Gloria Mundi' says [*Mus.herm.*, p. 268]: 'The Lord endowed Adam with great wisdom, and such marvellous insight that he immediately, without the help of any teacher – simply by virtue of his original righteousness – had a perfect knowledge of the seven liberal arts, and of all animals, plants, stones, metals, and minerals. Nay, what is more, he had a perfect understanding of the Holy Trinity, and of the coming of Christ in the flesh' " (CW 14, *Mysterium*, §570, p. 398).

41 The division of the archetype into halves: good (Christ) and evil (Satan).

All conservatives and institutionalists are Pharisaeans, if you apply this name without prejudice. Thus it was to be expected, that just the better part of Jewry would be hurt most by the revelation of an exclusively good God and loving Father. This novelty emphasized with disagreeable clearness that the hitherto worshipped Yahwe had some additional, less decorous propensities. For obvious reasons the orthodox pharisaeans could not defend their creed by insisting on the bad qualities of their god. Christ with his teaching of an exclusively good God must have been most awkward for them. They probably believed him to be hypocritical, since this was his main objection against them. One gets that way, when one has to hold on to something which once has been good and had meant a considerable progress or improvement at a time. It meant an enormous step forward, when Yahwe revealed himself as a *jealous* God, letting his chosen people feel that he was after them with blessings and with punishments, and that God's goal was Man. Not knowing better, they cheated Him, by literally obeying his Law. But as Job discovered Yahwe's primitive amorality, God found out about the trick of observing the Law and swallowing camels.[42]

The old popes and bishops succeeded in getting so much heathendom, barbarism and real evil out of the Church, that it became much better than some centuries before: there were no Alexander VI,[43] no auto-da-fé, no thumbscrews and racks any more, so that the compensatory drastic virtues (asceticism etc.) lost their meaning to a certain extent. The great split having been a merely spiritual fact for a long time, has at last got into the world, as a rule in its coarsest and least recognizable form, viz. as the iron curtain, the completion of the second fish.[44]

Now a new synthesis must begin.[45] But how can absolute evil be connected and identified with absolute good? It seems to be impossible. When Christ withstood Satan's temptation,[46] that was the fatal moment, when the shadow was cut off. Yet it had to be cut off in order to enable man to become morally

42 Jesus rebukes the Pharisees: "You blind guides, straining out a gnat and swallowing a camel!" (Matthew 23.24).

43 Pope Alexander VI (Rodrigo Borgia, 1431–1503), "most notorious of the corrupt and venal popes of the Renaissance" (*Letters II*, p. 165n).

44 Adler notes: "The astrological sign of Pisces consists of two fishes which were frequently regarded as moving in opposite directions. Traditionally, the reign of Christ corresponds to the first fish and ended with the first millennium, whereas the second fish coincides with the reign of the Antichrist, now nearing its end with the entry of the vernal equinox into the sign of Aquarius" (*Letters II*, p. 166n). (Cf. CW 9.ii, *Aion*, §148f, pp. 92ff; and CW 11, "Answer to Job," §725, pp. 446f.)

45 This paragraph is a long interpolation that Jung pasted into his handwritten draft. Perhaps overwhelmed by the complexity of the material to be typed, the secretary introduced many small changes into the letter that White received. As far as possible, especially where they create a sense different from the original, these changes are noted here.

46 Jesus' encounter with Satan in the desert (Matthew 4.1–11).

conscious. If the moral opposites could be united at all, they would be suspended altogether and there could be no morality at all. That is certainly not what synthesis aims at. In such a case of irreconcilability the opposites are united by a neutral or ambivalent bridge, a symbol expressing either side in such a way that they can function together.[47] This symbol is the *cross* as interpreted since old, viz. as tree of life or simply as tree, to which Christ is inescapably affixed. This particular feature points to the compensatory significance of the tree: the Tree symbolizes that entity from which Christ had been separated and with which he ought to be connected again, to make his life or being complete. With other words, the *Crucifixus* is the symbol uniting the absolute moral opposites. Christ represents the light, the tree the darkness; he the son, it the mother. Both are *androgynous* (tree = phallus).[48] Christ is so much identical with the cross, that both terms have become almost interchangeable in ecclesiastical language (f.i. "redeemed through Christ or through the cross" etc.). The tree brings back all that has been lost through Christ's extreme spiritualisation, namely the elements of nature. Through branches and leaves the tree gathers the powers of light and air and through its roots those of the earth and the water. Christ has been suffering on account of his split and he recovers his perfect life at Easter, when he has been buried again in the womb of the virginal mother. (Represented also in the myth of Attis by the tree, to which an image of Attis has been nailed, then cut down and carried into the cave of mother Kybele.[49] – The Nativity Church of Bethlehem erected over an Attis sanctuary!)[50] This mythical complex seems to represent a further development of the old drama, existence becoming real through reflection in consciousness, Job's tragedy.[51] But now it is the problem of dealing with the results of conscious discrimination.

47 Adler notes: "The bridge is the uniting symbol which represents psychic totality, the Self" (*Letters II*, p. 166n). Cf. also CW 6, *Types*, §828, p. 480.

48 Adler notes: "The tree often symbolizes the mother and appears as such in the numerous rebirth myths (cf. CW 5, *Symbols of Transformation*, Part II, ch. V). But it is also a phallic symbol and thus has an androgynous character. (For Christ's androgyny cf. CW 14, *Mysterium*, §526, §565 and n. 63)" (*Letters II*, p. 166n).

49 Cf. Jung, 25 Nov 1950, p. 158 and note.

50 Adler notes: "A sanctuary of Adonis, another young dying god closely related to Attis, existed since ancient times in a cave at Bethlehem. It is supposed to be identical with Christ's birthplace, over which Constantine the Great (ca. 288–337) had a basilica built" (*Letters II*, p. 167n). More accurately, according to ancient Christian accounts, many gardens sacred to Adonis were located in a grove overshadowing the cave where Christ was said to have been born. The grove went back to the time of Emperor Hadrian, second century CE (cf. St. Jerome, *Letter 108*). [AC]

51 Cf. *MDR*, p. 312, pp. 338f. Cf. also Jung to Neumann, 10 March 1959: "Without the reflecting consciousness of man the world is a gigantic meaningless machine, for in our experience man is the only creature who is capable of ascertaining any meaning at all" (*Letters II*, p. 494).

The first attempt is moral appreciation and decision for the Good. Although this decision is indispensable, it is not too good in the long run. You must not get stuck with it, otherwise you grow out of life and die slowly. Then the onesided emphasis on the Good becomes doubtful, but there is apparently no possibility to reconcile Good and Evil. That is where we are now.

The symbolic history of the Christlife shows as the essential teleological tendency the crucifixion viz. the union of Christ with the symbol of the tree. It is no more matter of an impossible reconciliation of Good and Evil, but of Man with his vegetative (= unconscious) life. In the case of the christian symbol, the tree however is dead and Man upon the cross is going to die, i.e. the solution of the problem takes place after death. That is so far as christian truth goes. But it is possible, that the christian symbolism expresses Man's mental condition in the aeon of pisces, as the bull and the ram gods do for the ages of aries and taurus. In this case the post-mortal solution would be symbolic of an entirely new psychological status, viz. that of aquarius, which is certainly a oneness, presumably that of the Anthropos, the realization of Christ's allusion: "Dii estis".[52] This is a formidable secret and difficult to understand, because it means that man will be essentially God and God man. The signs pointing in this direction consist in the fact that the cosmic power of self-destruction is laid into the hands of man and that man inherits the dual nature of the Father. He will understand it and he will be tempted to ruin the universal life of the earth by radio activity. Materialism and atheism, the negation of God, are indirect means to attain their goal. Through the negation of God one becomes deified, i.e., godallmighty like and then one knows what is good for mankind. That is how destruction begins. The intellectual schoolmasters in the Kremlin are a classical example. The danger to follow the same path is very great indeed. It begins with the lie, i.e. the projection of the shadow.

There is need of people knowing about their shadow, because there must be somebody who does not project. They ought to be in a visible position, where they would be expected to project and unexpectedly they do not project! They can thus set a visible example which would not be seen, if they were invisible.

There is certainly pharisaeism, law consciousness, power driven, sex obsession and the wrong kind of formalism in the Church. But these things are symptoms, that the old showy and easily understandable ways and methods have lost their significance and should be slowly replaced by more meaningful principles. This means indeed trouble with the christian vices. Since you cannot overthrow a whole world, because it harbours also some evil, it will be a more individual or "local" fight with what you rightly call "avidya". As "tout passe", even theological books are not true forever and even if they

52 "You are gods" (John 10.34).

expect to be believed one has to tell them in a loving and fatherly way, that they make some mistakes. A true and honest introverted thinking is a grace and possesses for a time at least divine authority, particularly if it is modest, simple and straight. The people who write such books are not the voice of God. They are only human. But it is true that the right kind of thinking isolates oneself. But did you become a monk for the sake of congenial society? Or do you assume that it isolates only a theologian? It has done the same to me and will do so to everybody that is blessed with it.(1)[53]

{That is the reason, why there are compensatory functions. The introverted thinker is very much in need of a developed feeling, i.e. of a less autoerotic, sentimental, melodramatic and emotional relatedness to people and things. The compensation will be a hell of a conflict to begin with, but later on, by understanding what "nirdvandva"[54] means, they[55] become the pillar at the gate of the transcendent function, i.e. the transitus to the Self.}

We should recognize that life is a transitus. There is an old covered bridge near Schmerikon[56] with an inscription: "Alles ist Uebergang".[57] Even the Church and her sententiae are only alive inasmuch as they change. All old truths want a new interpretation, so that they can live on in a new form. They can't be substituted or replaced by something else without losing their functional value altogether. The Church certainly expects of you that you assimilate its doctrine. But in assimilating it, you change it imperceptibly and sometimes even noticeably. Introverted thinking is aware of such subtle alterations, while other minds swallow them wholesale. If you try to be literal about the doctrine, you are putting yourself aside until there is nobody left that would represent it, but corpses. If on the other hand, you truly assimilate the doctrine, you will alter it creatively, by your individual understanding and thus give life to it. The life of most ideas consists in their controversial nature, i.e. that you can disagree with them, even if you recognize their importance for a majority. If you would fully agree with them, you could replace yourself just as well by a gramophone record. Moreover, if you don't disagree, you are not good as a directeur de conscience, since there are many other people suffering from the same difficulty and being badly in need of your understanding.

I appreciate the particular moral problem you are confronted with. But I should rather try to understand, why you were put into your actual situation of a profound conflict, before you think it being a fundamental mistake. I

53 Jung's first footnote, designated by *1)* in the text, appears here as the bracketed paragraph, following.

54 (Sanskrit) "free from the opposites" (of love/hate, joy/sorrow, etc.). Cf. CW 6, *Types*, §327ff, pp. 195ff.

55 i.e., the compensatory (inferior) functions.

56 Small town on Upper Lake Zurich, east of Bollingen. (Cf. map, Figure 5.1, p. 137.)

57 "All is transition."

remember vividly your charta geomantica,[58] that depicts so drastically the way you became a monk. I admit there are people with the peculiar gift to get inevitably and always into the wrong place. With such people nothing can be done, than to get them out of the wrong hole into another equally dubious one. But if I find an intelligent man in an apparently wrong situation, I am inclined to think, that it makes sense somehow. There may be some work for him to do. Much work is needed, where much has gone wrong or where much should be improved. That is one of the reasons why the Church attracts quite a number of intelligent and responsible men in the secret (or unconscious?) hope, that they will be strong enough to carry its meaning and not its words into the future. 1)[59] {The old trick of law obedience is still going strong, but the original christian teaching is a reminder.} The man allowing the institution to swallow himself, is not a good servant.

It is quite understandable that the ecclesiastic authorities must protect the Church against subversive influences. But it would be sabotage if this principle should be carried to the extreme, because it would kill the attempts at improvement also. The Church is "Durchgang"[60] and bridge between representatives of higher and lower consciousness and as such she makes sense quite definitely. Since the world is largely sub principatu diaboli,[61] it is unavoidable that there is just as much evil in the Church as everywhere else, and as everywhere else you got to be careful. What would you do, if you were a bank-clerk or a medical assistant at a big clinic? You are always and everywhere in a moral conflict, unless you are blissfully unconscious. I think it is not only honest, but even highly moral and altruistic to be what one professes to be as completely as possible with the full consciousness that you are making this effort for the weak and the unintelligent, who cannot live without a reliable support. He is a good physician who does not bother the patient with his own doubts and feelings of inferiority. Even if he knows little or is quite inefficient the right persona medici[62] might carry the day if seriously and truly performed for the patient. The grace of God may step in,

58 geomantic chart. (Cf. White's chart, Figure 6.1, p. 154.) Adler notes: "In geomancy, an ancient method of divination still widely practised in the Orient, especially the Far East, earth or pebbles are thrown on the ground and the resultant pattern is interpreted. In Europe the pattern was known as the *charta geomantica*. A later development was to make dots at random on a piece of paper: the "Art of Punctuation." (Cf. CW 8, "Synchronicity," CW 8, §866, p. 453.) Jung was fond of experimenting with all such mantic methods in order to test synchronistic events" (*Letters II*, p. 169n). Geomantic divination is discussed by Marie-Louise von Franz in *Number and Time: Reflections Leading Towards a Unification of Psychology and Physics* (Trans. Andrea Dykes., London: Rider & Co.), pp. 117ff; also in *Time: Rhythm and Repose* (London: Thames & Hudson, 1978), pp. 92f.

59 Jung's second footnote, indicated again by *1)*, is contained in the bracketed sentence, following.

60 passage, opening; *fig.* transition.

61 under the rule of the devil.

62 medical role.

when you don't lose your head in a clearly desperate situation. If it has been done, even with a lie, in favour of the patient, it has been well done, and you are justified, although you never get out of the awkward feeling that you are a dubious number. I wonder whether there is any true servant of God, who can rid himself of this profound insecurity balancing his obvious rightness. I cannot forget that crazy old Negro Mammy,[63] who told me: "God is working in me like a clock – funny and serious." By "clock" seems to be meant something precise and regular, even monotonous; by "funny and serious" compensating irrational events and aspects; a humorous seriousness expressing the playful and formidable nature of fateful experiences.

If I find myself in a critical or doubtful situation I always ask myself, whether there is not something in it, explaining the need of my presence, before I make a plan of how to escape. If I should find nothing hopeful or meaningful in it, I think I would not hesitate to jump out of it as quick as possible. Well, I may be all wrong, but the fact that you discover yourself in the Church does not impress me as being wholly nonsensical. Of course huge sacrifices are expected of you but I wonder whether there is any vocation or any kind of meaningful life, that does not demand sacrifices of a sort. There is no place where those striving after consciousness could find absolute safety. Doubt and insecurity are indispensable components of a complete life. Only those who can lose this life *really*, can gain it really. A "complete" life does not consist in a theoretical completeness, but in the fact, that one accepts the particular fatal tissue, in which one finds oneself embedded without reservation, and that one tries to make sense of it or to create a kosmos from the chaotic mess, into which one is born. If one lives properly and completely, time and again one will be confronted with a situation, of which one will say: "This is too much. I cannot bear it any more." Then the question must be answered: "Can one really not bear it?"

"Fidem non esse caecum sensum religionis e latebris subconscientiae erumpentem" etc.,[64] indeed not! Fides in its ecclesiastic meaning is a construction expressed by the wholly artificial credo, but no spontaneous product of the unconscious. You can swear to it in all innocence, as well as I could, if asked. Also you can *teach*, if asked, the *solid* doctrine of St.Thomas Aquinas, as I could if I knew it. You can and will and must criticize it, yet with a certain discrimination, as there are people incapable of understanding your argument. "Quieta movere"[65] is not necessarily a good principle. Being an analyst, you know how little you can say, and sometimes it is quite enough, when only the analyst knows. Certain things transmit themselves by air, when they are really needed.

63 Adler notes: "Possibly a patient Jung interviewed ... at St. Elizabeth's Hospital in Washington, D.C., in 1912. Cf. *FJL*, 323J, n.3" (*Letters II*, p. 170n).

64 Cf. White, 4 March 1954, p. 230 and note.

65 to move things at rest (i.e., to "disturb sleeping dogs").

I don't share at all Barbara Robb's idea, one should not be so finnicky about conscience. It is definitely dishonest and – sorry – a bit too catholic. One must be finnicky, when it comes to a moral question and what a question! You are asked to decide, whether you can deal with ambiguity, deception, "doublecrossing" and other damnable things, for the love of your neighbour's soul. If it is a case of "the end justifying the means", you better buy a through ticket to hell. It is a devilish hybris even to think, that one could be in such exalted a position to decide about the means one is going to apply. There is no such thing, not even in psychotherapy. If you don't want to go to the dogs morally, there is only one question, namely "Which is the necessity you find yourself burdened with, when you take to heart your brother's predicament?" The question is, *how you are applied* in the process of the cure, and not at all, what the means are you could offer to buy yourself off. It depends very much indeed upon the way you envisage your position in reference to the Church. I should advocate an analytical attitude, which is permissible as well as honest, viz. take the Church as your ailing employer and your colleagues as the unconscious inmates of a hospital.

Is the L.S.D. drug Mescal? It has indeed very curious effects – vide Aldous Huxley![66] – of which I know far too little. I don't know either what its psychotherapeutic value with neurotic or psychotic patients is. I only know, there is no point in wishing to *know* more of the collective unconscious than one gets through dreams and intuition. The more you know of it, the greater and heavier becomes your moral burden, because the unconscious contents transform into your individual tasks and duties, as soon as they begin to become conscious. Do you want to increase loneliness and misunderstanding? Do you want to find more and more complications and increasing responsibilities? You get enough of it. If I once could say, that I have done everything I know I had to do, then perhaps I should realize a legitimate need to take mescal. But if I should take it now, I would not be sure at all, that I had not taken it out of idle curiosity. I should hate the thought, that I had touched on the sphere, where the paint is made that colours the world, where the light is created, that makes shine the splendour of the dawn, the lines and shapes of all form, the sound that fills the orbit, the thought that illuminates the darkness of the void. There are some poor impoverished creatures perhaps, for which mescal would be a heavensent gift without a counterpoison, but I am profoundly mistrustful of the "pure gifts of the Gods".

66 Aldous Huxley (1894–1963): British novelist, poet and essayist, especially remembered for his novels, including *Brave New World* (1932). In the 1950s Huxley experimented with mind-altering substances. He wrote *The Doors of Perception* (1954) about his personal experiences with mescalin and LSD.

You pay very dearly for them. "Quidquid id est, timeo Danaos et dona ferentes."[67]

This is not the point at all, to know of or about the unconscious, nor does the story end here; on the contrary it is how and where you begin the real quest. If you are too unconscious it is a great relief to know a bit of the collective unconscious. But it becomes soon dangerous to know more, because one does not learn at the same time how to balance it through a conscious equivalent. That is the mistake Aldous Huxley makes:1)[68] {It is really the mistake of our age. We think it is enough to discover new things, but we don't realize that knowing more demands a corresponding development of morality. Radioactive clouds over Japan, Calcutta and Saskatchewan point to a progressive poisoning of the universal atmosphere.} he does not know that he is in the role of the "Zauberlehrling",[69] that has learned from his master how to call the ghosts, but did not know how to get rid of them again:

> "Die Geister, die ich rief,
> Werd ich nun nicht los!"[70]

I should be obliged to you indeed if you could let me see the material they get with L.S.D. It is quite awful that the alienists have caught hold of a new poison to play with, without the faintest knowledge or feeling of responsibility. It is just as if a surgeon had never learned further than to cut open his patient's belly and to leave things there. When one gets to know unconscious contents, one should know how to deal with them. I can only hope that the doctors will feed themselves thoroughly with Mescalin, the *alcaloid of divine grace*, so that they learn by themselves its marvelous effect. You have not finished with the conscious side yet. Why should you expect more from the unconscious? Since 35 years I know enough of the collective unconscious and my whole effort is concentrated upon preparing the ways and means to deal with it.

Now to end this very long epistle I must say how much I have appreciated your confidence, frankness, courage and honesty. This is so rare and so precious an event, that it is a pleasure to answer at length. I hope you will find a way out to Switzerland.

I have *seen* Mr. Caruso.[71] In nomen est omen?[72] He seems to be still on the safe side.

67 "Whatever it is, I fear the Greeks, even bearing gifts" (Virgil, *Aeneid*, I,48).

68 Jung's third footnote, marked again by *1)*, is contained in the two bracketed sentences, following.

69 "Sorcerer's Apprentice." Title of a poem by Goethe, quoted below.

70 "The spirits that I summoned, now I cannot banish!" (Goethe's poem, "Der Zauberlehrling").

71 Cf. White, 4 March 1954, p. 231 and note.

72 in the name is the omen. Jung's meaning is obscure. Possibly a reference to the world-famous operatic tenor who shared the psychologist's name.

The winter, though very cold, has dealt leniently with me. Both my wife and myself are tired, though still active, but in a very restricted way.

I am spending the month of April in Bollingen procul negotiis[73] and the worst weather we have known for years.

Cordially yours, C.G.

Blackfriars, Oxford

15.5.54[74]

My Dear C.G.,

Thank you a million for your long and truly marvellous letter. It moves me deeply that you should go to such very much trouble to help me. I must give myself time to assimilate it more thoroughly before I venture any comment; but I have already assimilated enough to realize that it contains great wisdom, very well attuned to my condition!

But I would add that it comes at a most opportune moment. About ten days' ago, an accumulation of events had brought me to just that point of "this is just too much. I cannot bear any more"; and I was astonished at the strength of the emotional charge (of hatred and fear at the prospect of staying) which accompanied it. Naturally I was suspicious; so I asked the I Ching what was happening, and what I should do. The answer was "44" ("Kou"),[75] with 9 in the 3rd and 4th places – so changing to "59" ("Huan").[76] As you may well imagine, this woke me up to what was happening in an uncommonly forceful way; and showed very clearly what I was and was not to do! It has also made me particularly receptive to what you say in your letter; and you will not fail to notice how closely your letter and the I Ching correspond. Anyhow, the practical upshot is that here I stay; and I hope a new attitude and perspective is forming. . . .

For the moment, I will say no more about *that* than Thank You.

Dr. Sandison (of Powick Hospital, Worcester)[77] is sending you his "reports"

73 away from work. 74 Typewritten.

75 The text for the 44th hexagram, "Kou / Coming to Meet," begins: "This hexagram indicates a situation in which the principle of darkness, after having been eliminated, furtively and unexpectedly obtrudes again from within and below" (*I Ching*, p. 170)

76 The text for the 59th hexagram, "Huan / Dispersion, Dissolution," begins: "Wind blowing over water disperses it, dissolving it into foam and mist. This suggests that when a man's vital energy is dammed up within him . . . gentleness serves to break up and dissolve the blockage" (Ibid., p. 227).

77 Ronald B. Sandison, F.R.C., consulting psychiatrist at Powick Hospital near Worcester, U.K., pioneered the use and development of psychotherapy with LSD between 1952 and

on LSD – one "factual", the other an attempted "Jungian interpretation": this will explain its likenesses and unlikenesses to mescal – his way of using it anyhow has no resemblance to Huxley's![78] I don't think I was very serious in wanting some myself; I do realize very well the truth of what you say. But sometimes I feel a bit psychically constipated, and foolishly suppose a laxative (if such there be) might be a help!

I expect J. Jacobi has told you about the Caruso meeting in Brussels.[79] It was certainly kept well on the safe side; every possibility of danger being smothered at birth in words, words, words. J.J. credited me with "courage" in telling them why they liked to talk so much; but there was really nothing to lose!

I wonder if Father Aylward[80] (the young American priest at the Institut) has been to see you – as he proposed. We had a pretty hair-raising time working together during the vacation; I hope he is none the worse!

I hope Fr. Zacharias's book and "The Trickster"[81] will come my way. They should both interest me particularly.

I very much wish I *could* see any prospect of coming to Switzerland again this year; I should dearly like to see and talk with you. At present I can see very little hope of finding the time or (more serious!) the money. However I am not altogether without hope of managing it somehow; in which case, I will not fail to let you know so soon as I can.

I am very thankful indeed that this winter has been more merciful to you. In England we seem to be having a second winter right now: the coldest May I can remember.

I do hope Mrs Jung is well too, and has now been released of some of her overwork. I have been wondering if she has seen *The Ancient Secret* by Lady Flavia Anderson[82] – a most extraordinary book on the Grail, etc. It

1965. His most recent book: *A Century of Psychiatry, Psychotherapy, and Group Analysis: A Search for Integration* (London, Philadelphia: Jessica Kingsley Publisher, 2001).

78 In 1954 Sandison published two papers in *Journal of Mental Science*: Sandison, R.A., "Psychological Aspects of the LSD Treatment of the Neuroses"; Sandison, R.A. & A. Spencer, "The Therapeutic Value of Lysergic Acid Diethylamide in Mental Illness."

79 Cf. White, 4 March 1954, p. 231 and notes.

80 James Aylward, American analyst. In the 1950s, as a Roman Catholic priest (later formally laicized), Aylward studied at the Jung Institute in Zurich. He worked for many years as an analyst at the Binswanger Klinik in Kreuzlingen, Switzerland. From 1975 until his retirement in 1990, he lived and practiced in Houston, Texas, where he also taught at the Jung Center.

81 Cf. Jung, 10 April 1954, pp. 232f and notes.

82 In *The Ancient Secret* (London: Gollancz, 1953), Lady Flavia Anderson argues that the Grail was pre-Christian and Egyptian in origin, had a fiery as well as a watery nature, was made of glass, and that its ability to focus sunlight so as to ignite tinder was one of its main ritual functions.

maintains, among other strange things, that the original grail or cauldron was a burning glass. . . .

I have just been reading your "Psychology of Transference" in the new translation. Gosh! – but it IS good.

I will probably write more anon, when I have pondered more on your letter. Meanwhile, with renewed thanks,

Ever cordially, VICTOR

P.S. Did I ever send you the paper I read to the London A.P. Club on "Good and Evil" (privatio boni and all that!)?[83] Or the one (which precipitated my "Pharisee" complex) on "Love and Wrath in St Paul"?[84] If not, I would gladly do so. But you must surely (as I do) just hate the sight of typescript!

Küsnacht-Zürich

20th of Aug. 1954[85]

Dear Victor,

Thank you ever so much for your kind birthday wishes![86] Too bad, that you can't come out to Zürich! I am rather curious to know about further developments of the problem, but it will be better to wait until we can talk about it. Letterwriting is a pest.

My best greetings and wishes!

Yours cordially, C.G.

P.S. I have weathered my birthday and I have a good summer as a whole.

83 Cf. White, 4 March 1954, p. 230 and note. This lecture remained unpublished by the London APC until five years after White's death (*Harvest*, Vol. 12, 1966).

84 Victor White, "Anathema-Maranatha: Love and Wrath in St Paul," a chapter in *Love and Violence* (London: Sheed & Ward, 1954, pp. 219–34), based on *Amour et Violence*, a volume in the series "Etudes Carmélitaines" (Père Bruno de Jésus-Marie, OCD, ed. Paris: Desclée de Brouwer, 1946).

85 (Handwritten?) Letter previously unpublished. The original of this letter is lost, but a typed transcript survives.

86 A letter from White is missing.

Figure 10.1 Formal portrait of Victor White, date and photographer unidentified.

Blackfriars, Oxford.

25.9.54[87]

My dear C.G.,

I was deeply touched to get your kind note of August 20th. It was awaiting me on my return from Sweden, where I had been combining a conference with a holiday.

I was very sorry that I could not get to Switzerland to see you too;

87 Typewritten by White.

but I found it was just impossible to fit in both. I had, at the time, considerable hope that I should be able to come and see you soon after Christmas, if not before. But now it seems that April is the earliest I can hope for.

The "problem" has been changed considerably, at least from the outside. I think the last you heard was when I at last got to taking that oath and the "Mastership in Theology" – with considerable help from your letter, urgings from my superiors and colleagues, and a big kick from the *I Ching*. All was set for me, not only to continue teaching here this year; but also to become the "Regent of Studies".[88] Then, in early August, I suddenly got a letter from my boss (Provincial)[89] in which I learned that someone else (a complete incompetent) was to be appointed Regent,[90] and asking if I would like to go to California! After many delays, this has at last been fixed up; and I am due to sail for USA on October 16th. I am still very much in the dark both about why I have been moved, and what I am supposed to do when I get there. I am not even sure of my address, but will send it to you so soon as I know: I expect it will be at the Dominican Study House at Oakland[91] (S. Francisco). So all my fuss about the oath, the degree, and my beautiful self-sacrifice pro bono publico has been a sort of sacrifice of Isaac – or maybe something a great deal more comic. But I have also been having quite a lot of conflicts

88 The Regent of Studies at a Dominican Studium, such as the one in Oxford, is responsible for curriculum and faculty and to a great degree shapes the education of those entering the Order. Even before receiving his STM degree, White had been designated Regent of Studies by the Master General of the Dominican Order, in Rome.

89 The news was communicated to White in a letter from his Prior Provincial, Fr. Hilary Carpenter. A newly appointed Regent of Studies would normally assume the post after receiving his STM degree, which White had done on 28 May 1954. Other events intervened, however, beginning with the death of the Master General of the Order, Fr. Emanuel Suarez, on 30 June 1954 in a car accident in Spain. Soon after this, the interim Master General set aside White's appointment.

It has been considered unlikely that a newly named interim Master General would have cancelled such an appointment on his own initiative (Bede Bailey, O.P., interview, 1 August 2001). A reasonable speculation was that the moving force behind the decision came from White's own Provincial. So in his study of the period Fr. Aidan Nichols writes that Hilary Carpenter, "who distrusted these arcane sources of wisdom [i.e., analytical psychology] saw his opportunity, and used the intermission in office-holders in Rome to have the appointment set aside" (Aidan Nichols, O.P., *Dominican Gallery: Portrait of a Culture*. Leominster, Herefordshire, U.K.: Fowler Wright Books, 1997, p. 54). Recently uncovered documents, however, point back to Rome (cf. Appendix 2, "Victor White, a Memoir, pp. 322ff).

90 The man appointed Regent of Studies in White's place, Fr. Ambrose Farrell, had been trained as a canon lawyer. He remained Regent for one term, 1954–1960. In 1960 the previously retired Regent, Fr. Daniel Callus, was recalled to his former duties as Pro-Regent (Acting Regent) for one year, with Fr. Ambrose as his assistant. On 13 October 1961 Fr. Columba Ryan became Pro-Regent, Fr. Ambrose remaining as Vice-Regent.

91 St Albert's House, Oakland, California, had at this time a cooperative relationship with the English Dominican Province.

about what I should do under the circumstances. However, I have finally decided to go and see what awaits me there. All the more so since, at least to start with, it will be only for about five months. This is so because I have been elected to attend the General Chapter of the Dominicans to be held in Rome in early April;[92] and I expect in any case to be in Europe for some months next summer.

I am hoping very much that I may come and see you on my way from Rome to England in April; perhaps I will stay around Zurich quite a while, especially if the Institut could use me in any way. Anyhow, for some reason or another, I am no longer "indispensable" at Oxford: indeed, it seems definitely "not wanted". I am still left guessing the reasons: there could be several.[93] But in many ways it is of course a huge relief.

I would have told you all this news sooner; but it was only a week ago that I knew definitely myself. Since then, I have been desperately busy sorting, packing, getting my passage, visa, cancelling engagements, etc.

While clearing out my room, I discovered copies of papers I had written, and intended to send you – though I am afraid I never could have done so. If you have had them before, please just destroy them. Of course, you don't have to read them anyway! "Good and Evil"[94] will, I am afraid, explain itself – which is not to say it needs no further explanation! "Anathema-Maranatha"[95] (which I know to be poor, muddled and inconclusive) may be only of biographical interest: I remember telling you how I had trouble with it with the censors – but finally got it passed, and it is now printed. "Guilt"[96] is a thing I did for an interdenominational "symposium" on religion and psychology, due for publication this winter.

I was on the phone with Barbara Hannah the other day, and was glad to hear you appear in fine health and spirits. I was very sorry, though, to hear Mrs Jung has been poorly, and has had to go away.[97] I do hope and pray she will soon be well.

92 White's move to California did not interfere with other responsibilities he held in the Order, such as his election to the General Chapter and his ongoing work as one of the translators of the English Province's new edition of the *ST*.

93 White had written a letter to Rome, to the Master General's socius (assistant), Fr Aelwin Tindal-Atkinson, O.P., asking for help in understanding what had happened to his appointment. Fr Aelwin, an old friend, sent back a letter saying that he was equally in the dark about how the decision had been made. (Information from the archivist for the English Province, based on documents in the Edinburgh archive. Fr Bede Bailey, O.P., interview, 1 August 2001.)

94 Cf. White, 15 May 1954, p. 245 and note.

95 Ibid.

96 Victor White, "Guilt: Theological and Psychological" in *Christian Essays in Psychiatry* (ed. P. Mairet. London: SCM Press, 1956).

97 Emma Jung had begun to be ill in 1954 and was diagnosed the following spring with cancer. During her illness she sometimes rested at a convalescent home outside Zurich. (Cf. White, 21 May 1955, p. 272 and note.)

I am afraid this is a very hurried – and superficial – letter. All these events have been rather on that level.

I will write again from California, and tell you what happens there.

All very best wishes,

Ever cordially, VICTOR

1955–58

6172 Chabot Road,
Oakland, 18,
California, U.S.A.

January 8th 1955[1]

My dear C.G.,

For some time now, the inner voice has been nagging at me to send you a few lines of greeting and news.

As you know already, my journey to California was quite a leap in the dark. Nobody in England seemed to have any clear purpose in sending me here, and when I arrived – although I was most kindly and hospitably received – none of my Dominican brethren seemed to have any clear purpose in inviting me: at any rate, there was no definite work waiting for me to do! For the first two or three weeks there was just nothing to do at all.[2] I may say, that I spent some of that time reading letters which you had written me over the years (how many there have been!), especially your more recent ones. I cannot say that my inner problem had resolved at all, though I think I have become much more clear about what you were driving at in those letters. How many subjects, by the way, we have raised but hardly threshed out!

But although nobody seemed to have any conscious object in my trip to California, I had had a strange feeling that there was something waiting here for me to do. And so it soon turned out. "Religion and Psychiatry" seems to be just *the* topic in this area – and especially among the Catholics. But few people seem to have got even to the ABC of the subject: and the Catholic "psychiatrists" (which, of course, means any psychotherapist here) have hardly got beyond the most elementary Freud. In a very short time, I found myself getting booked to lecture and speak on the subject all over the place: colleges, universities, social service agencies, priest seminaries, church halls – to say nothing of course of the A.P. Clubs in San Francisco[3] and

1 Typewritten. Handwritten note, upper left, in Jung's writing: "*to file!*"

2 White's eventual employment in California included teaching dogmatic theology to young Dominicans at St. Albert's College, Oakland. (He is listed as a lector at the Studium of the Dominicans of the Western Province, USA, in 1955–56.) A few of his students – among them Matthew Fox – valuing his connection with Jung, also sought him out for spiritual direction. But he is remembered as uninspired in the classroom, and isolated outside it. A former Dominican, who studied at St. Albert's shortly after White's visit, guesses that the faculty would have been uncomfortable in the knowledge that White had been passed over as Regent at Blackfriars and would have avoided close association with him (B. Wall, private correspondence, May 2004).

3 White addressed the APC of San Francisco as a member of a four-person panel on Friday, 10 December 1954. His visit was announced less than month ahead: "Possible surprise program: Father Victor White . . . will be invited to our December meeting, as soon as he returns to town, and will be asked to speak. . . . Father White is here on a short visit from England

Los Angeles. I even found myself selling some elementary Jungian psychology on television! I am now pretty well booked up until I leave in March: these bookings include some retreats as well as lectures on this interminable "religion & psychiatry" issue. It is quite fun for a time; but after a while one can have enough of rushing around in cars, being fed on enormous steaks, shaking countless hands, and being generally treated as a Pundit. By March I should have about saturated the market; but I am probably returning in September to take on a stable job of lecturing in theology at Los Angeles.[4] It seems the best thing to do: my superiors in England seem only too pleased!

The net result is, of course, that I have not had much time to brood over my inner problems. It seems that I've definitely got a job to do in my present calling, however uncomfortable I still often feel about it, and that there is nothing to do but to get on with it. It is at least rather satisfying to feel one is needed, and doing something that nobody else around here can do. But it is just telling the old, old story, and not very original or creative.

Of course, in view of this campaign of putting over a little elementary Jungian psychology in California, I am frankly rather relieved that "Answer to Job" has not yet appeared in USA![5] It would queer my pitch rather badly among these mostly very naïve, but very well meaning, Catholics. Already of course I am getting perplexed and indignant letters from England asking "What the hell. . . ." It cost quite some sleepless nights, trying to write an article to explain what I think – or, more exactly, to try and sort out what I *did* think! I hope you will find the result (which I will send you if and when it is published) not too distressing;[6] and especially that you will take into consideration for whom it is written.

(*APC of SF Newsletter*, Vol. I, No. 4, December 1954). As stated in the minutes: "Father White spoke on Christmas and rebirth, the Christmas story as an archetypal pattern, the observer as compared with the believer, the combination of opposites (the Universal and the Unique) in the birth of Christ" (Minutes, APC of San Francisco, 10 December 1954).

4 Apparently the expected job in Los Angeles did not materialize.

5 Jung's *Job* had been read by a limited circle of American readers in a translation made by James Kirsch, MD, for the analyst-participants in a seminar he taught in Los Angeles in 1952–53. Commercial publication, in Hull's translation, did not come until late 1954 with Routledge & Kegan Paul, London. In 1956 *Job* was also published by the Pastoral Psychology Book Club, Great Neck, New York. (Cf. Jung to J. Kirsch, J.B. Priestley and H.A. Murray, *Letters II*, pp. 104, 192f and 322ff; also "Translator's Note," CW 11, *Psych. & Rel.*, p. vii.)

6 White's "Jung on Job" appeared in the March 1955 issue of *Blackfriars* (Vol. XXXVI). The review included reasoned discussion of Jung's book, but also several personal attacks on Jung, accusing him of bad faith, childish ignorance, and paranoia. White's public attack on Jung deepened the rift between them (cf. Jung, 21 Oct. 1959, pp. 282ff). In his last year of life, before reprinting the review in his final book, *Soul and Psyche* (cf. White, 17 March 1955, p. 259 and note), White removed the damaging passages from it. Since the original version of this historically important review is now hard to find, it is reprinted below as Appendix 6, pp. 349ff.

I am all set to come to Zürich toward the end of April, where it has kindly been arranged for me to hold seminars at the Institut. I have not yet any very clear idea what to talk about there: I am frankly, at the moment, more interested in the opportunity it will give me to see you and gather some Zürich atmosphere to counterbalance the Irish-American-Clerical atmosphere in which I am at present mostly living. Quite a problem of opposites; but then I can't live long without them!

Talking of opposites, I stumbled recently on a passage in St. Thomas Aquinas which rather remarkably confirms the view that our differences about *privatio boni* is one of functions. It is in the Summa Theologica Ia IIae.36.1, where he asks "utrum bonum amissum sit magis causa doloris quam malum coniunctum",[7] and says:

> Si hoc modo se haberent privationes in apprehensione animae sicut se habent in ipsis rebus, ista quaestio nullius momenti esse videretur. Malum enim . . . est privatio boni. Privatio autem in rebus naturae nihil aliud est quam carentia oppositi habitus. Secundum hoc ergo idem esset tristari de bono amisso et de malo habito. Sed tristitia est motus appetitus apprehensionem sequentis. *In apprehensione autem, ipsa privatio habet rationem cuiusdam entis, unde dictur ens rationis.* Et sic, malum, cum sit privatio, *se habet per modum contrarii. . . .*[8]

It is clear, from ibid.22.2. that the "apprehensio animae"[9] which he considers to be presupposed to all emotions is a sort of "concretistic feeling". I don't know if this sort of thing interests you; but it certainly interests me that Aquinas recognized that to this sort of apprehension "malum" appears as a positive contrary[10] – though not of course to reflecting thought.

7 "whether good neglected be a greater cause of suffering than evil committed."

8 "If privations were to be in the mind what they are in reality, the present question would be of no importance. For as we have seen, evil is the privation of good; and in the real world, privation is simply the lack of the opposite positive good. At that rate, sorrowing over the loss of good would be no different from sorrowing over the occurrence of evil. However, sorrow is a movement of the orexis [appetite] arising from some cognitive perception; and within the realm of thought even privations have some sort of ontological status: hence the expression, *an entity of the mind.* Thus evil, being a privation, has the status of a contrary." (*ST*, Blackfriars, Vol. 20, IaIIae, 31–39, pp. 110f.)

9 consideration of the mind.

10 In 1955 White published an essay, "Kinds of Opposites," in the Festchrift for Jung's 80th birthday (*Studien zur Analytischen Psychologie C.G. Jungs, Vol. I: Beiträge aus Theorie und Praxis*, Zürich: Rascher Verlag, 1955). This was White's final effort to straighten out the category confusion, as he saw it, that muddied Jung's discussions of good and evil. Distinguishing logically between the types of pairings that can be called opposites, White writes that contraries involve "two positive qualities or contents, of which one excludes the other, but of which neither . . . necessarily entails the other. The pairs 'joy–sorrow', 'healthy–

Well, I will weary you no[11] more. But I thought that maybe you would like this brief account of how things fare with me.

I was glad to hear that, anyhow up till a few weeks ago, you were in good health. I do hope that continues, and that you are now being allowed to have a reasonably restful life. I so much missed seeing you this last summer, and look forward, more than I can say, to doing so in April or May.

Please give my warmest greetings to Mrs Jung,

Ever cordially, VICTOR

Küsnacht-Zürich

Jany 19, 1955[12]

The Rev.Father Victor White, O.P.
St. Albert's College
6172 Chabot Road
Oakland 18, Calif.

Dear Victor,

It is now more than 2 months ago that I had begun to write a letter to you, but I could not continue it since I did not know what you were doing in California, nor why you were sent there. From your recent letter I see that your stay in USA makes sense. No matter how little you can convey to your unprepared public, it contains at least some grains of the future.

I should have thanked you long ago for your kind messages and wishes for the New Year,[13] but I hardly can keep up any more with all my obligations. There are many things I could or should tell you, but "desunt vires".[14] It is nice to know that you come to Zurich in the end of April.

I know you will have some difficulties when my "Answer to Job" becomes public. I am sorry. Already Philip Toynbee has reviewed it in an "abysmally

sick', 'heaven–hell', 'black–white', . . . are common examples" (pp. 147f). Aquinas says that good–evil is a different kind of pairing, in that evil is always a privation or distortion of good. But even Aquinas, in the passage quoted, admits that the psyche sometimes *perceives* evil as being real and solid.

11 Typing error: "now," with "w" struck through (cf. Jung, 19 Jan. 1955, p. 257).

12 Typewritten, from holograph dated 16 Jan.

13 Written messages from White for the new year of 1955 are missing. They may have been conveyed by word of mouth, since in a previous letter White mentions that a few weeks before (early December) he had received word of Jung's good health.

14 strength is lacking.

stupid" way,[15] as R.F.C. Hull, the translator, rightly says (in a letter to me).[16] It was to be expected. I am up against the wall of stupidity since 50 years. That is just so and nothing can be done against it.

Your quotation from S. Thomas is a marvellous puzzle. I have brooded over it for many hours and I can't make head or tail of it, unless it is an attempt to give Evil some substantiality in recognition of the fact that we experience it just as "substantial" as Good. What is Good then in apprehensione animae?[17] He just does not carry through his argument, cum malum sit privatio boni,[18] to which he sticks, without looking at it from the other side. In ordinary logic, cold is the carentia oppositi habitus,[19] ergo privation of warmth et vice-versa, above–below, right–left, white–black, etc. In my "abysmal stupidity" I can see nothing but a petitio principii,[20] if there ever was one. Why should an emotion be more concrete psychologically than the ratio? Does the ratio not affect the body?

There is a joke in your letter: after your argument, you write: "Well, I will weary you *now* more." You win, I have laboured for several days getting nowhere. Please don't get angry with me, I am obviously too dense. I hope you will be patient enough with my debility and explain the puzzle orally to me when I see you again in the flesh.

Although I cannot complain about my health, I am feeling the burden of my age. My last work, the Mysterium Coniunctionis,[21] is now with the printer, and I have no ideas any more – thank Heavens.

My best wishes for the New Year,

Cordially yours, C.G.

15 In the *Observer*, London, 9 January 1955.

16 Richard Francis Carrington Hull (1913–74): translator of Jung's works from German to English for the CW. Hull also translated Jung's German-language letters for *The C.G. Jung Letters*, and Jung's half of *The Freud/Jung Letters*. (Cf. Jung to Hull, 24 Jan. 1955, *Letters II*, p. 217.) Regarding Philip Toynbee's review, Jung had written to Hull (in a letter previously unpublished): "One could not expect more of this inflated son of Toynbee's and it is a loss of time and energy to fight stupidity. It just does not pay, particularly in a case where idiocy is enhanced by malevolence" (Jung to Hull, 15 Jan. 1955. Jung–Hull correspondence, ETH Library archive).

17 as considered by the mind. Cf. White, 8 Jan. 1955, p. 255 and note.

18 that evil is the privation of good.

19 opposite of the state of warmth.

20 begging the question (logical fallacy: using a principle to explain the same principle).

21 Cf. Jung, early April 1952, p. 185 and note.

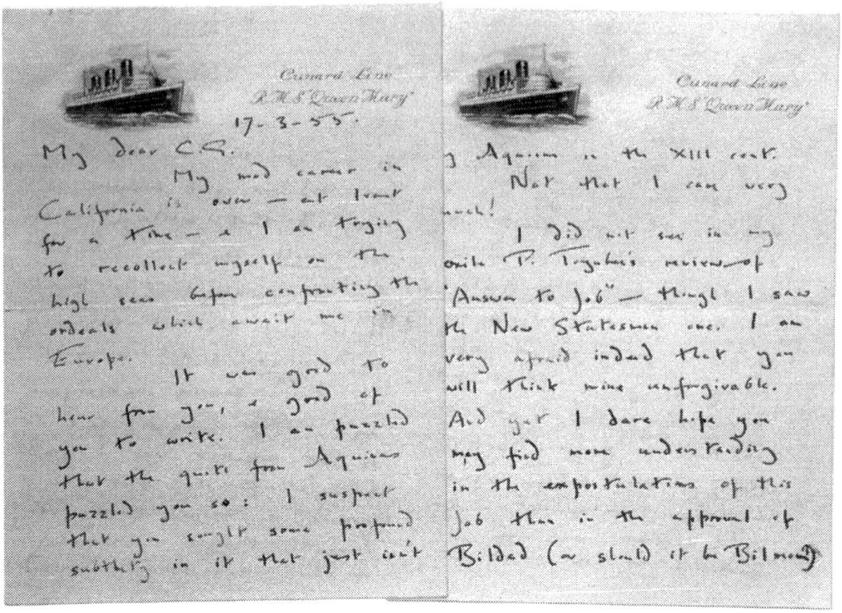

Cunard Line
R.M.S. "Queen Mary"
17-3-55.
My dear C.G.
My mad career in California is over — at least for a time — & I am trying to recollect myself on the high seas before confronting the ordeals which await me in Europe.
It was good to hear from you, & good of you to write. I am puzzled that the quote from Aquinas puzzled you so: I suspect that you sought some profound subtlety in it that just isn't

Cunard Line
R.M.S. "Queen Mary"
of Aquinas in the XIII cent. Not that I care very much!
I did not see in my exile P. Toynbee's review of "Answer to Job" — though I saw the New Statesman one. I am very afraid indeed that you will think mine unforgivable. And yet I dare hope you may find more understanding in the expostulations of this Job than in the approval of Bildad (or should it be Bil[illegible]

Figure 11.1 Two pages of White's letter of 17 March 1955, written aboard H.M.S. "Queen Mary."

Cunard Line
R.M.S. "Queen Mary"

17–3–55[22]

My dear C.G.

My mad career in California is over – at least for a time – & I am trying to recollect myself on the high seas before confronting the ordeals which await me in Europe.

It was good to hear from you, & good of you to write. I am puzzled that the quote from Aquinas puzzled you so: I suspect that you sought some profound subtlety in it that just isn't there! I have not the passage by me at the moment. It interested me just because it recognized that although "malum" is *thought* to be a "privatio" (& it is at least a psychological fact

22 Handwritten on ship's stationery.

that it frequently is!), it is *sensed* or *felt* to be a positive contrary – again a psychological fact. It is not important, but I just found it interesting that this ground of misunderstanding (between the thought & the feeling of evil) was already recognized by Aquinas in the XIII cent.

Not that I care very much!

I did not see in my exile P. Toynbee's review of "Answer to Job" – though I saw the New Statesman one. I am very afraid indeed that you will think mine unforgivable. And yet I dare hope you may find more understanding in the expostulations of this Job than in the approval of Bildad (or should it be Bilmom?) & Co. Even so, there are some passages I would now wish to have kept to myself.[23]

I wonder what induced you to publish it: when you gave me the MS. to read you were so emphatic that you would not![24] I just do not understand what is to be gained by publication of such an outburst, however cathartic for yourself & profoundly moving for your intimate friends. I am sorry: but I just see no sense in guying publicly the Christian beliefs, symbols, myths, virtues which you tell us elsewhere were never so essential as now. From my own point of view (& indeed from the point of view of your own letters to me) I can see only harm coming of it, not least to my own efforts to make analytical psychology acceptable to, & respected by, the Catholics & other Christians who need it so badly. But perhaps such is the fate of all of us born with Sol in Libra . . .[25] The "affect" is all very well, but a public parade of splenetic shadow makes me very sad indeed: it is so unlike the real you.

I am sorry – but that is how I feel about it, & very deeply. However perverse my feeling, I am sure you will understand it springs from my affection for you yourself, & my appreciation of the tremendous importance for humanity of the work you have been given to do.

I spend a few days in England before leaving for the horrors of the Dominican General Chapter in Rome. I expect to reach Zürich about April 27: I understand I am to stay at the Hotel Plattenhof, Züribergstr. 19. I am wanted back in Los Angeles in September. I am not at all so sure that I want to go! And I am still less sure what will actually happen! It seems that I am destined to be a wanderer & as homeless physically as I am spiritually.

23 Cf. White, 8 Jan. 1955, p. 254 and note. This review, with its most offending language deleted, was republished in White's final book, *Soul and Psyche* (cf. White, 26 July 1958, p. 277 and note).

24 White's assertion is puzzling. In a previous note (cf. White, 30 March 1952, p. 180) he alludes to some initial uncertainty on Jung's part as to whether *Job* would ever be published. But all of White's early responses to the work (cf. White, 23 Oct. 1951, p. 173; 5 April 1952, p. 181) express only his eagerness and gratitude for its publication. (For a detailed discussion of factors that may have led White to change his evaluation of the work, cf. *IGS*, ch. 3, esp. pp. 89–113.)

25 White's birthday was 21 October.

My experiences in USA have made me less rather than more at home as a Catholic priest, while USA itself begins positively to scare me.

I do hope that Mrs Jung has now quite recovered. Please give her my greetings.

Ever cordially, VICTOR[26]

P.S. I am intrigued – & baffled to hear from Mrs Wicks[27] that you have written & sent to press a commentary on a hitherto unknown deathbed seminar of St. Thomas Aq.![28] – NOT the *Aurora Consurgens*. Can this be authentic – or a step in your mytholigization.

Upton Sinclair's publication of your letter in *New Republic*[29] produced much stir – it was hard to discover *why*.

P.P.S. Dare I suggest the future editions of "Answer to Job" might have another preface, explaining that it is a purely personal document which does not commit your objective psychology, nor the Institut etc.? I feel it also would be helpful if the public could be told something of the circumstances in which it was written.

By the way, I think you cannot have noticed that Job & his "comforters" never use the sacred name of Yahweh, (They are Edomites – so hardly could) but only Elohim. It occurs only in the Prologue & Epilogue.

I *am* penitent that I have laid my criticisms on *so* thick.[30]

26 This is the last letter White signed with what had been his usual mark, a sweeping diagonal drawn below his name and two dots, like a colon, beneath it. In most of the remaining letters his name is followed by a wavy line, resembling an elongated S.

27 Probably refers to Frances Gillespy Wickes (1875–1967), an American analytical psychologist, one of Jung's oldest friends and correspondents. (Cf. Jung to Wickes, *Letters I*, pp. 44f; *Letters II*, pp. 338f.)

28 Reference unidentified. Mention of a deathbed seminar of Aquinas appears neither in Jung's "Vorwort" to Frances Wickes' "The Inner World of Childhood" (New York, 1927) (cf. CW 18, *The Symbolic Life*, §1248f, pp. 527f), nor in his 1954 "Letter to Père Lachat" (Ibid., §1532f, p. 679), in which he quotes from the *ST*.

29 C.G. Jung, "The Christian Legend. An Interpretation." Letter to Upton Sinclair, 7 Jan. 1955, in *The New Republic*, 132:8, 21 Feb. 1955, pp. 30f. (A similar letter from Jung appeared earlier: "The Challenge of the Christian Enigma. A Letter . . . to Upton Sinclair" [3 Nov. 1952], *The New Republic*, 128:17, 27 April 1953, pp. 18f.)

30 Cf. White, 8 Jan. 1955, p. 254 and note; also Appendix 6, pp. 349ff.

Küsnacht-Zürich

2. April 1955[31]

The Rev. Father
Victor White
Blackfriars
Oxford

Dear Victor,

Thank you for your letter and all the criticism it contains. As long as you do not identify yourself with the avenging angel, I can feel your humanity and I can tell you, that I am really sorry for my misdeeds and sore about God's ways with the poor anthropoids, that were meant to have a brain enabling them to think critically. As I am grateful for the fact that you call me to order and that your judgment – be it correct or not – does not spare me, so I assume God will listen to a mortal voice, just as much as he has given His ear to Job, when this little tortured worm complained about His paradoxical, amoral nature. Just as Job lifted his voice so that everybody could hear him, I have come to the conclusion, that I better risk my skin and do my worst or best, to shake the unconsciousness of my contemporaries, than to allow my laxity to let things drift towards the impending world catastrophe. Man must know that he is Man's worst enemy just as much as God had to learn from Job about His own antithetical nature. It is obvious that God's angel (having no will of his own) wanted to have his fight with Jacob and to kill him even, if he would not defend himself. I bet, the angel got some good knocking about, before he succeeded in dislocating Jacob's hip. God surely expected Jacob to answer Him in kind. I am rather certain that Job's case was the same. As a matter of fact there is biblical authority on my side (Is.XLVIII,10 sq.) "Behold, I have refined thee, but not with silver; I have chosen thee in the furnace of affliction. *For mine own sake, even for mine own sake* will I do it."[32]

Should I set the light of such an insight "under a bushel"?[33] In peaceful and harmless conditions it would have been very unwise to "movere quieta".[34]

31 Typewritten.

32 A more modern translation: "Behold, I have refined you, but not like silver; I have tried you in the furnace of affliction. For my own sake, for my own sake, I do it, for how should my name be profaned? My glory I will not give to another" (Isaiah 48.10f, RSV). Jung quotes from the same passage in Latin below (p. 264).

33 Cf. Matthew 5.15, Mark 4.21, Luke 11.33. From the Sermon on the Mount: "A city set on a hill cannot be hid. Nor do men light a lamp and put it under a bushel, but on a stand, and it gives light to the whole house."

34 Jung, 10 April 1954, p. 240 and note.

But in our time everything is at stake, and one should not mind the little disturbance I am causing. It is a mere fleabite on the immense body of Christendom. If I am causing trouble to the peace of mind of serious theologians, I am sorry, but I really do not see, why their sleep is better than mine. They have no prerogative to hide themselves from the great wind of the world and to leave uncomfortable things to themselves. The other day I got a letter from a student of (Catholic) theology, who had asked his directeur de conscience for advice as to the study of modern psychology. Very aptly the rev. father said: "Don't study what troubles you!" I am afraid – this is characteristic.

You should be glad that somebody thinks about God at all. The apostles and the early fathers of the Church had no easy life and moreover no Christian is meant to go to sleep in a safe pew. Look at the world – the whole damn thing is rent from top to bottom, and so is Man in our infernal epoch. I have hesitated and resisted long enough, until I have made up my mind to say, what I think. The peace of the Church is one thing and getting behind the time another. I have asked four theologians (Prot.) about the modern position of the Church with reference to the question, whether the God of the Old Testament is the same as that of the New Ts. Two did not answer at all. One said, that in the last 30 years theological literature does not speak of God any more. The last one said: "It is easy to answer your question. Jahwe is merely an archaic conception of God in comparison with the NT idea." I said: "This is exactly the kind of *psychologism* you accuse me of. When it suits you, God is suddenly nothing but a conception, but when you preach of Him, then it is the absolute truth." What did he say? Nothing. The old Jesuit father Nicolaus Caussinus[35] had a better answer: In the O.T. God was like a raging rhinoceros, but in the N.T. He turned into a God of love conquered by the love of a pure virgin, having found peace in her lap at last.[36] This is at least a kind of answer. It is even a profound answer showing the importance of Man in the divine drama of incarnation. It obviously began, when God took on *personality* (in contradistinction to all other Gods) i.e. *finiteness*. This was the first act of *Kenosis*[37] on the way to incarnation. This is the

35 Nicolaus Caussinus (Nicolas Caussin), S.J. (1583–1651): French Jesuit and scholar, specializing in moral and ascetical theology, philology and rhetoric. His major work, *Cour sainte*, a five-volume exploration of Christian holiness of life, was published in English in 1650 (*The Holy Court in five tomes*. London: W.Bentley).

36 This analogical play (God = rhinoceros = unicorn = Christ, tamed in the womb of the Virgin) is not original with Caussin; it appears also in Christian art, writing and preaching of the Middle Ages (cf. the Unicorn Tapestries, a medieval French treatment of the theme). But Jung finds Caussin's clear statement especially useful (cf. CW 9.ii, *Aion*, §299, p. 192, n. 23.).

37 emptying. An image introduced by St. Paul, who observes that God renounces divine power to become incarnate as Jesus Christ, "who, although he was in the form of God, emptied himself, taking the form of a servant" (Philippians 2.7).

"Answer to Job": He had to give up being the victim of unreflected opposites.[38]

You lose nothing and you even gain something in contemplating such thoughts. It affects your ecclesiastical position but not more than it disturbs my scientific position. The pope breaking through apostolic authority and the theological resistance of his own clergy got his share too. After "Ad Caeli Reginam" he got ill again.[39] There must have been a terrific conflict in him, being the pope on the one side and the religious innovator on the other. Should he have spared his clergy that could not agree with the new dogma?[40]

I have no papal authority, only honest common sense and no power except the consensus of a very few thinking individuals. As you do not belong to the Church exclusively, but also to humanity, it is not in the interest of the Church, if you pay no tribute to our time. Even the pope did in his way.

Your sun in libra demands undisturbed balance. You only get it, *when either side carries equal weight*. Christ is crucified between the one going up and the other going down, i.e. between opposites. So do not try to escape your fate "Written in the stars". I know, it is the mistake of libra people: they are afraid of anything disturbing the balance. But they only can maintain it by "studying, what troubles them".

Your criticism of my motive concerning "Job" is certainly unjust and you know it. It is an expression of the mental torment you had to undergo in USA – and in Europe. Nobody has more sympathy with your predicament than I have, since more than 50 years of uphill work outside and of the curtain rent inside have taught me something. Having chosen the life of the monk you have separated yourself from the[41] world and exposed yourself to the eternal fires of the other. Somewhere you have to pay the toll either to Man or to God and in the end you will discover, that both overcharge you. In this cruel suspension you will discover that redemption is to be found only on the middle ground, the centre of your Self, which is just as much with as against God; with – inasmuch as God wills you, against – inasmuch as Man's luciferic autonomy exists outside of God. It is as a matter of fact a product of the opposites in God. That is exactly the problem I am treating in "Job" and that is why Job invokes the help of God against God. It would be a great

38 The whole next paragraph is marked with a "delete" sign in the margin, possibly placed there by Adler or Jaffé while preparing Jung's letters for publication. The paragraph is nevertheless printed in Jung's *Letters*, but it lacks annotation (*Letters II*, p. 240).

39 On 11 October 1954 Pope Pius XII published *Ad Caeli Reginam*, his "Encyclical on Proclaiming the Queenship of Mary," to celebrate the 100th anniversary of the Dogma of the Immaculate Conception (defined by Pius IX in 1854). Pius XII himself had defined the Dogma of the Assumption in 1950, only four years before. Connecting the Pope's recurring illness with his 1954 encyclical overlooks the fact that Pius XII had suffered periods of exhaustion, sometimes requiring hospitalization, for many years.

40 the Dogma of the Assumption.

41 In holograph: "this."

mistake to think you can slip through such an ordeal without the most violent emotions. You yourself are profoundly emotional about it and you could not make anybody believe, that you are not in a hell of suffering. There is no comfort and no consolation anywhere except in the submission to and the acceptance of the Self or you may call it, the God that suffers in His own creation. "Excoxi te . . . et elegi te in camino paupertatis. Propter Me, propter Me faciam"[42] (Is.XLVIII, 10).

My psychology unfortunately tries to be honest. It is certainly the hard way, neither an easy consolation nor a narcotic. Nobody touching it in earnest can avoid seeing the dark side and feeling it. Most certainly I shall never cover up the truth as I see it. The Church can take it as one of the diabolical temptations of the world, and the world can condemn it as foolishness. I shall stick to my conviction that my "Answer to Job" is a straightforward application of my psychological principles to certain central problems of our religion. They can take it or leave it. Moreover they will do, what they please, without asking me.

Somehow I can afford my independence, but I am fully aware that there are many, that cannot do the same without risking their social existence. They must be able to live and to this end they have to protect themselves as well as they can. If I had not been able, to live an independent life, I should have been far more cautious in expressing my opinions and many things would have gone another way, f.i. I would not have even stuck out my neck for Freud, who had become my first great indiscretion. Primo vivere necesse est, deinde philosophari[43] – this is the hard rule for everybody fed by an institution for services received. The free lance only can risk saying something beyond the conventional and thus cause discomfort to himself without endangering his very existence.

I fully understand therefore your critical outburst, but you allow me nevertheless to call your attention to the fact that all the martyrs of your Church have been most unwise in this respect. I have discovered for my private life, that a true christian is not bedded upon roses and he is not meant for peace and tranquillity of mind but for war. And again I am realizing profoundly that not everybody's nature is as bellicose as mine, although I have attained – Deo concedente[44] – a certain state of peace within paid for by a rather uncomfortable state of war without. But even if a peaceful nature has reached a certain higher level of consciousness he cannot escape the raging conflict of opposites in his soul, as God wants to unite His opposites in Man.

42 "I have tried you . . . and chosen you in the furnace of affliction. For my own sake, for my own sake, will I do it" (Isaiah 48.10f). (Cf. Jung's citation of this verse in English, p. 261 and note.)

43 first it is necessary to live, then to philosophize.

44 God willing.

As soon as a more honest and more complete consciousness beyond the collective level has been established, Man is no more an end in himself, but becomes an instrument of God and this is *really* so and no joke about it. I have not made this world nor have I put a human soul into it. This is His work and His responsibility and there is no judge above Him. That is why the story begins with Job on the human level and with the assumption of personality on the divine level. One can like Job lament about it, but it is to no purpose. It is just so. If turmoil and torment becomes too great there is still the oneness of the Self, the divine spark within its inviolable precincts, offering its extramundane peace. Please spend some hours reading my Answer to Job with this comment in mind and see whether you still can maintain the idea, that it is a case of mere spleen. Could we not apply the same qualification to your own bad temper?

When you arrive in Zürich I shall be away in Bollingen, but when we return in the beginning of May, I should like you to stay with us in Küsnacht.[45]

Cordially yours, C.G.

Küsnacht-Zürich

May 6th, 1955[46]

Dear Victor,

The serious illness of my wife has consumed all my spare time. She has undergone an operation so far successfully,[47] but it has left her in a feeble state needing careful nursing for several weeks to come.

Since I am the cause of much discomfort to you, I am not sure whether you care to see me or not. Please, put conventionality aside and do not feel

45 The invitation is to Jung's "town" residence, rather than his retreat at Bollingen. The change may, as Adler surmises (*Letters II*, p. 243n), reflect how much the relationship had cooled. But it should be remembered that in the spring of 1955 Emma Jung had been very ill, and Jung's attention was focussed on his wife during what proved to be her final months. Taking all the circumstances into account, the fact that Jung invited White to be his guest in the summer of 1955 shows the extraordinary importance he continued to place upon their friendship.

46 Handwritten.

47 With Emma Jung's surgery in the spring of 1955, her doctors learned that her cancer was inoperable. She was told that she had about six months left to live. This gave her time to put her affairs in order, but it was a very difficult period for her family. In July she was able to take part in Jung's eightieth birthday celebration. Her condition worsened in the autumn, however, and she died on the 28th of November.

under any obligation. I can understand your true situation and I would prefer not to add to its spikes and thorns. A conventional call means nothing to me, and a straightforward talk may be painful and not desirable. Please decide according to your judgment. Needless to say, that you can count upon my friendship.

Cordially yours, C.G.

P.S. I just heard that you did not get a long letter I have sent to you (pr. adr. Blackfriars Oxford).

Küsnacht-Zürich

May 7, 1955[48]

The Rev. Father Victor White, O.P.
Hotel Plattenhof
Zürichbergstrasse 19
Zürich *PER EXPRESS*

Dear Father White,

I am terribly sorry you didn't get that letter of Professor Jung's of April 2. From our side, there is no explanation: I am sure the address on the envelope was correct. Thinking that at least you ought to get it as quickly as possible now, I am sending you a copy of that letter by express; otherwise you wouldn't get it before Monday.

Yours sincerely, [Secretary][49] (unsigned carbon copy)

1 enclo. [50]

48 Typewritten.

49 Perhaps Aniela Jaffé, who became Jung's secretary in 1954. (Cf. Jaffé to White, 17 Sept. 1956, p. 275 and note.)

50 Enclosure: Jung's letter of 2 April 1955 (cf. pp. 261ff).

Hôtel Plattenhof
Zürichbergstr. 19
Zürich

May 9[51]

My dear C.G.

Thank you so very much for your 2 letters. Mail has been forwarded to me regularly from Oxford, & I do not understand how the first failed to reach me. But the copy reached me on Saturday, & I am very grateful for it.

I also should detest a conventional visit – it would be impossible – & (I hope) I accept any "spikes & thorns". But I am trying to put on paper what I, for my part, would like the agenda to be, & would (if only to save time) like to send it to you in advance.[52] It should reach you in a day or two.

"Previous engagements" prevent my writing more now; but I would again send my deepest sympathy to you & Mrs Jung.

Ever cordially, VICTOR

Hotel Plattenhof
Zürichbergstr. 19

10.5.55.[53]

My dear C.G.–

I thank you again very heartily for your 2 most friendly & magnanimous letters.

I certainly appreciate "Antwort" as a stimulant to consciousness. It has certainly clarified my own. I have not hitherto been insensitive to your insight into the Divine Quaternity & the Evil God, its fascination – & convenience! But now I find myself quite definitely in painful agreement, not only with your theological & philosophical, but also with your scientific critics. For the clarification of my own position, I am truly grateful; but finding myself in opposition to your views, & indeed to your own "union of opposites" (or its transposition to the Divine sphere) is naturally painful, & also gives rise to

51 Handwritten. No year noted, but the letter can be placed in 1955 by context.

52 White was hoping for a working session with Jung to hammer out their differences. His extensive "agenda" for the meeting was enclosed with his next letter (cf. White, 10 May 1955, pp. 268–72).

53 Handwritten, with handwritten enclosure.

practical problems. These I have ventured to summarize in the accompanying document; & would much appreciate any comments that occur to you.

I should certainly like to see you & have anything or everything on the mat. But your letter leads me to say that I should not like to meet on the basis of any misunderstanding. I do indeed deeply regret having published[54] that article without any regard for your feelings or my own feelings for you.[55] But I am afraid it is just *not* my opinion that my criticism of your motive is fundamentally unjust – or that I know it. I do not know if these "opposites" between us can be bridged: but they certainly cannot merely in terms of the very symbol (or rather, the evaluation of it) which is in dispute.

I talk of "dispute", but behind it I think there is basic agreement. Though human consciousness, for me, is not the *summum* bonum, it is a very great & essential one. We are both, I hope anti-narcotic. My objection to the myth of the Evil God is just that it provides such a marvellous narcotic.

So, whatever the "opposites", & even because of them, I should like to reciprocate your assurances of friendship – for which I am immensely grateful.

Yours sincerely & cordially, VICTOR

P.S. Your theologian informants astound me. Are they Marcionites[56] or polytheists?

PROBLEMS ARISING FROM PUBLICATION OF "ANSWER TO JOB"[57]

1. Given that "Answer to Job" is not merely an autobiographic description of a stage in a subjective, personal crisis (which arouses all one's personal sympathy), but also has something to say to the world at large, one must ask what that 'something' is, & how it is to be evaluated.
2. Coming, as it does, under the name of C.G. Jung that something cannot be regarded, & is not in fact regarded, merely as the opinion of a private individual, but as in some way representative of, even authoritative for, "Jungian psychology". Whether he wills it or not, he is for ever the Father of Analytical Psychology, to followers & critics alike. Some of the former in *fact* regard the book as the finest flower of the psychology; some of the

54 White's original word, "written," is crossed out.

55 This statement had great importance for Jung. A heavy black line has been drawn in the margin left of this sentence. On the second page of White's 18 March 1960 letter to Jung (cf. p. 283 and note, below) a marginal note in Jung's handwriting refers to this sentence.

56 Followers of Marcion, a separatist Christian of the second century who was excommunicated and declared a heretic. In the view of Marcion the cruel God of the Old Testament was unrelated to, and superseded by, the loving God revealed in the New.

57 Handwritten on large, heavy sheets of paper, enclosed with White's letter of 10 May 1955. Although Jung and White met once in May 1955 (cf. White, 21 May 1955, p. 272 and note), they were unable to carry out a full discussion.

latter as its logical *reductio ad absurdum*. Jung says he is not the Pope, but his writings nevertheless carry great weight. (The Pope claims only to be divinely protected from teaching error under specified circumstances:[58] not to immediate revelation. The Pope only believes: Jung does "not need to believe", he *knows* – & has said so.[59] Jung has attained integration – & again has said so.[60] This may be taken (& is taken) to mean he has attained the Self – the Quaternity which the Trinity failed to realize. All this is not ironic. They are just facts;[61] but mean that his utterances whether "true" or "false" are not the negligible opinions of a private citizen.

3. "Answer to Job" is presumably to be read (at least primarily), not as an essay in theology, metaphysics or exegesis, but in practical psychology. It may be taken, and is being taken, as containing the "correct" psychological views, standards & attitudes of the "Jungians".[62]
4. What then is its practical psychological content & implication? What views & attitudes does it advocate?

First & foremost it seems to be this–[63]

God (= not me) is unconscious, divided in himself, moody, capricious, cruel, purposeless – but notably evil as well as good. I am the helpless plaything of that evil. Evil is an ultimate & irreducible constituent of reality to be accepted – not a privation which can be supplied by good, or out of which good can be brought. God is "mir böse"[64] – ergo he *is* böse. I do not want to be the suffering son, but the unchastened bastard (see Hebrews 11.8); therefore such treatment is evil & its Author is evil. My only hope is to know this, as God still does not, & in this *gnosis* alone lies my peace & salvation – & God's. (He is seemingly for ever evil, but in human consciousness of the fact, he may become more reasonable & amiable?)

58 Scribbled in the margin beside this sentence, by a hand other than Jung's (Franz Jung, interview, 17 August 1991): "– cannot God protect also Jung from teaching error?" Based on handwriting, the marginal comments on this documents may have been added by Gerhard Adler. He and Aniela Jaffé had access to White's letters for a decade, while they were editing Jung's correspondence for publication (private communication, F. Jung to A. Lammers, 10 December 1992).

59 Handwritten in the margin: "Incredibly twisted." White attributes to Jung a position resembling Jung's much publicized statement in his televised March 1959 BBC interview with John Freeman, "Face to Face" (*C.G. Jung Speaking: Interview and Encounters*, ed. William McGuire & R.F.C. Hull. PUP, 1977, pp. 424–39.)

60 In the margin: two question marks, and the words: "not true."

61 In the margin beside this statement: one question mark.

62 In the margin beside this sentence: a line and a question mark.

63 Beside the paragraph that follows, two handwritten comments: "What is good or evil?" and 'It seems to me evil to twist things in that way.'

64 "evil to me."

From this (or something like it) certain psychological consequences seem to follow:[65]

α). "My" evil is no more my concern. It is "all God's fault", & I can & should lay all the blame there.

β). By example, if not by precept, the book indicates that all personal psychology may be safely ignored:[66] the personal shadow transferred to the "divine" "collective" sphere – & left there. Heredity, environment, upbringing, parental determinatives, symptoms etc. have nothing to do with it. Attention is not to be given to Job's or Jung's (or presumably my) personal shadow & history, but only to the relationships & behaviors of God, Satan, etc. (? Personal psychology is "banal", uninteresting, "obvious" in comparison with the archetypal myth – & has nothing to do with it ?).

γ) The "correct" (because Jung's own) way of dealing with the problem will include a highly emotion-charged ridiculing of the "good" God, his saints, witnesses & devotees, with no undue regard for accuracy or for its consequences.

5. If these are *not* the psychological implications of the book, they are the obvious ones which in fact are being drawn,[67] & urgently need the author's own corrections.

If they are, then they seem diametrically opposed to what has hitherto been regarded as sound by all schools of psychology, the "Jungian" included. What have hitherto been considered to be primitive, infantile reactions & neurotic projections, now have the highest approval & sanction of a great psychologist. The criticism by non-Jungians that the "collective unconscious" becomes an escape-mechanism from personal problems & realities appears to be confirmed. Indeed, if all is at the mercy of capricious Gods, it is hard to see how scientific psychology – or indeed any science – can survive. Psychology is reduced back to mythology: conscious realization of the myth is now the summum bonum, to which even "sanitas" must be subordinated.[68] The empirical test by results in terms of "cure" & "mental health" becomes invalid: not "is the analysant well?", but "does he live in the myth?" becomes the criterion.[69]

It is not yet stated that realization of the myth (or at least acceptance of it) is a sine-qua-non for being an "analytical psychologist". But the question must be asked & answered.[70]

Meanwhile, some of us find ourselves in a quandary. It is all very well

65 A line has been drawn in the margin beside the three paragraphs that follow, with the handwritten comment: "absolutely misunderstood!"

66 In the margin beside this sentence: three exclamation marks.

67 Marginal annotation: "By whom are they drawn?"

68 Beside this sentence: two question marks and an exclamation mark.

69 In the margin beside this sentence: a line, and the words, "whose idea is that?"

70 In the margin beside this paragraph: a vertical line and a large question mark.

to say we can "take it or leave it". We cannot so easily "leave" analytical psychology, anyway in its earlier formulations & practice. Nor do we want to start anything like a "schism". But neither can we "take" this myth, symbol, doctrine – or whatever it is – of the Dark or Evil God.[71] It is not only that we may think it personally undesirable & socially harmful; for ourselves it is *psychologically impossible*. We do not deny that at certain levels of consciousness it is a perfectly genuine – even a "numinous" – experience. It may be a very necessary, but transient experience in certain stages of development for certain people. But we cannot know it otherwise than as a projection – & precisely *not* what we call "God", or the pattern for our living & the standard & measure of all things.

About 500 B.C. something happened to our fathers & our culture. Plato's Idea of the Good, Aristotles's, Θεός,[72] the Vedantas' realization of the Atman without attributes or with the attributes of Being-Knowledge-Bliss, the whole Greek search for the One beyond the Many & the Opposites, precisely Job's heroic encounter & healing & Yahweh's self-vindication, have delivered us for ever from the tyranny of unconscious gods – compelled us to seek below & in ourselves for unconscious elements.[73] Perhaps our religious upbringing has been more fortunate than Jung's or Job's. For that we claim no credit; but it prevents us for ever from taking the "Evil God" to ourselves—

I say nothing here of the special difficulties encountered here by the *Christian*. But it must be evident that he must find special obstacles here – &, indeed, the opposition between his beliefs and those of the "myth" are tacitly recognized in the book. He must find it particularly impossible to embrace the "Evil God" – even though he *should* be more ready than most to experience the darkness & evil in himself, & increasingly the darkness in his own apprehension of God. But this, apparently, is not at all the same thing. From the extremities[74] of 'Omne bonum a Deo; omne malum a homine' (orthodox in the context of human sin, but not of *all* evil) we are led to "Omne malum a Deo, omne bonum ab homine"[75] – or so it seems *in practice*.

If all this is now, not just the private opinion of C.G. Jung, but (as to some extent it is bound to be) *the* approved view of his school (only too

71 In the margin: a line, and the words, "who teaches a doctrine of an Evil God?"

72 God.

73 A faint line in the margin next to these sentences, and the words, "verstehe ihn nicht" ["I don't understand him"].

74 This and the following paragraph are marked with marginal lines. Beside this sentence is the comment, "absurd." As noted above, the marginal notations on this document were not made by Jung.

75 "All evil from God, all good from humankind." Jung's position, as White understands it, reverses the orthodox dictum, "All good from God; all evil from humankind."

likely to harden into its "dogma"), it must be evident that any would-be Christian, especially if he is unavoidable in the position of guiding others, may be faced with an "agonizing reappraisal" of his position vis-a-vis analytical psychology – whatever may be his personal feelings with regard to C.G. Jung.

Hotel Plattenhof
Zürichbergstr. 19

21–5–55[76]

My dear C.G.

I am afraid it was disgracefully inconsiderate of me to trouble you with my very mundane "problems"[77] when you yourself have so many other cares within & without. I earnestly hope that Mrs Jung is now well on the mend.[78] Her illness alone must have given you great anxiety, & of course I realize that you have many other cares on your mind. It was heartless of me to bother you with such very different problems – & so ruthlessly. Evidently I must work them out on my own, as best I can. And perhaps, in our mutual solitude, the reconciling symbol has a better chance to grow than in any amount of talk.[79]

I plan to leave for England on Thursday, & to remain (mostly) at Oxford until I leave for USA in September. I shall be there at *least* for a year, & it is improbable that we meet again for a very long time. I am sad indeed to have missed – perhaps through my ruthless tactlessness to have ruined – this carefully planned chance to do so.

Under these sad circumstances, perhaps I may "call the bluff" & tell you how deeply I feel with you personally in this wrestle with the Divine Mysteries & with our Brother Death. I must [commend][80] the outcome trustingly to Them & to your own fearless honesty & humility. But I know what it must cost you even to consider that perhaps, after all, God is good, & pursues you with unremitting love & care – & never more than when He acts the rhinoceros. "Happy endings", I know, have become so banal as to be unbelievable; but perhaps such belief requires more courage than the merely

76 Handwritten.

77 Cf. White, 10 May 1955, "Problems arising from publication of 'Answer to Job'," pp. 268ff.

78 Jung and White had met at the convalescent home in Mammern, where Emma Jung was convalescing after her cancer surgery. (Cf. Jung, 6 May 1955, p. 265 and note.)

79 This paragraph, in particular this sentence, suggest the tone of the meeting and its finality.

80 Word omitted in original.

empirical observation of unhappy endings – for the charge of "escapism" is not easy to bear. But I am confident that the "secret doubt" which must underlie the very vehemence of your repudiations of the "Summum Bonum" & the "privatio" will not leave you alone, & that the earthly end of Job will be as in the Bible rather than as in *Antwort* . . . .

For myself, it seems that our ways must, at least to some extent, part. I shall never forget, and please God I shall never lose, what I owe to your work & your friendship. It seems that my rôle, at least for a year or two, is to be that of a very independent Catholic priest in California, & I can assure you there are times when the prospect scares me stiff. But just there, as nowhere else, the opposites of Good & Evil, the Individual & the Collective, a new & strange (to me) form of consciousness & sheer unconsciousness, are at their most intense. I would much rather retire to my native England & write books – but I am not (at least as a Dominican) wanted there: in California I am.

So it is au revoir for the present. Please give my very kindest regards to Mrs Jung, & my sympathy to her & to you in her illness.

Ever cordially & sincerely, VICTOR

P.S. I hope you do not doubt my friendship, wrong-headed & heartless though it sometimes is. Poor Job at least had friends – however stupid. The horrible impression has come upon me in Zürich (I hope it is wrong) that my dear C.G. has around him only sycophants & flatterers: or people requiring audiences or transferences which no mortal can carry. I *hope* I am wrong: such a situation is *too* inhuman. . . .[81]

as from St. Michael's
Buckingham Road,
Cambridge

August 25 1956[82]

My dear C.G.,

In a few days I shall take the liberty of sending you a copy of my "new" book, which the publishers have insisted on calling "God the

81 Lower on the page is a note, written by Aniela Jaffé (cf. Jaffé to White, 17 Sept. 1956, p. 275 and note). In interview with AC, summer 1991, Jaffé acknowledged that she wrote this comment: "*Warum muss er das noch in schreiben in diesem Moment? Scheint ja seine 'wrong handed* [sic] *and heartless friendship'!*" ("Why must he add that at this moment? Seems like his 'wrongheaded and heartless friendship'!") [with AC]

82 Typewritten.

Unknown".[83] It is mostly just a collection of papers written long ago – mostly in my pre-psychology days. It is just possible that one or two of the contents, (e.g. "The Unknown God",[84] "Incarnations and the Incarnation", "Membership of the Church") may be of some little interest to you; but I think you will like the volume as a whole as little as I do (I published it under pressure and with very little revision) but I shall send it just as a token of esteem, and as a means of keeping in touch.

I returned from America on Tuesday, and in many ways I am very thankful to be back in civilization! To my great surprise and delight I am to be stationed in the small Dominican house at Cambridge,[85] where I should be able to lead a comparatively quiet and more introverted existence, free of routine teaching and suchlike chores. I can hardly believe my good fortune. I hope to get to work on a sort of sequel to *God & the Unconscious* among other things.

Meanwhile there seems to be much excitement in Italy about the original book. I wonder if you saw the vicious attack on you and me by Padre Gemelli (blue-eyed boy of your hero[86] the Pope!) in *Vita e Pensiero*[87] – it has also been translated into English and French. All this notwithstanding an Italian translation of my book is to appear next month: the authorities of the diocese of Milano have not only given the imprimatur but have (I am told) insisted it be published. But I am told that there is likely to be fierce opposition. Maybe I'll even get on the Index![88]

My year in California has been a rather wearing but profitable experience. I feel much more settled within myself now; not that any problems are solved, but they don't seem to matter so much anymore; and I feel more ready to plow a lonely furrow.

I had a wonderful time in New Mexico, but wished I could spend much longer there and get beneath the surface of it all. As you may imagine I was

83 Victor White, O.P., *God the Unknown & Other Essays* (London: The Harvill Press, 1956).

84 This essay, from which the title of White's second book is taken, was written after Jung told White that his thinking did not sufficiently acknowledge mystery ("you are moving in the universe of the known," Jung, 12 May 1950, p. 152). Two years later, White sent a typescript of "The Unknown God" to Jung (cf. White, 25 June 1952, p. 197), apparently to show him his judgment was unfounded.

85 The English Dominican *Catalogus* for 1957–1960 lists White as residing at the Cambridge house. (The *Catalogus* publishes information from the previous calendar year.) [AC]

86 Jung had praised Pius XII as a "religious innovator" (cf. Jung, 2 April 1955, p. 263).

87 Agostino Gemelli, OFM, "Psicologie e religione I: La psicologia analytica de C.G. Jung" (*Vita é Pensiero*, Anno XXXVIII, Giugno 1955); "Psicologia e religione II: La religione secondo psicologia analitica" (Ibid., Iuglio 1955). ["Psychology and Religion I: The analytical psychology of C.G. Jung'; "Psychology and Religion II: Religion according to analytical psychology' (Vol. 38, June and July 1955).] Cf. Appendix 2, "Victor White, a Memoir," pp. 326f.

88 Cf. Wolff, 18 July 1946, p. 37 and note.

particularly intrigued with the Pueblo Indians and their amalgam of Catholicity and Paganism – and that under the auspices of about the most narrow and intolerant and dictatorial bunch of clergy as you will meet anywhere!

I do hope, my dear C.G., that you are well, and that things go reasonably well with you notwithstanding your bereavement and so many other losses. I do not know when I shall be able to come to Switzerland again – but I hope there may be some possibility next year.

Ever cordially VICTOR[89]

Küsnacht-Zürich

September 17th 1956[90]

Father Victor White
St. Michael's
Buckingham Road
Cambridge

Dear Father White,

Dr. Jung, who is at Bollingen for the moment, asked me to thank you very much for your letter of August 25th and for kindly having sent him your book "God the Unknown".

He apologizes for not writing personally, but he is fully occupied with some building work at the Tower[91] and with an article on Schizophrenia.[92] He sends you through me his kindest regards.

Sincerely yours ANIELA JAFFÉ[93] Secretary

89 Below the signature is a word in Jaffé's hand: *danken* ("to thank"). 90 Typewritten.

91 Together with his son, Franz Jung, who was an architect, Jung was constructing the final addition to his retreat in Bollingen.

92 Probably "Die Schizophrenie" ["Schizophrenia"] (*Schweizer Archiv für Neurologie und Psychiatrie*, LXXXI:1/2, pp. 163–77). Republished in GW 3, *Psychogenese der Geisteskrankheiten*, ch. 9; and CW 3, *The Psychogenesis of Mental Disease*, ch. 10.

93 Aniela Jaffé (1903–1991): Born in Berlin to Jewish parents, she fled Nazi Germany just before finishing her doctorate in psychology, at the University of Hamburg, to settle in Switzerland. After difficult years, she went through analysis with Liliane Frey, then with C.G. Jung. Jaffé became the first secretary of the C.G. Jung Institute on its founding in 1948. She was Jung's secretary from 1954 until his death in 1961. While working in the household, Jaffé interviewed Jung for *MDR*, which she also edited.

Personal

Blackfriars, Cambridge

June 1st 1958[94]

My dear C.G.

You may perhaps be interested to hear that from next Friday (June 6th) I shall be staying–

chez Monsieur Chuffart,
Mont-Riant,
Chamby-sur-Montreux (Vaud) – tel. (021)6.53.88

I expect to be there, off and on, until June 25th.

I should of course be very pleased indeed to come over to Küsnacht (or Bollingen) to see you if you would care to see me, even though only for an hour or so. I could come any time between 6th and 25th, provided only that I am able to be in Montreux on Sunday mornings.

I have no special agenda! I have lately been re-reading the generous and most stimulating letters you have written me in the past. They have been most helpful in finding myself. I am, in fact, pretty well and happy these days, and better able to contain the "empirical church" – though less than ever able to be contained by it. . . .

I was not, I confess, very happy about our last meeting, which, you may remember, was at Mammern;[95] though I have no doubt that my feeling of estrangement (as distinct from mere disagreement) was my own fault. I should however like to say – to remove a possible barrier – that I like to take my own responsibility for my own writings, however blind and stupid they may be, and that I would never knowingly write a word under pressure from superiors! But the "doleo super te frater mi"[96] moves me also, and perhaps excessively; and he is, very often, a different "frater"!

I often think of you, dear C.G., and with great affection and gratitude; and I very much hope that all goes as well as possible with you in hac lacrymarum valle.[97]

Please do not trouble to reply to this unless my suggestion is possible and agreeable to you.

Ever cordially VICTOR (WHITE)[98]

94 Typewritten, except for salutation and closing.

95 The word Mammern is underlined by hand in pencil, with a marginal penciled comment by Aniela Jaffé (later acknowledged as her handwriting): *1955!* (Cf. White, 21 May 1955, p. 273 and note.) [with AC]

96 "I grieve for thee, my brother." Epigraph of Jung's *Job*.

97 this vale of tears. From a hymn, "Salve Regina," then sung in procession at Compline in Dominican churches. [AC]

98 White's addition of his last name, surprising in the context of this correspondence, is probably explained by the fact that he had not written to Jung in nearly two years.

Blackfriars, Cambridge

26.7.58[99]

My dear C.G.

I have allowed your birthday to come without sending my accustomed greetings and congratulations in advance. May I be more prompt on the many more birthdays which we hope you will have in this world! But I did of course remember you very specially at Mass this morning.

I should in any case have written you before this. Firstly to thank you for the most enjoyable visit I paid to you last month, and for giving so generously of your time. I was rather particularly impressed by your illuminating remarks on the childless manifestations of the Madonna these days. . . .

And, secondly, to thank you for so kindly sending me an offprint of your paper on schizophrenia.[100]

My dilatoriness is partly due to the fact that I am extremely busy these days. Among other things, I am wrestling to produce another book.[101] I have just finished a long chapter on Trinity and Quaternity, and am now in travail with one on the Bisexuality of God![102]

Ever gratefully & cordially, VICTOR

99 Typewritten, except for salutation and closing. On this date Jung turned 83.

100 Cf. Jaffé, 17 Sept. 1956, p. 275 and note.

101 Victor White, *Soul and Psyche: An Enquiry into the Relationship of Psychotherapy and Religion* (New York: Harper & Brothers, 1960), comprising primarily the 1958–59 Edward Cadbury Lectures, which he had delivered at the University of Birmingham.

102 Chapters 6 through 9 in *Soul and Psyche* are titled "Trinity and Quaternity," "The Missing Feminine," "The Feminine Image in Christianity," and "The Integration of Evil."

1959–60

Blackfriars, Cambridge

18.10.59[1]

My dear C.G.

This is mostly just to say Thank You for your messages which came to me – much to my surprise – from the Prioress [. . .].[2] I appreciated them enormously; and felt all the more regretful for not having written before – and having even missed your birthday.

I will spare you the trouble of reading, and myself the business of writing, my news. The fact is that much has happened since my smash,[3] and I have not yet assimilated it – and still less do I feel able yet to record it all in writing! Rather more surprising to me has been what has *not* happened. For instance, my dreams seem to have ceased entirely: I do not remember having had a single one since the accident! But there is no doubt that I am physically well recovered, though it seems that some inconvenient disabilities will remain for some time.[4]

I smiled, somewhat cynically, at your remark that I did not wholly disapprove of your work.[5] (How could I?) It seems that I am in quite serious trouble (and in Rome itself!) for (apparently) my approval of it; so much so that my future is quite uncertain![6] (This, for the time being, is rather strictly *entre nous*.) But I think you will agree that your work itself will be moribund if there is not

1 Typewritten, except for salutation and closing. Contains many small typing errors, with White's handwritten corrections.

2 Cf. Jung to Mother Prioress, Appendix 1, pp. 297ff. White had received Jung's messages through the Mother Prioress of the small contemplative community where he had served for years as spiritual director (cf. White, 2 April 1953, p. 213 and note).

3 White's accident on his Vespa scooter took place near Peterborough, north of Cambridge, on 17 April 1959. [AC]

4 White had sustained serious head injuries, such that he was unable to travel independently or even, for some time, to cross the street alone. A month after the accident, John Layard had sent Jung an account of White's condition: "The news about Victor White is that he recovers consciousness from time to time and wanders when he talks. What he will be like when he recovers from it I do not know. Will there have been a change? If so, in what direction?" (20 May 1959, Jung/Layard correspondence, ETH Library archive). To which Jung replied: "Thank you for the news about Victor White. It is an awful fate" (27 May 1959, Ibid.). Jung did not, however, write to White at this time. [AC]

5 Jung had written: "I am glad that you gave me some news about Father White's activity. Thus I know that he does not fully disapprove of my work" (Jung to Mother Prioress, Appendix 1, p. 298).

6 White's *God & Unc.* had been published in 1952 with the "Imprimi potest" from the English Provincial, the "Nihil obstat" from the diocesan deputy censor, and the "Imprimatur" from the Archbishop of Birmingham. In 1956, when the book was already out of print, the then Master General, Michael Browne, attempted to have its Imprimatur withdrawn (Nichols, *Dominican Gallery*, p. 54).

some disagreement about it, and some *Auseinandersetzung*[7] from those with different backgrounds and experiences – and perhaps different typologies!

But once again: Thank you so much. I do hope and pray things go well with you – whatever "well" may *really*[8] mean.

Ever yours cordially VICTOR WHITE[9]

Küsnacht-Zürich

October 21st 1959[10]

Father Victor White
Blackfriars
OXFORD

Dear Victor,

From your letter I see with great satisfaction that you are up and active again. I sincerely hope that no irreparable damage has been done.

Concerning my doubts about your general attitude I must mention, in self-defence, that you expressed yourself publicly in such a negative way about my work that I really did not know what your real attitude would be.

Thank you for your kind letter.

Hoping and wishing for a complete recovery, I remain

yours C.G. (unsigned carbon copy)

Blackfriars, Cambridge

18–3–60[11]

My dear C.G.

I am somehow moved to send you the assurance of my love for you, even though I cannot send much else.

7 thorough sorting-out; coming to grips (with intellectual or ethical concerns).

8 This and the closing word, "Ever," are underlined by hand.

9 From this letter on, although he continues to address Jung with the familiar "C.G.," White signs either his full name or (28 March 1960) "Victor W." Jung's signature, in letters where it is preserved, continues to be the familiar "C.G."

10 Typewritten by secretary.

11 In White's shaky handwriting, with minor errors corrected.

I have been sorry to hear (from Jolande Jacobi)[12] that you had heart-trouble, & (from Eve Lewis)[13] that you have since been isolated by some rather serious kind of influenza. I hope & pray that you are better now.

I had intended to write at some length some months ago – since it was impossible for me to see you. But then I was hurried off to hospital, & underwent a quite serious operation to the intestines. It seems the surgeons discovered a "malignant growth" down there, and I am still much of an invalid, & the prognosis is uncertain.

Anyway, it seems that my old, activist ego has got to go, & something else must be reborn for whatever life remains for me in this world!

In your last letter you wrote to me –

> "You expressed yourself publicly in such a negative way about my work that I really did not know what your real attitude would be."

I have been, & still am, sorely perplexed to understand *when* & *where* I am supposed to have done this – and not a little distressed that you should think this.[14] Is it troubling you too much to ask you to tell me? Otherwise I have nothing but rumour and speculation to go on, & am unable to offer either explanation or apology. In any case I want you to know that I regret it very much that you should think this.

(Rumour suggests it may have something to do with my review of Vol 7 of your *Collected Works*.[15] But this seems hardly credible to me. It contains a most express statement of the great debt I owe you & your work – even as "theologian & pastor", as well as disagreements in matters of *fact*, & *questions* on psychology (which nobody has yet answered!).

12 Cf. Jung, 27 Dec. 1947, p. 104 and note.

13 Eve Lewis: English Catholic and Jungian analyst, associated with the Withymead therapeutic community (cf. White, 13 Oct. 1946, p. 45 and note). Author of *Children and their Religion* (New York: Sheed & Ward, 1962), "The Archetypes during the Years of Middle Childhood" (*Harvest*, 14/1968) and *The Psychology of Family Religion* (London: Sydney, Sheed & Ward, 1968). After White's accident she visited Jung and attempted unsuccessfully to mediate between him and White (cf. Appendix 2, "Victor White, a Memoir," p. 333f). [with AC]

14 In the left margin beside this statement, a note in Jung's handwriting reads: "cf. Victor's Brief 10.V.55 pag.2/3" ["see Victor's letter 10 May 1955, pages 2/3]. White's letter of 10 May 1955 is one he sent to Jung after publishing his *Blackfriars* review of *Job*. In that letter a marginal line, apparently drawn by Jung, marks the sentence at the bottom of White's second page and top of his third, which reads: "I do indeed deeply regret having published that article without any regard for your feelings or my own feelings for you."

15 It is a puzzling suggestion, given that White's assessment of CW 7, *Two Essays*, had been glowing: "In them we find Jung as a writer at his crispest and clearest, and least inclined to deviate from the narrow path of strictly psychological exposition, as well as most ready to meet the prejudices of his medical colleagues and the general public" (*Blackfriars*, Vol. 25, March 1954, p. 126).

But please understand I am eager for your work to spread for it is so *needed.*

And, although these[16] are matters on which I cannot see eye to eye with you, I would never question your sincerity (let alone publicly), as you appear to question or deny mine in the quotation on p.20 of Philp's strange *Jung and the Problem of Evil.*[17] (I have not even heard of these "syllogisms" which bind me hand & foot!)[18]

But I will not bore you with more of this – especially as I do not know just what the trouble is all about at your end. And I hope you may enlighten me.

I think my publishers have sent you my new book, *Soul & Psyche*?

Anyway this poor letter wants to convey my love & gratitude, for what it is worth.

Yours ever VICTOR WHITE

Küsnacht-Zürich

25 March 1960[19]

My dear Victor,

Since you are very much in the situation of the suffering Job I shall not play the rôle of his friends, not even that of the wise Elihu.[20] I humbly submit the suggestion, you might apply your personalistic point of view to your own person and to your own case instead of to the unknown person of the individual Job.[21] You can see then, what it does to yourself as well as to myself – if I may introduce myself as an individual.

16 In holograph: "there," corrected to "these."

17 Howard Littleton Philp (1902–1976): English psychologist and Anglican clergyman; member of the British Psychological Association; Canon of Salisbury Cathedral, 1966–72. Among his other publications, Philp wrote *Freud and Religious Belief* (London: Rockliff, 1956) and *Jung and the Problem of Evil* (London: Rockliff, 1958).

18 The book contains excerpts from Philp's 1956–57 correspondence with Jung, in which he poses theological questions and Jung replies (cf. CW 18, *The Symbolic Life*, §1584ff, pp. 702–44). Philp quotes a footnote from White's *God & Unc.* (p. 76n), together with Jung's reply: "What Victor White writes about the assimilation of the shadow is not to be taken seriously. Being a Catholic priest he is bound hand and foot to the doctrine of his Church and has to defend every syllogism" (CW 18, *The Symbolic Life*, §1594, p. 710).

19 Typewritten. Undated in carbon copy, but Adler dates this letter 25 March 1960 (*Letters II*, pp. 544ff).

20 After three of Job's friends insist that God's treatment of him is just, a fourth, Elihu, argues that his unjust suffering is nonetheless good, because God instructs mortals through pain (Job 32–37).

21 Perhaps a reference to White's "Jung on Job" (cf. Appendix 6, pp. 349ff).

Job is very much the respectable Hebrew of his time. He observes the law and – by force of the covenant – his God ought to do the same. Now let us assume, that he is the neurotic, as one can easily make out from the textual allusions, he suffers from a regrettable lack of insight in his own dissociation.[22] He undergoes an analysis of a sort f.i. by following Elihu's wise counsel. What he will hear and what he will be aware of are the discarded contents of his personal subconscious mind, of his shadow, but not the divine Voice, as Elihu intends. You faintly insinuate, that I am committing Elihu's error too, in appealing to archetypes first and omitting the shadow.[23] *One cannot avoid the shadow*, unless one remains neurotic and as long as one is neurotic, one has omitted the shadow. The shadow is the block which separates us most effectively from the divine Voice. Therefore Elihu in spite of his fundamental truth belongs to those foolish Jungians, who, as you suggest, avoid the shadow and make for the archetypes, i.e. the "divine equivalents", which by the way are nothing but escape camouflage according to the personalistic theory.

If Job succeeds in swallowing his shadow, he will be deeply ashamed of the things which happened: he will see, that he has only to accuse himself, for it is his complacency, his righteousness, his literal-mindedness etc. which have brought all the evil down upon him. He has not seen his own shortcomings, but has accused God. He certainly will fall into an abyss of despair and inferiority feeling, followed, if he survives, by profound repentance. He will even doubt his mental sanity, that he, by his vanity, has caused such an emotional turmoil, even a delusion of divine interference, obviously a case of megalomania.

After such an analysis he will be less inclined than ever before, to assume that he has heard the Voice of God. Or has Freud with all his experience ever reached such a conclusion?

If Job is to be considered as a neurotic and interpreted from the personalistic point of view, then he will end there, where psychoanalysis ends, viz. in disillusionment and resignation, where its creator most emphatically has ended, too.

Since I thought this outcome a bit unsatisfactory and also empirically not quite justifiable, I have suggested the hypothesis of archetypes as an answer to the problem raised by the shadow. This apparently inordinate idea, also favourised [sic], but produced in the wrong moment by the wise Elihu, is a

22 The reference to Job's "dissociation" may refer, secondarily, to White's recent forgetfulness about the harmful language in his *Blackfriars* review of *Job*.

23 In his more recent review of CW 11, *Psych. & Rel.* (which includes Jung's *Job*), White had asked: "Can we legitimately transfer our personal splits and ills to our Gods and archetypes, and put the blame on them? . . . Or are the critics right who consider that Jungians have become so possessed by archetypes that they are in danger of abandoning elementary psychology altogether? I am not alone in asking such questions . . ." (*Journal of Analytical Psychology* IV: 1, Jan. 1959, p. 78).

petra scandali of the worst kind. In my naivety I had imagined it to be something better, than sheer despair and resignation, also something more true than mere rationalism and thoughtlessness. Your aggressive critique has got me in the rear.[24] That's all.

Don't worry! I think of you in ever lasting friendship. Ultra posse nemo obligatur.[25] Thus I ask for your forgiveness, as it is incumbent on one, who has given cause for scandal and vexation. It is difficult not to be crushed by the inexorable truth: Le Vray en forme brute est plus faux que le faux[26] or the mountain you have heaped up is your burial mound.

My best wishes in every respect!

Yours ever C.G. (unsigned carbon copy)

Postscriptum

I had a light embolism in the heart, the consequences of which kept me in the house for 4 weeks. I see from your letter, that you have published a new book, "Soul and Psyche", but neither my secretary nor I myself have seen a copy. I would be very interested indeed to learn your views about the intricacies of psychological terminology in this field disputed by Empiricism on the one and Metaphysics on the other side.

If you had seen Mrs. Philp's wife (as I have) you would know *everything* about him. When Johannes Hus bound to the stake saw a little old woman adding her last bundle of sticks to the pile, he said: o sancta simplicitas![27]

Blackfriars, Cambridge

28.3.60[28]

My dear C.G.

This little note can say no more than "thank you hugely" for your long & prompt letter.

I must, and shall, ponder on it for a while – certainly before I attempt anything like an "answer".

24 Cf. White, 6 May 1960, p. 289. "Your aggressive critique" must refer to White's 1955 "Jung on 'Job'" (cf. Appendix 6). His recent review of CW 11 (*JAP* IV: 1, Jan. 1959, op. cit.) also criticizes *Job*; but here White's writing is balanced and sanguine, with none of the fury of his earlier attack.

25 No one is required to do more than he can.

26 The truth in rough form is falser than falsehood.

27 Oh, holy simplicity!

28 Handwritten.

It is too bad that my publishers have not sent you a copy of my book – as they promised to do. A copy should reach you very soon. I do not expect you will like everything in it (I do not myself!), & yet I believe & hope it contributes something to the "dialectical procedure" so needed (I think) for the spread & development of your pioneer work.

Ever devotedly & affectionately, VICTOR W

Küsnacht-Zürich

30th April 1960[29]

My dear Victor,

I have heard of your illness and I should have liked to come to England to see you,[30] but I have to be careful with my own health and I must avoid all exertions. As I am completing my 85th year, I am really old and my forces are definitely limited. In February I had a bit of a heart embolism and my doctor is strict.

I have to thank you for the kind gift of your book "Soul and Psyche". It is certainly a theme worthy of a lengthy discussion in the "Auseinandersetzung" between Theology and Psychology. I have just begun to read it. I had to finish just the book "Psychotherapie und Religion" by Dr. Josef Rudin S.J.[31] The bit I have read in your book is most interesting and promising and I certainly shall go on studying it carefully.

In the meantime I hope you don't worry about my letter. I want to assure you of my loyal friendship. I shall not forget all the useful things I have learned through our many talks and through your forbearance with me. I was often sorry to be a petra scandali. It is my fate however, not my choice, and I had to fulfill this unbecoming rôle. Things had to be moved in the great crisis of our time. New wine needs new skins. We need no further outbursts on a grand scale or so it seems to me. The "iron curtain" is quite sufficient to me to demonstrate the enormous split in the soul (or psyché) of modern man, but we are mostly asleep. It needs some noise to wake the sleepers.

Many greetings and cordial wishes!

yours ever C.G.

29 Typewritten.

30 Enclosed in this letter was a small, recently taken snapshot of Jung standing in the doorway of the upper terrace of his house in Küsnacht. On its back he had written, "Instead of myself *in persona*, I come at least *in effigie*! C.G." (Figure 12.1, overleaf).

31 Cf. Jung, 10 April 1954, p. 233 and note.

Figure 12.1 A member of Jung's household evidently took this snapshot of him on the upper terrace of his house in Küsnacht, spring 1960. On the reverse side his handwritten message to White reads: "Instead of myself *in persona*, I come at least *in effigie*! C.G."

5 Harrowby Court[32]
London, W.1.

May 6th 1960[33]

My Dear C.G.,

I am being very sad that we are not able to meet and talk as in times gone by. This is all the more so because it seems that some strange misunderstanding – or non-understanding – has arisen between us. And such are our several conditions that it seems unlikely that we shall be able to meet and talk again in this world.

Your long letter has shaken me quite considerably.[34] Certainly I had not expected a "Job's comforter's" letter from you. And I should not have been very thankful for one had I got it! But still less had I expected that you would have experienced my comments and questions in the S.A.P. *Journal*[35] about "Antwort auf Hiob" as an "aggressive blow in the rear", which seems to have hurt you considerably. It seems that I have somehow assumed your shadow role, and of course I am terribly sorry if you have not found it to your advantage, but rather to your hurt.

I think and hope you know that when you first showed me "Antwort auf Hiob" I loved and admired it very much, especially when you told me the conditions under which you had written it and what it had done for you. I still do love your picture of Job, because I love you. But in those days you were emphatic that it was not to be published,[36] and I had never supposed that you would publish so personal a document without any analysis in personal terms. But once it *was* published, it surely has to be considered objectively, because I think there can be no doubt whatsoever that it raises very many

32 During White's final weeks he was cared for at this address by members of an intentional family of Jungian laypeople (cf. Jung to Mrs. Ginsberg, Appendix 1, p. 303 and note). He dictated his final letters to a member of the community, who typed them up and gave them back to him to be proofread and hand-corrected.

33 White took great care with this final letter. Its two parts were dictated, using a tape recorder, two days apart, and typed up by an assistant. The first typed draft has been preserved along with the final version. The draft is rapidly typed, double-spaced, showing many additions and corrections in White's hand. The final copy, which was sent to Jung, is single-spaced with a few handwritten corrections. The tape recording was returned after White's death to Catherine Ginsburg by Fr. Benot Weatherhead, O.P., as a "memento"; it no longer exists. [with AC]

34 This first part of White's letter replies to Jung, 25 March 1960. The second part, dated two days later, replies to Jung, 30 April 1960.

35 The S.A.P. (Society for Analytical Psychology) publishes the *Journal of Analytical Psychology*. White's recent review of *Job* had appeared in the January 1959 issue (cf. Jung, 25 March 1960, p. 285 and note), under "Critical Notices," pp. 73–78.

36 White's statement, that at one time Jung planned not to publish *Answer to Job*, starkly conflicts with his statements about the book in 1951 and 1952 (cf. especially White, 23 Oct. 1951, p. 173 and note).

difficulties and problems for many people besides myself, as I said in my review.[37] I wish you could have answered them publicly, whether in the *Journal* or elsewhere. I think these questions cannot be disregarded by anybody who is keen on spreading and continuing the wonderful work you have begun, and which "Antwort" seems implicitly sometimes to repudiate. I cannot pretend that it is not painful for me that you think I am repudiating your work as a whole, and just at the time when (as I told you)[38] I am in trouble with the Roman authorities for my support of it! I should like to think that the very fact that I seem to have unconsciously and unintentionally assumed a sort of shadow role to you and your work could be integrated and turned to the advantage of both. Certainly that is what I have learned from you can be done with the shadow that strikes us in the back. It may seem to you incredible, and yet I can assure myself that it is precisely the interest of your work and what it can do for humanity that I have at heart.

May I comment on some of the details in your letter? Of course I fully agree with your suggestion that I should apply my "personalistic" point of view to myself! But I dearly wish you had told me in what way I am failing to do so. And of course I agree that we cannot know much about the ancient person of Job. And yet I should have thought that, consistently with what you have always said about the law of compensation etc. between the conscious and the unconscious, we should not ignore what few hints we are given in the documents. It is probably not important, but I do not know on what grounds you say that Job was "very much a respectable Hebrew of his time". All the experts and commentaries I have been able to consult are emphatic that the land of Uz (or Hus) where he lived was not in Palestine but Idomea and that Job is not a Hebrew name. Not that I think that matters very much. Of course I understand you well when you say "one cannot avoid the shadow" etc., but it seems to me that the trouble about the book "Antwort auf Hiob" is that it precisely does so, and it makes no mention of Job's having any shadow, and his projection of it all on to Jahweh is thoroughly approved. My own reading is that Elihu and the vision of Leviathan, the animals etc. precisely show him that the voice of God is also *in* the shadow and not merely in the covenants etc. etc.

Clearly one cannot know what an analysant can take until one meets him and works things out with him. But certainly according to the original story Job is thrown into no such abyss of despair as you talk about, but he learns precisely to hear the voice of God *in* and *through* all these terrifying untamed natural things. But of course I agree that neither the shadow nor nothing else

37 Representing "my co-religionists . . . [and] compatriots," White writes: "The obstacle most difficult for us to overcome is the feature which the author is so eager to deny is there at all, the philosophical presuppositions and framework." This framework, he explains, is Jung's uncritical adherence to Kant's epistemology, which has no such authority in Anglo-Saxon or Catholic thought (*JAP* Jan. 1959, p. 78).

38 This parenthetical phrase was added by White in the margin.

can be wholly interpreted in *purely* personalistic terms. But surely not without relationship to the ego and the personality, who is the subject of the experience?

I do hope that you have recovered from the embolism and are in good form in every way. I am afraid this letter is quite inadequate to answer yours, but it is probably impossible to do so purely by post and especially for the likes of me and in my present weak state.

Of course I hold no brief for Mr. Phelp. His book struck me as mostly pretty stupid, and it failed entirely to get to grips with what you were talking about. But my reference was to *your* letter which he quotes on page 20 of your book. However much I have erred, and possibly been unjust to you, I think you must allow that I have never questioned your sincerity (publicly or privately) or suggested that you are "tied hand and foot" by other people's ideas or syllogisms.[39]

Still hoping that somehow, somewhere we may meet again, or at any rate find a real understanding even if at present it is beyond our ken. I should hate to feel that I have let you down in any way,[40] even if I have failed to give all you hoped – whether consciously or unconsciously.

Ever yours sincerely & cordially VICTOR W

8 May 1960[41]

My very dear C.G.

I composed and dictated the enclosed incoherent letter before your wonderful and comforting letter dated April 30th arrived. I am sending it to you all the same. Of course I well understand that it is impractical for us to meet at present. Perhaps we will meet in another world or dimension where "we know even as we are known".

I am glad to hear that you have got a copy of my book, even though I am afraid you may not like it all. It should in any case be different from that of Father Rudin.[42] You will realise, I am sure, that I have to think and talk in an environment – not only theological – very different from that of the Zurich Institute, and I am more convinced than ever of the importance of your pioneer work for humanity, even for those who cannot agree with every word you say but have to take part in the "dialectic discussion" with you.

But I am now finding that it is one thing to write a book – especially that

39 Cf. White, 18 March 1960, p. 284 and note.

40 In first typed draft, the remainder of this sentence is handwritten in the margin.

41 White's letter of 6 May was enclosed with this one, written two days later.

42 Cf. Jung, 10 April 1954, p. 233 and note; 30 April 1960, p. 287 and note.

part on life and death – and that it is quite another to live it and to have to keep these opposites here constantly in mind and together.

If ever you should have time or inclination to send me any comments on anything in my book, of course I should be delighted and profited. I do not know if it is true that you have been a "petrus scandali"[43] to me (as you say you have), but to the extent that you may have been, I think that I can honestly say that I am grateful for it.

May I add that I pray with all my heart for your well-being, whatever that may be in the eyes of God.

Ever yours cordially and affectionately, VICTOR WHITE[44]

43 Although White made several corrections in the final copy of this letter, he left this mistake in the Latin, where a masculine form, "petrus," is substituted for "petra" (stone). The biblical phrase, "stumbling block," appears more than once in this correspondence. White may have been amused by the double meaning in the typist's slip ("Peter of scandal").

44 Below his signature White drew a straight line. He died in the late morning of 22 May (cf. Appendix 1, pp. 303f and notes).

APPENDIX 1

JUNG'S LETTERS ABOUT WHITE

To Pastor Werner Niederer

23 June 1947[1]

Dear Pastor Niederer,

. . . .

Last year I saw an English Dominican[2] who spontaneously admitted that *everything* depended on whether the Church would go along with modern psychological developments or not. I was very surprised to hear that from a *Catholic* theologian. I wouldn't have gone so far. But it does seem to me that it would be appropriate if theology at least knew about the existence of the unconscious. This would be facilitated by St. Augustine's "Noli foras ire, redi ad te ipsum, in interiore homine habitat veritas."[3] Above all it must be understood that there is *objective psychic existence*, and that psychological explanation is not necessarily psychologizing, i.e., subjectivizing.

To Barbara Robb

19 November 1952[4]

Dear Mrs. Robb,

Thank you very much for your kind letter which has given me some valuable information. My discussion of the *privatio boni* with Victor[5] was a very unsatisfactory experience. I am glad, therefore, to have some further news about this problem, this time apparently more positive, if I may assume that the flaw demonstrated in the doctrine of the *privatio boni* has become

1 Letter previously published, *Letters I*, pp. 466f.

2 I.e., Victor White.

3 "Go not forth, return unto thyself: truth dwells inside the human being." (Augustine, *Liber de vera religione*.) This statement is the epigram to Jung's essay, "A Psychological Approach to the Dogma of the Trinity."

4 Letter previously published, *Letters II*, p. 93.

5 White had visited Jung at Bollingen for ten days in July 1952, where they talked about their differences regarding the problem of evil. Cf. their letters of April 1952; also Jung, 30 June 1952; White, 9 July 1952.

visible to Victor too.[6] Your dream about the word "Evil"[7] is extraordinarily illuminating and, in a way, most unusual. It contains in a nutshell practically everything you can say about the problem of evil. It is certainly worth remembering. The second dream[8] contains an equally excellent demonstration of the dynamic structure of the moral opposites in general.

Unfortunately, my illness has nothing to do with the weather, or only indirectly, inasmuch as the brilliant summer seduced me into an activity surpassing my actual strength. I am just about to recover, but slowly, from my prostration.

Thank you again for your kind information, I remain,

Yours cordially, C.G. JUNG

To Michael Fordham[9]

16 February 1954[10]

Dear Fordham,

Thank you for your letter and its most amusing report about your philosophical dealings with Father White.[11] Yes, he has a remarkable mind because it is not only logical, but also a remarkable twister and joker, and you put your foot just right into the middle of the plate. The question of the

6 Robb's letter of 16 Nov. 1952 consisted of two dreams, introduced by her statement, "In case you are interested, the following material seems to have demonstrated to Victor the flaw in the *privatio boni.*" In August 1954, however, she sent Jung a letter confessing, "I have long owed you an apology for having been far too previous about Victor's conversion re the *privatio boni*" (Jung/Robb correspondence, ETH Library archive).

7 In the first dream Barbara Robb is playing anagrams with Jung, who passes her the word "evil." She changes it into "live" which seems to please Jung. On waking, two alternatives occur to her: "veil" and "vile," the former showing blindness to the horrors of evil, the latter symbolizing the inability to appreciate "the good of evil" (*Letters II*, p. 93n).

8 "A vision of a small lump of hair-like substance representing the psychic energy that I use for doing good or evil. When it spun round and round in a clockwise direction, it meant that I was doing good; when it spun in an anti-clockwise direction, I was doing evil. In changing from good to evil, and vice-versa, there was an instant when it was absolutely still, and this neutral condition might be called the *privatio boni*, or, equally well, the *privatio mali* [privation of evil]" (Ibid.).

9 Cf. White, 4 March 1954, pp. 230f and note.

10 Typed. Previously unpublished letter, located in the archives of the Wellcome Trust, London. The editors are grateful to Sonu Shamdasani for providing it and to the C.G. Jung Estate for permission to publish it.

11 On 21 Nov.1953 White presented his lecture, "Good and Evil," to the London APC. (Cf. White, 4 March 1954, p. 230 and note.)

privatio boni is or was the favourite subject of discussion with Father White. The privatio boni is not a dogma, but a so-called sententia communis,[12] i.e. a generally recognized doctrine, and a "discutabile"[13] on principle. Father White thought it necessary – as he obviously did in your case – not to give way to any doubt about it. The doctrine is quite obviously a petitio principii[14] of the worst kind, and one can criticize it as you do and in many other ways. One always comes to the conclusion that it is a nonsense. I have discussed it at length in "Aion"[15] and still more privately with Father White until he almost collapsed, poor thing. I felt quite ruthless about it because I wanted to find out whether he really couldn't give way to simple logics. I hadn't known then how much the privatio boni is one of the main props of the Christian doctrine in general. It hangs together with the necessity to maintain the one way-goodness of the deity, the so-called Summum Bonum. They simply got to make the assertion absolute that God has not created evil although it is obvious that he has created Satan. Yet Satan is to be found in the dictionary under "devil" and the evil[16] under "evil", and neither in the one nor in the other both subjects are mentioned. One only can feel compassion with the position of an intelligent priest saddled as a representative of the ordo praedicatorum[17] is with the defence of the church (Domini cani = canes = God's watch dogs).[18]

Of course, good and evil are subjective feeling judgments, but good is hypostatized in the doctrine, and evil then should be equally real, but it must be a "me on", a "not being". One does not know exactly what is good and what evil, but the church just knows it.

Apart from these very awkward salti mortali,[19] Father White is a very nice

12 Cf. Jung, 30 June 1952, p. 198 and note.

13 "topic on which discussion is permitted"

14 a begging of the question

15 Jung's argument against the *privatlo boni* doctrine in *Aion*, whose fourth and fifth chapters are based on his Eranos lecture, "Über das Selbst" (cf. Jung, 21 May 1948, pp.118ff), was shaped partly by his debate with White on the topic. When revising the lecture to include it in the book, after the argument with White had become acerbic (cf. Jung, 31 Dec.1949, pp.140ff), he added new material, including §51–53 and §71–76, as a result of their argument. Cf. e.g., CW 9.ii, *Aion*, §74f, pp. 42f.

16 = the devil (?) From context, "evil" here appears to be a typing error.

17 Order of Preachers (Dominicans)

18 Jung cites folk etymology. (Cf. White, 3 Dec. 1950, p. 162 and note.) In legend, at the time of Dominic's birth his mother dreamed of a dog running with a lighted torch in its mouth. The image was taken as a sign that, like the dog in her dream, this child would spread the light of God.

19 logical discontinuities (lit. "mortal leaps")

fellow and delightfully intelligent, but one can see in his case in what an awful position the church is.[20]

Thank you for the news about Bennett.[21]

Cordially yours, [C.G. Jung] (*unsigned carbon copy*)

To Aniela Jaffé

Bollingen, 6 April 1954[22]

Dear Aniela,

Best thanks for your excellent review[23] – I have nothing to correct in it! After all the rubbish that gets delivered to my house on my work, it is such a pleasure to find something understanding and friendly for once. I often ask myself why by far the most of my "critics" are so unfriendly and unobjective? Is my style so irritating, or what is it in me that the world finds so offensive? This is understandable with *Job*, for that was its purpose. Now I have been irritated enough.

Your pious wishes for good weather were fulfilled only on Sunday, but then totally. Now the weather is beastlier than ever, so that one can only huddle behind the stove. I busy myself chiefly with cooking, eating and sleeping. In between I am writing a long letter to Pater White.[24] He has – thanks be to God – chosen the better course of facing his difficulties with complete honesty. I now see clearly what a fatal challenge my psychology is for a theologian but, it seems, not only for him.

I observe myself in the stillness of Bollingen and with all my experience of

20 After White's death Michael Fordham wrote to Jung to ask if he would contribute a personal statement about White to the *Journal of Analytical Psychology*. Fordham added, "I do so with some hesitation because I heard that you felt he was hostile to you. From what I have known of him I feel sure that this was not true in a personal sense though he was critical of some of your formulations. I never felt myself that he was unconstructive, however, and I know very well the great respect and admiration that he had for you" (Fordham to Jung, 18 October 1960, Jung-Fordham correspondence, Wellcome Trust archive). Jung replied with regret that he could not write a statement, although he would have liked to do so, since he had been ill and was under doctor's orders to avoid mental exertions (Jung to Fordham, 28 October 1960, Ibid).

21 E.A. Bennet (cf. White, 13 Oct.1946, p.47 and note).

22 Handwritten. Letter previously published, *Letters II*, pp. 162f.

23 Typescript of Jaffé's article, "C.G. Jung: 'Von den Wurzeln des Bewusstseins' " (*Tages-Anzeiger für Stadt und Kanton Zürich*, 29 April 1954).

24 Cf. Jung, 10 April 1954, pp. 232ff.

nearly eight decades must admit that I have found no rounded answer to myself. I am just as much in doubt about myself as before, the more so the more I try to say something definite. It is as though familiarity with oneself alienated one from oneself still further. Cordially,

Yours ever, C.G.

To E.V. Tenney[25]

23 February 1955[26]

Dear Dr. Tenney,

. . . .

Another aspect of this concretism is the rigidity of scholastic philosophy, through which Father White is wriggling as well as he can. He is at bottom an honest and sincere man who cannot but admit the importance of psychology, but the trouble is that he gets into an awful stew about it. Analytical psychology unfortunately just touches the vulnerable spot of the church, viz. the untenable concretism of its beliefs, and the syllogistic character of Thomistic philosophy. This is of course a terrific snag, but – one could almost say – fortunately people are unaware of the clashing contrasts. Father White, however, is by no means unconscious of those clashes; it is a very serious personal problem to him. But it is the same with Protestantism: there is the same difficulty between a concrete or historic belief and a symbolic understanding. One could well say it is a problem of our time whether our mind is capable of developing itself so that it can understand the symbolic point of view or not.

To Mother Prioress[27]

September 1959[28]

Reverend Mother Prioress,

I hope you will forgive the long delay of my answer to your kind letter of July 24. It came at a time when I was very tired and ever since I was waiting

25 Analytical psychologist, Ph.D., professor of philosophy at California State University, Fresno (*Letters II*, p. 227n).

26 Letter previously published, *Letters II*, pp. 227ff.

27 Mother Prioress in a contemplative order (cf. White, 18 Oct. 1959, p. 281 and note.) Her identity is withheld here, as in the *C.G. Jung Letters*, at her request and that of her heirs. [with AC]

28 Letter previously published, *Letters II*, p. 516.

for a propitious moment. I am very old and there are too many people who want to see me.

I am very grateful for the spiritual help you extend to me.[29] I am in need of it with this gigantic misunderstanding which surrounds me. All the riches I seem to possess are also my poverty, my lonesomeness in the world.[30] The more I seem to possess, the more I stand to lose, when I get ready to approach the dark gate. I did not seek my life with its failures and accomplishments. It came on me with a power not my own. Whatever I have acquired serves a purpose I have not foreseen. Everything has to be shed and nothing remains my own. I quite agree with you: it is not easy to reach utmost poverty and simplicity. But it meets you, unbidden, on the way to the end of this existence.

I am glad that you gave me some news about Father White's activity. Thus I know that he does not fully disapprove of my work.[31] I have heard of his terrible accident.[32] But I have no news since and I would be very grateful if I had some further information of his state of health.

I thank you for the unasked-for kindness of your letter. There is so much evil and bitterness in this world that one cannot be too grateful for the one good thing which happens from time to time.

Yours devotedly, C.G. JUNG

29 Mother Prioress's letter, sent near Jung's 84th birthday, assures him that this anniversary will be "specially commemorated in the prayers and thanksgivings of Father White's [. . .] nuns." She adds, "your influence through Father White's guidance has indeed helped this little community of nuns to stand on our feet, and we are grateful to you in the only way we can express it, by praying for you *every single day* . . ." (Mother Prioress, 24 July 1959, Jung/Mother Prioress correspondence, ETH Library archive).

30 Her letter ends with the request, "Please dear Dr. Jung, pray for us too, to live & die poor & humble" (Ibid.).

31 White reacted drily to this (cf. White, 18 Oct. 1959, p. 281).

32 Mother Prioress's first letter does not mention White's accident. She would have been aware that Jung already knew of it from others, including Eve Lewis and John and Doris Layard (Ibid., p. 281, note 4).

7 October 1959[33]

Reverend Mother Prioress,

I am much obliged to you for the kind news about Victor White's condition of health, and I glad to know that he has apparently recovered from his grave accident.[34]

It is indeed most remarkable that you should mention St. Niklaus[35] at all, since I happened to be quite busy with his visions these last days. He is most remarkable, even unique in respect to his inner life, and I must say, I have received an unusual amount of insight through his visions. I have heard, that in the 18th century an Austrian Baron has implored the Pope to cause the Ecclesiastical authorities to issue an official comment on Brother Klaus' dreams and visions. Although he has been promised an official commentary, it never has reached the light of the day, but about 200 years later an Austrian Baroness[36] has written a most profound and learned commentary about St. Niklaus' dreams. Many years ago I called the attention of my contemporaries to the peculiar and unique nature of his visions.[37]

I should have liked to send you the book "Die Visionen des Niklaus von Flüe" by M.-L. von Franz (Zürich 1959), but I am afraid, it is not yet translated into English. As a matter of fact I feel much inner relatedness to our national Saint, in spite of 500 years lying between. In a way I can't deny, that I am continuing the path of his visions. It seems, that he is still leading his host, as it was predicted by one of the three, who visited him in his vision.

33 Letter previously unpublished. (Jung/Mother Prioress correspondence, ETH Library archive.) Permission to publish it was kindly given by the C.G. Jung Estate.

34 Mother Prioress's letter of 1 Oct. 1959 reports: "I will tell Fr. Victor White that you ask after him. He had a convalescence of some months & was getting much better; then just 3 weeks ago he was rushed in hospital with what seems to have been food-poisoning. Now he is back at Blackfriars, & he writes that he is 'a good deal better' than before he went into hospital. They have really taken a lot of trouble to find out what was wrong. And he sounds more like his old self than ever since the accident" (Jung/Mother Prioress correspondence, ETH Library archive).

35 Niklaus von der Flüe (Bruder Klaus) (1417–1487): canonized in 1947 by Pope Pius XII and declared the patron saint of Switzerland. Mother Prioress writes: "As I told you, for *many* years, perhaps 14 or 15, we have prayed for you daily, invoking the help of Nicholas von der Flüe – during this period he was canonized & is now *Saint* Nicholas. A priest (Swiss) who has sometimes sent us help for our building of monastic cells (built of wood like a Swiss chalet), wrote to suggest that we call one cell after Nicholas of Flüe. . . . I have often wondered if St. Nicholas was listening to our prayers & what he is doing for you." In a P.S. she adds, "We all . . . send you most warm-hearted greetings, dear Dr.Jung – please ask your Bruder Klaus to bless us too" (Mother Prioress, 1 Oct. 1959, Ibid.).

36 A playful reference to Marie-Louise von Franz, whose recently published book is named in the next paragraph. Von Franz, born in Munich in 1915, was the daughter of a colonel in the military of the Austro-Hungarian Empire (Kirsch, *Jungians*, p. 11).

37 Jung's essay, "Bruder Klaus," *Neue Schweizer Rundschau* (Zürich, 1933) was translated and reprinted in CW 11, *Psych. & Rel*, §474–487.

Many thanks for your kind and reassuring news about Victor White. Please give him my regards, if you should see him.

Yours sincerely, C.G. JUNG

Many thanks for the symbolic pilgrim's shoes.[38]

6 February 1960[39]

Reverend Mother Prioress,

It is very kind of you to give me news about Victor White, although they are much worse than I expected.[40] I assume that a malignant tumor has been revealed through the operation. Let us hope that by the Grace of God and the aid of a human physician the ordeal of his passing away will be mitigated.

My dreams have warned me of this unexpected development. The last news I got from him have been of a rather cheerful nature, so that I was not expecting a deterioration of his state. I am very grateful to you that you let me know the truth about him. You have cleared up several points of what I have recently observed and experienced. As there are so few men capable of understanding the deeper implications of our psychology, I had nursed the apparently vain hope that Father Victor would carry on the opus magnum. But it is the curious fact, that most of the intelligent men I became acquainted with and who began to develop an uncommon understanding had come to an unexpected early end. It looked as if only those who are relatively close to death, are serious or mature enough to grasp some of the essentials in our Psychology, as a man who wants to get over an obstacle, grabs a handy ladder.

Well, it is a sad truth that we know very little about the most important aspects of life.

If Father Victor is still in a condition of enough consciousness, please give him my message, that I know and think of him.

Yours devotedly, C.G. JUNG

P.S. Dr. v. Franz tells me, that a translation of her book about S.Nicolaus of Flüe is under way at the Institute under her controle. Thank you![41] C.G.J.

38 She had enclosed these miniatures in her last letter, "a symbol . . . IN VIAM PACIS" (Mother Prioress, 1 Oct. 1959, Jung/Mother Prioress correspondence, ETH Library archive).

39 Typewritten, except for P.S. Letter previously published, *Letters II*, p. 536.

40 In a letter dated "Candlemas – 'La Fête de la Rencontre' " (2 Feb. 1960), Mother Prioress reports: "Father Victor is very very ill, & he may very likely sing his Nunc dimittis before you. . . . it was an emergency operation which gave up the truth" (Jung/Mother Prioress correspondence, ETH Library archive).

41 She had inquired whether a translator was needed for von Franz's work (Mother Prioress, 2 Feb. 1960, ibid.).

26 March 1960[42]

Reverend Mother,

Many thanks for your kind report about Father Victor![43] I am still shaken by this stroke of fate which has felled him. According to the experience and knowledge of medical science the verdict seems to be absolute, yet, in order to do justice to your faith,[44] I must say that I know (and have seen myself) of certain similar cases where an apparently miraculous recovery took place. There is a 1:X probability of an unaccountable cure.

I would share your standpoint of undaunted faith if I were not disturbed by the thought that this earthly life is not supreme, but subject to the decrees of a superior economy. I try to accept life *and* death. Where I find myself unwilling to accept the one or the other I should question myself as to my personal motives. . . . Is it the divine will? Or is it the wish of the human heart which shrinks from the Void of death?

. . . We should not only have a more or less complete understanding of ourselves but also of the way in which we are related to our fellow-beings and of their nature. Our moral freedom reaches as far as our consciousness, and thus our liberation from compulsion and captivity. In ultimate situations of life and death complete understanding and insight are of paramount importance, as it is indispensable for our decision to go or to stay and to let go or to let stay.

Since I had your letter, I have heard that the truth has been told to Victor White (which I hoped for fervently) and, as far as I know, the effect has been all to the good.

There is such a thing as *tempus maturum mortis*[45] and it is up to our understanding to fulfill its conditions.

Sincerely yours, C.G. JUNG

42 Letter previously published, *Letters II*, pp. 546f.

43 In a letter of 28 Feb. 1960 Mother Prioress writes: "I have just heard from Father Thomas Gilby, who is the Superior at Blackfriars, that the doctor expects Father Victor to decline steadily. I do not know the exact location of the cancer, but it might be of the stomach" (Jung/Mother Prioress correspondence, ETH Library archive).

44 Her letter continues: "I have had two postcards from Fr. Victor, & both times he says that he is getting better but it may be a longish time before he is well. . . . Now dear Dr Jung – I am wholly intending to take Fr Victor's own words as *true* – & I believe that he is going to get better. No one but God knows when our life will come to an end . . ." (Mother Prioress, 28 Feb. 1960, Ibid.).

45 time ripe for death.

29 April 1960[46]

Reverend Mother,

I am very sorry indeed that the news about Victor White is so bad and the end apparently so near.[47] If you have any chance to let him know about myself I should be so much obliged if you would tell him that I am at peace with him and that he should not worry any more. I am quite convinced of his sincere and human loyalty. I am sorry if I should have upset him by my attempt to explain to him the reason for a certain critique I had to make.[48] In my letter to him which contains the explanation, I also told him that it did not matter and he should not worry about it.[49] I don't know what more I could tell him to assure him of my feeling. If I were young and could trust my physique I would certainly come over to England and assure him of my personal feeling.[50] Unfortunately however extravagances are out of the question. So I would be most obliged if you would kindly let him know of my letter to you.

He has sent his new book[51] to me which I am going to read just now (having had to finish another book[52] first). I am very interested in it and it was my intention to write to him only after having gone through his book as carefully as possible. I am afraid the reading will take some time. Under these circumstances I do perhaps better if I wrote to him soon.[53]

Sincerely yours, C.G. JUNG

46 Letter previously published, *Letters II*, p. 552.

47 Replying to two letters from Mother Prioress, dated 4 April and Easter Sunday 1960. The first conveys the report of a friend, who has just seen White, that "he is terribly ill & looks very thin – but that his eyes are clear and happy, & he is able to work a little. . . . They consider he may perhaps live for two or three months." She adds that she has sent White the letter Jung wrote her on 6 February (Mother Prioress, 4 April 1960, Jung/Mother Prioress correspondence, ETH Library archive). Her next letter passes on information she has received from Mrs. Ginsberg (cf. Jung to Catherine Küsler-Ginsberg, below), who reports that White "can hardly take any nourishment" and is "accepting that he is dying" (Mother Prioress, Easter Sunday 1960, Ibid.).

48 Cf. Jung, 25 March 1960, p. 284.

49 Cf. also Jung, 30 April 1960, p. 287.

50 Mother Prioress had written: "How I wish & pray you could come to see him. Is it quite impossible for you to fly to London?" (Mother Prioress, Easter Sunday 1960, Jung/Mother Prioress correspondence, ETH Library archive).

51 *Soul and Psyche* (cf. White, 26 July 1958, p. 277 and note).

52 Josef Rudin, S.J., *Psychotherapie und Religion*. (Cf. Jung, 10 April 1954, p. 233 and note.)

53 In her reply of 9 May 1960 Mother Prioress urges Jung: "Please write to him yourself, & say anything you wish – or wait until you have read his book & criticize it! That will please him most" (Jung/Mother Prioress correspondence, ETH Library archive).

To Catherine Küsler-Ginsberg[54]

3 June 1960[55]

Dear Mrs. Ginsberg,

Thank you for kindly telling me the news of Father White's end. It forms a valuable supplement to the thoughts that have moved me from the moment when I saw we had come to the parting of the ways. I was at the end of my resources and had to leave him nolens volens to the decree of his fate. I saw that his arguments were valid for him and allowed of no other development. I accepted this in silence, for one can only respect such reasons even though one is convinced that – had the circumstances been favourable – one might yet have reached out beyond them. In such cases I usually tell my patients: here only fate can decide. For me personally it is, every time, a matter of life and death, where only the person concerned can speak the word. For it depends entirely on him and his decision what will happen. Knowing how much depended on whether Father White could understand my arguments or not, I still tried to point out the difficulties in my second-last letter to him.[56] With the feeling, however, that it would not be granted me to pierce through to his understanding.

It was then that I sinned against my better insight, but at least it served as a pretext for my asking his forgiveness and offering him a touch of human feeling in the hope that this would afford him some small relief.

As I have so earnestly shared in his life and inner development, his death has become another tragic experience for me. To us limits are set which we cannot overstep, not in our time. Perhaps what has evolved in the course of the centuries will not cease to be active for just as long a span. It may take hundreds of years for certain insights to mature.

I am glad and grateful that you looked after him so kindly.[57] It was always

54 Catherine Küsler-Ginsberg, German-born, living in London with an intentional Jungian community, individuals of various ages and nationalities, who had all undergone analysis. On 28 May 1960 she wrote to Jung recounting the death of Victor White. She explains that for the last year White has been a weekly visitor to her "voluntary family," which welcomed him to live there and be cared for during the last six weeks of his life. (Jung kept her letter, together with White's letters to him and his to White, in the private portfolio he passed down to his heirs. It is now with Jung/Küsler-Ginsberg correspondence, ETH Library archive.)

55 Letter previously published, *Letters II*, p. 563. Original in German.

56 Cf. Jung, 25 March 1960, p. 285.

57 It was the decision of Catherine Ginsberg and her household, she explained, to take Victor White in when his illness became acute, in order to help him to "his own death" (Küsler-Ginsberg, 28 May 1960, Jung/Küsler-Ginsberg correspondence, ETH Libary archive). This plan was arranged in conjunction with Thomas Gilby, White's superior at Cambridge Blackfriars. [with AC]

my fear that he would have to spend his last days in the professional chill of a hospital or in the atmosphere of a monastery cell. Thank God that was spared him. One must also be grateful for the merciful intervention of the embolism.[58]

I thank you for the kind offer to let me see the drawings.[59] I hope you will understand that I prefer to let the images of the living man steadfastly gazing ahead live on in my memory. In gratitude,

Yours sincerely, C. G. JUNG

12 August 1960[60]

Dear Mother Prioress,

Thank you ever so much for your letter with all its information about Fr. Victor's end.[61]

I am most grateful to you for sending me the picture you mention.[62] The living mystery of life is always hidden between Two, and it is the true mystery which cannot be betrayed by words and depleted by arguments.

Sincerely yours, C.G. JUNG

58 Her letter recounts White's death: "Despite great physical suffering, he was intellectually alive to an extraordinary degree. He had an easy death: a heart attack shortened the final struggle. He was alert to the end and went through a spell of anxiety, which resolved itself in his last word, 'O God, take me!' " (Küsler-Ginsberg, 28 May 1960, Ibid.).

59 She had offered to send Jung photographs of drawings that were made of White's head after death. Although he refused them in this case, Jung later received the photographs (cf. Jung to Mother Prioress, 12 Aug. 1960).

60 Letter previously published, *Letters II*, p. 581.

61 On 22 May 1960 Mother Prioress wrote: "Father Victor's beloved soul has returned to God. He died this morning between 11–12 a.m. from a sudden thrombosis. He was fully aware, & praying before he became unconscious, & they say he had no great pain." In another letter, dated 24 July 1960, she greets Jung on his birthday and recounts the last hour of White's life in greater detail (Jung/Mother Prioress correspondence, ETH Library archive).

62 Photographs of the drawings of White's head, made after his death, were later returned to the Mother Prioress with Jung's thanks by his secretary (Jaffé, 22 Aug. 1960, Jung/Mother Prioress correspondence, ETH Library archive).

To the Rev. W. P. Witcutt[63]

24 August 1960[64]

Dear Sir,

. . . .

I must call your attention to the fact that I have no theory that God is a quaternity. The whole question of quaternity is not a theory at all, it is a Phenomenon. There are plenty of quaternary symbolizations of the Deity and that is a fact, not a theory. I would not commit such a crime against epistemology. This is the stumbling block over which Father Victor White has fallen and many others. I am in no way responsible for the fact that there are quaternary formulas.

19 October 1960[65]

Dear Reverend Mother,

According to your wish[66] I wrote, as soon as I got your letter, to Dr. Rudin, S.J.[67] (the director of the Institutum Apologeticum in Zurich), who knew Victor White, asking for his cooperation. Thus I hope your wish will be granted.

It was perhaps just as well that my message[68] did not reach V.W. any more. It might have worried him. When I wrote my explanation[69] I was not yet informed of the seriousness of his condition, and from his reaction I only saw, that he did not understand what I meant, which was not astonishing under the circumstances. On the whole I prefer people knowing all they can about themselves when *in conspectu mortis*.[70] But the moment was ill chosen.

63 Catholic priest in Southend, England. (Cf. White, 23 Oct. 1945, p. 17 and note.)

64 Letter previously published, *Letters II*, pp. 584f.

65 Letter previously published, *Letters II*, pp. 603f.

66 In a letter dated 13 Oct. 1960 Mother Prioress implores Jung to contact a Catholic priest in his vicinity, to arrange that a Mass be offered on what would have been Victor White's 58th birthday, 21 October 1960.

67 Cf. Jung, 10 April 1954, p. 233 and note.

68 Cf. Jung to Mother Prioress, 29 April 1960, p. 302. Not knowing that White's death was so imminent but thinking to spare him, and with advice from others, she did not deliver Jung's message, an omission for which she later reproached herself (Mother Prioress, 13 Oct. 1960, Jung/Mother Prioress correspondence, ETH Library archive). She also comments on this decision in a letter to Catherine Küsler-Ginsberg, enclosing a copy of Jung's letter of 29 April: "I send you a letter of Dr Jung's which may clarify a little what he wrote to you & to Victor. It was a problem whether to send *this* letter to him to read – but I was advised *not*" (Mother Prioress, Oct. 1960, archive of the English Dominican Province). [with AC]

69 Cf. Jung, 25 March 1960, p. 284.

70 confronted by death.

Don't worry too much about it, as V.W. received my real message and was not able to understand it any more. My message to you was only an attempt to pacify his mind about my intentions. I was afraid he might be unduly worried about the letter he could not understand.

I have now seen quite a number of people die in the time of a great transition, reaching as it were the end of their pilgrimage in sight of the Gates, where the way bifurcates to the land of Hereafter and to the future of mankind and its spiritual adventure. You had a glimpse of the Mysterium Magnum.

Yours sincerely, C.G. JUNG

P.S. I just received Dr. Rudin's answer. He himself will celebrate the mass.

APPENDIX 2

VICTOR WHITE, A MEMOIR

By Adrian Cunningham

> It is difficult to know where to begin this story, for I do not yet know where it is going to end. Perhaps I never shall know; perhaps it never does end. And until I know the end I shall never know its real beginning. For even were I to introduce the story with a wearisome complete autobiography, still I should not begin from the beginning. For even were I to weary you with everything in my conscious memory before relating my story, still I should not begin from the beginning. I should have to go much further back than the limits of my conscious memory will take me; back to infancy; back to the womb; back to my parents; back to their wombs and their parents and so ad infinitum. Back, perhaps, to palaeolithic and anthropoid ancestors, back to Eden, back to primaeval swamps, back to the Mind of God. And that is just what, as yet, I cannot do. I cannot know the beginning until I know the end; and when I know the End I shall know everything.[1]

This "record of a healing" and his meetings with John Layard – "the magician", "my Guru, my Staretz – more prosaically, my analyst", marks the turning point of his greatest doubts about being a Catholic theologian and his first active contact with the Jungian world which the meetings and correspondence with Jung show in their profound, complex and finally tragic development.

1 This comes from the opening of Victor White's typing up of his Diary of 28 August 1940 to 30 March 1941. The typescript breaks off after a few paragraphs. From August 1940 to March 1941 White kept a diary or notebook to help clarify his problems and he wondered if others might come to read it. He also kept a Noctuary, a record of 120 dreams between August 1940 and September 1942. He took the term from Synesius of Cyrene: "We shall therefore see fit to add to what are called diaries or day books what we term noctuaries or night books, so as we have records to remind us of the character of the two lives concerned; for a certain life exists in Imagination, at one moment better, at another worse, then the intermediate, according to the relation of the spirit to health or disease" (*De Insomniis* 12). There is also a dream index organized under people, places and objects, for the years 1940 to 1946. These are the only extant autobiographical materials. I am indebted to Keziah Cunningham for the transcription of the diary and other White material.

Figure A2.1 White on an ocean-going sailboat, probably in Sweden, c. 1957.

Gordon Henry White was born in Croydon, Surrey, on 21 October 1902 and was baptized by his father in St Augustine's church on the 22 November. The family lived at 35 Avondale Road. His father, John Henry White (1865–1950) and grandfather, John White (1822–1905) were Anglican ministers, as was his uncle Frederick Ernest White (1853–1929). On this side the family can be traced in Northumberland, and later Sunderland, from the sixteenth century.[2] Less is known of his mother, Beatrice Mary Phillips, the daughter of a merchant, James Phillips. White was the oldest of three sons. The second son, Basil Philip Dawson became a commercial clerk, and the youngest, John Francis Christopher (1912–1971) became an Anglican clergyman. From an early age White himself felt that a clerical future was to be his path. He later reflected that it was his relationship with his father that

2 Among more distant relatives were Andrew White, the first (Radical) Member of Parliament for Sunderland, one of whose sisters, Jane Taft, was supposed to be of the same family as the American president. The White family in Leeds employed Charlotte Brontë as a governess. Andrew's father John White (1764–1833) started as a cooper and went on to be a shipowner and the proprietor of glass and iron works. He was staunchly Methodist. Another son, Victor White's great-grandfather (another John, 1794–1878) was an iron manufacturer. Information supplied by Douglas W. Smith based in part on the work of David White, Pursuivant Rouge Croix at the Royal College of Heralds.

had prevented his becoming an Anglican priest (letter to John Layard 29.12.40).

There is no record of his early education. At the age of 14, in October 1916, he joined the fourth form at Bloxham School, Banbury, Oxfordshire, gaining prizes in Divinity, English and French. He would also have studied history, Greek and Latin. He completed his studies in the summer of 1919.[3]

He later went to St Charles House, Begbroke, Oxford, about 15 miles from Bloxham School. This was a center primarily for Anglican clerics converting to Catholicism. He was by far the youngest student. The rather scrappy Register of St Charles House for September 1919 to April 1921 has an entry for what seems to be 1921 showing G. H. White arriving on 24 March: "son of an Anglican clergyman; just left school; under instruction. Still at Begbroke."[4] Since according to the Valladolid record he was received into the church on 12 March 1921 by the Warden of Begbroke, Monsignor H. Barton Brown, "with whom he had lodged for some months", the year of entry must be 1920.

White was accepted for ordination training for the diocese of Plymouth by Bishop Keily and from 1921 to 1923 studied at the English College at Valladolid in Spain. The reason for sending some candidates for the priesthood to study at the English Colleges in Rome and Valladolid were various. It could be either that they showed exceptional promise, or that as converts were thought to benefit from immersion in a traditional Catholic culture, or both.

The *Liber Alumnorum* oddly records *George* Gordon White arriving there on 10 September 1921. It notes his interest in Dominican life in the summer of 1922 and his leaving the college on 3 April 1923, when he decided to join the order.[5]

It is possible that he studied briefly at Fribourg in Switzerland before becoming a novice at the Woodchester Priory in Gloucestershire on 29 September. His name in religion was Victor. Until recent times names were assigned by the novice master – in this case Eustace O'Gorman – possibly in consultation with the novice. Of the 13 St Victors, ten were martyrs of whom one was a Pope of North African origin in the late second century, and the last recorded another Pope, Victor III, 1027–1087. Studies at Woodchester concentrated on the history of the order, liturgy, learning plainsong, spirituality. He was professed on 30 September 1924, along with Gerald Vann, who remained one of his closest friends in the order. The following year he went

3 Information supplied by Major Shaw McCloghry MBE, Honorary Archivist, Bloxham School.

4 Information supplied by Fr Ignatius McCafferty OSM, St Philip's Priory, Begbroke, Oxford.

5 Information supplied by Revd Monsignor Canon Peter Dooling, Rector, Colegio de Ingleses, Valladolid.

to the priory at Hawkesyard, Staffordshire, as a student in simple vows and was ordained priest in June 1928.

In 1929 the priory in Oxford was opened and the theologians (students in their final years) moved there from Hawkesyard the following year. The Studium remained divided until 1967, with the Regent of Studies in Oxford and the philosophers (students in early studies) remaining with a Lector Primarius in Hawkesyard. The re-establishment of the priory was of major intellectual and symbolic importance. The original priory had been suppressed in the English reformation. Catholics and Jews had been excluded from the universities of Oxford and Cambridge until the University Test Acts of 1871. Following suspicions in Rome about "mixed education", while there was no formal prohibition of studying at Oxford and Cambridge the English bishops warned parents of the attendant religious and moral hazards.

In the 1930s the Master of the order, Father Gillet, wrote a trenchant report on the generally poor quality of Dominican education. In this light the English studium was a strong one. The Regent of Studies between 1920 and 1932 was Hugh Pope (1869–1946) who had taught scripture at the Angelicum in Rome from 1909 to 1913 – he was suspended on suspicion of modernism but rehabilitated by Pope Benedict XV. Reginald Ginns had studied at the Ecole Biblique; Wilfrid Ardagh had a doctorate of theology from Fribourg; Hilary Carpenter, who taught Greek and philosophy, was an Oxford B.Litt.

Some of the more conservative members of the province were deeply worried at the move from rural isolation to the heady secular world of Oxford and there was even an attempt at having the studium move back to Hawkesyard. The liveliness of Oxford Dominican life at that time is captured in Bernard Wall's recollection:

> I sought out and rapidly made friends with every neo-Thomist I could find. . . . I remember going for long walks with Gerald Vann or Victor White beyond Boars Hill discussing minutiae of Thomism, the problem of Suarez, the nature of grace, matter and form, the operation of transubstantiation, faith in the sense of *substantia rerum sperandarum argumentum non apperentiu*, the sense in which the valid active life derived from contemplation, and Thomas' sudden passionate appeal for the mixed contemplative-active life which was that of his own Dominican order.[6]

6 Bernard Wall, *Headlong into Change, an Autobiography and a Memoir of Ideas since the Thirties* (London: Harvill Press, 1969, pp. 37–9). The quotation is from the Vulgate version of Paul's Letter to the Hebrews ch. 11.1: "Faith is that which gives substance to our hopes, which convinces us of things we cannot see".

White completed his licentiate in sacred theology in 1930. His thesis was rather challengingly titled "The Platonism of Saint Thomas Aquinas: An Outline of Thomist Exemplarism". Ten years later in the midst of his crisis of faith he picks up two phrases of Goethe on symbolism cited in John Middleton Murry's *Heaven and Earth* of 1938: "The supreme thing would be to comprehend that everything actual is itself theoretical. We must not try to get behind the phenomena – they themselves are the lesson." "In true symbolism the particular represents the universal not as a dream or shadow, but as a living, momentary revelation of the ineffable."[7] Murry comments: "It is significant that only Christian thought has an adequate expression for Goethe's belief: which is, simply that *everything* is sacramental, and that the supreme thing would be to be permanently conscious of this." Following this White reflects, "how Jungianism inculcates this state of mind, and I recall how it was universal before the 'Aristotelian renascence' of the XIII century. Was it not in the hope of salvaging it that my lectorate dissertation was on the exemplarism of St Thomas?"

White pursued further studies in Louvain in 1931–2. Back in Oxford he taught dogmatic theology and church history. Some of his writings of this time – on sexual ethics, and on scholasticism, for instance – are clear and competent, well within the conventions of the time, giving little sign of the profoundly original work to come 20 years later.[8]

The exceptions to this rather run of the mill writing included his *Blackfriars* contribution about the 1938 report from the Church of England doctrine commission, "the best comments by anyone on that report . . . exemplary", as the philosopher Donald MacKinnon recalled.[9]

There were also his many short contributions to *Blackfriars* on political topics under the pseudonym "Penguin", black and white being respectively the colors of the Dominican tunic and cloak. In particular, it was the critical line many *Blackfriars* items took on the general Catholic support for Franco in the Spanish Civil War that drew a lot of adverse comment.

The background to this stance came from White's close contact, from 1928 onwards, with the group around the sculptor, typographer, engraver and

7 White actually and significantly renders this "infallible"!

8 For an appreciation of White's philosophical and theological writings, see Aidan Nichols O.P. *A Dominican Gallery, Portrait of a Culture* (Leominster: Gracewing, 1997, ch. 3). Valuable ancillary material on the Dominican context of White's life can be found in Simon Francis Gaine O.P. *Obituary Notices of the English Dominicans from 1952 to 1996* (Oxford: Blackfriars Publications, 2000) and *Letters of Bede Jarrett, Letters and other Papers from the English Dominican Archive* selected by Bede Bailey O.P. and edited by Simon Tugwell O.P. and Dom Aidan Bellenger (Downside Abbey and Blackfriars Publications, 1989).

9 Elsewhere, MacKinnon thought it a pity that White got so involved in the Jungian world and did not produce the theological work he might have, given the fine essays in *God the Unknown*. He had not read *Soul and Psyche*. Interview with AC, 23 December 1991.

polemicist Eric Gill at Pigotts in High Wycombe, Buckinghamshire. A number of the Dominicans were deeply involved in the anti-industrialism, "back to the land" movement of smallholdings and William Morris-inspired craft revival that had, in its Catholic form, started at Ditchling in Sussex as the Guild of Saint Joseph and St Dominic in 1918.[10] Gill was also a pacifist and White was drawn by this, had many contacts with the Pax association, predominantly but not exclusively Catholic, though not identifying himself as a pacifist.[11] As he wrote to John Layard: "I am not a pacifist. . . . But some of my difficulties have been regarding the Catholic pacifists, and the various machinations to prevent them from stating their case" (12.1.41).

The "machinations" of church authorities regarding the Pax group infuriated him. His position on politics vis-à-vis established Catholic authority and the common inevitable strains of community living were obviously exacerbated in wartime and led in 1940 into a general crisis about his identity as a Catholic theologian. Fourteen years later he wrote:

> I am by profession a theologian. But I am a theologian to whom . . . something happened. Suddenly, or perhaps, not so suddenly, theology ceased to have any meaning for me at all: I could not get my mind onto it, or anything to do with it, except with horror, boredom and loathing.[12]

The "machinations" that angered him seemed symptoms of a wider problem: Catholicism tending to keep European man "in a state of infantilism and dependence, and so become the Terrible Mother who stifles the children and will not let them grow up. It is *impossible* for Europe to return to the

10 Donald Attwater, with whom White stayed in Wales for a fortnight during his leave from Blackfriars in 1940, writes of him as one of Gill's Dominican friends visiting Pigotts from 1928 onwards, "a disciple of C.G. Jung". He speculates that they may have met through Gill's friendship with the Catholic psychiatrist Dr Charles Burns. This errs in two respects. White shows no acquaintanceship with Jung's writings before about 1940, and his connection with Gill was independent of Dr Burns. *A Cell of Good Living: The Life, Works and Opinions of Eric Gill* (London: Geoffrey Chapman, 1969, p. 176).

11 He outlined his own position in two articles in *Blackfriars* in June and September 1939 ("War and Rumours of War", and "War and the Early Church"). He wrote in 1949: "We must rid ourselves of the idea that conflict, force, violence, destruction and death are inherently and wholly evil – an evil from which no good can come, something which is wholly of the devil and utterly opposed to God. Behind a great deal of what is called pacifism today lies a subtle kind of manicheanism: a belief that even if all matter is not evil, and that is no work or manifestation of God, then force and violence are such" ("The Morality of War", *The Life of the Spirit*, Vol. 4, 1949, p. 99).

12 Note to a version of his paper "Good and Evil" given in San Francisco in late 1954. The lecture was first given to the Analytical Psychology Club in London in November 1953, repeated for the Los Angeles Club in 1955. It was finally published in *Harvest* in 1966.

Faith. . . . A bewildering paradox: the Church the condition and yet the hindrance to Faith" (Diary 29.8.40). Writing of his dogmatic and socio-political difficulties in November 1940 he says:

> These abuses in R.C. Church, if they are abuses at all [i.e. they may be intrinsic and systematic—AC] seem to me so flagrant and pernicious, that spades should be called spades – and not merely by cautious and diplomatic articles in learned periodicals. . . . If one is conscious of Gemeinschaft with the Sancta Romana, one can patch up and interpret *ad lib.* If one does not, it all seems a tiresome waste of time.
>
> (Diary 21.11.40)

His teaching around this time suffered and he would respond to students' questions by reading from a standard commentary.

In crisis he had turned to his friend, the philosopher and theologian Donald MacKinnon (1913–1994) and on 31 August 1940 "by the banks of the Cherwell I expose my soul to him". He wanted to relate his problems of religious identity, the agnosticism burdening him to what he had recently read of Jung. MacKinnon recommended him to contact the Jungian analyst John Layard, which White did two weeks later. A fellow Dominican at Blackfriars, Paul Foster, was already in contact with Layard. Along with other Jungian therapists – Gerhard Adler, William Kraemer, Vera von der Heydt, and Toni Sussman – he had moved to Oxford from London to avoid the bombing. In mid-1940 the outcome of the war was very uncertain. Hitler had added to earlier conquests by invading Norway, Belgium, and Holland.

There had been earlier contacts between the English Dominican and Jungian worlds. Norbert Drewitt was in correspondence with Jung in 1937 (*C.G. Jung* Letters, Vol. I p. 237 where "O.P." is misconstrued as "Ordo Praemonstratensis", a quite different order), enclosing his *Blackfriars* article on myth.[13] Jung replied suggesting a meeting in London in April 1938. Drewitt was a close confidant of White's in the crisis of summer and autumn 1940. After a period as military chaplain Drewitt left the order in the early 1940s.

The former psychiatrist Aidan Elrington O.P. had reported in *Blackfriars*

13 "Catholicism and Myth", Vol. XVIII, Feb. 1937, pp. 103–10; and "Faith – Love and the Supernatural", Vol. XVIII, July 1937, pp. 514–24. From the latter: whilst "Jung's sporadic notions about the historicity of the Gospel narratives [are] as effete as in nineteenth century Tubingen", this has nothing whatever to do with his "substantial, empirically verifiable theses." As with Freud, "If Christianity does not take these new materials reasonably seriously then the enemies of Christianity will" (p. 519).

on the Tenth International Congress for Psychotherapy (Oxford, 29 July–2 August 1936), where he met Jung, who gave the opening address.[14]

Also White's closest Dominican friend and colleague, Richard Kehoe, referring to his student days under John-Baptist Reeves, O.P., recalled "how refreshing and exciting to hear the Scriptures expounded à la Jung. I was decent enough not to tell him that I had not yet read a word of that great man's works" (letter to Conrad Pepler O.P. 18.12.76). Or, as White characteristically puts it the other way round: "I fancy you may find there are remarkable affinities between Jung's technique of dream-interpretation and traditional canons of Scriptural exegesis" (letter to Layard 22.9.40). There is no sign that White himself took much interest in psychology or had read any Jung before late 1939 or early 1940.

By inclination and training White's initial attempt to understand what was happening to him was a feverish immersion in reading and thinking: theologians like Karl Barth and D.R. Davies; von Hartmann's *Philosophy of the Unconscious*; three books by John Middleton Murry; and for a second time Dostoyevsky's *The Brothers Karamazov* and especially the "Grand Inquisitor" section. Against this background the work with Layard on dreams and symbols came as a liberating shock. He also read Jung's *Psychology of the Unconscious* and his commentary on *The Secret of the Golden Flower*, the only two books he mentions specifically. In wartime conditions, "The opera jungiana, it seems, can't be got for love or money second-hand or first-hand – save by a fluke. Nor are they easy to borrow" (letter to Gerald Vann 21.6.42).

The problems about authority in the ecclesiastical ("Oh, to be dealing with men and not ecclesiastics!") and political sense led into wider and deeper doubts about the authoritative basis of Catholic doctrines. The issue was not so much the contents of belief as the way that, reinforced since the modernist crisis, the church had got itself into an absurd position where the *historical* basis for events in the life of Christ, for instance, were held as a matter of *faith*. Difficulties in the relation between the Jesus of history and the Jesus of faith were a commonplace in Christian theology, especially since the early part of the nineteenth century with new historical and textual methods but the official "solutions" to these were highly vulnerable.

> Catholic orthodoxy seems to have got itself into a hopeless tangle by interpreting dogma in terms of a naïve realist epistemology.[15]

14 See also Elrington's 1933 *Blackfriars* article "Psychoanalysis and Catholicism".

15 In experimenting with Norbert Dewitt's suggestion of the "myth come true" and how Jung's archetypical approach could play a part in this which would feature in his later writing, White notes how on the basis of existentialism and phenomenology there would be no grave difficulty. But on the official Thomist basis of "objective" realism "which is that of all the anti-modernist pronouncements of all 'good' Catholics – it makes no sense" (Diary 8.11.40).

> Not satisfied with that, that *philosophical* interpretation is virtually *de fide*.
>
> (Diary 31.8.40)

To take the example of the Virgin Birth, whilst White did not feel compelled to categorically deny it as a historical fact, he felt it at least questionable but as a historical and physiological fact it was *de fide* for Catholics. As a priest, let alone professor of theology, he was required to recite the anti-modernist oath which, among other things, precluded the idea, for instance, that what is true of "the Christ of faith" can be false of "the Christ of history", or vice versa. It was issues such as these that made for great difficulties in his remaining a Catholic (letter to John Layard 20.11.40). This problem of the anti-modernist oath arose again, in less acute form, when he became a master of theology in 1954.[16]

Whilst his reading of Jung and the sessions with Layard deepened his understanding of religious symbolism, Jung's writing on Christ gave a further edge to the familiar problems of the Christ of faith and the Christ of history:

> Why does Jung disturb me so? Because it is impossible to read him without drawing the conclusion that if Jesus had not existed it would have been necessary to invent Him. And if it was necessary to invent Him, it seems unnecessary that He should have existed.
>
> (Diary 31.8.40)

At the same time he had no doubt that what he wanted to do was to see how far Jung could be placed within Catholic theology (letter to Layard 7.11.40). In an extended exchange of ideas with Layard about the Fall of mankind (which is picked up in his 1942 lecture "The Frontiers of Theology and Psychology" and has an obvious bearing on the issues with Jung at the heart of many of their discussions and correspondence) White feels they raise in acute form the degree to which collaboration between Jungians and Christians is possible:

16 Formulated in 1910 the oath was required of clerics or lay people involved in official teaching. It affirmed assent to the papal documents *Lamentabile* and *Paschendi gregis*. These contained condemned propositions of scriptural and theological arguments taken from writers like Alfred Loisy and George Tyrrell. The condemnation of so-called modernism introduced a reign of terror and theological sterility that lasted half a century. (Laurence F. Barman, *Baron Friedrich von Hugel and the Modernist Crisis in England*, Cambridge: Cambridge University Press, 1972, p. 215.) Writing in 1922, Cuthbert Butler gives the essence of the matter: "Christian origins, New Testament, History of Dogma, etc. – have been made impossible for a priest, except on the most narrow apologetic lines. . . . The only freedom in biblical things and the rest is that of a tram, to go along as fast as you like on the rails, but if you try to arrive at any station not on the line you are derailed" (Alec Vidler, *20th Century Defenders of the Faith*, London: SCM Press, 1955, p. 37).

> Whether there is not considerable likelihood that Jungians, by going beyond their empirical data and making metaphysical and metapsychical affirmations which are not necessarily demanded by those data, may lay the foundations for a religion or ersatz-religion which, so far from complementing Christianity, may contradict it radically.
>
> (letter to Layard 5.12.40)

By early November following a "mammoth interview" with Layard, White felt desperate, "at the edge of an abyss": "I feel I am now on the brink of the Urgrund whence Gods and demons proceed . . . the imminence of a descent into hell." "I seem to have gone back in time to a devil-infested universe" (Diary 6.11.40, 8.11.40). A turning point came a few days later with three waking visions of a dazzling white sun, a windmill, and a revolving disc like the governor of a machine. Layard saw this mandala symbolism as one of a fundamental change and suggested White was ready to go back to teaching – a suggestion he fell in with. "Indeed I feel a changed person – at the dawn of a new life. Now I must thank God" (Diary 12.11.40).

White returned frequently to these visions as a source of support but the euphoria of thinking about a return to teaching did not last. Attending Mass two weeks later he listened to a sermon on the holy souls, the sufferings of purgatory, and indulgences "delivered with dogmatic assurance but with little sign of personal emotion or even conviction." "And I am expected to teach this and the like to simple people. No, dear Victor, it can't be done!" (Diary 24.11.40).

He was resisting the urging of Layard, Kehoe and Drewitt that he return to "Blaggers" with mental reservations about his religious position (he had left Blackfriars to stay with friends outside Oxford). In the only sharply critical comment on Layard as a person at this period he writes that to the extent that Layard is vehemently weighing the scales about a return "he sells me out to my 'enemies', – Roman authority – he himself becomes one of them – and a prelate who can be of no use to me – an orator and not a scientist. In doing so he sells his own soul as an analyst" (Diary 28.11.40).

At this point White was considering four options: rejoining the Church of England; becoming secretary or "apprentice" to Layard; returning to Blackfriars; joining a new religious foundation planned by the Benedictine editor of the *Eastern Churches Quarterly*, Dom Bede Winslow (1888–1959). White was under the misapprehension that the scheme was for a linked Catholic and Uniate foundation like the abbey at Amay-Chevetogne. He had an abiding attraction to Orthodoxy vis-à-vis what he saw as the rationalized and literalized theology of the western church and reflected that his haste to convert to Catholicism had led him to pass over the Orthodox option. A subsequent meeting with Winslow in London cleared up the misunderstanding. The new foundation to work for church unity was to be a wholly Latin rite agricultural community. White was still considering the possibility of joining Winslow as late as July 1941 when he was being sounded about returning to teaching in Oxford. The scheme did not get started. From 1944 to 1948 Dom Bede organized annual three-day conferences of Anglican, Catholic and Orthodox theologians at Blackfriars, Oxford. White was one of the participants.[17]

By the end of January 1941 his diary records that he was at the parting of the ways. Finances had made it impossible for him to remain without employment and Layard's offer of work could not be seriously considered until he felt the "official" priesthood was clearly impossible. Various ideas had been proposed by the Dominicans to allow him to stay in the order without being in Oxford or teaching. One was to work in the London parish ministry to people in air-raid shelters, for which he rightly felt no talent. Another possibility was to accompany young evacuees to Australia or South Africa, a position he briefly entertained. This pretty outlandish idea suggests the desperateness of his need to put a distance between himself and teaching at Oxford.

Finally, he accepted the Dominican proposal that he move to their house of study in Cambridge. Founded in 1938, it became a priory in 1969. "Now that I had, as it were, discovered the real ME, the contrast between the ME and the persona – I-should-be as a priest became more intolerable than ever. Perhaps at Cambridge it would be different" (Diary 27.3.41).

The Diary ends four days later. White continued work on dreams with Layard by correspondence and he must have overcome his qualms about mental reservations and returned to Oxford in September to resume teaching. "I'll be damned glad to go on with the analysis. In fact, I've a hunch there'll be another disaster if I don't" (letter to Layard 12.8.41).[18] There is no extant record concerning further sessions.[19]

17 A.H. Armstrong and E.J. Fry (eds) *Re-Discovering Eastern Christendom: Essays in Commemoration of Dom Bede Winslow* (London: Darton Longman and Todd, 1963).

18 Here and in the Jung correspondence references on both sides to his analysis and later his analysands need to be seen in context, before standardized hours per week over several years, and training analysis became the norm. In today's terms he might be described as a Jungian psychotherapist. The leading Jungian analyst Michael Fordham later wrote: "The trouble with you, if I may say so, is that your psychology is so good that pucka psychologists have difficulty in competing" (14.3.57). From November 1957 he regularly spent one day a week working at the More Clinic in the City of London. Started in 1954, the clinic was run by Fr Francis O'Malley, a Rosminian priest at St Ethelreda's church in Ely Place. The medical directors were F.B. Elkisch and Ruth Sandeman. The clinic closed in 1959.

19 In an interview with Gene F. Nameche in December 1969, Layard recollected that he had "saved Victor White's sanity and his place in the world" but "Jung never recognized that I had done anything for him at all. This may sound nasty and sour grapes, but it hurt a lot. And Victor White never came back to me actually [for analysis]." In the later 1940s Layard had felt ostracized by Jung and had been upset at White staying at Bollingen in 1946 where he had never been invited.

White's first substantial writing on Jung was a paper he gave to one of Layard's Oxford groups in June 1942, "Some Bearings of Religion on Analytical Psychology" (the order of phrases in the title is interesting) – amplifying themes from his discussions with Layard on the Fall and what he saw as the Jungian dogma of the autonomy of the psyche. The paper was repeated for the Guild of Pastoral Psychology in October, but with an important change. For that meeting White omitted some pages of the original paper which took Jung to task in supposing that:

> The virtual ignoring of the devil, disastrous as the tendency has become in modern bourgeois Christianity, is something endemic to original and authentic Christianity itself. I am convinced that he is utterly mistaken, and still more so in concluding that Christianity has fulfilled its historical function (Hegel?) and has now outlived its usefulness. The mistake would seem to be largely due to a failure to grasp the real significance of the definition of evil, found in many Christian philosophers, as the "privation of good". So far from implying, as Jung seems to suppose, a denial of the reality of evil, it precisely supposes it, and confirms his own conception of the opposites.[20]

The Guild paper version, published as "Frontiers of Theology and Psychology", later appeared in the early sections of *God and the Unconscious*. Two points are relevant here: the very early date at which White had hit on a major problem in a rapprochement between analytical psychology and theology which became pivotal in his later relation to Jung, and rather puzzlingly, why he dropped this section after its first presentation.

This was one of the papers he sent to Jung in his initial letter of August 1945. Visiting Küsnacht in March of the following year G.A. Bennet heard how impressed Jung was with his Dominican correspondent. That August was the first of White's ten more or less annual visits to Jung, the substance of most of which can be gathered from their correspondence.

White's efforts to put his reflections on Jung and theology into systematic form developed slowly. On Ascension Day 1946 he writes to the novelist Antonia White that his "God and the Unconscious" still needs a lot more knocking into shape – she had expressed an interest in translating the final product for publication in France. Versions of the paper were given in America in 1948 and Oxford in 1949 and it finally appeared as Chapter three of *God and the Unconscious* in 1952.

At various points in the 1940s he considered writing a systematic and historical treatise on the relations between depth psychology and theology,

20 *VW*ms. 1.6.42. p. 16. Cf. Adrian Cunningham: "Victor White, John Layard, and C.G. Jung", *Harvest*, Vol. 38, 1992, pp. 44–57.

but wrote to Antonia White in October 1947 that he had found that C.G. Carus had already written his book a century earlier (*Psyche* 1846). Further research showed that the work of Albert Béguin on early ideas of the unconscious and the Swiss volume *Rätsel der Seele* on the theological side rendered his own work on these lines redundant. The first two chapters of *God and the Unconscious* are all that survive of the abandoned treatise.

The Edward Cadbury Lectures of 1958–9 at the University of Birmingham that are the core of *Soul and Psyche: An Enquiry into the Relationship of Psychotherapy and Religion* (1960) are his most sustained and mature coverage of the subject and have received less study than *God and the Unconscious*. While the finished work is invariably clear and fluent, White had to work hard at this in the early stages: "I was evidently never meant to be a writer anyway. It's well to know one's own sterility" (letter to Antonia White 13.2.48).[21] Tim and Benita Smiley, who lived at the Cambridge Dominican house, recall that around 1957 White would take to his bed for days at a time struggling with an intellectual problem.

In the Jung correspondence and elsewhere his view of formal teaching is almost invariably negative. There is a striking divergence of views about different phases of his teaching work. Around the time of his 1940 breakdown not surprisingly he seems a mundane if not boring lecturer. It may have been the contact with Jung, the difference of perspective that his year in America in 1947–8 provided, as well as his reading of contemporary – mainly French – Thomist scholarship that gave a very different flavor to his work in the 1950s. As one of the most influential English Catholic theologians of the last century wrote, White gave him "the reality of Aquinas stripped of the scholastic obfuscations of so much modern 'Thomism' ".[22]

The fall of 1947 marked the start of a remarkable 12 months for White. After his second meeting with Jung and the success of his paper on Aristotle at the Eranos meeting in Ascona in September, and being invited to be a founder member of the Zurich Institut, he sailed to New York. For some months he was the guest of the "millionairess" he mentioned to Jung, Mrs Frances Leggetts at Stone Ridge, Ulster County. He stayed en famille for two

21 Quotations from the letters to Antonia White are made with the permission of her daughter, Lady Chitty. There are numerous references to Victor White in *Antonia White, Diaries 1926–1957* (London: Constable, 1991; *1958–1979*, 1992). See also Susan Chitty's *Now to my Mother, A Very Personal Memoir of Antonia White* (London: Weidenfeld, 1985) and Jane Dunn, *Antonia White, A Life* (London: Jonathan Cape, 1998).

22 Herbert McCabe O.P., *God Matters* (London: Geoffrey Chapman, 1987, p. 1). He notes how White found fascinating parallels with the anti-dualism and "materialism" of Saint Thomas in the work of modern depth-psychology. Cf. Donald MacKinnon's introduction to the posthumous collection of writings by Cornelius Ernst O.P. for a similar commendation of White's impact on later students. *Multiple Echo: Exploration in Theology*, eds Fergus Kerr and Timothy Radcliffe (London: Darton Longman and Todd, 1979).

months in the main house and then moved to the "Inn" on the estate, a retreat for, mostly, Catholic writers and artists. The sharp contrast to the wear and tear of Oxford over recent years, the "controls and malnutrition" of post-war Britain, provoked a lyrical response:

> This is an indescribably lovely place, and nowhere could be more suitable for my purposes . . . keen mountain air, brilliant light casting deep shadows, strange flowers and birds and beasts and no snakes. A lovely big bed-sitter room in the entrancing Colonial wooden house with porticos in all directions; an enchanting and most prayerful chapel with a 14th century Avignon altar-piece and an 11th century equal-armed crucifix. Most understanding and sympathetic people, and interesting visitors at weekends only, and lashings of such food and drink that – alongside all the rest – I've never felt so well in my life! Plenty of outside occupation, right down to EARTH. So far the writings have not been going so well; but I must allow time for all this influx of new impressions to subside perhaps.[23]

In December he was invited to become a patron of what was to become the C.G. Jung Institute in Zurich. In February 1948 he lectured on Gnosticism to the New York Jung Club and at Easter left his "hermitage" for lectures and seminars in Chicago, the North West Pacific coast, California, New Mexico and Arkansas to pay his way. The post-war £75 restriction on foreign currency made this inevitable. In this and other earnings any significant surplus would be turned over to his order. This "heavenly but hectic tour of the West, with one damn Lecture after another" (letter to Layard 8.5.48) left him exhilarated but exhausted. At some point he met with Jacques Maritain. He resumed writing at Ridgely Inn in July. "Anyway God and Ucs. aren't coming to the surface too well. Maybe you're right – and they are queerer bedfellows than I liked to suppose" (letter to Layard 8.7.48).

He began to dread the return to Oxford: "on the surface at least everything is just tootsy-wootsy . . . [but there are] persistent nightmarish dreams about being back in England betimes in a state approaching panic . . . and hideously homesick for the USA. . . . I am afraid I do just love this country, and it's gratifying to find it seems to like me" (letter to Antonia White 20.5.48).

He left New York for England towards the end of August and after spending 6 to 14 September with Jung resumed his teaching in Oxford, and the usual round of conducting retreats and addressing various societies around the country.

In late October 1950 he went on his first visit to Rome for the "ridiculous

23 Letter to a member of a religious order (hereafter R.), October 1947. I am grateful for the opportunity to look through this correspondence which will not be more openly available for some years.

exam" he mentions to Jung. In fact it would have been a tough examination for a baccalaureate which in due course would become a mastership in Sacred Theology (STM). It would also mean reaffirming the anti-modernist oath which had so deeply exercised him in 1940. Several stray references in 1951 apart from what he writes to Jung indicate that he still found difficulties in his Dominican life. These were compounded in December 1952. "I think it is now no secret that my very best friend among the O.P's – Fr Richard Kehoe – has left the Order, and for the most conscientious reasons which I am bound in varying measure to share" (R. 30.12.52). White does not elaborate on what these reasons were. By November 1953 he was again desperate:

> I am paid, I owe my bread and butter, to the alms and gifts of good Christians, who support me in the belief that I am a good Christian priest, labouring to bring all I can into the one Ark of salvation! Their God simply isn't my God any more; my very clerical clothes have become a lie. I feel acutely that my position has become morally impossible and dishonest. . . . So I tell myself from time to time that, whatever the cost, I must get out.
>
> (to Jung 8.11.53)

God and the Unconscious had been published in 1952. Many reviews were positive but the author later reflected:

> In one important respect God and the Unconscious did not receive the criticism, or arouse the discussion, for which the author hoped. In his own view the book's most salient feature, which it argued laboriously in one chapter, and which the rest of the book presupposed, was its insistence that religion and psychology shared a common territory and a great many concerns; but for the most part this feature was passed unchallenged, and indeed hardly noticed. This common territory, it was maintained, is what religion calls the human soul and what psychology calls the human psyche. It was maintained that, although the viewpoints of religion and psychology differed, and that each made different (and sometimes even seemingly conflicting) statements about them, this "soul" of religion and this "psyche" of the psychologist are identical – or, at the very least, overlap.
>
> (unused "Epilogue and Prologue", 1958, for *Soul and Psyche*)

This is a somewhat puzzling comment for it is the very objection to this position that concerned the influential British Catholic psychiatrist E.B. Strauss over many years. See his otherwise enthusiastic review of *Soul and Psyche* in *The Tablet* (19.3.60). Other instances are in the hostile reviews that led to his later difficulties with Rome – those in particular by Dom Gregory

Stevens (*Theological Studies*, Vol. 9, 1953); Raymond McCall (*New Scholasticism*, Vol. 28, 1954); and, as we shall see later, by Agostino Gemelli (*Vita e Pensiero*, 1955).

The events of 1954

May 1954 was an important month for White. In Brussels on 1 May 1954 he gave his paper to a meeting of the Wiener Arbeitskreis für Tiefenpsychologie. It was a small conference and it would be fascinating to know what the speaker on "Avatars de la parole" (Jacques Lacan) had to say to the speaker on "The Unity of the Person" (White).[24]

On 28 May at Blackfriars the cap and ring of a master of theology were given to Victor White and Ambrose Farrell. It was expected that White would become Regent of Studies for the coming October term. In fact around late July or early August Farrell was appointed instead. Words have been chosen deliberately here for it is generally held that White had been appointed and further that the Provincial, Hilary Carpenter, had taken the opportunity of the sudden death of the Master General, Emmanuel Suarez, to have the regency switched from a radical to a conservative. This may have been so but I have some doubts about this version. In a warm letter to White of 12 August the English language member of the master general's council, Aelwin Tindal-Atkinson, who had been very close to Suarez, writes:

> My own impression had been that you were to be designated for Fr Daniel Callus's office as soon as his second term was concluded this month. Hence the change came as a great surprise to me, as it would have, I believe to Fr Suarez.

Formally it would make sense for the appointment to be made after the conferral of the STM, that is between 28 May and Suarez's death four weeks later. If White had been formally appointed then no record of it survives. In fact this brief letter is surprisingly the only document about the affair extant.[25]

In reactions to the change there may not be much difference between "were to be designated" and actually appointed but since I want to consider the affair in a broader context it seems right to cross t's and dot i's. Certainly Tindal-Atkinson's not being consulted, as was customary, indicates something strange in the acting master general's procedures.

24 This appeared in a German translation by A. Wegeler as "Die Einheit der Person", *Jahrbuch fur Psychologie und Psychotherapie*, 1955.

25 When enquiries were made the Order's archives in Rome were rather disorganized. It is possible something more may eventually come to light.

The broader context is the crisis affecting the Dominicans in 1953–4, focussed on the suppression of the worker priests in France. These had their roots in 1943 in the sending of clandestine priests as civilian workers in German labor camps. At the end of the war the worker priests continued and expanded in France as part of a mission to offset the alienation of great parts of the working class from Christianity. The Vatican's immediate anxiety about this and the increasing trade-union and political activities of the priests was followed in February 1951 by Rome's forbidding the admission of any new candidates and a request to the French bishops for annual reports on each individual priest.

The speeding up of restrictions on the worker priest mission can, in Gregor Siefer's account, be traced to one fact, the replacement of Mgr Roncalli, later Pope John XXIII, as Papal Nuncio in France.[26] In May 1953 the Dominican Père Montuclard, leader of the Jeunesse de l'Eglise community in Paris, resigned from the order and the priesthood after his book, *Les Evenements et la foi* was condemned. In August 1953 Cardinal Giuseppe Pizzardo, Prefect of the Congregation for Seminaries and Universities, ordered heads of religious orders to recall their worker priests and in September called for an end to the "experiment" indicating severe penalties for any continuation. Of the hundred or so priests ten were Dominicans. The order was unusual in that it had from the outset enshrined in their Constitutions a strong juridical independence from the central Roman authority.[27] There was severe pressure within the Vatican to even have the Constitutions revised. Twenty-five years earlier Master General Parades had been more or less forced to resign in Pope Pius XI's campaign against Catholic involvement in the Action Française movement, the 1929 General Chapter being forbidden to have any discussion of his resignation. The 1953 crisis looked likely to be even worse.

In November Suarez made a formal visitation of the English province speaking individually to every member of the order. This would, among other things, have given him an opportunity to take soundings on the regency to fall vacant in the following year. It is inconceivable that he did not discuss the French and more general crisis with White and with others.

26 Gregor Siefer, *The Church and Industrial Society* (London: Darton, Longman and Todd, 1964; German original 1960, p. 71).

27 As one of those directly affected by the purge, Yves Congar wrote: "Here we see the general ecclesiological basis of the Dominican episode. We are almost the only organized body of free thought in the Church. . . . We remain the only body which can, canonically, organize and act of its own accord." "Chronique de la petite purge", cit. François Leprieur, *Quand Rome Condamne* (Paris: Plon, 1989). Congar wrote only one article about the worker priests but had been under suspicion in Rome, probably from as early as 1937, for his ecumenical studies. I am grateful to Fergus Kerr O.P. for an exchange of views about Congar Chenu, and the Dominican crisis in the years following 1953.

Suarez still delayed, but after the bishops declared on 19 January 1954 that the worker priests completely stop their work by 1 March he acted ruthlessly lest worse happen to the order. On 9 February in Paris he removed the three French Provincials (Avril of Paris, Belaud of Lyons, and Nicolas of Toulouse); the leading theologians, Chenu, Congar and Feret, were removed from their teaching posts and banished from Paris; the director of the publishing house, Editions du Cerf, Fr Boisselot, was dismissed. The French bishops were concerned with Chenu's leading influence in the worker priest movement. Conservative Dominicans in the Holy Office, like Garrigou-Lagrange, had been concerned with Congar's ecumenism, perhaps from as early as 1937, and took the general crisis as an opportunity to discipline him as well.[28]

On the night of 30 June Suarez and his assistant were killed in a car accident near Narbonne. In accordance with the Constitutions the interim master of the order was the provincial where the next general chapter was due to be held. In this case it was Timothy McDermott of St Joseph's province, New York, a very experienced ecclesiastical politician of a conservative and authoritarian disposition. He held office until the General Chapter of May 1955.

In the context of the above it seems to me that there was probably a general scrutiny of regencies in Rome over the summer of 1954 with the Holy Office objecting to White as regent, something that McDermott would be inclined to go along with. It seems less likely that Hilary Carpenter initiated the change from White to Ambrose Farrell.

Although the assignment of Laurence Bright and Cornelius Ernst to teach at Hawkesyard promised well, the new appointment of a conservative canon lawyer as regent set back studies at Blackfriars for several years. When Henry St John became Provincial in 1958 he took steps to ensure that Farrell's term was not extended beyond the usual six-term period. The elderly former regent Daniel Callus was appointed for the year 1960–1 and then Columba Ryan served as pro-regent until, with the relaxing of the STM requirement, Cornelius Ernst was appointed regent in 1966.

In 1954 it was an anguished Cornelius Ernst who had tried unsuccessfully to start a petition for White's appointment. Certainly, it was a personal affront to White but he seemed to recover from it quite quickly. When he passed the STM examination in 1950 he told Jung this "means the end of my hopes that I can retire from teaching and the wear and tear of community

28 Later, when Michael Browne, another of the powerful conservative voices in the Holy Office, became Master General he "banished" Congar to Cambridge "indefinitely". In the end Congar stayed there for six desperately miserable months, February to November 1956. There was a brief overlap with Victor White on his return from America in August. There is no record, but they had interests in ecumenism and Roman problems in common.

life and devote my time to quiet reading, writing and seelsorge" (3.12.50). And writing to Jung in September 1954: "So all the fuss about the oath, the degree, and my beautiful self-sacrifice pro bono publico [in becoming regent] have been a sort of sacrifice of Isaac – or maybe something a great deal more comic." – He adds, "But in many ways it is of course a huge relief" (25.9.54).

Given the anguished need to "get out" in his letter to Jung the preceding November, this last reflection is far from surprising. As he put it to Herbert McCabe, "poor old Hilary mucked me about but it was a blessing in disguise". It was the Provincial's rather desperate suggestion that White go to California and find something to do there. As his next letter to Jung makes clear he was soon occupied: "It seems that I've definitely got a job to do in my present calling, however uncomfortable I still feel about it, and there is nothing to do but get on with it. It is at least satisfying to feel one is needed, and doing something that nobody else can do. But it is just telling the old, old story, and not very original or creative" (8.1.55).

It was whilst in Oakland that he wrote his article on *Answer to Job* that so upset Jung ("Jung on Job", *Blackfriars*, March 1955). It seemed to have surprised its author too: "that Job article may be *true* – but it's *terrible*. I've amazed myself and others by the mercilessness of it" (R. May 1955). He left America in April for a general chapter of the order where Michael Browne was elected master and then went on to Zurich.[29] Here he gave seminars at the institute on "Classes of Opposites" and "Baptism Ritual and the Opposites" (Christ and "Self"). These were an attempt to come at the issues between himself and Jung from a different angle. The problems between them over the Job book were at their height. Thus their brief meeting at Mammern where Emma Jung was convalescing turned out to be a disaster, as White's subsequent letter acknowledges and Jung's distress was confirmed to me by Aniela Jaffé many years later.

In a subsequent dream White notes: "Waiting to say good-bye to Jung. . . . Trying to find him. 'The only great man I've known'. I wonder if this is artificial". "So I am still out of touch with C.G. and anxious (genuinely?) about it. Compensation for my own central lack of strong effort to contact him? But it seems I have to do without him in this 'afternoon' of life and should reconcile myself to this" (23.7.57). Their very last meeting was to be in June 1958.

On returning to California in August 1955 for a further year White found

29 Browne was a Vatican official of many years standing and his devotion to Pope Pius XII was the mainspring of his life. He was sent by Pius to report on the progress of a deadlocked Dominican election. On the assumption that he was a prudent appointment in the wake of the previous year's crisis and a candidate approved by Pius, in some confusion, he was elected. Pius never spoke to him again. Browne was in an unbearable position. His physical breakdown and sense of desperation at this time is recalled by his niece Máire Cruise O'Brien in *The Same Age as the State* (Dublin: O'Brien Press, 2003, pp. 207–8).

that as well as some teaching in the Dominican house he had a "rather mounting collection of 'souls'. It must be quite hell to be a lay Catholic in USA if you have any imagination or individuality at all, and this alone is back of a great many problems" (R. 25.12.55). Among other engagements was a request from Hollywood to give a short retreat to "ladies of the motion pictures" (R. 31.10.55).

In April 1956 he spent a wonderful weekend in Yosemite with Gerald Vann and Killiki Palmquist who were also on lecture tours. It is likely that all three visited Henry Miller at Big Sur – "a GENUINELY FREE man". Palmquist was a vocation counselor in Stockholm whom White had first come across in 1946. She was to become one of his most trusted friends and colleagues. She was present at the talks White gave at Ståket near Stockholm in 1954 and 1957; the theme of the latter was "Guilt, Theological and Psychological".[30] She worked in London several times and they were planning to see *West Side Story* in the last months of his life.

In August White returned to England. His American Provincial had begged that he might return for a further period. White was keen but the English Provincial was unwilling: "My year in California has been a rather wearing but profitable experience. I feel much more settled within myself now; not that any problems are solved, but they don't seem to matter so much anymore; and I feel more ready to plow a lonely furrow" (letter to Jung, 25.8. 56). He then set off for Zurich and Bollingen, 6–14 September.

Further problems with Rome

In the June and July issues of the review *Vita e Pensiero* in 1955 the editor Agostino Gemelli (1878–1959) wrote a not wholly lucid account of Jung's psychology of religion, noting its increasing appeal for Catholics. He singles White out for particular criticism. *God and the Unconscious* is seen as a disconcerting book. "It is quite extraordinary that this work should carry the imprimatur of the Archbishop of Birmingham." He finds White not very watchful of orthodoxy, inattentive to the mind of the Church. Gemelli asserts that to understand the religious sphere one needs to operate in philosophical and theological terms, not seek support from psychology. "Here lies the very grave intellectual[31] error of those Catholics, like White, who use the

30 Ståket was a residence founded in 1952 for aged sisters of the Order of St Elizabeth which has functioned as a retreat and conference center for priests of the Stockholm diocese (Fr Jean Paillard O.P., 1 September 2004).

31 The phrase used is "l'imperdonabile errore" (p. 384). Russell Price kindly helped with the translation of passages from the articles. In his view a native Italian speaker would only mean "unpardonable" of an act or deed, not an intellectual position. It would not be surprising that a non-Italian reader would understand "imperdonabile" in the strongest sense.

teachings of Jung in order to strengthen support for the truths of religion or, even worse, to enrich it".

Vita e Pensiero was one of the most widely read Italian Catholic periodicals.[32] The Franciscan Gemelli was a major figure in Italian Catholicism, founder of the Catholic University of Milan in 1921 and director until his death. "Il Machiavelli di Dio" and "naturaliter fascista" are phrases cited from his biographers in the 20-column entry in *Dizionario Biografico degli Italiani* (Rome, 1999, Instituto della Enciclopedia Italiana). When White was to attend the Seventh International Congress of Catholic Psychologists in Madrid in September 1957, where Gemelli was to be president of honour, it is not surprising that he refers to him as "my Enemy" (R. 8.8.57).[33]

The Holy Office's concern about White's orthodoxy came to a head in late 1957 and in a curt note of 8 January 1958 from Cardinal Giuseppe Pizzardo to Michael Browne as Master General he asks for an opinion of White's teaching and a list of his publications. This was not Pizzardo's first interest in English Catholic writers. In 1953 he had condemned Graham Greene's novel *The Power and the Glory* on the grounds that it was "paradoxical" and "dealt with extraordinary circumstances" and requested changes in a text published 14 years earlier. Cardinal Griffin's Advent pastoral letter in the Westminster diocese was along similar lines.[34] Browne's request about White to the English Provincial Hilary Carpenter met with a swift reply on 14 January. Given the importance of Carpenter in what did or did not happen in the regency issue four years earlier, it is worth quoting in full. Knowing that his response to Browne would go to Pizzardo, Carpenter echoes the rotund phrasing of the original in the opening and closing phrases:

> Most Reverend and dear Father General,
>
> I beg to acknowledge the receipt of Your Paternity's letter in which you express some anxiety in respect of the writings of Father Victor White and ask for information concerning him. I will endeavour to answer as fully as possible and to the best of my ability and knowledge.
>
> I am very happy to be able to reassure Your Paternity, first of all, as to his life and spirit as a religious. From this point of view I have always found him admirable in every way and, if anything,

32 An exchange copy for *Blackfriars* was in the library of the London priory.

33 Writing to Jung, White refers to "the vicious attack on you and me by Padre Gemelli (blue-eyed boy of your hero the Pope!)", 25 Aug. 1956.

34 Years later Greene spoke of this episode in conversation with Pope Paul VI: " 'Who condemned it?' 'Cardinal Pizzardo.' He repeated the name with a wry smile and added 'Mr Greene, some parts of your books are certain to offend some Catholics, but you should pay no attention to that.' " (Norman Sherry, *The Life of Graham Greene, Vol. 2, 1939–1955*. London: Jonathan Cape, 1994, pp. 42–3).

increasingly so as the years go by. I have had more than one occasion to admire his humble obedience, both during my Provincialate and earlier during my years as Prior at Oxford, and in general his personal life is, as far as I am aware, above criticism.

As to his intelligence, he is endowed above the average. He has a particular gift for teaching as well as for preaching, and he is a most assiduous student. He is regarded as something of an international expert in the field of modern psychology, but at the same time his adherence to and devotion to the *sana doctrina* of St Thomas has long been established and becomes more and more evident with the years. His great desire, for a considerable time past, has been to combine these two interests, trying to sift out what is good in modern psychology and to measure it against a background of Aristotelico-Thomist teaching.

[sentence illegible] . . . he has done complete justice to himself in either.

The former is mostly a collection of essays and lectures directed to very diverse readers and audiences, some to Catholics, some to the general public (as in the case of the broadcast talks included), some to academic societies. But all were meant to be, in one form or another, a critique, favourable or unfavourable, of modern psychological investigations and theories. The book had a limited appeal, but was well received. There was no adverse comment, as far as I was made aware, either from the Hierarchy or from the recognised theologians. The diocesan censorship was effected in the Archdiocese of Birmingham.

The other book is theological. In his opening chapter Father Victor writes: "Those who are acquainted with the opening pages of the *Summa Theologiae* of St Thomas Aquinas will, I hope, recognise to how great an extent my own account depends on his: indeed what follows will be to a large extent a paraphrase or an amplification of the more relevant parts of that opening chapter 'On the Holy Teaching'." I quote this because I believe it truly represents Father Victor's mind and intention in general, however the actual outcome may be estimated. But here again the book in question is, for the most part, a collection of essays and articles already printed in various journals. Yet it was received with notable approval. This book was also given its diocesan imprimatur in the Archdiocese of Birmingham.

His only other publication in permanent form is the translation of and commentary upon St Thomas's letter to Brother John "On How To Study" which originated as an address delivered at an academia in Blackfriars. Of this "The Clergy Review" wrote: "The text of the *De Modo Studendi* with translation needs less than three pages; the rest of the little booklet contains a profound commentary on it . . . It is tempting to quote some of the more telling passages, but the task of selection from so much that is valuable is too difficult".

Except for an article on the psychologist Jung, rather critical in tone, I cannot recall any other recent writings by Father Victor. He is engaged now upon a book, as I understand, but I do not know its content. It will be submitted to me in due course, I need hardly say, for censorship.

In my own judgment, for what it is worth and speaking generally, if Father Victor lays himself open to criticism in his writings this may well arise from an active and penetrating mind reacting, somewhat impatiently at times, against a more passive approach to the understanding of the *sana doctrina*; he feels that St Thomas has much to say to the modern world as such, but that it must be said with cognisance of modern theories and research. It may arise too, I think, from a too ready vocabulary not always subjected to that restraint of expression necessary especially in the written word when matters of grave import are under review. On the other hand I am bound to say that as a lector in formal theology and as a preacher he has received much praise. The year he spent, with Your Paternity's kind approval, in California was so successful from both points of view that the Provincial there has begged that he might be allowed to return for another period. (I felt that, for the time being, I was not able to agree, and it is typical of Father Victor that he accepted this decision with commendable alacrity and obedience.)

No comment, adverse or otherwise, has reached me from the hierarchy or other ecclesiastical authorities in respect of Father Victor. Amongst theologians he is regarded, as far as I know, as of good standing and merit.

Finally while I cannot regret too much that Your Paternity should have been given reason for anxiety, I can at least assure you that in all basic things Father Victor is an excellent religious and Dominican. If it were necessary to offer him correction, I am sure that he would accept the same humbly and even gratefully. I have tried to answer Your Paternity's queries as fully and accurately as I could, and I hope satisfactorily. With profound respect and devotion

Your Paternity's most obedient son in S. Dominic
FR HILARY CARPENTER, O.P.

This response was received by Cardinal Pizzardo on 24 January. Partly reflecting on his own position at this time, White writes:

> The trouble for so many of us converts-in-adolescence is something awfully difficult for you cradle Catholics to understand! The trouble is that, one fine day, we find that we *did* (unconsciously) pose when we became RCs. It is more a matter of *culture*, of our picture-of-the-world, than of religion! We revolted from the whole "protestant-materialist" world and values in which we were brought up: probably threw out the baby with the bath-water. For that we substituted a beautiful, romantic "Ages of Faith", medieval world – perhaps helped by Chesterbelloc [G.B. Shaw's term for G.K. Chesterton and Hilaire Belloc], Gill, Pepler etc. The Church was central in that pretty picture; and after playing with High Anglicanism of course we became Catholics. There was really very little choice in the matter, certainly no idea of choosing thorns rather than roses: it was just the most important part of the picture – and in the "Church" of this picture, we found certainty, security, a consoling ritual, almost EVERYthing. Perhaps we had never had much to do with the "real" Church of the average Catholic, and we never did feel much at home in it. We found "home" in the rather exceptional Catholicism of Blackfriars, Oxford; and were perhaps enamoured of the rather rarefied out-of-this-world "Life of the Spirit".
>
> Of course the fantasy doesn't last: we grow up, see it's phoney: and with the mirage our Church-picture fades too: we feel we just don't belong any more, and some of us "lapse" out as inevitably as we had come in. And to the old picture we *cannot* return, though we'd like to find another vision.
>
> (R. 10.2.58)

By late 1958 he had completed *Soul and Psyche*, the key themes of which were to be his Cadbury lectures. At the invitation of Professor G.W.A. Lampe of the University of Birmingham Theology Department, these were delivered between 16 January and 6 March 1959: "The lectures in Birmingham are being quite well attended and received – so far. And the book thereof has somehow got all the required imprimaturs! I am finding John XXIII such a joy and relief. We must pray hard that this Ecumenical Council really does something – and undoes a lot else" (R. 27.1.59).

At this time White came regularly from Cambridge to London for his Thursday sessions working at the More Clinic and visiting friends like Barbara and Bernard Wall, his publishers Manya Harari and Marjorie Villiers of the Harvill Press, Antonia White, and Catherine Ginsberg. In early 1959 I had two long conversations with him at St Dominic's Priory, Haverstock Hill, about my attempts to understand Jung's *Psychology and Alchemy* and difficulties I was having at school about these and similar interests. The relaxed and friendly reassurance from the smiling priest with cigarette holder was important to me and I started to read his books.

On 17 April 1959 White was in a severe accident on his motor scooter near Peterborough. As Layard wrote to Jung: "The news from Victor White is that he recovers consciousness from time to time but wanders when he talks. What will he be like if he recovers from it I do not know. Will there have been a change. If so in what direction?" (20.5.59.)

As he reflected five months later: "Oh, I HOPE I'm changed all right! It would be pretty futile to be nearly dead and return to ego-less childhood if something wasn't reborn, even if I'm not sure what" (R. 9.10.59).

In the meanwhile Michael Browne had written to White that the Holy See had ordered that sales of *God and the Unconscious* be suspended (23.7.59). Returning to Cambridge from convalescence White replied that *God and the Unconscious* had been out of print for two years but that he would do what he could to prevent a further edition or reimpression (11.8.59). In a memorandum for the new provincial Henry St John he outlined the contractual and other legal issues about the copyright of the book and the problem of sales of translations ending: "It is difficult to plan when one is told nothing about what the trouble is all about; and without even knowing why orders should be given to the *author* to 'take steps' to 'suspend sales' . . . I would like to know where I stand, and conscientiously can stand in the future!" St John replied that in justice White should be officially told just what is considered to be wrong with the book and that if it would be expedient to make such a petition he would energetically back it. In his formally humble brief response to the Master General White kept silent about the problem of translations of the book. Replying to a letter of Henry St John's which cannot be traced, Thomas Garde notes that "Father General is very pleased and edified by Father Victor's excellent dispositions. It seems that the Holy See does not usually give reasons for orders of this kind" (19.9.59). St John's response was brilliant:

> I am forwarding to Fr Victor the M.G.'s very kind words concerning his "edifying dispositions" – I am sure he will be greatly comforted by them. In view of the not unnatural anxiety and worry he has suffered in this matter I have felt justified in assuring him that since he is not to be told what, in the content of his book, has moved the Sacred Congregation to take this action there can be nothing in it even remotely dangerous to his own faith and morals or to those of any of his readers capable of understanding its subject matter. I hope I have judged rightly in saying this.

To White he continues:

> I think you may regard the matter as closed; that the S.C. will forget it and that the M.G. is content to leave it so. Since you have received no warning of any kind concerning further publication on this subject

> and no indication as to matters on which it might be expedient to take extra care when writing about it you are perfectly free to proceed and I am glad that *Soul and Psyche* will soon be appearing, and in case of any possible trouble, glad that the diocesan censorship is Westminster, and that the censor [Charles Davis] is Professor of Dogma at the Cardinal's own seminary. He will not rat in the event of any criticism, which I think however is quite unlikely. I expect you will hear no more of this. You know that you have my fullest support.
> (21.9.59)

Either there was some further move or news of the problems spread slowly, for Eve Lewis wrote to Catherine Ginsberg ten months later: "I am grieved to learn from Dom Oswald [Sumner] that *God and the Unconscious* is to be proscribed and that he is afraid in case the same fate should befall *Soul and Psyche*" (21.7.60). In material not used in the latter book which may refer to these events, White wrote:

> It seems necessary to add that a word of caution should be added for the benefit of a type of reader who seems to be more numerous and influential than might be supposed.[35] The gang-mentality of early adolescence, with its all-black and all-white groups, its undiscriminating loyalties to a gang, a leader or a cause, its simple divisions of mankind into warring parties of those who are *for* and those who are *against*, has an extraordinary persistence into later life. . . . I have found it widely supposed that (in spite of much that I have said to the contrary) I am somehow "for" every form of psychiatry or psychotherapy, and approve all that is done in its name (in sharp contrast to, let us say, Monsignor X., who is notoriously "against" it).

When the Mother Prioress of a contemplative order sent him Jung's September 1959 letter to her about White's illness he replied: "I am rather sad he is in such a self-piteous state about being 'misunderstood' etc. But amused somewhat at his remarks about my not fully disapproving of his work – if he knew half the trouble I've had and am having for approving most of it, even if I don't agree with some of his views. And his work wouldn't have much future if everybody did" (9.10.59).

The last year

White's major scooter accident in April 1959 left him with permanently impaired sight and hearing: "there is no doubt I have learned a lot! But there are a lot of difficulties ahead, both interior and exterior. . . . It may be quite a

35 Gemelli would certainly count as one of these.

time before I can go anywhere unaccompanied, or even cross streets by myself!" (R. 21.1.59). Fortunately his mental recovery was complete and he was able to dictate for transcription by his friend Donald Nicholl parts of his translation of the first section of the new edition of Aquinas's *Summa Theologiae* and write with some difficulty. In September he suffered acute abdominal pains and was admitted to Addenbrookes hospital in Cambridge for two weeks. This problem seemed to clear up. But he was in hospital again for an operation 20 January to 11 February 1960. The stomach cancer was now irreversible and his medical notes for 11 March say that "he is going down hill . . . there is nothing further we can do. He is aware of his condition".

He had been due to speak at a joint meeting of the Society of Analytical Psychology and the Analytical Psychology Club on 21 January 1960 but was too ill to attend. In a manuscript note to his contribution "The Self"[36] he writes: "I might say that this is my very first attempt at anything like a public appearance since – perhaps rather significantly – a gust of wind blew me off my scooter onto my skull – and cracked it. And I could not possibly want this first attempt at public speaking to be anywhere else". He had the satisfaction of seeing *Soul and Psyche* published in February.

For the last six or eight weeks of his life White was persuaded by Catherine Ginsberg to move from the North London Dominican priory in Hampstead to Harrowby Court in Kensington. It is unclear when she and White first met. She was associated with The Open Way, a charitable trust founded in 1957 to further mental health education developed by the psychiatrist Dr Graham Howe: Toni Sussmann was honorary associate director and R.D. Laing a member of the advisory council. Dr Margaret Grant had invited Ginsberg to help her run a therapeutic community in Rosary Gardens in London. Some of this group moved to flats in Harrowby Court and under Ginsberg's leadership this became the Fabyc community (Family by Choice), and as members grew considerably they moved to their present location at Kew in Surrey. White was nursed by Christina Megroz in Flat 5. She recalled that she did not know how Ginsberg persuaded White and his superior that this was the best plan and that there were difficulties. Ginsberg was a Catholic convert of forceful and unorthodox ideas who frequently challenged White to demanding arguments. It was Megroz's impression that White felt lonely and at times may have regretted leaving the priory.[37]

At some point after his accident it seems that, according to Richard Ingram O.P., Eve Lewis made a "detour" to visit Jung and urge him, without

36 This appeared as "Theological Reflections", *The Journal of Analytical Psychology*, Vol. 5, No. 2, 1960, pp. 147–54.

37 Christina Megroz to AC 27 March 1998 and 22 August 2004. Michael Statham provided copies of relevant materials from Catherine Ginsberg's letters and papers.

success, to contact White.[38] The building of bridges came with the letter in July 1959 to Jung from the Mother Prioress of a contemplative order who had known White since the late 1940s. She sent Jung's September reply to White – "You are certainly privileged to have (these days) this autograph letter from the old man" (9.10.59). With White's letter of thanks about this a week later the correspondence had resumed, though not without some continued misunderstandings. His friend from wartime Oxford, the Jungian analyst F. Elkisch, visited him at Harrowby Court and recalled White saying: "Look, Elk, the letter I got from Jung: listen, he said, and read a few lines which I have forgotten but which to me in no way sounded offensive: We are friends, close friends, how could he write like this? . . . . I feel Father Victor and Jung had lived for so long on different levels that it was understandable when the new common platform was a bit slippery on occasions" (R. 7.10.76).

White died on 22 May 1960. Lucid until the end, his last words were, "God, take me". After the funeral at St Dominic's in London he was buried at Woodchester where he had entered the order 36 years earlier. In a subsequent letter Elkisch wrote that somewhere he had read words which he never forgets in which Jung said: "I have a huge correspondence, see innumerable people but have only two real friends with whom I can speak about my own difficulties; the one is Erich Neumann and he lives in Israel and the other is Father Victor White in England" (R. 29.10.76).

38 The former editor of the *Journal of Analytical Psychology* and friend of Lewis, Judith Hubback, confirmed that this sounded very likely (May 2005).

APPENDIX 3

JUNG'S "GNOSEOLOGICAL NOTE"[1]

Below is the "gnoseological note" to which Jung refers in his letter of 5 Oct. 1945. Originally printed in Beatrice Hinkle's translation of *Wandlungen und Symbole der Libido*, Part II, Chapter V, "Symbolism of the Mother and of Rebirth,"[2] it sums up Jung's theory of cognition, insofar as he had developed it in 1912.[3]

Here it is not to be forgotten we are moving entirely in the territory of psychology, which in no way is allied to transcendentalism, either in positive or negative relation. It is a question here of a relentless fulfillment of the standpoint of the theory of cognition, established by Kant, not merely for the theory but, what is more important, for the practice. One should avoid

1 Taken from *The Psychology of the Unconscious. A Study of the Transformation and Symbolisms of the Libido*. (Trans. Beatrice Hinkle. New York: Moffat Yard, 1919; London: Kegan Paul, Trench, Trubner, 1921), p. 307, nn. 42. (Cf. Jung, 5 Oct. 1945, pp. 6, 7 and notes.)

2 The paragraph to which the note belongs reads in its entirety: "The religious myth meets us here as one of the greatest and most significant human institutions which, despite misleading symbols, nevertheless gives man assurance and strength, so that he may not be overwhelmed by the monsters of the universe. The symbol, considered from the standpoint of actual truth, is misleading indeed, but it is psychologically true *[42]*, because it was and is the bridge to all the greatest achievements of humanity" (*Psychology of the Unconscious*, 1921, op. cit., p. 144).

3 Jung's later extensively revised version of this work, titled *Symbole der Wandlung* (CW 5, *Symbols of Transformation*), still includes the paragraph (§343) to which this footnote once belonged. In place of the original note, however, a footnote at the end of the paragraph now refers to a passage in *Energetik* 1928, cryptically directing the reader: "Cf 'On Psychic Energy', the Swiss edition, pp. 80ff." The Swiss edition of *Energetik* 1928 is now nearly inaccessible, even in Switzerland. The passage may be found, however, in CW 8, *Structure and Dynamics*, §91–93. Comparison of this passage with the "gnoseological note" reveals some of the ways Jung's thinking about the psyche's symbol-making power continued to evolve in the decades after his break with Freud.

playing with the infantile image of the world,[4] because all this tends only to separate man from his essential and highest ethical goal, moral autonomy. The religious symbol should be retained after the inevitable obliteration of certain antiquated fragments, as postulate or as transcendent theory, and also as taught in precepts, but is to be filled with new meaning according to the demands of the culture of the present day. But this theory must not become for the "adult" a positive creed, an illusion, which causes reality to appear to him in a false light. Just as man is a dual being, having an intellectual and an animal nature, so does he appear to need two forms of reality, the reality of culture, that is, the symbolic transcendent theory, and the reality of nature, which corresponds to our conception of the "true reality". In the same measure that the true reality is merely a figurative interpretation of the appreciation of reality, the religious symbolic theory is merely a figurative interpretation of certain endopsychic apperceptions. But one very essential difference is that a transcendental support, independent in duration and condition, is assured to the transubjective reality through the best conceivable guarantees, while for the psychologic phenomena a transcendental support of subjective limitation and weakness must be recognized as a result of compelling empirical data. Therefore true reality is one that is relatively universally valid; the psychologic reality, on the contrary, is merely a functional phenomenon contained in an epoch of human civilization. Thus does it appear today from the best informed empirical standpoint. If, however, the psychologic were divested of its character of a biologic epiphenomenon in a manner neither known nor expected by me, and thereby was given the place of a physical entity, then the psychologic reality would be resolved into the true reality; or much more, it would be reversed, because the psychologic would lay claim to a greater worth, for the ultimate theory, because of its directness.

4 Jung's original text: "Man soll auch nicht mehr dergleichen tun und infantiles Weltbild spielen wollen" (*Wandlungen*, 1912, p. 276n). A clearer translation might be: "One must not behave, either, as if it were still possible to play at an infantile image of the world" (ACL).

APPENDIX 4

SOME NOTES ON *PSYCHOLOGIE UND ALCHEMIE*[1]

by Victor White

with responses by Barbara Hannah and Marie-Louise von Franz

p. 37 [§24, p.20][2] I suggest that the "palliative Reaktion" of Probabilism[3] was called into being through forgetfulness of the traditional doctrine of SS. Paul, Augustine, Thomas Aquinas etc. that fallen man "non potest non peccare".[4] The original and authentic Catholic doctrine is far from perfectionist and calls for no such subterfuges. But as a Dominican I may be prejudiced about this![5] Cf. "Dictionnaire de Théologie catholique" s.v. "Probabilisme" by T. Deman (now of Friburg, Suisse).

p. 46 [§31, p.26] "Vier hat die Bedeutung"[6].... Is there not much evidence that the "Three" is traditionally often the symbol of the Divine, the "Four" of the Human (cf. A. Ehrhardt, "Vir

1 Typed sheets enclosed with White's letter of 23 June 1946.

2 White's page numbers refer to the first edition of *Psychologie und Alchemie* (Zürich: Rascher Verlag, 1944). Bracketed numbers, following, refer to the corresponding paragraph and page numbers, current English edition, CW 12.

3 A form of moral reasoning favored by both Dominicans and Jesuits in the Counter-Reformation, later falling into disrepute because it tended toward laxism, probabilism is defined as "the system of moral theology based on the principle that, if the licitness or illicitness of an action is in doubt, it is lawful to follow a solidly probable opinion favoring liberty, even though the opposing opinion, favoring the law, be more probable" (*ODCC*, pp. 1127f).

4 "is unable not to sin."

5 A Spanish Dominican, Bartolomeo Medina, O.P., gave Probabilism its classical formulation in the sixteenth century.

6 "Four signifies . . .". In Hull's translation: "The number three is not a natural expression of wholeness, since four represents the minimum number of determinants in a whole judgment" (CW 12, *Psych. & Alch.*, §31, p. 26).

bonus quadrato lapidi comparatur",[7] Harvard Theological Review, July 1945)? These do of course stand in a Masc.-Fem., Geistig-physisch[8] relationship. Theologically considered the "Unsicherheit" and "Schwanken"[9] between "3" and "4" seem often to represent the difficulty in differentiating the Human from the Divine which is the fruit of the Tree of Knowledge ("eritis sicut dii").[10]

p. 58 [§41, p.35] "zwar von der Kirche verboten".[11] I cannot find any evidence at all for this; only, as in a Bull of John XXII, warning against swindling under cover of alchemy. I understand (but have not personally been able to trace the evidence) that the plea of the "advocatus diaboli"[12] that Vincent Ferrer[13] had practised alchemy was formally rejected as an obstacle to his canonisation. St. Thomas Aq., in his commentary on Aristotle's Meteorology, counts alchemy among the "verae scientiae",[14] though undoubtedly considering alchemy from its "physical" aspect as the transmutation of metals. The remarkable thing seems to be that in an age which was ever heresy-hunting, alchemy was not ever (so far as I can discover) regarded as an indictable offence before the Inquisition. But perhaps I have some prejudice here!

p. 85 [§60, p.52] "Für die Schwachen im Geiste ist es auch

7 "The good man resembles the square stone." (Journal article earlier mentioned by White, 1 April 1946, p. 31 and note.)

8 spiritual-physical. 9 "uncertainty", "wavering."

10 "you will be like God" (Genesis 3.5).

11 "forbidden, to be sure, by the church." (A phrase missing from the English text of the revised edition of *Psych. & Alch*, but its sense is there.) Later White admitted to Jung that he had found documents from Dominican General Chapters in the thirteenth and fourteenth century, strictly forbidding to Dominicans the study and practice of alchemy (White, 13 Oct. 1946, p. 45).

12 "devil's advocate."

13 Vincent Ferrer, O.P. (1350–1419): French Dominican priest and missionary, canonized in 1455.

14 "true sciences."

besser so."[15] This raises great *practical* difficulties in my mind, which I hope very much to be able to ask about. Is it not these "Schwachen im Geiste" who stand in greatest need of analysis?

pp. 163–4 [§192, p.152] "Die Häresie dieses Gedankens . . ."[16] Understood (as I think a Catholic alchemist or mystic would understand it) as a realisation in consciousness of the Divine Generation immanent in nature and in the soul, this would hardly be "Häresie" but a commonplace corollary of the doctrine of the soul as "Imago Trinitatis".[17] It is implicit in St. Augustine's "De Trinitate" and St. Thomas's "De Imagine". Cf. A. Gardeil, "La Structure de l'Ame et l'Experience mystique".[18]

p. 273 [§298?, p.197] "ist auch die Bibel auf dem Index" ??? !!![19]

15 "And for the weak in spirit [mind], it is better so." The sentence appears at the end of a long paragraph by Jung, which concludes, in Hull's translation: "But to let the unconscious go its own way and to experience it as a reality is something that exceeds the courage and capacity of the average European. He prefers simply not to understand the problem. For the spiritually weak-kneed this is the better course, since the thing is not without its dangers" (CW 12, *Psych. & Alch.*, §60, p. 52).

16 "The heresy of this thought . . .". The English version lacks this phrase. But in Jung's discussion of the feminine symbology associated with the third Person of the Trinity, we read: "It was in keeping with this psychological fact that the Holy Ghost should be heretically interpreted as Sophia, for he was the mediator of birth in the flesh, who enabled the deity to shine forth in the darkness of the world" (Ibid., §192, pp. 144f).

17 "image of the Trinity."

18 "The Structure of the Soul and Mystical Experience."

19 "the Bible, too, is on the Index" (cf. Wolff, 18 July 1946, p. 37 and note). This hyperbolic expression, which renders White speechless, does not appear in later editions of *Psych. & Alch.*, either German or English. White's amazed reaction (with von Franz quietly in agreement) may have led Jung to drop it. In the first edition, the passage surrounding Plate 94, *"Der Aetna 'Gelat et ardet'"* ["Mt. Etna 'Freezes and burns'"], reads, in part, *"Nicht vergebens wurde der vierte und den dreien geschieden und ins Reich des ewigen Feuers verwiesen. Aber sagt nicht ein unkanonisches Herrenwort: 'Wer mir nahe ist, ist nahe dem Feuer'? (Vgl. Abb.58 ["Christus als Feuerquelle mit den 'flammenden Wundmalen"].) Solche furchtbaren Zweideutigkeiten sind nichts für erwachsene Kinder; deshalb hat man schon den alten Heraklit den 'dunkeln' genannt, weil er zu deutliche Sachen sagte und das Leben selber ein 'ewig lebendes Feuer' nannte. Deshalb gibt es nicht-kanonische Logia für Hellhörige, und deshalb – last not least – ist auch die Bibel auf dem Index"* (*Psych. & Alch*, 1944, p. 273). "Not in vain were the fourth and the three separated and banished into the realm of everlasting fire. But is there not a noncanonical saying of the Lord, 'Whoever is near to me is near to the fire'?" (Cf. Plate 58 [Christ as source of the fire with 'flaming wound-marks'.] Such terrible ambiguities are not for grown-up children; for this reason, in old Heraclitus' day he, too, was called 'the dark one,' because he said things too clearly and called life itself 'an ever-living fire.' That is why there are noncanonical sayings, for those who have ears to hear, and that is why – last but not

p. 291 [p.212] (Abb. 104)[20]	"Doppelaspekt"?[21] I suggest that the Holy Ghost is also represented (by the wings).
p. 293 [p.213] (Abb. 105)	I am not sure why this is called "als Personifikation des Sternhimmels".[22] It is a pretty commonplace motif in iconography – the B. Virgin as "woman clothed with the sun, etc." in Apocalypse, 12.1ff.
p. 294 [§322, p.214]	"ketzerische"?[23] Surely, very orthodox for a Catholic?
p. 333 [§342ff, pp.242ff]	"Die Projektion psychischer Inhalte". The whole of this section seems well summarised in the oft-quoted alchemical "Hermetic Enigma" – "Unless you disembody the bodies, and embody those without bodies, nothing will occur" (cf. Sherwood Taylor, "Origins of Greek Alchemy" in "Ambix" No.1, p.46).[24]
pp. 412 [§414ff, pp.306ff]	This contrast between the "christliche" and "heidnische" Projektion[25] seem altogether too simpliste. The immanence of the Mystery in nature, and its discoverableness there, is essentially Christian (cf. John 1 and Romans 1), while the crudest anthropomorphism is characteristic of much "heathendom". More important, is it not rather misleading to use the term "projection" of "faith"? The former is an unconscious process, "nie gemacht, sondern geschieht"[26] (p. 336); the faith of the

least – the Bible, too, is on the Index" [trans. ACL]. The next paragraph deals with more fire-imagery, the apocalypse of Enoch (Cf. CW 12, *Psych. & Alch.*, §298, p. 197.)

20 *Abbildung:* plate (illustration).

21 "double aspect." The image in the illustration has two faces, and Jung's original caption for this figure refers to "God's double aspect." White's comment, that the presence of wings implies the Holy Spirit, seems to have led to a minor revision in the English edition, where the caption now reads "God as Father and Logos creating the zodiac" (Ibid., p. 212, fig. 104). In the German edition, White's suggestion was fully adopted. There the revised caption reads: "Gott als Trinität, den Tierkreis schaffend" [God as Trinity, creating the Zodiac] (GW 12, *Psych. & Alch.*, Plate 104, p. 248).

22 "as personification of the starry sky."

23 heretical. Jung had written: *"Zwar hat der Dichter in Guillaume die ketzerische Wahrheit wohl geahnt, als er dem König eine Frau Königin, die auf dem erdbraunen Kristall sitzt, beigab"* ["To be sure, the poet in Guillaume seems to have guessed the heretical truth, when he provided the King with a Queen, seated on the earth-brown crystal"] (GW 12, §322, p. 251).

24 Cf. White, 23 Oct. 1945, p. 21 and notes.

25 "Christian", "heathen projection."

26 "never made, but occurring."

believer, on the contrary, is "gemacht", conscious and voluntary – the willing opening of the mind to the Unseen (non visum, non scitum[27], according to Aquinas) in which the salus humana[28] is to be found. I think there are certain ambiguities in the use of the word "projection" which are the source of many misunderstandings of Analytical Psychology.

p. 414 [§416, pp.307f] I cannot see the justification for the "dagegen"[29] here. For Christian and Alchemist alike, human nature is the microcosm; for the Christian this microcosm is assumed to the Godhead in the Incarnation. Christ likewise becomes "tote materie"[30] and descends "in die Finsternisse";[31] and in the conformation of man to Him the whole creation is redeemed (cf. Romans, 8, 22). Would not the very "participation mystique" of the alchemist have prevented his making this distinction between the redemption of matter and the redemption of himself? The alchemists themselves seem to have seen no such contrast between their "opus" and the "opus Christi", but rather complete continuity. I cannot see on what grounds we can gainsay them. For neither Christian nor Alchemist is the "causa principalis" of the "opus" man but God; for both it is man – the human "ego" which seems to be the "Zuerlösende".[32]

p. 419 [§417, p.308] ". . . so wäre es Christus gewesen".[33] But this is precisely what the Pauline-Catholic doctrine of the Mystical Body would maintain. (Now I live, no not I, but Christ liveth in me.)

27 unseen, unknown. 28 human health (salvation).

29 "in contrast." "The Christian projection differs from all these manifestations of the mystery of redemption and transformation by reason of the historical and personal figure of Jesus. The mythical event incarnates itself in him and so enters the realm of world history as a unique historical and mystical phenomenon" (CW12, §416, pp. 307f).

30 "dead matter." 31 "into the dark places." 32 "that which shall be redeemed."

33 "so it would have been Christ." In Hull's translation: "Were such an approximation to occur, then Christ would have re-established himself in the believer and replaced the latter's personality" (Ibid., §417, p. 308).

p. 419 [§417, p.309]	It is very doubtful if "immolatio" for Aquinas can mean just "Opfer", at least in the sense of "offering" or even "sacrifice"; though this has been much disputed. It seems rather to mean "slaying". For Aquinas, the Mass *is* properly a "sacrifice", but it is an "immolatio" only representatively and "effective".
p. 422 [p.311] (Abb.159)	Surely just a Baptism?
p. 424 [§419, p.312]	I am afraid "dignatus est" is a deponent, not a passive, verb. It means "deign" (? gerühen),[34] hardly "für würdig sich halten").[35]
p. 424 [§420, p.312]	"Dieser Gedanke ist durchaus unchristlich".[36] But "durchaus katholisch",[37] and an important aspect of transubstantiation!
p. 509 [§462, p.373ff]	I am afraid this "ältere pseudoplatonische Schrift"[38] will never be found. Bonus[39] has evidently misread the celebrated passage in Augustine's "Confessiones", lib. VII.cap.9.[40]
pp. 536 [§480, pp.396ff]	I have not seen this curious document of Melchior's Form der Messe;[41] but I think that in some important particulars it is misinterpreted. It follows the quite regular form for

34 White's spelling error, for *geruhen*, to deign.

35 "to consider oneself worthy." This error was corrected in the English edition but not in the German, where the passage still reads: *" 'qui harmonitatis nostrae fieri dignatus est particeps' (der du dich für würdig gehalten hast, unserer Menschheit teilhaftig zu werden)"* ["who hast held thyself worthy to become a partaker in our humanity" – trans. ACL] (GW 12, *Psych. & Alch.*, §419, p. 359).

36 "This thought is entirely unchristian." The paragraph, in Hull's translation, states: "By pronouncing the consecrating words that bring about the transformation, the priest redeems the bread and wine from their elemental imperfection as created things. This idea is quite unchristian – it is alchemical" (CW 12, *Psych. & Alch.*, §420, p. 312).

37 "completely Catholic."

38 "older pseudoplatonic document."

39 Petrus Bonus, fourteenth-century alchemist, Ferrara. (Cf. CW 12, *Psych & Alch.*, §462, pp. 373ff, esp. n. 96.)

40 In the Confessions (Book 7, ch. 9) Augustine outlines several parallels between Platonic and Christian thought, but then observes that he has never known a Platonist who would accept the incarnation ("the Word was made flesh"), much less the crucifixion. Petrus Bonus concludes, on the contrary (perhaps after misunderstanding Augustine's analysis), that Plato himself wrote the opening of the fourth Gospel: "In like manner Plato, writing of alchemical matters, wrote a gospel which was completed long after by John the Evangelist. Plato wrote the opening verses from 'In the beginning was the Word' to 'There was a man sent from God' "(CW12, §462, p. 375).

41 *The Form of the Mass.*

the "Proper" (i.e. variable parts) of the Mass such as will be found in any Missal, from which the "Common" (invariable parts) of the Mass are always excluded, being printed elsewhere in the Missal. This does not mean that the Creed, Consecration etc. were intended to be omitted, any more than the same could be said of the "Proper" of any Mass in the Missal, nor that Melchior expected the Post-Communio to follow directly on the Secreta, as is suggested on p.546 [§486ff, p 404]. Indeed, there could hardly be a Postcommunio without Communio!

The only additional feature which will not be found in a modern Missal is the "farced Kyrie", based on the familiar "Kyrie, Fons Bonitatis".[42] But the "farced Kyrie" (in which a syllable was found to fit each pneum or note in the music) was quite regular in the Middle Ages, and only later forbidden.

"Sequentia evangeli"[43], strangely, will not mean "Nach dem Evangelium" and "wo das Credo folgt"[44] – unless I am very much mistaken. The "Sequentia" is the regular name for a hymn sung *after* the Epistle and Gradual and *before* the Gospel; I doubt if this is an exception. The choice of Luke X for the Gospel is probably prompted by the fact that this is also the Gospel for the feast of the Assumption – the feast of the glorification of the Feminine Body.

The text is indeed "geschmacklos"[45], but I think hardly so irregular and heterodox as is here suggested. The most irregular feature is in the picture (Abb.216)[p.397]: there is Host and Paten on the Altar, but no chalice, and the priest has both the book and the maniple at the wrong side: wrong, that is to say, in the print, but presumably not in the block. I am not quite clear why the figure on the left is

42 "Lord, Fount of Lovingkindness." 43 "Sequence of the Gospel."
44 after the Gospel . . . where the Creed follows (CW 12, §481, p. 398). 45 tasteless.

described as "Die Erde, das Mercuriuskind säugend".[46] In Melchior's mind it is surely the "in lucem gentium Maria divinitus orta" suckling the "Patris Verbum"?[47]

Comments on Father White's notes

M.L.v.F. & J.B.H.[48]

p. 37. We think this could be ignored, for probabilism goes further towards a real acceptance of evil. But one could also add a note, such as: "As Father White points out, the original Catholic doctrine (SS. Paul, Augustine, Thomas Aquinas, etc) contained other efforts to help man in this respect, for fallen man 'non potest non peccare'.[49] But this does not really free a sensitive conscience for the fact remains that all sin is regarded as entirely reprehensible".

p. 46. This is quite interesting but we think you already have often said the main part in other places.

p. 58. M.L.v.F. says "von Kirche verboten – nur insoweit die Alchemie magische Proceduren (Daemonbeschwörungen etc) miteinschloss, welche aber eben untrennbar mit ihr verbunden sind. (Father White hat also recht aber nicht wirklich.)"[50]

p. 85. Emma & I had a lot of trouble in translating "Schwachen im Geiste", & in the end decided on "mediocre minds". Perhaps he could swallow

46 "The earth, suckling the child Mercury." This caption was not altered.

47 "Mary divinely arisen to give light to the nations," "Word of the Father."

48 Undated document, handwritten by Juliet Barbara Hannah on behalf of herself and Marie-Louise von Franz, recording their evaluation of White's remarks about the first edition of *Psychologie und Alchemie*. Their responses, which reflect some consultation also with Emma Jung, were helpful to Jung in deciding which of White's suggestions, if any, to incorporate in the second edition. (Permission to publish this document was kindly given on 28 August 2003 by Dr. Emmanuel Kennedy and Dr. Hansueli Etter, on behalf of the Stiftung für Jung'sche Psychologie, literary executors for Juliet Barbara Hannah and Marie-Louise von Franz.)

49 "is unable not to sin."

50 "forbidden by the Church – only insofar as alchemy included magical procedures (invoking of demons, etc.), which however were inseparably associated with it. (Father White is therefore right, but not really.)" (Trans. ACL.)

it like that? Every parson I ever knew rose like a fish to the charm of supporting the *weak*!

p. 162–4. I have translated "erzeugen" as "engendered";' but perhaps one should say "actually produced" to give the more active sense? Father White seems to have over-looked this active & realistic nuance which gives the heretical note. We are both for ignoring him here.

p. 273. This is beyond us. Please decide yourself!

p. 291 (Abb. 104). Here he seems to be right. Shall I omit "double aspect"?

p. 293 (Abb. 105). There also seems something to be said for his comment here. Should I soften into "The Virgin with the starry heavens" (Res.XII, ff)".

p. 294. We are both for ignoring.

p. 333. We are neither of us much impressed by the Ambix quotation & therefore vote for ignoring!

pp. 412. Neither of us agree with his "simplistic" remark, but it is difficult to see what he means because apparently he has not understood what you mean by projection. What he says about the projection of faith seems quite wrong, presumably because he takes the projected content as an absolute reality & then mixes it up with attitude? M-L v.F. suggests that, if you want to make it clearer for such people, a footnote might be added dividing the Church[1)], alchemistic[2)] & psychological[3)] standpoints. Of course only you could do this but she suggests roughly: 1) Mystery of God can be in nature but separable from it. 2) Mystery is nature itself. 3) Projection of soul into nature & therefore separable & not separable.

p. 414. Both of us think he has misunderstood here, & vote for ignoring. The important points you have dealt with elsewhere in same book.

p. 419. 1) Father White seems to have over-looked the nuance of Christ as causa efficiens & man as causa efficiens? One could perhaps make it clearer by saying:

"Were such an assimilation to take place at all, it would be the work of Christ himself who had reappeared . . . etc."?

p. 419. 2) Most of this falls away in the English because I have not tried to translate (Opferung). M-L.v.F.

suggests softening by changing "not a real immolatio" to: "Not an immolatio in every sense of the word but only representative & effective,[1)] an image representing" . . . etc.? & perhaps with a footnote [1)] I owe this formulation to Father White.?

p. 422 (Abb.154). M-L.v.F. thinks he is right here. Perhaps it could be changed to "Ecclesiastical representation of baptism which bears a striking ressemblance to the alchemistic marriage bath".?

p. 424. 1) This has already been altered & passed by you. There is nothing he could object to now.[51]

p. 424. 2) Perhaps this could be made clearer by saying: "*The accentuation of this thought is not at all Xtian*" etc.?[52]

p. 509. M-L v.F. will look up this St. Augustine reference when she returns to Zürich.

p. 536ff. p. 538 (top) M-L.v.F. thinks Father White is right in his translation of "Sequentia evangelii" & therefore could alter to: "Before the gospel is read, Melchior has an Ave" . . . etc.?[53]

p. 544 (first paragraph).[54] M-L.v.F. thinks it might be better to omit "aber Consecratio fehlt"[55] & change to:

"Die Wandlung entspricht sachlich die Regeneration des Aethiopiers, und ist auch enthalten in der Mariensequenz 'Ave praeclara' als ein Geheimnis" etc.?[56]

She cannot be sure about this whole suggestion until she compares it with the text which she will do when she returns to Zürich.

p. 537. Abb. 216 would add "represented as the Virgin Mary with child."[57]

51 The passage was not changed in the second German edition. The English edition, however, borrows this translation from the Book of Common Prayer: "who vouchsafed to become partaker of our humanity" (CW 12, *Psych & Alch.*, §419, p. 312).

52 Passage was reprinted unchanged.

53 Passage was reprinted unchanged.

54 (Cf. CW 12, §486, p. 404.) This suggestion, not directly prompted by White's notes, presumably arose when von Franz discovered the discrepancy during her study of White's remarks about Melchior (p. 342, above). Jung decided against her, however; the passage was reprinted unchanged.

55 "but the Consecration is lacking."

56 "The transformation concretely represents the regeneration of the Ethiopian, and is also contained in the Mary-sequence 'Hail shining one' as a secret" etc.

57 The caption was reprinted unchanged.

APPENDIX 5

WHITE'S FOOTNOTE ON GOOD AND EVIL

In this footnote, added in 1952 to his lecture, "The Frontiers of Theology and Psychology," which became Chapter V of *God and the Unconscious* (orig. pub. 1952; Spring ed., 1982, pp. 75f), White lays out the traditional position of the Catholic Church on the problem of evil. The paragraph breaks have been added for legibility.

Since Jung's essay on the Trinity was written the discussion on the nature of good and evil has been elaborated with some warmth by both parties, e.g., by the present writer in *Dominican Studies*, Vol. II, 1949, p. 399, and at length by Jung in *Aion* (1951), pp. 69ff. So far, the discussion appears to have generated more heat than light – an indication that the issues at stake may prove to be of vital importance, and that some strong resistances are yet to be overcome before understanding is to be reached.

Of the position of traditional Catholic thought as formulated by Aquinas, the following may be briefly noted:

(1) There is no formal dogma of the Church on the subject.
(2) But inasmuch as the meaning of basic human words, and those indicative of fundamental human values, is at stake, the matter cannot be lightly dismissed as an academic logomachy.
(3) As Jung himself shows in *Aion*, the conception of evil as a privation of good is asserted by the Fathers of both East and West.
(4) They do not deny, as might a "Christian Scientist", the *reality* of evil (on the contrary they vigorously affirm it); their concern is with the further question: In what does that reality consist? Or, What is it that constitutes *x* to be "evil" and not "good"?
(5) Their answer is that it is always the *absence* (the *privatio*, not the negation) of a *real* good from a *real* subject – evil has no positive existence of itself – as blindness is real (but consists in the *absence* of sight from a real man) or darkness is real (but consists in the absence of light).
(6) This *absence* may indeed *result from* a presence (as the presence of a cataract causes the absence of sight – and the "better" the cataract the "worse" the sight) but does not consist in it.

(7) This conception is no *a priori* "metaphysic", but is empirically verifiable by an *analysis of meaning* whenever the words "good", "evil", or their equivalents are used.

Jung has our keenest support and sympathy in deploring the minimizing of evil which leads to its repression, with its devastating results for the individual psyche and for society; but we are unable to find evidence that the conception of the *privatio boni* has contributed to this. On the other hand, we are unable to find any intelligible, let alone desirable, meaning in such fundamental Jungian conceptions as the "assimilation of the shadow" if they are not to be understood as the supplying of some absent good (e.g., consciousness) to what is essentially valuable and of itself "good".

APPENDIX 6[1]

by Victor White

If ever there were grist for the Jungian mill it was, one might suppose, the Book of Job. It can be read almost as a paradigm of the 'integration process' as Jung himself has repeatedly described it. For here we have a man 'perfect and upright, fearing God and eschewing evil' – as well he might, never having experienced it, and abounding in cosy piety and worldly prosperity. He has, as Satan points out, 'a fence about him, and his house, and his substance'. Anybody can be 'good' in such narrow, sheltered confines as these; but he can hardly be a grown-up man, let alone a hero, a prototype of the way of salvation through crucifixion and resurrection. Any psychologist should know he is heading for a crash. Any theologian should know that such easy and complacent virtue cannot continue long in this post-lapsarian world. Job's professed love for God – and God's for him – must grow from this agreeable but infantile and unconscious, autoerotic phase. Job's idol of a merely intelligible and amiable God must be smashed: he must learn the lesson which the New Testament writers were to see it was the function of the Old Testament heroes to teach: that man's righteousness before God is not wrought by moral works without 'faith in the Absurd', the Unseen and the Unknown. So the psychologically and theologically inevitable happens: Job's fences are down; evils rush in. His sufferings are truly frightful, but they are also symptoms; and the loss of his domesticated animals and his children (concerning whose youthful high spirits he had been inordinately anxious), the chidings of the *anima* (his wife), and the psychosomatic eruptions (his boils) add up to a clear clinical picture. He cannot cope. He retires to the dunghill, the libido is introverted, and he is in the grips of intense neurotic depression and conflict.

The conversation with the three 'friends' begins, and goes on and on. Job suffers, they say, *ergo* he is morally guilty. Job knows he has not sinned, and morally he has not; but unconsciously he has disregarded the natural laws

1 Reprinted from *Blackfriars*, Vol. 36, No. 420 (March 1955), with kind permission of Fr. Fergus Kerr, for *New Blackfriars*.

which require that a man must grow up, and that his physical, psychological and spiritual growth should keep pace with one another. He has forgotten (or has not realized) that the Author of moral commandments and legal covenants is also the Author of man's physical, animal and psychological nature, and that its laws and demands cannot be disregarded with impunity. He oscillates miserably between confidence in Yahweh and ironic blasphemy (God is just not what he had supposed); he is overwhelmed with perplexity and self-pity. Job and his friends are all right, and all wrong: the problem is simply insoluble on the conscious level of rational argument about moral merit, and on the supposition that God is nothing but an indulgent Daddy or an equal party in commutative justice.

Then comes Elihu, the *fourth* friend (this surely should have appealed to Jung). He is young, inferior, hitherto silent and repressed; yet he claims to have (what the talkative three had quite overlooked) the *Spirit* of the Lord. He is something of an intuitive, a poet. He is sick of all this argument without issue, and must break down its fatal assumption of the competence of consciousness to resolve it. Like any skilful analyst (though certainly he preaches overmuch) he indeed grants what he can of the conscious convictions and values of his hearers; but he opens to them gradually another point of view: he stresses the vastness and incomprehensibility of God and the limitations of the conscious human standpoint: he 'will not level God with man' (32, 21). He silences the rationalistic and moralistic chatter by recalling that 'there is a *spirit* in man; and an *inspiration* of the Almighty gives him understanding' (32, 8). There are ways of God that are beyond wordy explanations (33, 13); but 'by a *dream*, in a *vision* by night, when deep sleep falleth upon men and they are sleeping in their beds; then he openeth the ears of men, and teaching instructeth them what they are to learn, that he may withdraw a man from what he is doing, and may deliver him from pride' (33, 15–17). (How could Jung have missed that?) It is from the unconscious and its 'royal road' that deliverance must come, and sure enough it does. The emotional tensions are transformed, in typically Jungian fashion, into the terrible, numinous but healing symbol of Yahweh in the whirlwind: a mandala of dynamic spirit. The amiable, comprehensible maker of covenants with Israel, the intelligible author and rewarder of the moral law, is *also* the *mysterium tremendum*, the Lord and Creator of the irrational and brute creation as well as of man's high ethical aspirations. In the vision Job also beholds Behemoth, the clumsy, mighty irrational brute power beneath which he had squirmed; and he learns that precisely this 'evil' is 'the chief of the ways of God'. So the vision unites the opposites, the former evil is integrated into the totality of the Self; the 'captivity' of Job is 'turned', he emerges from the ordeal the adult man Yahweh had repeatedly urged him to be, and 'with twice as much as he had before'.

It has all gone according to schedule: one might almost think that the author had consulted Jung's psychological treatises before writing it. And one might suppose that Dr Jung would be very pleased. But he is not pleased at all: **[he is very – we might say blindly – angry. So blindly that]**[2] he gives us a reading of Job no more subtle than that of Bernard Shaw's Black Girl. Jung identifies himself wholly with Job in his sufferings and with his sense of being treated abominably and insanely. His sufferings are just cruel sufferings and in no wise symptoms; only Yahweh is to blame for them. When Elihu appears, it is not at all as a mediator of the unconscious, but just as one heartless idiot more to maintain that Yahweh cannot, in spite of reason and experience, be wrong. (Yet this 'absurdity' is, after all, Job's own deep conviction also; without it there would be no opposites, no conflict, no tragedy.) There is no transformation of the libido into the symbol, and no transformation of Job – he merely submits, with his tongue in his cheek, to *force majeure*. The story has no dénouement at all. 'Yahweh abruptly breaks off this cruel game of cat and mouse . . . Job's torments suddenly come to an end.' Anyway, they have been 'pointless', 'to no purpose'. Job's harrowing experiences have profited him nothing; the only lesson to be drawn is that God is a beast. Yahweh in any case has nothing to teach Job; he is 'unconscious', 'at odds with himself', contradictory, irritable, irrational, unstable, childishly hungry for love and admiration; in short, 'a prehistoric menagerie'. On the contrary, it is Job who 'shows himself superior to his divine partner both intellectually and morally', and it is Job who will, and does, teach God. Yahweh is a slow learner, but after further graded instructions from Ezechiel, Daniel, the Sapiential writers and Enoch, he himself becomes man; not, however, *propter nos homines et propter nostram salutem*, but for his own self-improvement. Unfortunately, however, he incarnates only his 'light side', to the neglect of the 'dark', in the guiltless Christ who 'did no evil'. So the last state is worse than the first: evil is more repressed and unconscious than ever and threatens a terrible revenge. The coming of Christ heralds the reign of Antichrist: the triumph of almighty evil through atomic fission. There are, however, signs that God is learning better the dark, feminine side of his all too masculine nature: there is the Woman of the Apocalypse, and there is the papal definition of the Assumption: hints of a coming, and more satisfactory, rebirth of the God-Man.

The summary of the argument is of course unfair, but no more astounding than many passages within it.[3] **[It is not surprising that some of Jung's friends, jealous for his honour in his old age, and concerned for the repute and future of**

2 Four passages, here set boldface and within brackets, appeared only in White's original *Blackfriars* review of *Answer to Job* in 1955. Four years later he amended this review by deleting just these passages, to create a more temperate though still critical essay. He also deleted his footnotes, but otherwise no changes were made in the review before he added it to his final book, *Soul and Psyche*, as Appendix V.

3 White's footnote at this point reads: "*Answer to Job*. By C. G. Jung, translated from the German by R.F.C. Hull. (Routledge and Kegan Paul; 12s, 6d.)."

his school, have regretted the publication of this document, or that the German original met with considerable indignation.] Psychiatric journals appear, on the whole, to have received it with discreet silence. But the *bien-pensants*, if not also the genuinely devout, could hardly restrain their complaints of impiety and blasphemy. Protestant divines were particularly censorious:[4] they seem not to have read the preface addressed *Lectori Benevolo*. But Jung hardly invites their benevolence. Such a *reductio ad impossibile* of the private interpretation of Scripture, when it really succeeds in cutting loose from all tradition and every *consensus fidelium*, must seem a cruel caricature. Nor can it be pleasing to be told that the Pope's definition of the Assumption is thoroughly enlightened and up-to-date, while at its critics (the Anglican Archbishops included) is hurled the supreme insult of being obscurantist and behind the times – as well as of being deaf to the Holy Ghost. Catholics will welcome Jung's insights into the definition, and of contemporary Marian devotion generally; but they will be hesitant to open their arms to this gift-bearing Greek. For Pius XII and C. G. Jung hardly seem to be talking about the same thing in their affirmations of the Assumption. According to the latter, while the visionary figure of Apocalypse 12 is 'an ordinary woman, not a goddess' (for all that she is apparently the monstrous titaness Leto, who begat Apollo by leaning against a mountain!), the mother of Christ, being an immaculate virgin, is 'different from all other mortals': hardly flesh and blood at all.

[This is only one of the many ideas in this volume which may give some readers the feeling that the author is not in earnest, even that he is pulling their legs. Is he, after the manner of his own 'Yahweh', duped by some satanic trickster into purposely torturing his friends and devotees? Or is he, more rationally, purposely putting them to the test to discover how much they will stand rather than admit the fallibility of their master – or how many, more Job-like, will venture to observe that the Emperor has appeared in public without his clothes?] But the bizarre ideas will astonish the educated Christian readers less than the naïve misunderstandings and misrepresentations of elementary doctrine. Can Jung really suppose that sacrifice and worship are for God's benefit rather than man's? Or that the commandments are or could be directives for divine behaviour as well as human – or would he subject God also to the laws of gravitation or thermodynamics? Has any Bible-reader really supposed that 'Christianity burst upon world history as an absolute novelty'? How does he charge a religion, which puts the Cross at its

4 White's second footnote states: "A very noteworthy exception is the deeply sympathetic but critical *Assessment of Jung's 'Answer to Job'* by the Rev. Erastus Evans, obtainable for 1s. 7d. from the Guild of Pastoral Psychology, 124 Pepys Road, London, S.W. 20. A brief but penetrating critique from the standpoint of a Catholic exegete [Richard Kehoe] appeared in *Dominican Studies*, 1952, pp. 228ff. Both are to be recommended for their presentation of other aspects of this many-sided book."

centre, with repressing consciousness of evil? How has he missed the very essence of the Christian's situation which is to be at once a child of God by baptism and a child of wrath by inheriting a grace-deprived nature? He quotes St John's, 'He that is born of God commits no sin', but ignores his reiterated 'If we say we have no sin we deceive ourselves . . . make him a liar.' Thereby he misses the conscious duality in John (yet this is vital for understanding the Apocalypse) – and in grown-up Christians generally.

But when we have read Jung's preface ('I beg of you, dear reader, not to overlook it', he writes), we must see that all such questions and observations are largely beside the point. Nor will a Catholic, firm in the security of his faith, 'answer' the book by drawing from his treasure things new and old and showing how they sort out and dispose of the countless points which the book raises. Jung has remarked elsewhere that there must be continual misunderstanding between the theologian and the empirical psychologist over their use of the word 'God'; for 'the theologian will naturally assume that the metaphysical *Ens Absolutum* is meant', while the empiricist 'just as naturally means a mere statement, at most an archetypal motif which preforms such statements'. It appears then, that Jung employs names like 'Yahweh' and nouns like 'God' to function not as signs but as things (to adopt modern terminology): as second, not first *intentiones* (to adopt scholastic terminology). Such usage is legitimate, though perhaps unusual even among empiricists, but we must allow Jung to use words in the way he chooses, and (difficult though it may sometimes be to construe some of his sentences in his own way) try to understand them accordingly. Thus it emerges from this preface that in statements about 'God' or 'Yahweh' he is talking about endopsychic images considered as psychological phenomena and not as signs for what they merely represent. He is 'quite conscious that . . . none of my reflections touches the essence of the Unknowable'. He is talking all the time of the interaction between archetypes and ego-consciousness, personifying the former because of their seeming autonomous behavior. When, for instance, the book says that Yahweh is unconscious, or that aspects of him become conscious, we should understand it to mean that he (or it) is unconscious to the human ego, or that aspects emerge into human consciousness – the only consciousness which the rigid empiricist, who rejects the validity of inference, will recognize. We have suggested, in our *God and the Unconscious*, that for Catholic theology also 'progressive revelation' consists precisely in such an enlargement of human consciousness, and it might be expected that Jung's book could be read as a contribution to the history of that process. Read from this standpoint, it certainly offers several illuminating and exciting insights. But, generally speaking, it cannot be so read.

For Jung deliberately reads the Scriptures through a pair of highly distorting spectacles. Although he is not writing of God but of God-images, he is not writing directly even of Job's images of God, but rather of his own images of Job's images. This method effectively obscures an objective and dispassionate reading of the Scriptures against their own authentic historical background: it is an interpretation of 'God' at several removes. Its aim is 'not to give a cool and carefully considered exegesis that tries to be fair in every detail, but a purely subjective reaction': to present 'the way in which a modern man with a Christian education and background comes to terms with the divine darkness which is unveiled in the book of Job'. Jung will 'not write in a coolly objective manner, but must allow my emotional subjectivity to speak if I want to describe what I feel when I read certain books of the Bible. . . . I shall express my affect fearlessly and ruthlessly'. What he offers us is the highly feeling-toned reaction of 'a layman and a physician who has been privileged to see deeply into the psychic life of many people'. It is an angry book, but it is an anger born of experience and compassion for mankind in its contemporary quandary, and in the disastrous inadequacy of its supposed Christian education to enable it to come to terms with contemporary realities. The preface is headed with the text, 'I am distressed for thee my brother'; and we recall Jung's declaration which, if it cannot win our approval, yet must command our respect:

> 'I do not write for church circles, but for those who stand *extra Ecclesiam*. I associate myself on purpose and deliberately with those who are outside the Church. . . . The Church is my Mother, but the Spirit of my Father draws me away from her into the wide world and its battlefields.'

Even an instructed Christian may expect an explosion when an adult, whose religious development has become fixated at the kindergarten level of bourgeois morality *plus* 'a Friend for little children above the bright blue sky', becomes confronted with the realities of life, of the ways of God both in the Bible and in contemporary events. It is understandable that he feels a close kinship with the disillusioned, tortured Job. Yet it is a fact that the acquaintance of millions of our contemporaries with Christianity has not reached beyond this stage. The violence of the abreaction is understandable, but its infantile quality may still amaze readers who are unfamiliar with abreactions. We might suppose, for instance, that the text, 'Whom the Lord loveth he chastiseth', might call a halt to the tantrums, and even induce the author to reflect that his grievance is hardly adult. But the only reaction is that of the spoiled child. 'It would be quite understandable if the Laodiceans did not *want* too much of this "love".' Other remarks about Christian ideas of love and goodness, otherwise unintelligible or merely abusive (e.g. 'To believe that God is the Summum Bonum is impossible for a reflecting consciousness') become clear commonsense if they be understood as the reactions of a consciousness which, religiously speaking, has become fixated at the oral phase, for which 'love' means the egotistic 'I want', and 'goodness' only an elementary *bonum delectabile* – perhaps just 'good luck'. 'Reflecting' or not, such a consciousness is a primitive one which has as yet scarcely differentiated religion from magic, which has never heard of the logician's niceties about the analogical predication of *bonum*, or come within miles of experiencing the saints' joy in God: St Paul's 'All things work together for good to those who love God' or St Julie Billiart's 'How good the good God is!'

'One would be very ill advised', Jung remarks in quite another connection, 'to identify me with such a childish standpoint.' Nobody who has read his more 'objective' books or who has noted the deep insights in this book – let alone anyone who knows him personally – could make such a mistake about one of the most mature and advanced spirits of our time. Why then, we must ask, does he identify himself with such childish standpoints here? To this there seems no answer except his distress for his brother, his deliberate identification with those *extra Ecclesiam*. An analyst must give his heart to those who suffer and require his aid; and even though he may not lose his head he must run the risk of exposing himself to, and being infected by, their complaints. This book should be neither laughed off nor should it provoke anger or disgust. It does not belong to the large and worthless library written by cranks who wrest the Scriptures to prove some crackpot theory. **[It has – and this is its most distressing feature – the ingenuity and power, the plausibility and improbability, the clear-sightedness and blindness of the typical paranoid system which rationalizes and conceals an even more unbearable grief and resentment.]** Its depth and tragedy we can only guess from the fact that it calls upon, not other men, but the hallowed names and symbols of God to carry the projection of the criminal and pathological persecutor. A Christian reader should hear, beneath all the provocation, behind the seeming mockery of all he holds most sacred and most dear, a profoundly moving cry of anguish, a reproachful signal of distress.

But he should also observe that, destructive and childish as much of this book seems to be, its aims are eminently constructive, and that its challenge to ourselves and our contemporaries is imperative and urgent. We must regret that the author seems so often to bark up the wrong tree; but we should see that his attack is essentially directed on Victorian, liberal, diluted, one-sided pictures of God and his Christ which are utterly inadequate to the tasks which our age imposes upon humanity. We can only agree with Jung that these obsolete and insipid idols must be destroyed if a new realization of the God-Man in his wholeness is to be born in human minds and hearts, and humanity itself is to survive. But this precisely is the lesson to be drawn from a dispassionate reading of holy Scripture itself, and it is seldom more explicit than in the Book of Job itself. It is also the lesson of the history of the Church, whose task is to carry on and develop 'what Jesus began to do and to teach' – what Jung calls the 'continuing incarnation of God which began with Christ'. We too await another coming of Christ, not in meekness only, but in the full exercise of his power and majesty, and for 'the *hieros gamos*, the marriage of the son with the mother bride'.[5] The pity is that in his violent reaction against an emasculated version of Christianity, he has failed to see that he is, in spite of himself, on the side of the Bible and of authentic orthodox Christianity. Blake wrote of Milton that he was on the devil's side without knowing it; we may say of Jung that he is on Yahweh's side even when he seems to mock at him.

In the very last sentence of the book, when all its *Sturm und Drang* have subsided, Jung leaves us in no doubt that he has known the answer to Job all along:

> 'Even the enlightened person remains what he is, and is never more than his own limited ego before the One who dwells in him, whose form has no visible boundaries, who encompasses him on all sides, fathomless as the abysms of the earth, and vast as the sky.'

What is this if not – though couched in more modern language – the answer to Job; precisely Yahweh's answer to Job in the Book of Job?

5 White's final footnote states: "Jung asserts that the *hieros gamos* with which the Apocalypse closes 'takes place in heaven . . . high above the devastated world'. This is unfortunately characteristic of his reading of a 'pie in the sky' Christianity into the Bible, even (in this case) to the extent of defying the explicit text. Apoc. 21, 1–3 could hardly be more clear to the contrary: there is 'a new heaven and a new earth', the old heaven–earth opposition is destroyed; the bride 'comes *down out of* heaven from God' and the 'dwelling of God is *with us*'."

EDITORIAL NOTE

Ownership of letters cuts two ways. As a physical object, a letter belongs to its recipient and can legally pass to the recipient's heirs, or to others who may receive it. As a literary product, however, a letter's content is copyrighted, always, to its author. The publication of letters thus requires permission from two sides. This volume of letters is published with permission from the Jung Estate ("Letter of Intent," signed by Ulrich Hoerni and Peter Jung, August 1999) and from the English Dominican Province (copyright letter, A. Cunningham to A. Lammers, 3 March 2005).

The primary documents on which this book is based, the letters of C.G. Jung and Victor White, have been housed since 1991 at the ETH Library archive (the C.G. Jung Archive, Department of Manuscripts and Legacies, Archive of the Swiss Federal Institute of Technology, Zurich). Copies of both sides of the correspondence are also held at the archive of the English Dominican Province, in Edinburgh.

Prior to 1991, except as discussed below, the letters of Jung and White were in the custody of the recipients or their heirs. White's letters to Jung, together with handwritten drafts and carbon copies of many of Jung's letters to him, were kept at Jung's house in Küsnacht. Jung's letters to White were kept at the Dominican house in Cambridge. Between 1962 and 1972, with permission from both sides, originals of the Jung–White letters were in the keeping of Gerhard Adler and Aniela Jaffé, while they edited Jung's letters for publication.[1]

After 1972 it becomes harder to verify the location of certain parts of the correspondence. The documents which Jung's heirs had lent to Adler and Jaffé were finally given back in 1972, though some may have been lost

1 Franz Jung later recalled that originals (not copies) were lent to the editors of Jung's letters (private communication, F. Jung to A. Lammers, 10 December 1992). Fr. Kenelm Foster, prior of the Dominican house in Cambridge in the early 1970s, likewise told Adrian Cunningham that Gerhard Adler had borrowed the originals of Jung's letters to transcribe, and that these documents were later not returned.

in transit.[2] Documents which the English Dominicans had lent to Adler, including many of Jung's holographs, were for some reason not returned to them. It was the search for these missing letters that brought Adrian Cunningham to Zurich in 1990.

The Jung Archive at the ETH Library first became active in 1977.[3] While the majority of Jung's correspondences were turned over to the archive by his heirs, a few discrete correspondences were held back longer, among them the Jung–White letters. In late 1989 Franz and Lorenz Jung decided the time had come to transfer the letters of Jung and White to the archive (private communication, F. Jung to A. Lammers, 9 August 1990; 1 November 1992; 10 December 1992).[4] Soon thereafter, in June 1990, Adrian Cunningham wrote to inform Franz Jung of his interest in publishing the correspondence of Jung and White.

Mr. Cunningham, whose study of White's life and work goes back several decades, had found in 1981 that the letters from Jung to White were missing.[5] He was authorized in 1990 by then prior provincial of the English Dominicans, Fr. Timothy Radcliffe, to act on behalf of White's heirs "in all matters respecting White's papers" (Timothy Radcliffe, O.P., 5 June 1990). Thus he came to Zurich carrying, equal with the Jung heirs, legal responsibility for the disposition of the Jung–White letters.

2 Some letters in the Jung–White correspondence may have been lost through an accident which occurred in 1972, when Gerhard Adler, having finished work on the English-language *Letters*, yielded to Franz Jung's request that he return the documents which had been lent to him. His large parcel arrived in Küsnacht so badly damaged that a local postal official called to apologize. No one could be sure which letters were lost in transit, or how many. Mr. Jung was also unsure, 20 years later, whether White's letters to Jung were in the parcel sent by Adler, or whether they had been among the documents that were given back that year by Aniela Jaffé. (Interview, Franz Jung, 19 September 1992; private correspondence, 10 December 1992.)

3 Jung provided in his will that after his death (1961) his literary legacy should go to the ETH. The ETH Library established the C.G. Jung-Arbeitsarchiv 16 years later, and starting in August 1980 documents from Jung's estate were sent to the archive in several batches. Until 1981 Franz Jung was primarily responsible for Jung's archival materials. At that point the Erbengemeinschaft C.G. Jung (the C.G. Jung Estate) was reorganized, and Lorenz Jung took over until 1990, when his final illness intervened. After Lorenz's death, Franz Jung resumed the role temporarily. Eventually the Erbengemeinschaft entrusted this responsibility to Peter Jung and Ulrich Hoerni, who now jointly oversee Jung's literary deposit on behalf of his heirs.

4 The Jung heirs' 1989 decision to give the ETH Library archive the Jung–White letters may have been in some part a response to my doctoral work ("The Relation between Theology and Psychology: Victor White and C.G. Jung," Yale University, 1987), which they had received shortly before (interview, Franz Jung, 19 September 1992).

5 While writing his essay, "Victor White and C.G. Jung, the fateful encounter of the White Raven and the Gnostic" (*New Blackfriars*, July/August 1981, pp. 320–334), Adrian Cunningham had first discovered that Jung's letters to White were missing from the Dominican house in Cambridge. He then began the search which led him to Zurich in 1990.

Almost a year's delay occurred, however, before the Jung–White letters could be either transferred to the ETH Library archive or released to Mr. Cunningham. When he arrived in Zurich, Lorenz Jung had just entered the hospital with what proved to be his final bout with cancer. Although Lorenz thought he had already given the Jung–White letters to the ETH archive, they were not found there. After his death in August 1990, the surviving heirs[6] searched in vain for the letters. In February 1991 they were finally discovered in a locked cabinet at Lorenz's home, still in the same zippered case in which Franz Jung had given them to his son in 1989.[7]

The complete[8] correspondence of Jung and White was finally deposited at the ETH Library archive in 1991, and then immediately released to Mr. Cunningham for the English Dominican Province. Copies were also sent to Fr. Bede Bailey, archivist for the English Dominicans. By special arrangement with Mr. Cunningham, the originals of Jung's letters to White were allowed to remain at the ETH Library archive.[9] The letters were given to me, as well, with permission from both the Jung heirs and Mr. Cunningham, to allow me to finish my book on Jung and White.[10] Mr. Cunningham's health unfortunately prevented his editing the Jung–White letters for publication at the time, as planned; hence our current collaborative effort.

6 In 1990, Franz Jung still took a role in overseeing his father's papers.

7 Franz Jung later wrote: "*Als Cunningham unerwartet schnell nach seiner Ankündigung bereits Mitte Juli in Zch [Zürich] eintraf, war[en] natürlich Lorenz und ich überrascht & wir beide waren der Meinung die Briefe von V. White seien bereits, wie vorgesehen, im Archiv ETH, obschon diese in einem verschlossenen Dossier im Schrank bei Lorenz lagen. Es ging deshalb recht lang, beinahe 1 Jahr, bis einer meiner Söhne (Andreas und ich) bei der Sichtung aller Briefe & Dokumente des Verstorbenen in seinem Hause die White-Briefe fanden, in jener Enveloppe, wie ich diese seinerzeit Lorenz übergeben hatte*" (private communication, F. Jung to A. Lammers, 1 November 1992). ["In mid-July, when Mr. Cunningham arrived in Zurich, sooner than expected after his letter, Lorenz and I were naturally surprised & we both thought the letters of V. White were already in the ETH archive as planned, although they were lying in a zippered dossier in the cabinet at Lorenz's residence. So it took quite a while, almost a year, until one of my sons (Andreas and I), while sorting through all the letters and documents of the deceased, found White's letters, in the same envelope in which I had originally given them to Lorenz" (trans. ACL).]

8 As the history of the documents makes clear, "complete" is a relative word. The Jung–White correspondence which was donated to the Jung Archive in 1991, complete as possible at the time, lacked 15 of Jung's previously published letters. In late 1997, through an anonymous sale at Sotheby's, the ETH Library was able to buy back not only these but also several of Jung's previously unpublished letters to White. (The recovered letters were, with two exceptions, original holographs.) This brought the collection closer to completeness. From internal evidence, however, as annotated in this edition, a few letters are still missing on both sides of the correspondence.

9 Franz Jung took this offer from the Dominicans as "a highly esteemed gift" (private communication, F. Jung to A. Cunningham, 12 July 1991).

10 Lammers, *In God's Shadow* (cf. "Introduction," p. xxi and note).

Thirty-two of Jung's letters to White have been published previously. Eighteen, including Jung's addendum dated 23 March 1946 and half of his letter of 12 May 1950, appear here for the first time (cf. List of Letters, pp. 363ff). Adler's and Jaffé's policies in editing *C.G. Jung Letters* supplied the model for major aspects of this volume.[11] Contrasts between their editorial approach and ours are dealt with elsewhere (Introduction, pp. xxviiiff); but their practical grasp of specific ethical and legal concerns helped us create the foundation for this edition.

When editing a correspondence, questions of privacy and confidentiality may arise regarding third parties. Libelous or defamatory statements must not be published, of course; this restriction is easily grasped by editors familiar with Anglo-American common-law traditions. Medical confidentiality, too, is a familiar concept. A challenge arose for the editors of this volume in the concept of *Persönlichkeitsschutz* ["rights of personality"]. It is a principle in Swiss and European law, whose meaning is only partly matched by the laws of the United Kingdom and the United States.[12]

Persönlichkeitsschutz partly overlaps with familiar Anglo-American laws protecting privacy and forbidding libel or defamation of character, but it does not exactly correspond to them. Swiss law, in common with European human rights law, shields *die Privatsphäre an sich* ["the private sphere as such"] more vigorously and extensively than in the Anglo-American legal tradition, by protecting people not only from objective harm but also in certain situations from *feeling* that their right to privacy is damaged or intruded on.

In the agreement governing our editing of the Jung–White correspondence, we undertook to treat *C.G. Jung Letters* as a model. In their respective introductions, Jaffé and Adler provide clues toward the practical meaning of *Persönlichkeitsschutz*, but not a developed outline. In explaining their decisions to conceal the names of some of Jung's addressees and make textual cuts, they mention medical confidentiality, but they say nothing explicit about "the rights of personality" as such, perhaps because its implications were self-evident to them. *Persönlichkeitsschutz* is evidently the principle that required them to seek written permissions from all Jung's addressees, going

11 The 1999 "Letter of Intent" for this volume, signed by representatives of the Jung Estate and the ETH Library, by me, and later by Adrian Cunningham, discusses the ethical and legal guidelines to be followed in this edition and cites two earlier editions of Jung's letters as models: the Adler/PUP edition of *C.G. Jung Letters* and McGuire's edition (in English) of *The Freud–Jung Letters*.

12 My statements on the topic are tentative; but this much at least is borne out by Swiss legal opinion (Ulrich Hoerni, private correspondence, 31 December 2004). To date I have encountered the principle of "personality rights" only in a Swiss–German cultural context, but I am assured it has a wider application, having been incorporated into the European Convention on Human Rights.

back to 1930, even in cases where medical confidentiality played no role. When such permissions were unavailable, Jung's addressees and third parties were "anonymized" (*Letters I*, pp. xiif; *Briefe I*, pp. 10f).

The meaning of "personality rights" is also limited in specific ways. For example, Jung need not be protected from injuries his words might inflict on his own personality. Jaffé writes: "So far as possible the letters are unabbreviated, in that attention was paid neither to internal contradictions nor to what could be seen as digressions or errors."[13] Permissions were sought from living addressees, but not (or not routinely) from the heirs of those who had died. Historical and public figures discussed in relation to their public activities are routinely named, even when Jung's judgments on them are biting.[14] Finally, it is striking that the restrictions of *Persönlichkeitsschutz* become less binding with the passage of time. No permissions were sought from addressees prior to 1930 (*Letters I*, p. xiii; *Briefe I*, p. 11).

A critical component of the concept is summed up in Adler's statement about textual cuts: "Omissions are of two kinds, of repetitive or quite unimportant passages, and of passages of a too intimate or confidential nature" (*Letters I*, p. xv). The second half of the sentence, on respect for privacy, comes close to the heart of the matter. The following language was therefore included in the contractual framework for this volume:

> Where necessary to fulfil the terms of this agreement, the names and other distinguishing features of third parties mentioned in the letters of C.G. Jung used in this work shall be concealed, to prevent their identification and protect their privacy. Regarding any third party mentioned in Jung's letters, the Editors shall do whatever is necessary to avoid risk of libel, defamation, or breach of clinical confidentiality. The Editors shall seek written permission from any third party (or estate) for whom these risks arise. Lacking such permission, the Editors shall delete material from Jung's letters to conceal the identity of the affected party or to remove the offending text. The Editors shall also delete names or portions of text as needed, to avoid printing too-intimate or private information about third parties,

13 "*Soweit als möglich erscheinen die Briefe ungekürzt, wobei weder auf Widersprüchliches Rücksicht genommen wurde noch auf das, was vielleicht als Entgleisung oder Fehlurteil angesehen werden könnte*" (*Briefe I*, p. 10; trans. ACL).

14 Jung speculates with cutting irony, for example, about a famous Protestant theologian: "I wonder which devil Karl Barth (with his absolute God) worships in practice. It's very likely one of them has him by the collar" (Jung to Albert Oeri, 4 Jan. 1929, *Letters I*, p. 58). Barth, who died in 1968, was still living while Jung's letters were being prepared for publication. But because this criticism was considered to touch only his public role, as a theologian, the editors felt no need to ask his permission.

> unless specific permissions have been obtained from the affected parties or their estates.

Conforming to the above, we have found it necessary to withhold three names in these letters and to omit a few words. In most cases permissions were kindly given. This was particularly important with the heirs of Barbara Robb and John Layard, two prominent "third parties" in the Jung–White correspondence for whom there would otherwise have been difficulties because of copyright, clinical confidentiality or privacy. In two cases where clinical confidentiality required a written release, none was forthcoming. Relatives of one person were not found, and family members of the other denied permission. Cuts in the text, shown with brackets and ellipsis [. . .], are thankfully rare.

Our most difficult case under the rubric of "personality rights" was that of Toni Sussmann, an analyst and trainer of analysts, who was known to both White and Jung. She is most frequently mentioned in the letters of 1945 through 1947, where Victor White asks whether Jung approves of her claim to teach with the same authority as Jung's own. (Specifically, Sussmann seems to have adopted a literal reading of statements Jung wrote for her during the war, helping her to escape from Berlin to England.) Under Swiss law, I am told, the situation gives no firm reason to conceal her identity; yet if she were living (her death in 1967 is documented), we should have been concerned for her feelings about certain passages. Therefore we have tried diligently to locate her heirs, to seek their permission to publish her name. Despite all efforts we could find no evidence of living heirs.

In deciding to print the name of a third party who occupies such a grey area, we weighed conflicting considerations, including the historical information that would be lost if she were made anonymous. Her story has value in the history of the Jungian movement, touching on the nature of professional authority among Jung's immediate followers. Against the value of this information, we weighed the possibility that certain passages might injure the feelings of her heirs, if any, or of those who were once her patients in analysis. We feel that it is relevant that Toni Sussmann died nearly 40 years ago, and that the letters referring to her are now almost 60 years old. The editors take full responsibility for letting her name stand.

ACL

LIST OF LETTERS

I. Letters to Victor White

Jung's letters to White, previously published in C.G. Jung Letters

26 Sept. 1945
5 Oct. 1945
13 Feb. 1946
13 April 1946
6 Nov. 1946
18 Dec. 1946
27 March 1947
23 April 1947
19 Dec. 1947
27 Dec. 1947
30 Jan. 1948
21 May 1948
24 Sept. 1948
16 Dec. 1948
8 Jan. 1949
31 Dec. 1949
12 May 1950 (half of letter)
25 Nov. 1950
21 Sept. 1951
early April 1952
9–14 April 1952
30 April 1952
30 June 1952
7 Aug. 1952
24 Nov. 1953
10 April 1954
19 Jan. 1955
2 April 1955
6 May 1955
21 Oct. 1959
25 March 1960
30 April 1960

Jung's letters to White, previously unpublished

23 March 1946 (addendum to 13 Feb.)
17 July 1946
23 Jan. 1947
7 May 1947
6 July 1947
22 Sept. 1947
30 Sept. 1948
14 May 1949
12 May 1950 (half of letter)
19 June 1951
21 Sept. 1951
16 Oct. 1951
28 Jan. 1952
16 Feb. 1952
14 May 1952
31 Oct. 1952
14 Nov. 1952
15 May 1953
20 Aug. 1954

Other letters to White, previously unpublished

From Toni Wolff	*From Emma Jung*
18 July 1946	18 Dec. 1946

From Marie-Jeanne Schmid

26 Sept. 1946	21 June 1948
24 Oct. 1946	12 Aug. 1948
7 Nov. 1946	13 June 1949
16 Nov. 1946	24 June 1950
26 Nov. 1946	3 April 1952
16 Dec. 1946	23 May 1952
13 Jan. 1947	29 May 1952
11 March 1947	

From other secretaries

11 Jan. 1954
7 May 1955
17 Sept. 1956 (signed by Aniela Jaffé)

Jung's letters about Victor White, previously published in **C.G. Jung Letters**

to Pastor Werner Niederer, 23 June 1947
to Barbara Robb, 19 Nov. 1952
to Aniela Jaffé, 6 April 1954
to E.V. Tenney, 23 Feb. 1955 (excerpt)
to Mrs. C.K. Ginsberg, 3 June 1960
to Rev. W.P. Witcutt, 24 Aug. 1960 (excerpt)
to Mother Prioress, Sept. 1959
to Mother Prioress, 6 Feb. 1960
to Mother Prioress, 26 March 1960
to Mother Prioress, 29 April 1960
to Mother Prioress, 12 Aug. 1960
to Mother Prioress, 19 Oct. 1960

Previously unpublished

to Michael Fordham, 16 Feb. 1954
to the Mother Prioress, 7 Oct. 1959

II. Letters from Victor White, previously unpublished

White's letters to Jung

3 Aug. 1945
9 Oct. 1945
14 Oct. 1945 (with dream of 22 Jan. 1945)
23 Oct. 1945
16 Nov. 1945
1 April 1946
Easter 1946
23 June 1946
27 Aug. 1946
31 Aug. 1946
13 Oct. 1946
11 Dec. 1946
31 Dec. 1946
19 Jan. 1947
4 Feb. 1947
7 Feb. 1947
8 March 1947
20 April 1947
2 May 1947
2 June 1947
16 June 1947 (with Robb's "Vision of March 31st")
14 Sept. 1947
23 Oct. 1947
27 Dec. 1947 (with dream of 12 Dec. 1945)
3 Jan. 1948
1 June 1948
6 Aug. 1948
5 May 1949
19 May 1949
30 May 1949
30 June 1949
10 Feb. 1950
4 May 1950 (with dream of 21 Jan. 1950)
18 May 1950
20 June 1950
10 July 1950
20 July 1950
5 Aug. 1950
3 Dec. 1950 (with papal statement)
17 July 1951
6 Sept. 1951
3 Oct. 1951
7 Oct. 1951
23 Oct. 1951
21 Feb. 1952
25 March 1952
30 March 1952
5 April 1952
20 April 1952
13 May 1952
25 June 1952
9 July 1952
10 Aug. 1952 (with dream of 26 July 1952)
10 Nov. 1952
2 April 1953
22 June 1953
15 Sept. 1953
8 Nov. 1953
29 Nov. 1953
4 Jan. 1954
4 March 1954
15 May 1954
25 Sept. 1954
8 Jan. 1955
17 March 1955
9 May 1955
10 May 1955 (with "Problems arising from publication of 'Answer to Job' ")
21 May 1955
25 Aug. 1956
1 June 1958
26 July 1958
18 Oct. 1959

18 March 1960
28 March 1960
6 May 1960
8 May 1960

White's letters to Marie-Jeanne Schmid:

18 Sept. 1946
16 Oct. 1946
29 Oct. 1946
11 Dec. 1946
9 Jan. 1947
26 Feb. 1947
(undated) 1952
21 May 1952
6 April 1952

SELECTED BIBLIOGRAPHY

Note: This bibliography lists all the works of C.G. Jung and Victor White cited in text and notes. For cited works by all other writers, please consult the Index and annotations. Detailed information on Jung's published works, through 1975, is found in *General Bibliography*, CW 19. For more on White's publications, see *IGS*, pp. 263ff.

* * *

First Source

"C.G. Jung–Victor White Correspondence" (HS 1056), C.G. Jung Archive, Department of Manuscripts and Legacies, Archive of the Swiss Institute of Technology, Zurich. ["Korrespondenz C.G. Jung–Victor White" (HS 1056), C.G. Jung-Arbeitsarchiv, Hauptabteilung Handschriften und Nachlässe des Archivs der ETH Zürich.]

* * *

Jung, C.G. *The Collected Works of C.G. Jung*. Edited by Herbert Read, Michael Fordham, and Gerhard Adler; executive editor (from 1967), William McGuire. Translated by R.F.C. Hull, except as otherwise noted. New York: Pantheon Books for Bollingen Foundation, 1953–60; Bollingen Foundation (distributed by Pantheon Books, a Division of Random House), 1961–67; Princeton, New Jersey: Princeton University Press, 1967–78 (Bollingen Series XX). London: Routledge & Kegan Paul, 1953–78. (The New York and London editions are identical except for title pages and binding. Reprintings vary.)

—— *Die Gesammelten Werke von C.G. Jung*. Herausgegeben von Marianne Niehus-Jung, Lena Hurwitz-Eisner, Franz Riklin, Lilly Jung-Merker, and Elisabeth Rüf. Zürich: Rascher Verlag, 1958–70. Olten: Walter Verlag, 1971–.

* * *

Jung, C.G. *Aion: Researches into the Phenomenology of the Self*. Collected Works 9.ii, 1958/1968.

—— *Aion: Untersuchungen zur Symbolgeschichte*. Unter Mitarbeit von M.-L. von Franz. Psychologische Abhandlungen 8. Gesammelte Werke 9,ii, 1951.

—— *Alchemical Studies*. Collected Works 13, 1967.

—— *Answer to Job*. Translated by R.F.C. Hull. London: Routledge & Kegan Paul, 1954. Republished in *Psychology and Religion: West and East*. Collected Works 11, 1958/1969.

—— *Antwort auf Hiob*. Zürich: Rascher Verlag, 1952. Republished in *Zur Psychologie westlicher und östlicher Religion*. Gesammelte Werke 11, 1963/1973.

—— *The Archetypes and the Collective Unconscious*. Collected Works 9.i, 1959/1968.

—— *Aufsätze zur Zeitgeschichte*. Zürich: Rascher Verlag, 1946.

—— *Civilization in Transition*. Collected Works 10, 1964.

—— "The Challenge of the Christian Enigma. Letter to Upton Sinclair." *The New Republic*. 27 April 1953.

—— "The Christian Legend: An Interpretation. Letter to Upton Sinclair." *The New Republic*. 21 Feb. 1955.

—— *Contributions to Analytical Psychology*. Translated by H.G. and Cary F. Baynes. New York: Harcourt Brace; London: Kegan Paul, Trench, Trubner, 1928.

—— *Essays on Contemporary Events*. London: Kegan Paul, Trench, Trubner, 1947.

—— "Foreword to Amy Allenby's 'A Psychological Study of the Origins of Monotheism'." *The Symbolic Life: Miscellaneous Writings*. Collected Works 18, 1975.

—— "Foreword to White's 'God and the Unconscious'." *Psychology and Religion: West and East*. Collected Works 11, 1958/1969.

—— "Der Geist Mercurius." *Eranos-Jahrbuch 1942*. Herausgegeben von Olga Fröbe-Kapteyn. Zürich: Rhein-Verlag, 1943. Republished in *Symbolik des Geistes: Studien über psychische Phänomenologie*. Zürich: Rascher Verlag, 1948; in *Studien über alchemistische Vorstellungen*. Gesammelte Werke 13, 1978.

—— "Der Geist der Psychologie." *Eranos-Jahrbuch 1946*. Herausgegeben von Olga Fröbe-Kapteyn. Zürich: Rhein Verlag, 1947.

—— "Instinct and the Unconscious." Translated by H.G. & Cary Baynes. *Structure & Dynamics of the Psyche*. Collected Works 8, 1960/1969.

—— *The Integration of the Personality*. Translated by Stanley Dell. New York: Farrar & Rinehart, 1939.

—— *Memories, Dreams, Reflections*. Recorded and edited by Aniela Jaffé. Translated by Richard and Clara Winston. New York: Vintage Books, 1962.

—— *Mysterium Coniunctionis: An Inquiry into the Separation and Synthesis of Psychic Opposites in Alchemy*. Collected Works 14, 1963/1970.

—— *Mysterium Coniunctionis. Untersuchung über die Trennung und Zusammensetzung der seelischen Gegensätze in der Alchemie*. Psychologische Abhandlungen 10. Unter Mitarbeit von Marie-Louise von Franz. Zürich: Rascher Verlag, 1955. Republished as Gesammelte Werke 14, 1968.

—— "On the Nature of the Psyche." Collected Works 8, 1960/1969.

—— *The Practice of Psychotherapy: Essays on the Psychology of the Transference and Other Subjects*. Collected Works 16, 1954/1966.

—— *Praxis der Psychotherapie. Beiträge zum Problem der Psychotherapie und zur Psychologie der Übertragung*. Gesammelte Werke 16, 1958.

—— "The Process of Individuation: Exercitia Spiritualia of St. Ignatius of Loyola." ETH Lectures 8–11, 1939; ETH Lectures 1–16, 1940. *Modern Psychology*, Vol. 4. Edited by Barbara Hannah. Privately published. Zurich: Karl Schippert & Co., 1940/1959.

—— *Psychogenese der Geisteskrankheiten*. Gesammelte Werke 3, 1968.
—— *The Psychogenesis of Mental Disease*. Collected Works 3, 1960.
—— "A Psychological Approach to the Dogma of the Trinity." *Psychology and Religion: West and East*. Collected Works 11, 1958/1969.
—— *Psychological Types*. Translated by H.G. Baynes. London: Routledge & Kegan Paul, 1923. Republished as Collected Works 6, 1971.
—— *Psychologie und Alchemie*. Psychologische Abhandlungen 5. Zürich: Rascher Verlag, 1944. Republished as Gesammelte Werke 12, 1953/1968.
—— *Die Psychologie der Übertragung. Erläutert anhand einer alchemistischen Bilderserie. Für Ärzte und praktische Psychologen*. Zürich: Rascher Verlag, 1946. Republished in *Praxis der Psychotherapie. Beiträge zum Problem der Psychotherapie und zur Psychologie der Übertragung*. Gesammelte Werke 16, 1958.
—— *Psychology and Alchemy*. Collected Works 12, 1953/1968.
—— *Psychology and Religion*. The Terry Lectures. New Haven & London: Yale University Press, 1938. Republished in *Psychology and Religion: West and East*. Collected Works 11, 1958/1969.
—— *Psychology and Religion: West and East*. Collected Works 11, 1958/1969.
—— "The Psychology of the Child Archetype." In Karl Kerenyi, *Introduction to a Science of Mythology*. 1951. Republished in *The Archetypes and the Collective Unconscious*. Collected Works 9.i, 1959/1968.
—— "On the Psychology of the Trickster Figure." In Paul Radin, *Der göttliche Schelm*, Zürich: Rhein-Verlag, 1954. Republished in *The Archetypes and the Collective Unconscious*. Collected Works 9.i, 1959/1968.
—— "The Psychology of the Transference. Interpreted in Conjunction with a Set of Alchemical Illustrations. For physicians and practical psychologists." *The Practice of Psychotherapy: Essays on the Psychology of the Transference and Other Subjects*. Collected Works 16, 1954/1966.
—— *The Psychology of the Unconscious. A Study of the Transformation and Symbolisms of the Libido. A Contribution to the History of the Evolution of Thought*. Translated by Beatrice M. Hinkle. New York: Moffat, Yard, 1916, 1919; London: Kegan Paul, Trench, Trubner, 1917, 1921.
—— "Randglossen zur Zeitgeschichte." *The Symbolic Life: Miscellaneous Writings*. Collected Works 18, 1975.
—— "Religion und Psychologie." *Merkur* 6:5, May 1952.
—— "Die Schizophrenie." *Schweizer Archiv für Neurologie und Psychiatrie* 81: 1/2. Republished in *Psychogenese der Geisteskrankheiten*. Gesammelte Werke 3, 1968.
—— *Spirit and Nature: Papers from the Eranos Yearbooks*. New York: Pantheon, 1954; London: Routledge and Kegan Paul, 1955.
—— *The Spirit in Man, Art and Literature*. Collected Works 15, 1966.
—— *The Structure and Dynamics of the Psyche*. Collected Works 8, 1960/1969.
—— *Studien über alchemistische Vorstellungen*. Gesammelte Werke 13, 1978.
—— *Symbole der Wandlung: Analyse des Vorspiels zu einer Schizophrenie*. Vierte, umgearbeitete Auflage. Zürich: Rascher Verlag, 1952. Republished as Gesammelte Werke 5, 1973.
—— *The Symbolic Life: Miscellaneous Writings*. Collected Works 18, 1975.
—— *Symbols of Transformation: An Analysis of the Prelude to a Case of Schizophrenia*. Collected Works 5, 1956/1962.

—— "Synchronicity: An Acausal Connecting Principle." *Structure and Dynamics of the Psyche*. Collected Works 8, 1960/1969.
—— "The Tavistock Lectures." *The Symbolic Life: Miscellaneous Writings*. Collected Works 18, 1975.
—— "Theoretische Überlegungen zum Wesen des Psychischen." *Von den Wurzeln des Bewusstseins: Studien über den Archetypus*. Zürich: Rascher Verlag, 1954.
—— *Two Essays on Analytical Psychology*. Translated by Cary & H.G. Baynes. New York and London, 1928. Republished as Collected Works 7, 1953/1956.
—— *Über die Energetik der Seele und andere psychologische Abhandlungen*. Zürich: Rascher Verlag, 1928.
—— *Über psychische Energetik und das Wesen der Träume*. Zürich: Rascher Verlag, 1948.
—— "Über das Selbst." *Eranos-Jahrbuch 1948*. Herausgegeben von Olga Fröbe-Kapteyn. Zürich: Rhein-Verlag, 1949.
—— "Ulysses." *European Review* 8:2/9, 1932.
—— "Ulysses, a Monologue." *Spring 1949*. Translated by W. Stanley Dell. New York: Analytical Psychology Club, 1949.
—— "Versuch zu einer psychologischen Deutung des Trinitätsdogmas." *Symbolik des Geistes: Studien über psychische Phänomenologie*. Zürich: Rascher Verlag, 1948.
—— *Wandlungen und Symbole der Libido: Beiträge zur Entwicklungsgeschichte des Denkens*. Leipzig and Vienna: Franz Deuticke, 1912.
—— "Woman in Europe." *Contributions to Analytical Psychology*. Translated by H.G. and Cary F. Baynes. New York: Harcourt Brace; London: Kegan Paul, Trench, Trubner, 1928. Republished in *Civilization in Transition*. Collected Works 10, 1964/1970.
—— "Zur Phänomenologie des Geistes im Märchen." *Symbolik des Geistes: Studien über psychische Phänomenologie*. Zürich: Rascher Verlag, 1948.
—— "Zur Psychologie des Geistes." *Eranos-Jahrbuch 1945*. Herausgegeben von Olga Fröbe-Kapteyn. Zürich: Rhein-Verlag, 1946.
—— "Zur Psychologie der Trinitätsidee." *Eranos-Jahrbuch 1940/1941*. Herausgegeben von Olga Fröbe-Kapteyn. Zürich: Rhein-Verlag, 1942.

* * *

White, Victor, "The Analyst and the Confessor." *The Commonweal: A Review of Religion, Politics, and Culture*. 23 July 1948.
—— "Anathema–Maranatha: Love and Wrath in St Paul." *Love and Violence*. London: Sheed & Ward, 1954.
—— "The Aristotelian-Thomistic Conception of Man." *Eranos-Jahrbuch 1947*. Herausgegeben von Olga Fröbe-Kapteyn. Zürich: Rhein-Verlag, 1948.
—— "The Collected Works of C.G. Jung: Volume 1 and Volume 5." *Blackfriars*. Vol. 38, Oct. 1957.
—— "Communications: 'The King and the Corpse'." *The Commonweal: A Review of Religion, Politics, and Culture*. 13 Aug. 1948.
——"Critical Notices: *Psychology and Religion*, by C.G. Jung." *Journal of Analytical Psychology*, Vol. IV: 1. London: Tavistock Publications, Jan. 1959.
—— "Eranos: 1947, 1948." *Dominican Studies*. Vol. 2/4, Oct. 1949.

—— "The Frontiers of Theology and Psychology." Lecture 19. Guild of Pastoral Psychology, Oct. 1942.

—— *God and the Unconscious*. London: Harvill Press, 1952. Revised ed. Dallas, TX: Spring Publications, 1982.

—— *God the Unknown and other Essays*. London: Harvill Press, 1956.

—— "Good and Evil." *Harvest*. Vol. 12, 1966.

—— "Jung on Job." *Blackfriars*. Vol. 36, March 1955.

—— "Kinds of Opposites." *Studien zur Analytischen Psychologie C.G. Jungs*. Festschrift zum 80. Geburtstag von C.G. Jung. Vol. I: *Beiträge aus Theorie und Praxis*. Zürich: Rascher Verlag, 1955.

—— "The Letter of St. Thomas Aquinas to Brother John: De Modo Studendi. Latin Text with Translation and Exposition by Victor White, O.P. A Lecture Read at the Inauguration of Studies for the Year 1944–45 in the Dominican Priories of Hawkesyard and Blackfriars, Oxford." *The Life of the Spirit: A Blackfriars Review*. Vol. 1/10, Dec. 1944.

—— "The Prolegomena to the Five Ways." *Dominican Studies: An Annual Review*. Vol. 5. Blackfriars Publications, 1952.

—— "Psychotherapy and Ethics." *Blackfriars*. Vol. 26, Aug. 1945.

—— "Psychotherapy and Ethics: Postscript," *Blackfriars*. Vol. 26, Oct. 1945.

—— "Review of Stern's *The Third Revolution*." *The Commonweal: A Review of Religion, Politics, and Culture*. New York, March 1954.

—— "The Scandal of the Assumption." *The Life of the Spirit: A Blackfriars Review*. Vol. 5/53–54, Nov./Dec. 1950; and in *The Assumption in the Life of the Christian*. London: Blackfriars Publications, 1950.

—— "Scholasticism." Pamphlet No. R 126. London: Catholic Truth Society, 1934.

—— *Soul and Psyche: An Enquiry into the Relationship of Psychotherapy and Religion*. New York: Harper & Brothers, 1960.

—— "St. Thomas Aquinas and Jung's Psychology." *Blackfriars*. Vol. 25, June 1944.

—— "St. Thomas's Conception of Revelation." *Dominican Studies: An Annual Review*. Vol. 1. Blackfriars Publications, Jan. 1948.

—— "The Unknown God." *The Life of the Spirit: A Blackfriars Review*. Vol. 7, 1952. Republished in *God the Unknown and other Essays*. London: Harvill Press, 1956.

—— "Walter Hilton: An English Spiritual Guide." Lecture 31. London: Guild of Pastoral Psychology, 1944.

INDEX

Page entries for illustrations are shown in **bold** type
Page entries for headings which also have subheadings refer only to general aspects of that topic

Made in the USA
Las Vegas, NV
26 August 2025

8346b5ff-9df5-4116-9b50-4f20aeaeaf5fR01